The Coercive Utopians

Contents

Acknowledgments

This book owes a great deal to a great many.

Much of the material on which it is based cannot be found in libraries, which do not subscribe to the journals or collect the other written materials of many of the groups whose activities are chronicled here. We have therefore depended on the generosity of those who have accumulated the literature of these groups, in some cases over a period of many years. We would like to thank John and Louise Rees for giving us access to their remarkable collection. To Peter Metzger we are grateful not only for opening his extensive files to us, but also for giving us permission to use his title "The Coercive Utopians." We are also deeply grateful to David Asman, Susan Crowley, David Jessup, Mary Kiss, George and Alice Massay, Bill Perkins, Gerald and Natalie Sirkin and John Train for making materials available to us.

In some areas we have depended on specialized libraries and the collections of organizations and foundations. We are in debt to the Swarthmore Peace Collection, the Tamiment Collection of New York University, the library of Union Theological Seminary, the Conservative Caucus Educational Foundation, the Foundation Center, the Institute on Religion and Democracy, the Foundation for Public Affairs, the Media Institute and the Heritage Foundation. Kerry Ptacek of the IRD was especially helpful and William Poole, formerly of the Heritage Foundation, went beyond the call of duty in supplying us with material that has been invaluable in the preparation of this book.

This book has also benefited greatly from critical readings. For this we are much indebted to Leo Raditsa and Miro Todorovich. Peter Metzger and his talented assistants Richard Westfall and Carol Ann Calamia helped to forestall errors in one chapter. Roger Gerber provided much appreciated comments. Our sons Gideon and Gamaliel were tough and valued critics, chapter by chapter. Of course none of our readers are in any way responsible for remaining defects.

Finally we would like to thank our good friend Virginia Armat for her help in a host of ways.

FOR GIDEON AND GAMALIEL,

sons and critics

I

Who Are The Coercive Utopians?

In April 1980, $18,000,000, assigned by Congress to the Community Services Administration, to help low-income and elderly people pay their fuel bills, was given instead to anti-business activist lawyers and other programs never contemplated by Congress. (After half the money had been allocated, the decision was repealed by the same judge who had originally consented to the arrangement. He said he had been misled by the Community Service Administration's lawyer.)

David Jessup, an AFL-CIO official and a member of the United Methodist Church, submitted a 40 page summary of Methodist contributions to political groups to the 1980 General Conference of the Church. Mr. Jessup began his report as follows: "Most Methodist churchgoers would react with disbelief, even anger, to be told that a significant portion of their weekly offerings were being siphoned off to groups supporting the Palestine Liberation Organization, the governments of Cuba and Vietnam, the pro-Soviet totalitarian movements of Latin America, Asia and Africa, and several violence-prone fringe groups in this country."

Decisions on the leasing of coal on federal lands were taken out of the hands of the Department of Interior for a period of several years and in practice given to the private environmental pressure group, the Natural Resources Defense Council.

In May 1980, the taxpayer-funded Public Broadcasting Service showed an anti-CIA documentary, "On Company Business." Chief figure in the film was co-producer Philip Agee, a CIA defector who has published the names of hundreds of CIA agents around the world.

Coal leasing. Church donations. A television documentary. Grants by a government agency. The items would appear to have little in common. But, they are deeply interwoven. They reflect the activity of what scientist-journalist Peter Metzger calls the coercive utopians,[1] whose programs, if implemented, will accelerate the decline in our standard of living, erode our democratic system, and may well result in the loss of genuine national independence.

Why do we borrow Metzger's term "coercive utopians?" Most of the diverse groups we will describe are utopian because they assume that man is perfectible and the evils that exist are the product of a corrupt social system. They believe that an ideal social order can be created in which man's potentialities can flower freely. They are "coercive" because in their zeal for attaining an ideal order they seek to impose their blueprints in ways that go beyond legitimate persuasion.

If they believe that society is perfectible, the utopians also believe that the society in which they live is deeply flawed, indeed hateful. And if one has to identify the single aspect of American life that they find most repugnant, it is our economic system. The reason for the abhorrence of capitalism varies among utopian groups. Churchmen, who have adopted a utopian perspective, believe that it fosters competition rather than the cooperation they define as a religious ideal. The militant wing of environmentalism believes capitalism is inherently wasteful, compelled to produce ever more products which people do not need to satisfy basic wants, and thus destructive of the environment. Consumerists believe capitalism produces ever more unsafe, shoddy and unnecessary goods in the pursuit of profit.

The utopians do more than reject our economic institutions: ultimately, their attack is directed against modern technology and science itself. In a very real sense, the coercive utopians are twentieth century Luddites. They do not smash machinery in the crude fashion of their forebears, but in a more sophisticated way demonstrate, lobby, propagandize and bring suit. Their rebellion against technology is the more striking because the resurgence of utopianism in the last hundred years was based upon *belief* in technology. Marxist utopianism, with its promise that eventually each would give according to his capacities and receive according to his needs, rested on faith in the unlimited potentialities of technology. Marx foresaw technological progress reaching so high a level that production would be almost wholly automated and man's relation to the machine would become that of scientific guidance.

The efforts of the present day utopians are two-pronged. Where public fear can be mobilized, the utopians work to stop the technology cold, as in the case of nuclear energy and genetic engineering. More fundamentally, the utopians seek to reorganize the economic system in such a way that complex technology can be eliminated. If there is one shibboleth which almost all the utopians invoke it is "appropriate technology." The term sounds as if the attitude toward technology is positive, for who can dispute that technology like any other human activity should be appropriate to its target? But what is meant by appropriate technology is a technology appropriate to the human condition, as the utopians define that condition. In the words of E.F. Schumacher, who coined the term "appropriate technology," "Man is small, and, therefore, small is beautiful." Large coal-fired plants are no more appropriate to man's nature than nuclear power plants for they too leave the individual, as utopian philosopher Amory Lovins points out, "humiliated" every time he turns on the light. That flip of the switch, as Lovins sees it, brings home to the individual his dependency on far off bureaucrats and technicians who can cut him off at their pleasure.[2] What the utopians reject is market-controlled large-scale industrial civilization. Since that civilization runs on energy, it is through transforming the energy system that the utopians believe they can transform society.

The United States, as the most successful producer of goods and food, is seen by many of the utopians as literally the worst society in the world. In so far as the utopians have real life models, they are places like Cuba, Vietnam, Nicaragua and China (at least until it moved toward the West). The glorification of socialized Third World poverty reflects the romanticism of the utopians. Rural communal life, the outward show of worker participation in workplace assemblies, the rhetoric of egalitarianism, the block level of civic control which is seen as an expression of neighborhood solidarity and self-governance, the very absence of consumer goods, make these societies immensely appealing. That their chief distinguishing characteristic is the desire of vast numbers of their citizens to leave at almost any price does not daunt the utopians.

Since Americans still want progress, economic growth, expansion of opportunity and social mobility, the utopians deny values cherished by the majority. And so, understandably, they do not openly call for a halt to technological advance and a return to human labor in place of the machine. Rather they couch their appeals in terms of values that Americans share. The source of their strength has been their invocation of purposes that Americans, to their credit, want to achieve—social justice, peace, a pollution-free and safe environment, equality between the races and sexes, the reduction of risk, greater control of the individual over the decisions that affect his life.

Who are the coercive utopians and where do we find them? Many of them are intellectuals in the definition used by the great economist and analyst of both capitalism and socialism Joseph Schumpeter: "people who wield the power of the spoken and written word" and do so "in the absence of direct responsibility for public affairs." Others are strategists and organizers, who develop and implement programs based on the ideas of utopian intellectuals.

Utopians dominate the leadership and professional staff of the mainline Protestant denominations and their related organizations, including the National Council of Churches, the umbrella body representing 32 Protestant and Eastern Orthodox churches. They are the leaders of almost all the peace groups, including the pacifist ones, like the War Resisters League and the American Friends Service Committee and those that, while not opposing all forms of violence in principle, seek to reduce the risks of war, like SANE, Clergy and Laity Concerned, Physicians for Social Responsibility, etc. They are the intellectuals in a number of institutes and think tanks that have flourished in the soil of so-called "revisionist history," which places the blame for world tensions after World War II primarily on the United States. They people community action organizations like ACORN and National People's Action. They are in government bureaucracies, and have been especially attracted to agencies like the Department of Education, ACTION (in the Carter years) and the now defunct Community Services Administration, most of whose personnel have been transferred to other agencies. They are prominent in the legally independent, but wholly government-funded, Legal Services Corporation and in the similarly constituted Corporation for Public Broadcasting. While the leaders of some environmental organizations have limited goals and cannot be classified as utopians, they play an important role in the environmental movement, especially in newer national organizations like Friends of the Earth and Environmental Action, and in the host of local enviromental groups which, spurred by the issue of nuclear energy, have burgeoned around the country. They lead the consumer organizations established by Ralph Nader. They are in the colleges, and are particularly prominent in the law and social science faculties of elite universities.

The coercive utopians, let it be said immediately, are not a cabal of conspirators parcelling out areas of action to different groups in a coordinated onslaught on American institutions. They come from diverse backgrounds and traditions. The environmentalists among them go back to the older wilderness movement. Protestant churchmen hearken back to the Social Gospel movement dating back to the turn of the century. Seeing the harsh impact of industrialization, many churchmen had concluded that capitalism was fundamentally flawed. The consumer movement can point to forebears early in this century who envisaged an economic system in which neither capital nor labor would control production. Rather consumers, through cooperatives, would reign over the economy of a consumer-cooperative commonwealth.

One characteristic all the utopian groups have in common is that most members have at best a partial idea of the goals of the leadership. For this reason, utopians are able to mobilize large numbers of people who would be out of sympathy with the organization's broader—and often hidden—agenda. Many, presumably most, who contribute to the multi-million dollar war-chest of Nader's Public Citizen do not feel themselves part of a movement to transform the basic structure of the corporation. Similarly, few who rally to the cause of the nuclear freeze know that the groups who created the freeze movement seek unilateral U.S. disarmament and see the United States as the greatest force for evil in the world. But once an individual becomes part of one of these groups or movements, the leadership has an opportunity to "educate" him. Members receive publications; they may attend meetings; depending on the type of organization, they may even take part in demonstrations. As they become active, they are caught up in a web of social and political activity which as much as more formal educational devices commits them to goals they earlier did not think deeply about.

The mainline Protestant denominations offer a dramatic example of a leadership wholly out of touch with its constituency. Acknowledging the gap, the leadership sees it as a sign of its failure to communicate, interpret and educate (they hire ever more specialists in this area), not as significant of any flaw in the substance of what they communicate. And while it is possible to dismiss the position of the hierarchy and their professional staffs as that of a small minority, British student of religion David Martin points out that it is not enough to be a silent majority. The command posts of pronouncement and communication (and, one might add, of church resources) have been captured.[3] The coercive utopians in the churches that are affiliated with the National Council of Churches can speak and act in the name of 42 million Christians.

While the focus of the utopians is primarily on the evils of the present social order, there is a surprising similarity in the portraits that are provided of the ideal society. It is above all one that will be shaped by a new relation to energy. Barry Commoner, Amory Lovins, and Jeremy Rifkin are among the most familiar figures forseeing a society built around new energy technologies and new attitudes toward the use of energy. What Amory Lovins calls "the soft path" will do away with "difficult large scale projects." Even the language reveals that what is involved is more philosophical than technological: the "soft path" connotes gentleness and ease in contrast to the "hard path" which suggests unpleasantness and difficulty. (The hard path comprises fossil fuels and all complex technology, including complex solar technology.)

An interesting version of the future order was provided by Ernest Callenbach in his 1975 literary utopia *Ecotopia.* In Ecotopia, humans take their "modest place in a seamless, stable state web of living organisms, disturbing that web as little as possible." Basic necessities are "utterly standardized" and ecologically offensive consumer items are not produced. If a new device is invented, a law requires that pilot models be given to a panel of ten ordinary people. Only if everyone of them can repair anything that might go wrong with the invention, is manufacture permitted. Not surprisingly, life is strikingly egalitarian. The nuclear family is in process of disappearance, being replaced by communal groups of up to twenty people. Population is in steady decline, although not rapidly enough for some of the "radical thinkers" of the ruling party, who believe the proper population size would be "the number of Indians who inhabited the territory before the Spaniards and Americans came."

While the Ecotopians closed all their oil and gas-fired power plants, they have kept some of their nuclear power plants open. It is interesting, given the enormous importance the struggle against nuclear energy has assumed for all the utopian groups we will describe, that in Callenbach's view, nuclear energy is the least offensive of "hard path" power generating technologies. Of course, there is also solar energy, and Ecotopians are said to delight in their windmills and rooftop wind-driven generators. But what is most noteworthy about Ecotopia is that energy is *not* cheap and abundant. Indeed, Callenbach tells us that it is three times as expensive as it is outside Ecotopia. This may represent the honesty of an author who sees himself addressing the initiated. But it is also part of the ideology of the utopians that cheap and abundant energy is not desirable. Amory Lovins, for example, has said: "It would be little short of disastrous for us to discover a source of clean, cheap abundant energy because of what we might do with it." Professor Paul Ehrlich, a guru of the zero population growth movement, puts it even more sharply: "Giving society cheap abundant energy . . . would be the equivalent of giving an idiot child a machinegun."[4]

Ecotopia's appeal goes beyond the environmental movement. Ralph Nader's reaction was that "none of the happy conditions in Ecotopia are beyond the technical or resource reach of our society." While Ecotopia's unusual family structure would presumably have little appeal to churchmen, the energy policy statement passed by the National Council of Churches in May 1979 sounded as if it could have been composed in Ecotopia. It declares that energy technology should be labor intensive and "appropriate to human nature." What is appropriate to human nature is in turn defined as renewable energy sources that are also comprehensible to the average citizen, "esthetic, pleasing to the sense, and enjoyable to work with." This almost sounds like a direct reference to Ecotopia, with its windmills that are a source of joy to the inhabitants.

There are strong similarities between the Ecotopian ideal and the visions of an ideal society put forward by the New Left. Although the New Left of the 1960s was accused of lacking any alternative to the institutions it was intent on destroying, in fact some of its leaders had a vision of what they wanted. It was difficult to articulate, however, and seemed impossible to implement. And so most of those determined to act out their protest against existing society contented themselves with creating new life styles. Students, rejecting technology and seeking to recover the authenticity of creative man, turned to communes or individually rejected the "rat race" for farming or handicrafts. Still, the vision was articulated in such books as *Being and Doing,* written in 1971 by Marcus Raskin, co-director of the Institute for Policy Studies, the major think tank of the utopians. Raskin described the reconstructed society that would follow "the dismantling of that system of economics and politics which presses man forward in a technology that spells its own doom." It was to be based on cooperative communities. All decisions were to be made in face-to-face local meetings. What was to be produced would be determined locally and workers would operate their own industries, whose products would be confined to those fulfilling "human needs."

With the Arab oil embargo of 1973, the New Left utopian vision for the first time began to assume the character of practical politics. The discomfort of Americans and the ugliness that surfaced as a result of the long lines at gas stations in the wake of the Arab oil boycott suggested that Americans were unable to cope with energy shortages and that solutions to the energy problem would have to be found for social peace as well as economic health. And why not a society where the satisfactions of "participatory democracy"—the New Left's favorite rallying cry—substituted for technological abundance? By this time the campus New Left was no more than a memory, but its graduates were in universities, in foundations, in the media, in government at all levels. So that when the prospect of scarce energy became the newly discovered key to creating a plausible utopia, there was a potential sympathetic audience. And the notions fit in perfectly with the environmentally-grounded Ecotopian vision, also built on the idea of scarce energy, small autonomous communities and control by the citizen of all the decisions that affected his life.

It may be asked: "What is wrong with utopianism?" After all, the utopian seeks a better world and if he believes he can achieve more than is possible, does this not merely give him the energy to keep up the struggle where others, less optimistic about human possibility, would give up in the face of difficulties? There is merit in this argument. The problem is that utopianism, by its inherent logic, leads to coercion. The utopian begins with a belief that the world is perfectible. John Collins, for example, a Methodist clergyman who serves both as head of the Methodist Federation for Social Action and as co-chairman of Clergy and Laity Concerned, one of the leading peace organizations, describes his vision of a world in which there is clean air and water, no nuclear weapons or energy, and a job for everyone. In addition, racism and sexism would be eliminated; there would be no rich or poor nations because resources would be equitably divided; and decision-making would be so decentralized that people would participate in all the decisions that affect their lives. Because he can imagine this world, Collins is convinced that it can be created. And so he asks:

"If such a world is achievable, and most people want it, why is it so difficult to achieve . . . Jack Nelson, in his book *Hunger for Justice,* has showed us, for instance, that the system of corporate capitalism prevailing today *needs* a hungry world to enable it to operate 'efficiently.'" (Italics in original)[5]

Utopians are forced to a devil theory to explain the gap between the desired and the real. Here, it is the corporate "system" which is the villain, but utopians may also place the blame on government or the military establishment. Collins, himself, is ready to broaden the locus of responsibility saying it is necessary to "identify more clearly the centers of corporate and governmental power which actively oppose the steps needed to realize the vision." But if the vision can be realized, and all that stands in the way is greedy and/or corrupt economic and political institutions, it follows that the utopian has the responsibility to work to abolish the institutions that stand in the way of realizing an ideal order, in which no one is hungry and everyone is materially and spiritually nourished. Of course where utopians have succeeded in abolishing existing institutions, they have found that it is not as easy as they thought to create an ideal system. Utopians rapidly discover that human nature is not as malleable as they had assumed, and that people must be transformed to fit the ideal scheme of their imagination. And so utopians become coercive, sometimes concluding that one generation must be sacrificed to create an ideal system for a future one.

While the utopians fail to understand human nature and the impossibility of creating a society of free men according to their prescriptions, they have an excellent understanding of the mechanics of power and how to obtain it and are well versed in the tactics of political pressure. Under President Carter, utopians moved into leadership positions in the bureaucracy, became heads of such government agencies as ACTION and filled a whole series of sub-cabinet posts. These people were then in a position to siphon government funds to utopian organizations and programs, despite the fact that these expenditures were in no way authorized by Congress.

Perhaps most important, the utopians have had an enormous impact on the way we think. They write many of the articles we read in opinion-setting magazines, on the Op-Ed pages of the *New York Times* and *Washington Post.* We watch them on the panels that interpret current events for us on television. We hear them from the pulpit and our children listen to them in college classrooms. To a large extent, they have set the fashions in thought, and fashion is every bit as tyrannical in ideas as in clothes. Publishers churn out their books. (To take only one example, let any reader go to a bookstore and compare the number of books attacking nuclear energy with the number supporting it.)

In so far as the ideas of the utopians can be fitted into a traditional political framework, they reawaken what had become the dormant tradition of anarchism. While there had been a strong strain of individualist anarchism, particularly in the United States, which finds current expression in libertarianism, the utopians are in the tradition of collectivist anarchism.

There is a widespread misconception that anarchism means the absence of government. But as political scientist Donald McIntosh observes, anarchism is really a form of government in which decisions are the product of unanimous agreement among the governed.[6] Far from dispensing with coercion, anarchism has to avail itself of a coercive and oppressive process to achieve unanimity. Orwell has written that there is a

> totalitarian tendency . . . implicit in the anarchist or pacifist vision of society. In a society where there is no law and in theory no compulsion, the only arbiter of behavior is public opinion. But public opinion, because of the tremendous urge to conformity in gregarious animals, is less tolerant than any system of law. When human beings are governed by 'thou shalt not,' the individual can practice a certain amount of eccentricity; when they are supposedly governed by 'love' and 'reason,' he is under continuous pressure to make him behave and think exactly the same way as anyone else does."[7]

For anarchists all forms taken by the state are illegitimate, with democracy only a milder variant of what is nonetheless oppression. Proudhon argued that the people were declared sovereign by a trick when in elections they actually abdicated their power anew every few years. Similarly Bakunin argued that universal suffrage was only a mask behind which lurked "the really despotic power of the State based on the police, the banks, and the army."[8] We will encounter very similar perspectives among our utopians.

In the anarchist model, the commune is the basic unit. Further levels of solidarity are to be achieved through the federation of communes, moving from the local to the regional to the national to the international level. The model is strikingly similar to the one put forward by Marcus Raskin in *Being and Doing*.

Anarchism also appeals to the utopians because of its built-in anti-technological bias. The expert, integral to scientific technological society, represents authority, and anarchism rejects the notion of superiority this implies. Complex technology also requires a division of labor, which produces the social stratification anarchists are intent on avoiding. As Corinne Jacker points out in *The Black Flag of Anarchy,* there is a kind of asceticisim inherent in the anarchist critique of urban technological society, a desire to be rid of what are seen as superfluous material objects.[9] Leo Tolstoy, a pacifist anarchist, questioned if raising the standard of living was beneficial, since in exchange for loss of liberty and healthy labor, people obtained more and more useless goods, and developed a greater appetite for them. In addition, in anarchist thought there is an everpresent awareness that a size limit is necessary for both industrial and agricultural units to make collective decision-making a possibility.

While drawn to anarchist thought, the utopians are also attracted to the one teaching which provides a comprehensive secular explanation for all social ills—namely Marxism. As a form of secular messianism which assumes that perfect social arrangements will produce a new man, Marxism strikes a responsive chord in utopian hearts. Church bureaucracies and peace movement leaders have been especially prominent in providing support for third world Marxist liberation movements, whose victory, they believe, is essential for the creation of a global, just, peaceful, social order. Of course, Marx, too, foresaw anarchy as the ultimate form of social organization. (Many of the utopians who use Marxist social analysis do not accept the idea of an interim dictatorship of the proletariat, but envisage going straight from the collapse of the present order to a community of communities.)

In *The American as Anarchist,* David de Leon argues that anarchism is the true native American radicalism. While the utopians can thus be considered to stand in a major American tradition, there are important differences between the new anarchism and the old. One is that the utopians are not open with us. Their goals are put forward in such a way as to evoke a broad favorable consensus. Because much of the agenda of the new utopians is known only to the initiated, the public is in effect coerced into courses of action that a majority would reject if it were aware of their full implications. How many who march against nuclear energy want to restrict all sources of energy, including coal, oil and water? How many who rally to the cause of greater corporate responsibility want to use only products they can make and repair themselves? Because of its double face, the new utopian movement has chalked up successes in the political arena unknown to earlier, more forthright representatives of utopian movements in this country.

There is another way in which the new utopian anarchism is different from its forerunners. The old anarchism existed in a country with a relatively low level of international responsibilities and with a relatively high state of security. The present day movements have developed in a United States vulnerable to outside threat and with commitments to other states. This has forced these groups to deny the reality of external danger. They emerge consistently as apologists for Soviet actions and affirmers of the benign character of Soviet intentions. They are pushed to defense of the Soviet Union because if there were a genuine Soviet threat, the United States would have to organize to meet it. The anarchist model, with no central organization, with all decisions made in face-to-face local meetings, with technology scaled down to "appropriate" and "human scale" would scarcely seem the most suitable with which to counter the Soviet war machine. But by defining the Soviet Union's actions as essentially defensive, the utopians can push for unilateral disarmament, emasculation or outright abolition of our intelligence agencies, the elimination of whole energy technologies and the severe restriction of others.

Thus the new utopian anarchism, unlike the old, employs a double standard. Anarchists were the most trenchant early critics of Marxism, foreseeing the inevitable direction of a regime based on its principles. Proudhon foresaw that state communism would mean "the absorption of all local and individual life into the administrative machinery, and the destruction of all free thought."[10] Bakunin similarly understood where the supposedly "interim" dictatorship of the proletariat would lead: "to the vilest and most dangerous lie of our century . . .: Red Bureaucracy."[11] But our utopians show a remarkable restraint when it comes to Soviet society and Soviet actions. Although nuclear technology, whether used for energy or weapons, is the focus of utopian indignation in the United States, the Soviet deployment of nuclear weapons directed against Western Europe and its extensive use of nuclear energy, without the safeguards used in the United States, do not draw the utopian's anger or even attention. The typical rationalization of the utopians is that they can only deal with the problems of their own society. (The National Council of Churches offers this same excuse for its double standard in explaining why it condemns human rights violations by El Salvador—and not in Vietnam. El Salvador receives support from the United States.)

Finally, the methods of the new movements do not recall traditional anarchist methods. Anarchists wrote, preached, formed model communities and threw bombs at the symbols of authority. They did not seek to exploit the political machinery as a means of bringing about the great social change. It took anarchists in the United States nine years simply to organize the Chicago Black International of 1881, so opposed were the various anarchist groups to any kind of central authority. But the attitude toward power of the new anarchists is far less straightforward. Inveighing against centralized power, they seek to take over that power. The goal, as is quite clear in the literature of these groups, is to bring down the system through the system. After power is obtained, what a leader of one group called ''our own political wreckers groups'' can bring down existing institutions and inaugurate the ideal order. (That speaker, incidentally, headed two groups that have been the recipient annually of hundreds of thousands of dollars of Federal funds.) In the interim, finding themselves in a growing number of key administrative positions, the thrust of their activity has been to augment the powers of the central government by an elaboration of administrative rules and the development of regulatory mechanisms from whose coercive power there is no easy appeal.

Thus, the visionaries of the modern anarchist paradise have accommodated their vision to a powerful central government, run by themselves, as an intermediate state. While this differs sharply from earlier American utopian conceptions, it forcefully recalls the fate of other utopian visions, which on the way to the withering away of the state, have created the most coercive state systems known to man.

The utopians would not have had the success they have enjoyed if it were not for the malaise within this country's leadership that followed the Vietnam War. The utopians were articulate and self confident; they offered new ideas and direction, a moral center, a vision of the future. They fed upon the leadership's sense of guilt that somewhere, somehow, they had gone astray or the Vietnam disaster would not have happened. The Carter administration was prepared to give virtue and conviction a chance, and utopians trooped into key regulatory and policy-making positions.

Although the public has not been aware of the role of the utopians, the Republican victory was in part a repudiation of their achievements.

The Reagan administration was committed to an anti-utopian thrust. Nonetheless, if the utopians were downcast at the Republican victory, it made them redouble their efforts, and they have been successful in undercutting key administration initiatives in the area of environmental regulation, defense and foreign policy. The utopians remain in key government bureaucracies. They have a strong, even dominant voice in the media. The utopians will remain a powerful force in our midst—it is time we knew more about them.

REFERENCES

1. H. Peter Metzger, "The Coercive Utopians," Presented at the National Meeting of the American College of Nuclear Medicine, April 28, 1978 (updated June 1979) Public Service Co. of Colorado, Denver, Colorado, p. 14
2. Amory Lovins, "Energy Strategy: The Road Not Taken," *Foreign Affairs,* Oct. 1976, pp. 91-92
3. David Martin, "Revs and Revolutions," *Encounter,* January 1979, p. 11
4. Quoted in Joseph Shattan, "The No-Nuke Wind Ensemble," *The American Spectator,* March 1980, p. 7
5. Jack Collins, "Approaching the Millennium." *CALC Report,* Jan./Feb. 1980, p. 2
6. Donald McIntosh, "The Dimensions of Anarchy," in J. Roland Pennock and John W. Chapman eds., *Anarchism,* New York: New York University Press, 1978, pp. 243-44
7. Quoted in Ibid., p. 256
8. Daniel Guerin, *Anarchism,* New York: Monthly Review Press, 1970 pp. 17-18
9. Corinne Jacker, *The Black Flag of Anarchy,* New York: Charles Scribner's Sons, 1968, p. 4
10. Daniel Guerin, op. cit., p. 16
11. Ibid., pp. 25-26

II

Sanctifying Revolution: Churches in Pursuit of Perfection

In January 1980, the research office of the National Council of Churches of Christ circulated to upper level staff a study called "Profiles By Faith." Recipients were warned to keep the study secret:

> "Although we may all agree that public opinion does *not* set our marching orders, there are those who will see some of these findings as showing how 'out of step' the NCCC is with its own constituency and censure us for it. To those who are hunting for such ammunition we need not supply a 'silver bullet.'"[1]

"Profiles By Faith" analyzed 1972-1978 data from the general Social Survey conducted annually by the National Opinion Research Center in Chicago so as to throw light on the attitudes of church members toward some of the issues taken up by the National Council of Churches. The study found that in denominations belonging to the NCC, the proportion of members who characterized themselves as liberal was smaller than the proportion in any of the other categories to which they were compared: Protestants in denominations that do not belong to the Council, Catholics, Jews, and non-affiliated individuals. Although the NCC passed a resolution against the death penalty in 1976, 68.1 percent of members of Council-affiliated denominations favored the death penalty, more than in any other group, except

Catholics. Although the NCC had passed a policy statement on the criminal justice system accusing it of undue severity, by an overwhelming 81.5 percent, members of Council-affiliated denominations considered the courts insufficiently harsh in handling criminals. Busing, supported by the NCC, was opposed by 78.3 percent of those questioned in the survey, but by 82.3 percent of members of Council-affiliated denominations.

An article that appeared in the January 1983 issue of *Reader's Digest* (by one of the authors of this book, Rael Jean Isaac) and a segment on the popular "Sixty Minutes," devoted to the World and National Council of Churches, shown a few weeks later, first made millions of Americans aware of the extent to which mainline Protestant denominations had become supporters of revolutionary activism, both in the United States and abroad.

While some denominational money has gone directly to terrorists via the Program to Combat Racism of the World Council of Churches, much more church money has gone to political support groups for terrorist organizations and for totalitarian states, and for field work designed to raise consciousness of oppression and to organize the oppressed against their designated oppressors. Contributions in cash and in services come from the World Council of Churches, the National Council of Churches and many of its member communions, including the United Methodist Church, the Episcopalian Church, the United Presbyterian Church and the United Church of Christ. While the most famous World Council of Churches' donations have been to terrorist groups in southern Africa, the Program to Combat Racism over the last years has given $672,500 to almost 40 groups within the United States, including support groups for revolution in Puerto Rico and the United States itself. These grants are made, according to the Program's director Anwar Barkat, on the ground that in the U.S., "racism is the predominant reality."[2]

The climate in some church agencies has grown so fevered that they have literally become breeding grounds for terrorists. The FBI uncovered a Puerto Rican FALN cell operating out of the Episcopal Church's National Commission on Hispanic Affairs. The FALN has taken responsibility for 120 bombings, including the bombing of the historic Fraunces Tavern in New York City, which killed four and injured dozens more, and the bombings in New York, on New Year's Eve of 1983, that seriously wounded three policemen. The FBI was led to the cell in 1976 when it found stationery from the Hispanic Affairs

Commission, along with a bomb factory, in the home of Carlos Alberto Torres. Torres, a former Hispanic Affairs Commission member, joined the FBI's most wanted list and another former member of the Commission, Oscar Lopez Rivera, was sought with him.

The Hispanic Affairs Commission, which had been established in 1970 by the General Convention of the Episcopal Church despite warnings that it might be used as a revolutionary device in Puerto Rico and elsewhere in Latin America,[3] seems to have unwittingly been funding the FALN. When the FBI examined the Commission's files, it discovered that the dates and places of various FALN bombings coincided with the travels of Commission members at church expense.[4] Vehicles rented by the Hispanic Commission were also apparently used for terrorist actions and a typewriter in the New York offices of the Commission matched the typing on two FALN communiques.[5]

Not long after the exposure of Torres, the Hispanic Affairs Commission's former Northeast Regional representative, William Morales, lost his fingers and part of his jaw while inexpertly making bombs for the FALN in his apartment. Morales filed a $1.2 million lawsuit against New York officials, charging them with confiscating his fingers as evidence after the explosion rather than arranging for them to be resewed. Although Morales won his suit, he did not stay around to collect, escaping from a prison ward at Bellevue a month after being sentenced to a 29-89 year prison term. According to the National Committee to Free Puerto Rican Prisoners of War, it was through the Episcopal Church's Hispanic Commission that Morales "became familiar with the oppressive condition of other Spanish-speaking people in the United States." (Morales, also wanted in connection with the New Year's Eve bombings, was captured by Mexican police in May 1983.)

The attitude of the churches to these discoveries is instructive. The Hispanic Affairs Commission's Executive Director and her secretary went to jail rather than testify before a grand jury concerning what they knew of the whereabouts of Torres. The National Council of Churches filed a legal brief on their behalf, issued a resolution demanding that they be promptly released and urged church authorities in similar cases in the future to support employees who for "reasons of principle" defied the law. The NCC also cooperated with the Episcopal Church in paying the legal fees of the two women who were given $40,000 in church funds on their release. The Interreligious Foundation for Community Organizations (IFCO), then part of the NCC, argued that although some might contend it was the duty of church people to aid the authorities to apprehend criminals "that may be true *so long as the trail does not lead through the church.*"[6] (Italics in the original)

The once staid Episcopal Church, the economic well-being of whose members earned it the sobriquet, "The Republican Party at Prayer", became a center of counter-cultural as well as political radicalism in the late '60s and early '70s. The great Episcopal cathedrals, St. John the Divine in New York City and Grace Cathedral in San Francisco, became centers of what Episcopal Canon William Rauscher has called "the church in frenzy." Well known political scientist and Episcopal layman Paul Seabury has described how St. John the Divine was made available for light shows, Shinto rites, Sufi workshops in Dervish dancing, ceremonies for striking farm workers and for Indians at Wounded Knee, special anniversary masses for the musical *Hair* and political protest rallies. On the other side of the continent, Bishop Kilmer Myers welcomed to Grace Cathedral light shows, guitar liturgies, nature festivals and pagan ceremonials. Seabury writes of one nature ceremony in the cathedral in 1971:

> "The cathedral dean was dimly seen through marijuana smoke, wrestling atop the high altar to remove a cameraman, while movie projectors simultaneously cast images of buffalo herds and other endangered species on the walls and ceiling to the accompaniment of "rock music."[7]

The Episcopal Church's political radicalism was not confined to the Hispanic Commission. Seabury notes that by the late 1960s:

> "National church authorities were dispensing millions of dollars of missionary funds collected from parishes and dioceses to radical political movements across the land—Black Power groups, migrant farm workers, Afro-American thespians, native American organizers, Puerto Rican nationalists, Marxist documentary film producers, and Third World liberation movements."[8]

In 1977 the Church appointed the former spiritual adviser to the Black Panthers, the Reverend Earl Neil, to head its Coalition for Human Needs, responsible for giving money to minority community action groups. The 44 member Executive Council of the Church voted in 1980 to commend Fr. Paul Washington for participating with Ramsay Clark in Iranian hearings on the crimes of America.[9] In 1983, when five leaders of the Puerto Rican independence movement, described by the FBI as "the remaining unincarcerated leadership of the FALN,"[10] refused to testify before a grand jury investigating the New Year's Eve bombings in New York City, Episcopal Bishop Paul Moore charged the grand jury was being used for a "witch hunt."[11] One of the five was Maria Cueto, the former executive director of the Episcopal Church's Hispanic Commission, who had earlier refused to testify about the whereabouts of Torres.

While the church leadership on the whole sees itself as part—if an unwilling and penitent part—of the oppressors, Episcopal Bishop Robert DeWitt, editor of *The Witness,* sees the church as part of the oppressed. DeWitt likens the United States to the Roman Empire and Pharoah's Egypt. The agents of enslavement are supermarkets, insurance companies and banks, which he calls local precincts of the empire. The clergy is not exempt from servitude because its members drive, shop and buy insurance. Bishop DeWitt is not without a certain optimism, however, for he says this is the way it was in the land of Egypt until someone preached "Let my people go."[12] DeWitt edited a Study Action Guide designed for use by groups within the church that declares "the system which creates and sustains much of the hunger, underdevelopment, unemployment and other social ills in the world today is capitalism."[13] The Guide is full of enthusiasm for both the Soviet Union and Maoist China, especially for the Cultural Revolution with its "very pragmatic goal of accelerated nation-building by an aroused, motivated people with new skills, awareness, and a sense of purpose." Bishop DeWitt's ideas dominate the Episcopal Urban Caucus, established in February 1980. Its governing board is composed largely of the board of the *Witness,* with the former associate editor of the magazine heading the staff. The keynote speaker at its foundation meeting announced that members were being asked to join a "revolution;" funding was to be obtained from the Convention of the Episcopal Church.[14]

Much is known about the funding of radical political groups by the Methodist Church thanks to the pioneering work of a young Methodist layman, David Jessup.[15] In April 1980 Jessup presented to the United Methodist Church's General Conference a report on contributions made by several agencies of the church to radical political groups between 1977 and 1979. (Detailed in Chapter I.)

In seeking to discredit Jessup's study, the Board of Global Ministries of the Church suggested that his criticism represented "right wing extremism."[16] But Jessup is scarcely a conservative. He works for the AFL-CIO's Committee on Political Education and was active in the Peace Corps in Peru and in the civil rights and farm worker movements in California. Anxious to work for refugee aid within the church, Jessup first became aware that something was amiss when in 1977 his children came home from Sunday school with "rice bags" which the family was supposed to fill with money to be used to buy wheat for Vietnam. Jessup's wife Linda had been reading about the way the Communists were using food as a means of forcing compliance with the new regime.[17] Spurred to investigate, Jessup wrote to various agencies of the Methodist church, asking them to detail the grants they had given to outside political groups. Simply from the agencies that responded to his inquiry Jessup documented $442,000 in direct grants, much of it to terrorist and totalitarian support groups, and he calculated that in-kind services to these groups went into the millions.

Jessup asked the General Conference of the United Methodist Church to establish a Committee on Accountability to examine the dollar value of support given by the church to such groups and to consider carefully whether anti-democratic groups should be funded at all. The Conference refused. Instead, the Methodist bureaucracy prepared an answer to Jessup's study, rationalizing support of these groups. The Board of Global Ministries and Board of Church and Society of the Methodist Church defended the grants on the grounds that they conformed to the social principles and social issues resolutions of the General Conference and were consistent with the Church's mission.

What was this mission? The church's reply to Jessup defined it as "solidarity with the poor and the powerless." According to the reply: "In the ministry and message of Jesus, the way in which we treat 'the least of these' transcends the question of whether the political system is totalitarian or democratic."[18] Actually, since in totalitarian states all but a small elite are powerless to control their fate, any group that proclaims itself for the poor then becomes a theologically appropriate beneficiary of Methodist funds. Since Marxist groups inevitably do this, they qualify. Methodist Bishop Roy Nichols, President of the Board of Global Ministries, in his introduction to the church reply to Jessup admits as much: "When the church commits itself to identification with the poor and oppressed, we may sometimes become involved with people whose blend of Marxist interpretation and Christian theology may be different from our own."[19] Since a number of groups receiving church funds professed no Christian theology at all, presumably Marxist ideology in and of itself was sufficient.

A number of the groups cited by Jessup's study were propaganda operations for Communist states, especially Cuba and Vietnam. (That these "progressive" states produce flotillas of refugees does not seem to darken their image as havens of the oppressed.) The Methodist Board of Global Ministries gave money to five organizations that produce pro-Cuba propaganda. The most influential of these is the North American Congress on Latin America (NACLA), founded as the research arm of the SDS, the revolution-minded campus movement of the 1960s. American churches provided the start-up funds for NACLA; its initial headquarters were in the National Council of Churches; many of its founders were seminary students; and one of the initial incorporators was the well-known Presbyterian theologian Richard Shaull. Its church connections and funding has not stopped NACLA from viewing the church as a prime instrument of imperial oppression. NACLA developed a "Church Project" designed, in NACLA's own words, to show how the churches, by and large, function as the "velvet-gloved counterparts of the iron fist of capitalist violence and exploitation."[20]

The Board of Global Ministries also sponsored tours to Cuba and participated in Cuban-sponsored international conferences, which according to one glowing Methodist report "deal with the liberation of people from oppressive political, economic and social systems." Even the forcible transfer of thousands of children as young as seven from Africa to Cuba for training as revolutionary cadres for Soviet-backed regimes was praised by Methodist officials. One tour participant wrote admiringly of the Cuban program that it would produce "highly trained and disciplined leaders [who] will be a decisive force in the future direction of their nations."

Although many in the anti-war movement subsequently condemned human rights violations by the victorious North Vietnamese, the Methodist Church financed organizations that uncritically endorsed Vietnam. These included Friendshipment and the Indochina Resource Center. Pat Patterson of the Board of Global Ministries staff was part of a Friendshipment delegation to Hanoi. At a May 1977 press conference, she explained that she had learned from the Vietnamese that their reeducation process was "a way to make people ready for a new society." The Indochina Resource Center for years was distinguished by its defense of the Pol Pot regime. The testimony by Gareth Porter, coordinator of the Center from 1974-1976, in 1977 Congressional hearings so offended liberal Congressman Stephen Solarz that he compared Porter to the writers who denied that Hitler killed six million Jews.

The only terrorists directly obtaining Methodist money were in southern Africa. The United Methodist's World Division at first funded both Bishop Muzorewa's group and that of Robert Mugabe. But after Bishop Muzorewa accepted an internal settlement in 1979, the Methodists gave money only to the Patriotic Front which was employing terror against the Muzorewa-led government. Since Bishop Muzorewa was head of the Zimbabwean Methodist Church, it is little wonder that he expressed hurt anger when he learned of the Methodist action:

> "We just can't understand why the American church sides with our enemies. Doesn't it seem strange to you that our brothers and sisters . . . would support people who want to close our churches?"

The Methodists also funded the Soviet-backed African National Congress and the Southwest Africa People's Organization as well as American support groups for these organizations. While in the worldview of Methodist church leaders, this money doubtless goes to fight racism and colonialism, it is noteworthy that the African countries subject to Soviet colonialism, sometimes via Cuban troops, have been singled out in Methodist resolutions as deserving of economic aid from the United States.

The Methodists have aided the PLO via its support-groups in the United States. One recipient has been the Middle East Research and Information Project (MERIP) whose main problem has been in deciding with which branch of the Palestinian revolution to identify. MERIP's publications were included in the Methodist resource packet *Middle East Mosaic* distributed to church study groups. Another recipient was the Palestine Human Rights Campaign, the chief PLO support group in the United States. Palestine Human Rights Bulletin #12, included in the Methodist resource packet, calls for a PLO state on the West Bank and in Gaza as a transitional goal toward the "secular democratic" state which is the PLO's euphemism for Israel's destruction.

Jessup identified over forty similar groups which received Methodist funds.[21] Some were concerned with domestic issues—a number denied legitimacy to any intelligence activities by the United States within or outside the country. Several, like the American Indian Movement, cooperate with Soviet efforts to publicize the "plight of American political prisoners." What they all have in common is promotion of the view that America is an evil society.

In funding primarily support groups, rather than those who actually handle weapons, the Methodists perform a far more valuable service than they would if they supplied the guns. The "liberation" groups in Africa, the Middle East and Latin America supported by the Methodists all receive arms directly or indirectly from the Soviet Union. They need legitimacy, acceptance in the United States as positive forces for needed social change, so as to inhibit any action being taken against them, whether overtly or covertly, by the United States government.

Although Jessup did not obtain the committee on financial accountability he asked for at the United Methodist Church's 1980 General Conference, the Jessup Report had two major consequences. The Conference did agree to require the boards and agencies of the church to make full disclosure of all cash and in-kind contributions to outside organizations beginning in 1981. The first report was duly released in 1982, revealing a curious pattern. The usual liberal organizations such as Common Cause, the National Organization of Women, or the NAACP, were conspicuous by their absence. The fringe groups of the radical left, on the other hand, continued to be well represented. Beneficiaries of the Women's Division included a varitable Who's Who of the far left, ranging from PLO fronts to groups attacking the U.S. as a repressive and racist society. For example, the Women's Division in 1979 gave $64,000 to Operation Najdeh of the Palestine Aid Society, an organization which not only engages in anti-Israel activities in the United States but, as a reporter for the *Jewish Week* discovered, shared the offices of the U.S. Peace Council, U.S. branch of the international Soviet front, the World Peace Council.[22]

The second major consequence of the Jessup Report was the establishment of the Institute on Religion and Democracy (IRD), which includes on its board Jessup and distinguished ministers and laymen, including Methodist evangelist Edmund Robb, who is its chairman, Lutheran theologian Richard Neuhaus, Baptist minister and founder of *Christianity Today* Carl Henry, Catholic layman Michael Novak and sociologist of religion Peter Berger among others. The IRD has provided an indispensable source of leadership, organization and research in the battle to force the mainline churches, not to abandon social activism, but to include as a vital component of that activism a concern for fostering human freedom.[23] Not least of the advantages of the IRD in this campaign was that it included many political liberals, who spoke the language of their opponents in the churches, whom they saw as having betrayed genuine liberalism. (The Church League of America, created by political conservatives, had long criticized the mainline churches in a vocabulary so foreign to its target that the criticisms had no effect.)

The United Methodist Church provides more money than any other denomination (in 1981 over $5 million) to the budget of the National Council of Churches in which it has a correspondingly important voice. The NCC includes 32 Protestant and Eastern Orthodox communions and is even more detached than the Methodist bureaucracy from the views of lay church members.

The actions of the NCC are supposed to flow from its policy statements. Given the pains that are taken over these, it is worth examining a couple of them for the light they throw on the NCC's perspective. The NCC's policy statement on criminal justice developed out of a series of hearings by a Council task force in five regions of the country to which 120 people gave testimony.

According to the policy statement, our legal system reflects "the interest and privilege of the powerful." It is a tool "to suppress non-violent political dissent, to cope with social problems, and to provide cheap labor." Our legal system oppresses the poor and racial minorities who "sometimes serve a scapegoat function for society." By the end of the twelve page document it transpires that there are three levels of culpability. Least at fault is the criminal; partly culpable is the unjust criminal justice system; but most culpable is society itself whose injustices have created the criminal.

The only concrete change the paper suggests is the substitution of restitution for imprisonment. "Incarceration should only be imposed with a formal, legally prescribed demonstration that no acceptable alternative exists." Instead "a constructive social relationship" is to be established between the victim and the offender. The criminal and his victim will negotiate the resolution to their conflict "with appropriate safeguards against vindictiveness and intimidation." One has visions of an old lady in a Bronx housing project sitting in her living room over tea "negotiating" with the thugs who robbed her. How the NCC expects to prevent her from being intimidated in the absence of penal sanctions is unclear.

But the NCC does not really believe in the thugs terrorizing low income housing projects. The true criminals are those who represent the institutions that oppress the poor, forcing them into what is interpreted as criminal behavior. Thus the NCC-linked Interfaith Center on Corporate Responsibility, its offices also at 475 Riverside Drive, is zealous for criminal sanctions and prison penalties for corporation executives, upon whom they wish to fasten personal responsibility for damage caused by corporate actions, i.e. unsafe toys, cars etc. In the NCC world view, social determinism applies only to the poor and minorities. Those higher on the social scale possess freedom, responsibility, culpability—and should go to jail.

Given the NCC's views on our criminal justice system, it is not surprising to find that its President from 1979-81, Rev. William Howard, visited "political prisoners" in the United States. According to Howard: "One of our favorite beliefs in this country is that we have no political prisoners" when "much of our prison population is comprised of people who are victims of the social, economic and political structures of our society."[24] In deciding which prisoners to visit, Howard was guided by the research of the National Conference of Black Lawyers,'[25] a U.S. affiliate of the International Association of Democratic Lawyers (IADL), which is listed by the CIA as an international Soviet front organization. (The National Conference of Black Lawyers' director, Lennox Hinds, is the permanent representative to the UN for the IADL.) A strange guide for an American church leader, the National Conference of Black Lawyers directed Mr. Howard to such "political prisoners" as convicted murderer Larry Jackson of the Republic of New Africa.

In 1980 the NCC passed a policy statement on the Middle East, the main point of which was to urge the U.S. to recognize the PLO. But in the course of the statement it becomes clear that for the NCC the real villain is neither Israel nor the Arabs but the United States. For the NCC the "deepening dependence of nations" on oil has only made the Middle Eastern states more the victim of great power "intervention and exploitation." The NCC does not blame the Arab states for using their oil income to buy arms, but the United States and "transnational corporations" for selling them. Bizarrely, the United States is berated for its supposed mistreatment of Muslims and Jews in the United States who, according to the policy statement, suffer from "violence and deprivation of civil rights."

The NCC looks upon the United States as an oppressor, both at home and abroad. In an enthusiastic 1975 message of greeting to the newly victorious FRELIMO, the Marxist group that seized power in Mozambique, William Howard, then chairman of the NCC's Fifth Commission on Justice, Liberation and Human Fulfillment, spoke of minorities in the U.S. having in common with FRELIMO their suffering under "a greedy, domineering, global oppressor." Howard could only have been referring to the United States. Howard's replacement as head of the NCC's Fifth Commission is in full agreement. At a conference called by the NCC's Agricultural Missions program she declared: "In Puerto Rico we are born into colonialism, we think colonialism, we speak colonialism, we behave colonialism, we study colonialism, we eat colonialism, we breathe colonialism, we live colonialism, we die colonialism."[26]

NCC leaders identify the economic system as a primary cause of this supposed pattern of global exploitation. In 1975 an Ecumenical Consultation on Domestic Hunger sponsored by the NCC passed a statement which said there was a basic contradiction between capitalism "and the Biblical values of justice, mercy, stewardship, service, community and self-giving love."[27] Warren Day, the NCC's Director of News and Information, points out that such statements do not reflect the official view of the NCC, which is expressed formally only by the Governing Board. Nonetheless the statements passed by such conferences are revealing of the attitudes of NCC staff, who determine who shall be invited to them and then disseminate their conclusions.

The most important way in which some of the NCC's member churches confront corporations is through the Interfaith Center on Corporate Responsibility, which is loosely connected to the NCC as a "sponsored-related movement." The Interfaith Center's chief weapon is the stockholder resolution. Donald J. Kirchhoff, President of Castle & Cooke, a company that has been the target of Center-coordinated resolutions, says that the Center pursues an "anti-corporate strategy" using the annual meetings of corporations as a "primary battleground for divisive and abrasive political issues."[28] Herman Nickel, in a *Fortune* article on the Interfaith Center aptly called "The Corporation Haters" observes that the Center represents "the confluence of radical Christian and radical Marxist thinking."[29]

But if the United States functions as a negative ideal, the NCC leadership also finds countries that serve as a positive ideal. Astonishingly, these are Marxist third world countries that have either severely restricted or all but eliminated religion. Paul Hollander in his study *Political Pilgrims* has chronicled none more remarkable than the ministers who find in countries whose official policy is to extirpate religion an embodiment of religious ideals. In 1977 the NCC sent a ten man delegation to Cuba which reported on its return that it had been "challenged and inspired repeatedly by the determination and the success of the Cuban people to build, against great odds, a society characterized by economic equity, justice and human dignity." The delegation insisted that it was convinced "that the churches enjoy full freedom of worship and suffer no persecution, contrary to what many members of our constituency believe."[30] Yet in Cuba children are indoctrinated in atheism in schools; all public evangelism is forbidden; and no one who professes belief in God can be a member of the Communist party or advance in his career. As one party official admitted, in Cuba, as a practical matter "a Christian cannot be a boss." These measures have been sufficiently effective to bring the proportion of the population openly belonging to the Catholic Church down to just 1.5% of the country's 10 million population. The Protestant population has been reduced to a tiny minority estimated at 65,000.[31]

NCC leaders have embarked on yet stranger pilgrimages. Eugene Stockwell, director of the NCC's Division of Overseas Ministries, reported that his 1979 visit to China challenged his Christian faith. He said he was not "led to abandon faith in Jesus Christ" but had to ask himself "whether Christian nations can provide nothing better than injustice while an atheist nation struggles mightily to secure a fair modicum of justice."[32] Yet at that time in China, as Stockwell himself reported in an interview with Protestant bishop K.H. Ting, Christians had been deprived of all church buildings and educational institutions. Ting reported that in China, Christianity had become "a world view" consisting of small groups of people who met informally, not on Sunday because that was a workday, but in private homes once every few weeks "to share insights."[33]

Even Marxist prisons look good to some NCC leaders. In 1977 Paul McCleary, director of the NCC's relief and development arm, Church World Service, testified before Congress on the excellent conditions in a Vietnamese "reeducation camp" he had visited. At the same hearings Nguyen Van Coi, a survivor of eighteen months in three different reeducation camps described living conditions.

> "I was given two small bowls of rice twice daily, plain rice with salt. The cell in which I was detained was 11 feet by 22 feet. There were around 81 prisoners in my cell. We had to lie on our side because there was not enough room to lie on our back during the night."

Nonetheless, McCleary insisted to the Congressional committee that the Vietnamese camps were an improvement over the way Americans treated draft dodgers and deserters. "As a churchperson, I would have to identify with the Vietnamese as those who have chosen the better way to heal the wounds of war."[34]

In view of the NCC's idealization of third world communist regimes, it comes as no surprise that the NCC's human rights resolutions are marked by a pronounced double standard. Although on its own estimate the NCC has issued 120 such resolutions, most of the great human rights outrages have been passed over in silence by the NCC's governing board—the atrocities of Idi Amin, the killing of half a million non-Moslems by Moslems in the Sudan, Vietnam's creation of almost a million boat people, the cultural revolution in China, the Soviet invasion of Afghanistan. The NCC governing board did condemn the Cambodian genocide but in its resolution laid as much blame on the U.S. government as on the Pol Pot regime. The NCC reserves most of its indignation for right wing governments. The Governing Board has condemned El Salvador, Turkey, Nicaragua (under Somoza, not the Sandanistas), Chile, South Korea and Guatemala.

In the wake of publicity about the weakness of the NCC for despotisms of the left in *Reader's Digest* and "60 Minutes", the *United Methodist Reporter,* the largest independent Methodist newspaper, conducted its own study and found that there was indeed a 4-1 disproportion in the number of resolutions critical of non-Communist countries as against Communist countries. Moreover the *Reporter* found these figures understated the difference, because criticisms of Communist countries were confined on the whole to a narrow issue (e.g. condemnation of the refusal of the Soviet Union to allow Pentecostal families who had taken refuge in the U.S. embassy basement out of the country), while condemnations of non-Communist countries were sweeping. The *Reporter* noted that the NCC's double standard on human rights was especially apparent when it called for an end to all economic aid for El Salvador on the grounds of that government's violation of human rights while the NCC itself, through Church World Service, was pouring economic aid into Vietnam.[35]

While the enthusiasm of NCC leaders for Soviet Third World satellites does not carry over to the Soviet Union, NCC leaders have been eager to carry on dialogue with Soviet churches. In 1979, for the first time, the NCC issued a joint proclamation on disarmament with Soviet churchmen. The problem with this sort of activity is that while NCC leaders are free to criticize their government, the Soviet church leaders permitted to engage in dialogue with the NCC without exception defend all actions of their own government. The NCC's sharp condemnation of the Reagan administration for increasing military spending (an NCC resolution condemned Reagan's defense policies as "utterly in conflict with the Gospel of Christ") was not, needless to say, followed by condemnation of the Soviet arms buildup by any Soviet church leaders with which the NCC maintains dialogue.

The Soviet use of churches as propaganda instruments is particularly obvious in the Christian Peace Conference, ostensibly an independent international organization concerned with peace, but actually a Soviet-controlled front. Nonetheless the NCC allowed an American group, Christians Associated for Relationships with Eastern Europe and the Christian Peace Conference (CAREE) to become a subcommittee of one of its own divisions and the NCC's President James Armstrong joined CAREE's board. CAREE selects candidates for positions on the Christian Peace Conference's working committee, International Secretariat, Executive Committee and various commissions. CAREE can thus not avoid all responsibility for what the CPC does. One of its most recent activities was to try to expel all Jewish nongovernmental organizations accredited to the UN on the grounds that Jewish organizations support Israel despite "Israel's sinister alliance with South Africa." It is also interesting that CAREE met in Chicago at the moment when the military junta in Poland was dissolving Solidarity—and said not a word of protest.[36]

The NCC's relief and development work has been affected by its ideology. In part the effect has simply been to make programs less efficient. Church World Service, the NCC's relief and development agency, is easily the most popular NCC program with churchgoers, a popularity reflected in its budget, which is roughly 70% of the NCC total. In 1973 a "consultation" was held concerning CWS at which it was proposed that the organization commit itself to "liberation and justice." When its long time director James MacCracken refused to reorient the agency from its traditional mission of helping the poor and hungry, he was summarily fired by Eugene Stockwell, director of the Division of Overseas Ministries of which CWS is a part.[37] According to a former executive of CWS, a great deal of time under MacCracken's successor, Paul McCleary, is spent on writing issue papers and trying to identify the root causes of poverty. This executive notes that the Division of Church and Society used to do that sort of thing while CWS "delivered the goods and took care of the victims."

The NCC sees one of the major functions of its overseas aid program to be the creation of rural leadership cadres to struggle against "oppression" by their governments and "transnational corporations," which, in the words of an NCC resolution "hold people in bondage to poverty and hunger." According to the report of the Division of Overseas Ministries, its Agricultural Missions program places its main emphasis on supporting "local indigenous movements that tended toward total liberation of rural people—spiritual, economic and political."[38] Agricultural Missions has no use for "agrarian reform" programs, which it describes as "tools for the repression of rural leaders."[39] It seems clear that when the NCC's Agricultural Missions program talks about "liberation" it means movements of the sort carried out by the Sandanistas and the Marxist guerillas in El Salvador, and it reports arranging "face-to-face contacts between the churches and persons who are directly involved in peoples' liberation struggles."[40]

Consciousness raising and networking of political activists is a major program direction of the NCC's "development" work. NCC leaders see this as progress over previous efforts in the war against hunger, such as sending of food, seeds, tools and agricultural experts. (Fortunately, despite its low opinion of such efforts as not going to "the roots of hunger", the NCC has not dispensed with them altogether.)

The sympathy of CWS leaders with Marxist regimes has led them to fund such questionable schemes as the New Economic Zones established by the Vietnamese government. These are one of the coercive schemes typical of Communist countries, and "political undesirables," without farming experience, have been herded into them. It was fear of being moved into these zones that propelled many ethnic Chinese to brave death at sea. Church World Service, through a World Council of Churches organized consortium, sent half a million dollars for two New Economic Zones, one in an area inhabited by Montagnard tribesmen into which the Vietnamese were sending people from Hanoi.

The literature published by the NCC's Friendship Press and used in the educational programs of member denominations is so blatantly hostile to American institutions and supportive of Third World Communist regimes that it has served as a catalyst in mobilizing a number of people who have become leaders in the effort to counter the revolutionary activism of their denominational leadership. For example, George Massay, a minister in the Disciples of Christ, who with his wife Alice initiated a group called Christian Mission Awareness in an attempt to reorient the church to traditional priorities, first became aware something was wrong when he read an enthusiastic church publication describing Castro's Cuba.

Typical of this literature is the People and System series which consists of a series of pamphlets on Cuba, China, Tanzania, the United States and Canada. Health care, education, work, religion and the status of women are compared. In Cuba we are told people work because "Work is not alienated; it has been made *human*." The Cultural Revolution, which even the present regime in China admits had a devastating impact, is praised for having "deepened and continued" the process of moving China to socialism by uprooting "mutant social growths." Similarly, in Tanzania we are told "freedom is work" and there is "exploitation by none." Only in the United States, we learn, workers feel "alienated and exploited."[41]

Per capita the largest contributions to the National Council come from the Presbyterian Church, whose leadership has also displayed marked sympathy for radical causes for over a decade. United Presbyterian national headquarters made a $10,000 donation to the Angela Davis defense fund at the time of her murder trial. (The hierarchy gave no funds to her less radically chic non-Communist co-defendant Rushell McGee.)

In 1980 the General Assembly of the Church voted to set up an Emergency Fund for Legal Aid for Racial and Intercultural Justice to provide financial assistance to individuals from racial minorities for costs related to litigation. Substantial sums promptly went to various individuals accused (in some cases already condemned) for murder and robbery. After American hostages had been held in captivity in Iran for 231 days, the General Assembly passed a resolution that called for their release, but expressed embarrassment at "our quickness in expressing righteous indignation when our own people are hurt, but our slowness to do so when brutal indignities are imposed on others with our tacit support."[42]

The United Church of Christ may well be the most radical of the larger churches. It had the distinction of receiving a $10,000 award from the People's Bicentennial Commission, a radical and bitterly anti-business group formed in opposition to the official bicentennial celebrations. It was bestowed upon the Church for "evidence likely to lead to the arrest and imprisonment of the chief executive officer of a Fortune 500 company." The Church had turned over to the group documents obtained from an avowedly Communist (white) group in the Union of South Africa allegedly showing that Mobil Oil had supplied fuel to (then) Rhodesia despite trade sanctions in force against it. The Church was promised another $15,000 if Mobil's head should actually go to jail.[43]

In 1978 the United Church of Christ responded to the allegations of then Ambassador to the UN Andrew Young (himself a United Church of Christ minister) that there were political prisoners in the United States, not with the outrage of most Americans, but with a list of political prisoners compiled for them by yet another United Church of Christ member, the Reverend Ben Chavis, then in jail as one of the Wilmington 10 accused of firebombing a grocery store in North Carolina. Prominent in the group Chavis compiled were jailed Puerto Rican terrorists. That laws were broken, bombs thrown, or people killed cut no ice with the United Church of Christ. If people are politically *motivated,* they are political prisoners.

Officials of the United Church of Christ are among the most prominent radical activists. The church's Barry Lynn conducted a national signature campaign "to register against the draft" as chairman of the National Committee against Registration and the Draft. Ben Chavis served as Washington director of the United Church of Christ's Commission for Racial Justice from his North Carolina cell. By 1978, the church had poured $425,000 in churchgoer funds into the defense of Chavis and others of the Wilmington Ten. The conviction of the group was set aside, but Chavis had little use for any aspect of U.S. justice or society. He became co-chairman, with U.S. Communist Party leader Angela Davis, of the National Alliance Against Racist and Political Repression. Speaking at the February 1980 rally of the National March against the Klan in Greensboro, North Carolina, Chavis vowed that there would be no draft: "If we're going to fight, we're going to fight right here in the U.S." And Chavis shouted: "We're going to march; we're going to keep on marching until we tear this system down."[44]

Although the churches are second only to the government in the amount of money that passes through their hands each year, except for the United Methodists little is known concerning the way the mainline denominations spend their funds. Churches do not have to file annual reports with the IRS the way other tax exempt organizations do. And they don't have to account to their membership how their funds are spent. Church financial reports at national assemblies are typically vague. Groups have been formed within a number of churches seeking to make them follow the lead of the United Methodists in providing detailed information to church members on financial expenditures. At this writing, no other church has followed the Methodist example.

If the emphasis here has been on Protestant churches rather than on synagogues or the Catholic church, it is not because Jewish and Catholic religious leaders have been impervious to revolutionary enthusiasms. Among Jews the Reform movement has been the most susceptible. The Union of American Hebrew Congregations, the official organization of Reform temples, belongs to the Methodist-created Coalition for a New Foreign and Military Policy. But the fact that the Human Rights Working Group of the Coalition includes the chief PLO support groups in the United States puts Reform on the defensive with its own members. Reform is in the position of dipping its foot in, but hesitating to immerse itself.

In the case of the Catholic church, while individual priests and orders have been prominent among radical activists—the Berrigan brothers are probably the best known religious radicals in the country and the Maryknoll order has been a strong supporter of revolutionary action—the problem has not been as pervasive. That may be changing. The disarmament movement seems likely to push the Catholic hierarchy further into an adversary stance to United States institutions. (That movement is even having an impact upon evangelical churches, notably the Southern Baptists, who have resisted the social activism of the mainline denominations.)

Thus far we have not addressed the most interesting question: Why? That fringe groups within the churches should be caught up in cultural eddies in the broader society is not surprising, but why should the leadership of mainline churches support revolutionary groups? Why is this leadership so critical of United States economic, social and political institutions? Why are Marxist regimes, although they violate human rights far more massively than the governments these churchmen attack, exempt from criticism? Why, on the contrary, are such regimes praised, and their support groups given financial aid? Why should Marxism exert any attraction at all for churchmen when the antipathy of Marxism to religion is one of its best known characteristics?

Rev. Isaac Rottenberg of the Reformed Church in America, who was part of the NCC world for twelve years before he was dismissed for criticizing it publicly in a letter to the *New York Times* in 1978, casts some light on this puzzling question. "These are immensely romantic people, often quite naive."[45] There is ample evidence of this naivete in relation to Communist governments. For example Dr. Kirk Alliman of Church World Service declared:

> "I think part of the reason that Church World Service has what I consider to be a fairly bright future with Kampuchea is because the three of us (Kirk Alliman, Doug Beane—CWS Indochina Regional Representative and Perry Smith, acting Kampuchea Director) were prepared to spend hours listening and sympathizing with government officials who sensed in us the same kind of concern for human dignity and the value of life that they have."[46]

Although the Heng Samrin government refused to permit a "land bridge" of trucks by international relief agencies and the death toll in the first year of that regime was equal to the worst year of the Pol Pot regime,[47] Perry Smith, director of CWS's relief operation in Phnom Penh said: "In 16 years of work in relief with CWS, I have never had better cooperation with a government than I got from the Kampuchean government."

Rottenberg notes too that the Interchurch Center at 475 Riverside Drive, which houses the NCC and most of the national church bureaucracies, has had an effect that is the reverse of that originally intended. While the idea in bringing church leaders together in one building was to promote dialogue, instead, says Rottenberg "people in the bureaucracies start feeding on the same ideas from floor to floor. They go to the same conferences and repeat the same phrases. And NCC phrases become very much the phrases of the Third World—the oppressed, liberating the oppressed."

In part totalitarian societies may be attractive to some churchmen precisely because they make the practice of religion so difficult. Those who remain Christians sacrifice secular advancement for their faith, may actually suffer martyrdom. American churchmen, accustomed to flocks who take their church for granted, may see Christians in Marxist countries as more satisfying congregations, recalling early days of the church, when believers were persecuted but vibrant in faith. Preaching in Moscow, in May 1982, Billy Graham seemed to be expressing this notion when he referred to the packed church and said you would not find this on Sunday in North Carolina. (A *Washington Post* reporter at the service noted the congregation's size owed much to the very large contingent of KGB agents in the church.) At the same time that the state restricts religion, in many churchmen's view, it bears a sort of unconscious Christian witness by working for what they consider to be justice and equality and attending closely to all aspects of the individual's life. This characteristic of totalitarian societies seems to be interpreted as "caring" by these churchmen.

But while ignorance, romanticism, bureaucratic isolation and naiveté may all play a part, the behavior of the mainline Protestant denominational leadership can only be understood in the light of the history of the ecumenical movement. The battle for the soul of the mainline churches, spearheaded today by the Institute on Religion and Democracy, has been fought before. There are, to be sure, differences this time round. While the dislike of capitalism and the attraction of Marxism is old, the hatred of the United States is new. While the yearning for major social transformation is old, the acceptance by churchmen of the idea of violence is new. That the equivalent of today's utopians lost the first time was in large part due to the influence of a single "convert" from the utopians of an earlier period, Protestant theologian Reinhold Niebuhr.

The predecessor of the National Council of Churches, the Federal Council of Churches, established in 1906, became the center of what was known in the years between World Wars I and II as "The Social Gospel." And the churches most zealous for revolution today were those most active in support of the Social Gospel: the Methodists, United Presbyterians, Episcopalians and Congregationalists (now part of the United Church of Christ). The Social Gospel's first major expression within the Federal Council was in a report called *The Church and Industrial Reconstruction* which the Council published in 1920. The report was a scathing attack on capitalism. Capitalism depended on the conflict between capital and labor, emphasized competition, self-interest and the profit motive, treated people as tools, and produced stunted personalities. Capitalism was contrary to the teaching of Christ that human personality was of sacred worth, that brotherhood was the proper relationship between men, that cooperation and not greed should guide men's actions, and that social behavior should be guided by loving service.

In contrast, the Soviet experiment, newly launched in that period, seemed closer in spirit to the Christian vision of an ideal economic order, for its stated goal was absolute equality and human brotherhood. In 1919 Methodist minister Harry Ward wrote in the Methodist Federation's Social Service Bulletin: "The aim of the Bolsheviks is clearly the creation of a state composed of producers and controlled by producers. This is manifestly a Scriptural aim.''[48] William B. Spofford Sr., director of the Episcopal League for Industrial Democracy, saw the Soviet Union as ''a star in the East'' that ''wise men will follow as far as its beams cast light and do so without fears merely because its color happens to be red.''[49]

When time brought knowledge of purges and the destruction of the peasantry, the Soviet Union continued to be judged leniently by many in the forefront of the ecumenical movement. The very loftiness of Soviet goals served to excuse performance. It was argued that it was so difficult to transform man and society that mistakes were bound to occur. The United States on the other hand was judged by its flawed performance. Not surprisingly, the depression of the 1930s made that performance seem all the more unsatisfactory. Among churchmen the depression evoked a sense of the immediacy of inevitable historical change, a sense that this was ''the fullness of time,'' which made them even more receptive to Marx's analysis of the ''revolutionary process of society which is taking place before our very eyes.'' In 1931 *The Christian Century,* the leading organ of the Social Gospel, asked when America would begin social planning.[50] The New York East Conference of Methodists in 1932 unanimously endorsed social ownership of the means of production. Other conferences stressed that ''the only alternative to the present system is one in which social ownership and control is gradually and widely inaugurated.'' A district meeting of the Methodist's Evangelical Synod announced the disintegration of capitalism and called for nationalization of industry and resources.[51]

What prevented the majority of Social Gospel leaders from adopting in toto the Marxist critique of capitalist society was the Marxist insistence on violent revolution. The vanguard of the Social Gospel opposed violence. The Kingdom of God and the Christianization of the social order were to occur through love and not through class warfare. In addition, the Social Gospel leaders preferred the idea of cooperative ownership of productive resources to centralization and state-controlled public ownership.

The pacifism of many Social Gospel leaders, combined with their detestation of capitalism, led them into isolationism. They were resigned before even such calamities as the fall of France to Hitler. Charles Clayton Morrison, editor of *The Christian Century,* wrote:

> ''Can Hitler give the rest of the world a system of inter-relationships better than the trade-strangling and man-exploiting system of empire capitalism?''

Morrison was not optimistic that Hitler could, but found compensations for France in her defeat:

> "In a united Europe governed from a German center, with a unified planned economy covering the continent, France will be able to find compensation in terms of human values."[52]

France, wrote Morrison, might experience "a genuine and creative revival of economic freedom."

That many advocates of the Social Gospel awoke from their illusions was due largely to the intellectual transformation of Reinhold Niebuhr, who had shared them. Niebuhr was a central figure in the Social Gospel movement. A member of the Fellowship of Reconciliation which brought together pacifists and adherents of the Social Gospel, Niebuhr for a brief period became a committed Marxist, and a favored speaker for Communist front organizations. Yet Niebuhr's thought was not Marxist. For while Marxism assumed that a perfect society would eventually emerge, Niebuhr argued in *Moral Man and Immoral Society* that there was no possibility of a truly moral social order. Man could choose only the relatively good—the absolutely good was a chimera.

As the threat of Hitler loomed ever larger in the 1930s, Niebuhr was prepared to attack the two utopian delusions from which he and so many other Social Gospel figures had suffered: pacifism and Marxism, and to defend democracy. Niebuhr berated the churchmen who argued that all societies were imperfect and not worth defending by force. Niebuhr was also prepared to confront the totalitarian nature of Soviet society and after the war, in words that resonate especially strongly today, insisted that nuclear weapons had made pacifism no more acceptable for Christians:

> "There is nothing in the Christian faith which would enable Christians to evade a tragic dilemma which other men face. The development of atomic weapons has heightened the moral dilemmas which periodically generate the pacifist revolt against responsibilities which embody moral ambiguities. But it has not solved them."[53]

But if Niebuhr could be called "the father of us all" by one of America's foremost "realists" of the cold war, that realism was swept aside by churchmen in the post World War II period. The National Council of Churches named an adjoining street Reinhold Niebuhr Plaza and obeisance done, proceeded to ignore the man whose thought had guided so many of the new organization's leaders. Once a Niebuhr disciple, John C. Bennett became President of Union Theological

Seminary and assumed a leading role in the new variant of the Social Gospel. He observed in an essay published in 1970: "The forward-looking social activism of the Social Gospel is with us again, but in a much more radical form."[54]

And there's the rub—in a much more radical form. One reason that Niebuhr was able to persuade many churchmen to abandon their pacifism was because fundamentally they *did* believe the United States was worth defending. The members of the Federal Council saw the United States, for all the defects of its capitalist system, as purer than other nations. As historian Donald B. Meyer points out, it was their "deep expectations about the special qualities of American society" that had "allowed them to criticize in the first place."[55] This contrasts sharply with the view that has gained adherents among activist churchmen today that the United States is uniquely evil, the oppressor and exploiter of Third World countries and peoples.

The growing willingness to believe the worst about the United States led activist churchmen to apply to this country the kind of critique applied by German theologians to the church's role in permitting the rise of Nazism. The witness a courageous few like Friedrich Bonhoeffer, Martin Niemöller and Karl Barth bore against the Nazi state became identified with the witness of radicals in the United States facing the American juggernaut. The absurdity of the analogy between the protester against government policy in the United States and the individual who stood up to virtually certain death from the Nazi murder-machinery does not seem to have occurred to those who saw themselves modeled on the heroic anti-Nazi figures. That Niemöller and Barth became increasingly anti-American enhanced their influence with radical American churchmen (Barth actually claimed it was a religious duty to support the Vietcong.)[56]

Even more influential than the anti-Nazi German Protestant theologians have been the theologians of what has variously been called "revolution," "hope" and "liberation." Although historian Gunther Lewy points out that this theology is so ecumenical in spirit that it is impossible to point to specific denominational elements, its impact has been specially felt in Catholic Latin America, where it has become wedded to Marxism. Peruvian Catholic theologian of liberation Gustavo Gutierrez asserts that Marxism, by liberating man from his temporal oppression, frees God to usher in his kingdom. Marxist revolution becomes a precondition for salvation. The theology of liberation transforms key symbols like incarnation, revelation and resurrection, so that they do not point to a past event but to political liberation in the here and now. According to American Presbyterian theologian Richard Shaull, only at the center of the revolution can men "perceive what God is doing."[57] Brazilian Protestant Ruben Alves thinks man must meet the liberating event of Christ's resurrection as co-creator of his own destiny through political revolution. Catholic priest Camilo Torres carried theory into action. Torres stated his belief that "only violent revolution could put properly oriented decision-makers into positions of power"[58] and took to the hills where he and his band met death at the hand of Columbian government forces. Four years later he was followed by Father Domingo Lain who issued a manifesto to Columbians calling upon them "to prepare themselves for the final struggle." (The manifesto, with its dateline "from the mountains" was published in full by the North American Congress on Latin America,[59] one of the groups already mentioned as receiving Methodist funds.) While only a few priests have actually taken to the hills, the priests of the Golconda Movement in Columbia have taken up the perspective of the guerilla-priests, arguing that even a theoretical Marxist Christianity "cannot respond to the revolution, for theology is done in action."

Whether formulated by native or foreign clergy (including American churchmen) the theology of revolution has a distinctly anti-American cast. Ironically, much of what is believed to be characteristic of Latin American liberation theology is, as Edward Norman has observed, the work of North American and other foreign missionary and staff priests. So noticeable is this that one measure taken by beleaguered Latin American governments is to try to keep out foreign priests. In El Salvador, where priests have been active in revolutionary movements, Bishop Aparico, conducting a mass, said "foreign priests should ask the Most Holy Virgin to grant the grace that they return to their own countries, there to find the hate and resentment they want to instill in our people." Ironically the United States (and several Western European democracies) have become exporters of revolution in a far more fundamental sense than the Soviet Union.

The dialogue opened between Marxists and Christians, especially in Latin America, opens the way for the utopians to understand how mischievous the role of the United States has been. In the words of John C. Bennett ". . . the dialogue and collaboration between Christians and Marxists in the Third World and especially in Latin America may have a transforming effect on Christian understanding of the U.S. role in the world."[60] The traditional conflict between Marxism and

Christianity is presented as the fault of the churches. Bennett believes not only that "Marxism has been the bearer of a true revolutionary imperative" but that "its anti-religious stance is a judgment upon the churches."

Revolutionary change in the United States is essential because only such change will remove this country, in Professor Bennett's words "as a counterrevolutionary force from the backs of the third world countries."[61] The "third world" takes on a metaphorical meaning, applicable not only to a geographic area but to the oppressed and exploited everywhere. In the United States blacks, Spanish-Americans and American Indians take on the honorary designation of Third World peoples. The Christian task becomes to identify with the oppressed and actively to support them in both the geographical and metaphorical third world.

The belief that violence is an appropriate means for achieving social change underlies liberation theology. Heavily influenced by liberation theology, the Uppsala Assembly of the World Council of Churches in 1968 declared that "at times 'law and order' may be a form of violence" and that the "covert violence of those with power may at times have to be overcome by the overt violence of those who are their victims." In 1969, responding to the wave of black rioting in U.S. cities, the National Council adopted this view and announced "there was an ethical difference between the violence used by the oppressed and that used by the oppressor." Said the Council: "Each use of violence is to be viewed on its own merits." Dr. Robert McAfee Brown in 1979 asserted that while nonviolence was useful as a technique, it was dangerous as an ideology. To urge non-violence "on Third World people *or on minority groups at home* [italics added]" was irresponsible.[62] The churchly revolutionaries make no distinction between the government of an Idi Amin and that of the United States. Indeed, judging from their response to Amin's Uganda and to this country, the United States is more in need of revolutionary violence.

Even peace churches can condone violence once the definition of violence has been broadened to include the injustice that drives men to violence. In a curious way, for groups like the Quakers, violence becomes the touchstone for identifying the worthy. The more violent the group the greater the injustice from which it must suffer and the more it must be in need of support.

The idea of Revolution is so attractive precisely because it allows cooperation with Marxists without committing churchmen to Marxist scientific materialism. The Marxist does not present clear or consistent images of the future. "What socialism will be we just don't know" said Lenin.[63] To the Christian radical this is confirmation that the future could be a Christian future and that the traditional Marxist attack on religion was directed against churchly establishments that had made their peace with an oppressive order.

In seeking models for a pure, revolutionary and uncompromised Christianity, some of the theologians of revolution have become fascinated by the heretical millenarian movements of medieval or early modern times such as the Brothers of the Free Spirit, Edomites, Joachimites and Puritan Fifth Kingdom Men.[64] These millenarians, believing the travails of their times to be unprecedented, followed leaders who promised a cataclysmic birth of a redeemed world. Claiming divine inspiration, and in the case of the Free Spirit, to have become divine themselves, the leaders set out to purify the world of sin in preparation for the coming of the millennium, often in very bloody fashion.

The modern Christian left combines millenarian temperament with a social and political analysis and action program which is hardly distinguishable from Marxism-Leninism. The present situation is defined as one of unparalleled suffering everywhere. In "every part of the world the inner contradictions . . . have given rise to struggles within and against the established order" and that order has reached "the End of the Road" says Richard Shaull. Such descriptions of a universal revolutionary situation differ from Communist tracts only in their occasional use of traditional religious phraseology.

The destruction of the old order is to lead to the birth of a New Man and to the creation of new Christian communities. While secular utopians do not forsee specifically Christian communities, they, too, forsee a new man in a new order based on absolute equality, brotherhood and simplicity of life. And, as we shall see, they set out to woo church leaders. For secular utopians see the churches not only as sources of money for their myriad projects, but view churchgoers as a potential mass base to be organized.

REFERENCES

Profiles by Faith or Surveying the Religious Landscape," Office of Research, Evaluation and Planning, NCC, Jan. 1980, p. 2

2. Joseph Harriss, "Karl Marx or Jesus Christ?" *Reader's Digest,* August 1982, p. 132
3. Dorothy Faber, "The Revolutionary Movement in Puerto Rico and the Church Connection Part I," *The Christian Challenge,* September 1979, p. 6
4. *New York Times,* April 17, 1977; Dorothy Faber, "The Revolutionary Movement in Puerto Rico—and the Church Connection, Part II," *The Christian Challenge,* October 1979, p. 6
5. *Information Digest,* January 14, 1983
6. "Grand Jury: A Legal Monster on the Loose," *IFCO News,* May-June 1977, p. 7
7. Paul Seabury, "Trendier than Thou," *Harper's,* October 1978, p. 43
8. Ibid., p. 40
9. Rev. William H. Ralston Jr., "They're at It Again," *The Christian Challenge,* November 1980, p. 10
10. *New York Times,* Jan. 20, 1983
11. Ibid.
12. Robert L. DeWitt, "Editorial," *The Witness,* Feb. 1979
13. *Struggling with the System, Probing Alternatives: A Study/Action Guide,* Church & Society Network/the Witness Magazine, September 1976, p. 24
14. Rev. Jerome Politzer, "Will Pecusa Be Transformed into Medusa?" *The Christian Challenge,* September 1980, p. 5
15. David Jessup, "Preliminary Inquiry Regarding Financial Contributions to Outside Political Groups by Boards and Agencies of the United Methodist Church, 1977-1979," April 7, 1980, p. 1
16. "The Use of Money in Mission—an Opportunity for Understanding," United Methodist Communications, October 17, 1980, p. 5
17. Evidence on this issue comes from Nguyen Long (with Harry H. Kendall), *After Saigon Fell: Daily Life Under the Vietnamese Communists,* Institute of East Asian Studies, University of California at Berkeley, 1981, p. 105
18. "The Use of Money in Mission—an Opportunity for Understanding," op. cit., p. 1
19. Ibid., p. 6
20. *NACLA's Latin America and Empire Report,* December 1973, p. 1
21. See David Jessup, op. cit., passim
22. *The Jewish Week,* Sept. 10, 1982
23. See *Christianity and Democracy; A Statement of the Institute on Religion and Democracy,* Wash. D.C. 1981
24. *Human Rights Perspectives* (published by National Council of Churches), March 1980, p. 5
25. The Fifth Commission: A Monitor for Third World Concerns, Vol. 5, No. 4, Fourth Quarter, 1979, p. 3
26. Rev. Eunice Santana de Velez, "Puerto Rico—the Colony," *The Christian Rural Mission in the 1980s—a Call to Liberation and Development of Peoples,* Agricultural Missions, National Council of Churches, 1979, p. 52
27. *The Presbyterian Layman,* Nov./Dec. 1975
28. S. Prakash Sethi, "Interfaith Center on Corporate Responsibility," mimeographed, 1980, p. 25
29. Herman Nickel, "The Corporation Haters," *Fortune,* June 16, 1980, p. 126
30. "Statement by the National Council of Churches Delegation to Cuba" released by Communication Commission, News and Information Services, National Council of Churches, December 8, 1977
31. New York Times, April 19, 1981

32. Eugene Stockwell, "Spirituality and Struggle for Fullness of Life," *Missiology,* January 1979, p. 55
33. Eugene L. Stockwell, "The Life of Christianity in China: An Interview with Dr. and Mrs. K.H. Ting," *The Christian Century,* February 23, 1977, p. 169
34. Statements of Paul F. McCleary and Nguyen Van Coi, Human Rights in Vietnam, hearings before the Subcommittee on International Organizations of the Committee on International Relations, House of Representatives, 95th Congress, 1st session, June 16, 21, and July 26, 1977, pp. 61-70, 74
35. *The United Methodist Reporter,* special edition, April 1983
36. *Religion and Democracy,* Jan. 1983, p. 5
37. Doug Hostetter and Michael McIntyre, "The Politics of Charity," *The Christian Century,* September 18, 1974, pp. 845-50; "National Council Church Official Fired for Refusing to Politicize Relief," *The Presbyterian Layman,* February 1975
38. *Hopes and Realities,* Division of Overseas Ministries, National Council of Churches 1976/78, p. 12
39. Annual Report, Agricultural Missions 1981, p. 4
40. Ibid.
41. *Cuba: People Questions,* p. 22; *China: People Questions,* pp. 21-22; *Tanzania: People Questions,* p. 24; *United States: People Questions,* p. 10. All are published by Friendship Press, New York, n.d.
42. *Presbyterian Layman,* June-July 1980
43. *New York Post,* June 22, 1976
44. *The News and Observer,* Raleigh North Carolina, Feb. 4, 1980
45. Interview, Isaac Rottenberg, Dec. 1, 1981
46. *Service News,* Church World Service-CROP, Vol. 33, No. 1, Jan. 1980, p. 1
47. Stephen Morris, "Vietnam Under Communism," *Commentary,* September 1982, p. 45
48. Donald B. Meyer, *The Protestant Search for Political Realism 1919-41,* Berkeley and Los Angeles: University of California Press, 1961, p. 146
49. Ralph L. Roy, *Communism and the Churches,* Harcourt, Brace & Co., N.Y. 1960. p. 330
50. Donald B. Meyer, op. cit., p. 170
51. Ibid., p. 173
52. Ibid., p. 380
53. Jacob van Rossum, "Remembering the Answers: Reinhold Niebuhr's Case Against Pacifism" *This World,* Summer 1982, p. 21
54. John C. Bennett, "Christian Responsibility in a Time that Calls for Revolutionary Change," in John C. Raines and Thomas Dean eds., *Marxism and Radical Religion: Essays Toward a Revolutionary Humanism,* Philadelphia: Temple University Press 1970, p. 49
55. Donald B. Meyer, op. cit., p. 4
56. Frederic Spotts, *The Churches and Politics in Germany,* Connecticut: Wesleyan University Press, 1973, p. 238
57. *Time,* Dec. 26, 1969
58. Frederick C. Turner, *Catholicism and Political Development in Latin America* Chapel Hill: University of North Carolina Press, 1971, p. 144
59. *NACLA Newsletter,* March 1970, pp. 8-10
60. John C. Bennett. op. cit., p. 61
61. Ibid., p. 56

62. Robert McAfee Brown, "15 Commandments for Liberals," *The Witness,* February 1979
63. Melvin J. Lasky, *Utopia and Revolution,* Chicago, Chicago University Press, 1976, p. 50
64. John C. Raines and Thomas Dean, op. cit., xii; Herbert Marcuse, "Marxism and the New Humanity: An Unfinished Revolution" in Raines and Dean, pp. 3-10

III

The Environmental Utopians

Student of public policy Irving Kristol has described the environmental movement as a reform movement that is being transformed into a fanatical and self-defeating crusade.[1] But actually, as Paul Johnson has noted, the environmental revolution began as an ecological panic, and thus from the beginning lacked the sense of balance and proportion that is associated with a movement of reform.

Ecological panic struck the United States in 1970. The earth, up to then, a comfortable, taken-for-granted dwelling place, suddenly seemed in imminent danger of becoming uninhabitable. And just as millennial sects provide a date for the world's end, so the enthusiasts of the ecological crisis offered a limited time span—unless radical steps were taken immediately—for the continuance of life. "We are already 5 years into the biosphere self-destruct era" read a sign in the Berkeley office of Ecology Action, one of the two hundred environmental groups that mushroomed in the San Francisco area alone during the panic.[2] "The generations now on earth may be the last" read the cover of *The Dying Generations,* a book of readings published in 1971. Even such normally dreadful accusations as neglecting the poor and minorities for the new cause did not evoke guilt. "It would be the ultimate cop-out to give all our money to the Black Panthers and then have them all die in 20 years because they couldn't drink the water" was the confident retort of the editor of *Earth Times,* one of the vast number of publications that now appeared devoted to the ecology crisis.[3]

Protest against pollution took forms ranging from teach-ins to car burials. At San Jose College, students contributed $2500 to buy a new yellow Maverick, planning to bury it at the climax of a week-long survival fair. Some students complained that the burial of a non-biodegradable object was ecologically unsound and black and chicano students argued the money for the car could have been better spent on them. In the end the car was buried with a biodegradable box of grapes in the back seat. The grapes symbolized support for then striking farm workers.[4]

Public emotion reached its peak on April 22 with Earth Day, in which millions of Americans took part. Congress closed down as its members fanned out to make speeches on the environment to their constituents. Traffic was sealed off in downtown New York and reporters estimated that a hundred thousand people poured into Union Square at 14th Street for Earth day exhibits and songs. Thousands crowded into a block-long polyethylene bubble to sample pure air: a reporter noted, however, that within half an hour the pure air carried the unmistakable odor of marijuana. Mayor John Lindsay addressed the throng with a level of sophistication typical of that being brought to the problem. The environmental issue, said Lindsay, could be summed up simply: "Do we want to live or die?" Other parts of the country produced more imaginative demonstrations. In Bloomington, Indiana, coeds dressed as witches, pelted participants in the Earth Day rally with birth control pills.[5]

Those whose feelings could not be adequately expressed in demonstrations resorted to more active measures. A man in the Chicago area, calling himself "the Fox," dumped sewage in the corporate offices of polluters and a Miami group, dubbing itself "the Eco-Commando Force '70," dumped dye in the waste vats of the city's sewage treatment plants, turning half the city's inland canals yellow.

Why did an ecological panic sweep the country in 1970? The explanations offered seem thin and unconvincing. In his *Environmental Awakening,* Rice O'Dell, of the Conservation Foundation, chronicles what he sees as the movement's precipitants. In 1969, there had been a series of dramatic incidents: an oil blowout off the Santa Barbara coast fouled eighty miles of beaches; the Cuyahoga River in Cleveland, brimming with oil sludge and other industrial effluents, caught fire;

U.S. marshals seized 22,000 pounds of fresh salmon because of excessive DDT concentrations; due to air pollution, people in Los Angeles were warned not to engage in outdoor activities that involved deep breathing. But while the Santa Barbara oil spill was unusually dramatic, oil spills were familiar. So surely was smog in Los Angeles. Seizure of food because of unacceptable levels of some chemical were also not new. There was nothing here or in other of the items mentioned by O'Dell to explain the emotional wave of urgency that gripped a broad public.

More poetic—and more plausible—explanations were offered by some of the young men and women who participated in Earth Day 1970. One young man asserted that watching the moon shot had been decisive for him: it showed how vulnerable the earth was. Another said that Vietnam showed him "the system" was at fault, preparing him to see how the system also produced the pollution that could end human life. Yet another spoke in frankly religious terms. Technology and rationality had buried spiritual values and ecology restored them.[6]

In *Risk and Culture,* social anthropologist Mary Douglas and political scientist Aaron Wildavsky underscore the fundamentally amazing character of the ecological panic by noting "the rise of alarm over risk to life" occurred "at the same time as health is better than ever before." Once the source of safety, science and technology had now been reperceived as "the source of risk."[7]

But whatever the reasons why masses suddenly joined together to avert destruction of the earth, and panics, like other forms of mass behavior can rarely be satisfactorily "explained," the ecology panic would have faded away if it had not been for certain special conditions that fostered the movement. Unlike some mass hysterias, this one had a basis in fact. While the planet was in no danger, pollution was a genuine problem and steps could be taken to reduce it. The existence of long-established wealthy conservation organizations gave the movement ready-made institutional backing. But also very important, the movement was welcomed by diverse constituencies, including the Republican politicians at the nation's helm. Indeed, politicians of *both* major parties saw the environmental issue as a unifying force. The Vietnam War was still tearing the country apart in 1970 and politicians could not help but welcome a problem that called for cooperative action by all Americans. Then Secretary of the Interior, Walter Hickel, urged President Nixon to declare Earth Day a national holiday on the explicit grounds that this would align the administration more closely with youth.[8] Such was the eagerness of local politicians to climb on the environmental bandwagon that the California legislature had difficulty passing a resolution that urged the Federal government to halt oil drilling off the California coast. Republicans and Democrats squabbled over who would get credit for the bill. Only after the list of the bill's authors was expanded so as to satisfy everyone could the measure be passed—unanimously.[9] But if politicians initially embraced environmental issues because they distracted public attention from political problems like the war in Vietnam, the effect was to build an illusion of consensus around issues which had profound long range political implications that were not thought through or even acknowledged in the political arena.

Support from the broad public, a support which encouraged the enthusiasm of politicians, was based on the widespread belief that pollution was dangerous to health, and specifically was a major cause of cancer. Starting in the 1950s scientific studies appeared linking cancer with the environment. John Higginson, founding director of the World Health Organization's International Agency for Research on Cancer, hypothesized an environmental component in cancer causation as high as 80%. Stimulated by the environmentalists, the public put two things together. The environment was polluted. Cancer was environmentally caused. Therefore pollution caused cancer. Appealing as this logic sounds, it was, as we shall see, faulty. But the public's conviction that its health was at stake made the charge of elitism, which increasingly was hurled by critics at the environmental movement, deflect harmlessly. As journalist William Tucker noted in an acerbic article in *Harper's*,[10] the chief beneficiaries, when Storm King Mountain in New York was saved from the "visual pollution" of a proposed Con Ed pumped storage plant designed to supply energy at time of peak demand, were the wealthy estate owners in the area, while the chief losers were the New Yorkers who suffered blackouts a decade later—one of them to cost the city over half a billion dollars. But as long as the public saw environmentalists as protectors of the public's health, the charges of elitism did not bite deeply.

Begun in an atmosphere of panic, the environmental revolution was conducted from the beginning in an ill-considered rush, with only the haziest understanding of what the dangers to public health were. As a result, huge costs were imposed upon industry, and, of course, ultimately upon the public, many of them unnecessary and serving largely symbolic goals.

Congress set out to legislate pollution out of existence. Laws laid down absolute objectives of zero pollution. Completely ignored were warnings like those of Dr. H.E. Stokinger, then chief of the laboratory of toxicology and pathology at the National Institute for Occupational Safety and Health, who protested against "the ruinous concept of 'zero tolerance' for pollutants." Stokinger insisted: "Man has never, before he was a man, or ever after, survived in an unpolluted void."[11] Oblivious, Congress issued the laws that were to produce the perfect environment, in a veritable flood: the Clean Air Act, the Clean Water Act, the Clean Air Act Amendments, the Clean Water Act Amendments, the Federal Water Pollution Control Act Amendments, the Surface Mining Control and Reclamation Act, the Critical and Endangered Species Act, the Toxic Substance Control Act, the Environmental Protection Act, the Occupational Health and Safety Act, to name only a few.

In their study *Clean Coal, Dirty Air,* Bruce Ackerman and William T. Hassler chronicled the counterproductive methods used in the war against pollution. The EPA mandated scrubbing of coal, in 1971, even though there were only three operational scrubbers in the United States. The mandate was predicated on scrubbing seventy percent of sulfur out of the average eastern coal.

One trouble with this was that all coal in the United States does not have an equal sulfur content. Western coal is predominantly low in sulfur, eastern coal high in it. As a result midwestern and eastern utilities had an alternative: they could burn low sulfur western coal, absorbing the cost of transportation, rather than high sulfur eastern coal, where they should have to absorb the even higher cost of scrubbing. Predictably, eastern coal producers became frantic as they saw the market for their coal in danger of dwindling rapidly as more and more new plants were built. (The restrictions on older plants were different and less onerous.) Surprisingly, at this point they found an ally in the environmentalists. It was surprising because from the environmentalist's viewpoint, the whole point of environmental regulation is to force producers to bear the social costs of their enterprise. From that perspective, high sulfur coal had so far enjoyed an unfair competitive advantage over low sulfur coal because the harm it caused the environment had not been reflected in its price.[12] Nonetheless the environmentalists joined with the dirty coal producers in a bizarre alliance against the utilities to persuade Congress to take away the advantage of low sulfur producers by enforcing universal scrubbing.

But the end result of universal scrubbing is more pollution, not less. For one thing, scrubbers do not work well on low-sulfur coal so that the sulfur the technology is supposed to eliminate has to be added artificially to make the scrubbers work. Furthermore, scrubbers produce huge quantities of sludge, which requires the permanent removal of thousands of acres of land, often productive farmland, from any future use. Scrubbing also requires large quantities of water, creating both thermal and chemical water pollution, and exacerbating water-scarcity problems in the arid West. Moreover, forcing new plants to scrub lengthens the life of dirty plants as utilities postpone the evil day when they have to install the costly new technology.

After passage of the 1977 Amendments to the Clean Air Act, the EPA was again left with decisions on how to implement them. A section within the Agency argued that Congress wanted full scrubbing and full scrubbing it should get. But computer models revealed that full scrubbing would be one of the costliest ventures ever imposed in the name of a cleaner environment, costing an extra 4.1 billion dollars a year by 1995 and much more thereafter as more new plants were built.[13] Moreover, the computer studies showed that full scrubbing would yield very modest nation-wide reductions in sulfur dioxide. In the end, the EPA decided to promote a new technology, the dry scrubber. Preliminary research suggested a dry scrubber could operate more cheaply than the wet scrubber as long as it did not have to eliminate more than 70% of the sulfur content of coal. (The wet scrubber by now could go up to 90%.) The dry scrubber, note Ackerman and Hassler, served as a symbolically satisfying way of justifying partial universal scrubbing. There was just one difficulty with the dry scrubber. There was not a single one operating on a full-sized power plant anywhere in the United States. And there were experts to point out that the state of knowledge of dry scrubbing in 1980 was akin to the state of knowledge of wet scrubbing in 1970, when the costs were thought to be half of what they turned out to be.[14]

But the ironies were still greater. Despite the enormous costs that were mandated for yet another unknown technology, no one knew if its target, sulfur dioxide, was harmful to health. In fact the growing consensus among scientists was that not sulfur dioxide, but the sulfate compounds into which sulfur dioxide can be transformed over time were damaging.[15] But if that were the case, a quite different strategy was called for. To begin with, knowledge was needed of how sulfates of different kinds and quantities do harm us, how they are produced and transformed in transport. But while the EPA was planning to invest some millions of dollars a year on sulfur research, the energy consumer was going to be spending billions a year for forced scrubbing. Without any real knowledge of what the health risks were, the EPA was railroading the public into spending vast sums for a strategy that might not be appropriate to ends that might not themselves make sense. Of course the EPA was in turn impelled by Congress, which was in turn pressured by the environmental lobby, supported in its turn by a citizenry aroused to fear of an imminent hazard to health and indeed life on earth.

Similarly there is mounting evidence that auto emissions devices, despite their great cost, whether measured in money or in increased energy consumption, have made only a minor contribution to cleaner air and that the catalytic converter may in fact be a major contributor to the growing problem of "acid rain."[16] Paul Langerman, an analyst on environmental problems for the Heritage Foundation, argues that the whole federal auto emissions control program is "based on skimpy scientific data reflected in archaic standards, a questionable federal automobile testing procedure, an ill-conceived and wasteful state-monitored inspection and maintenance program, and the retention of pollution control devices that work only on paper or in an artificial laboratory environment." Langerman believes most of the improvements in air quality, in recent years, are not due to pollution controls, but to the shrinking average car size: smaller cars emit a lower amount of pollutants because of their lighter weight and smaller engines. Langerman estimates that changes in the standards "could save the American consumer between $5.4 and $15.2 billion and put 152,000 automobile workers back to work."[17]

What the environmental crusade has completely ignored is a simple dictum advanced by Aaron Wildavsky: "Richer is safer." Wildavsky observes that both between nations and within nations there is a strong inverse association between mortality and income. According to Wildavsky the real question is: "How much safety can come from measures to reduce hazards for particular populations and how much from overall improvement in the standard of living?"[18] For the middle class environmentalist, a drop in GNP may mean inability to travel abroad. But for others, the drop in GNP means jobs, less heat in winter and other involuntary changes in lifestyle that can be extremely threatening to health. Every society assigns priorities in the avoidance of risks: under the impact of the environmental movement, the risk of economic failure and loss of prosperity has been shunted aside in favor of single-minded concentration on the risks of pollution. But this may be no more rational than the "risk priorities" of the Lele people of Zaire. Douglas and Wildavsky note that while they suffered all the usual devastating tropical ills, including gastroenteritis, tuberculosis, leprosy, pneumonia etc., the Lele *worried* about being struck by lightning and one disease—bronchitis.[19]

The costs to the public of fighting pollution have been staggering. A 1970 *New York Times* survey found that industry planned that year to spend what was then defined as the impressive sum of almost $2 billion to fight pollution. By 1979, economist Murray Weidenbaum (who became chairman of Reagan's Council of Economic Advisers) calculated that fighting pollution was costing industry $100 billion annually, and the costs would go up as industry met future legislated targets.[20]

Particular industries have been disproportionately hard hit, especially steel, coal, aluminum, zinc, lead and copper. Innovation has been discouraged as a substantial portion of the research budget is shifted to meeting regulations. The head of General Motors Research Laboratory complained: "We've diverted a large share of our resources—sometimes up to half—into meeting government regulations instead of developing better materials, better manufacturing techniques and better products . . . it's a terrible way to waste your research dollars." More and more, corporations are compelled to rely on their lawyers, who serve as experts on regulation. As Paul Johnson puts it: "A big corporation now resembles a quasi-elective social institution rather than an organization geared to maximize production and profit. At the boardroom level, engineers, technocrats, salesmen and leaders are being replaced by lawyers, especially those with experience in handling government."[21]

Small companies are the most likely to fall by the wayside. Editor of the pro-energy development newsletter *Access to Energy,* Petr Beckmann notes that "whether mining coal or drilling for oil, it is, of course, the small independent operations that are being driven out of business first by the so-called environmentalists. A Wyoming independent oil man told us that before he could file his environmental impact statement, he had to pay $1400 to have forty acres searched and certified free of Indian arrowheads . . ."[22] As a result of water pollution regulations, as Harvard economist Robert Leone has pointed out, the metal and finishing industry was reduced from 70,000 to 5,000 factories.[23] Leone discovered that water pollution regulations had the same effect on tissue-paper manufacturers. Firms with larger plants and bigger profits were better able to absorb the costs of water-pollution control equipment. In the end bigger firms were left with a larger share of the market.[24] Some critics have argued that the most significant result of the environmental era may be industrial concentration and business oligopoly. The severe impact on small business is the more ironic in that the environmentalists, at least rhetorically, seek to promote small business.

There is a cost to society at large, not merely to the small businessman, for innovation historically has come disproportionately from small companies. As William Tucker sums it up:

> "A 1977 study by the National Science Foundation showed that small firms produce four times as many industrial innovations per research dollar as medium-size firms, and twenty-four times as many as the largest firms. A long study by the Panel of Invention and Innovation for the Department of Commerce found that more than half the major technological advances during this century have been developed by individual inventors and small businesses. The first working model of what became the Xerox machine was developed in a small laboratory over a bar. Individual inventors and small companies also produced insulin, the vacuum tube, Kodachrome, power steering, the self-winding wristwatch, the helicopter, cellophane, the ballpoint pen, FM radio, shrink-proof knitted wear, the Polaroid camera, and the zipper.[25]

The cost of some environmentalist victories will only become apparent in the future. Vast areas have been withdrawn as wilderness and even more removed from economic development. The Alaska Land Bill removed 46% of that mineral-rich state from development.

Although the environmental movement of today is often considered successor to the conservationist movement that arose late in the nineteenth century, in fact, as Tucker points out, it is a *rebellion* against that movement. Conservationists wanted efficient and careful use of resources: their efforts resulted in the National Forests, the Bureau of Land Management Reserves and the Bureau of Reclamation territories. They won out over the rival preservationists of the wilderness movement, whose goal was to exclude all human activity. Environmentalism has revived the preservationist ideal; much of the land, now under conservationist management, it seeks to redesignate as "wilderness" excluding all roads, mining and logging.[26]

The lumber industry has been one casualty—and with it the home buyers. Under conservationist programs, forests were "managed," with both planting of new and logging of mature forests considered part of proper management. But as environmentalists have waged their battle for ever more wilderness designations, producing tie-ups in sales from National Forest lands, the United States, despite its vast timber resources, has become an importer of logs. Not surprisingly prices have shot up. Between 1972 and 1980, the price of a Douglas fir in Oregon increased 500%. Ironically, in "wilderness" areas, fires are allowed to rage (fighting them would constitute human intervention) which consume millions of board feet. Harvesting of mature forests has the same effect of clearing the way for new growth with much less damage to forest soils—while providing lumber for human needs.[27]

Although the environmental movement is sharply opposed to nuclear energy, leaving coal, oil and gas as the only viable alternatives for the next decades, environmental organizations have tried to inhibit coal, oil and gas exploration as well. According to Eugene Guccione, editor of *Coal Mining and Processing,* it takes from 8-10 years from the time a coal producer in the West decides to open a mine and the time he can take his first ton of coal from it, as a result of the weight of regulations. On federal lands, new coal leases were all but frozen early in the 1970s. During the first two years of the Reagan administration, the Interior Department issued coal leases for 119,000 acres of Federal land. But while this was more than twice the total leased in the four years of the Carter administration, as Interior Secretary James Watt pointed out, it was far less than the 252,000 acres leased during the last two years of the Johnson administration, when a staunch environmentalist, Stewart Udall, was Interior Secretary.[28]

While hundreds of old leases exist, few are legally mineable, since 95% of them were issued prior to 1970 and thus prior to the passage of all the rules, laws and regulations that now apply to them.[29] The Independent Petroleum Association asserts that, as a result of law or administrative procedures, 500 million Federal acres, or close to a fourth of the U.S., have been placed off limits to oil and gas development.[30] Currently, environmentalists are trying to "save" from energy development the geological strata running through Colorado, Wyoming and Montana (called the "Overthrust Belt") by having the whole area designated "wilderness."[31]

Some costs may never be assessed—the projects that are cancelled or never begun because of regulatory requirements. Standard Oil of Ohio (Sohio) spent five years assembling over 700 permits needed to construct a pipeline from a terminal in Long Beach, California to Midland, Texas. It gave up in 1979 after spending $50 million. Under California law, it had to win any lawsuits growing out of the project, including lawsuits brought purely for purposes of harassment, by July 1, 1979, obviously an impossible proposition. (It had to win them by that date because the non-discretionary sanctions of the Air Pollution Act Amendments then went into effect, making construction illegal under federal standards. Before that date, the project was allowed, under a complicated system in which Sohio had negotiated with other industries so that the pollution created by the new terminal would be more than offset by improvements in pollution control in other area industries.)[32]

No law has been so abused to stop development as the Endangered Species Act of 1973. While the Act was originally passed out of understandable concern for the dwindling numbers of buffalo, whooping cranes, sperm whales and other increasingly rare creatures, it has been exploited by those eager to stop energy and other projects. The most famous single case is probably that of the snail darter which almost sealed the fate of the Tellico Dam. The fish was identified as a separate species by Dr. David Etnier, a University of Tennessee ichthyologist opposed to the dam. When the Endangered Species Act was passed, he went to the dam's site along the Little Tennessee River, and, as Tucker notes, "discovered the snail darter in one morning's work." (That it had never been found before was probably because no one had ever bothered to look before, since another population was discovered in a neighboring river in 1979.)[33] It took a special act of Congress to enable the almost completed Tellico Dam to go ahead.

The Furbish lousewort, an obscure plant, held up the proposed Dickey-Lincoln Dam in northern Maine. Antioch, California, a wealthy beach community near San Francisco, went to work to head off in advance any possible development proposals that might affect their community by finding an endangered butterfly, two rare lizards, ten varieties of local insects and two local plants to qualify as endangered species.[34]

Entrepreneurs in endangered species sprang up. Robert Zappalorti, a biologist at the Staten Island Zoo, set up Herpetological Associates in 1979 and was soon pocketing fees of $10,000 for spending a few weeks scouring proposed construction sites for endangered species. Tucker notes: "Within a few months, Herpetological Associates had furnished ammunition to help the town of West Milford, New Jersey, block a proposed housing project on a reservoir site owned by the City of Newark, and had assisted the Township of Parsippany-Troy in blocking a sewage plant planned by a rival regional sewer authority."[35] Tucker points out that there are a million animal and 350,000 plant species. While the official U.S. list "only" includes 296 endangered species, in principle there can be unlimited additions to it. Moreover once a species is found to be endangered, any population of that species can stop any project receiving any federal aid, even if only a few birds, for example, are involved and there are large populations of the same bird elsewhere.

If, generally speaking, "richer is safer," then clearly the costs to health of environmental protection measures must be compared to their benefits to health. But environmentalists treat financial considerations as if they were automatically *opposed* to public welfare. Rice O'Dell writes: "Despite the inherent logic in cost effectiveness analysis, it is difficult to imagine a more Orwellian intrusion on individual freedom than for a government to set a dollar value on someone's life or good health."[36] (Similarly Ralph Nader says: "It seems anomalous that institutions bent on private greed need not apologize for their polluting activities, whereas agencies that are devoted to the protection of public health, under due process of law, must apologize in terms that it is good for the economy."[37])

Heads of government agencies self-righteously adopted the same attitude in the Carter administration. Belatedly, explicitly ordered to perform cost-benefit analyses, Occupational Safety and Health Administration (OSHA) head Eula Bingham insisted the law said nothing about considering costs, and she would not do it. But the problem was that the agency not only had no interest in costs, but no notion of benefits. An appeals court threw out OSHA's proposed standards on benzene exposure because the agency had set them at the lowest level technologically feasible without attempting to show that such a low level of exposure "was reasonable, necessary or appropriate to provide safe and healthful employment."[38] No reasonable standards satisfy the perfection-seeking environmental organizations. The Environmental Protection Agency, in setting standards for clean, healthy air, has ruled that air must be clean enough not to affect asthmatics, who make up about 4% of the population. Not content, the Environmental Defense Fund wants air safe for people suffering from cystic fibrosis, which affects .005% of the population or around 11,000 people. One economist, calculating the price of similar standards to protect angina patients, suggested it would be cheaper to buy every victim of the disease a $200,000 condominium in the Florida keys.[39]

Even when government agencies under Carter reluctantly began to make cost-benefit analyses, they did not figure large in agency decisions. The government established a Regulation Analysis Review Group (RARG) in 1978, but the first year it was only able to review nine regulations. In the Carter years, the only real constraint upon the agencies was public uproar when a regulatory agency came up with something absolutely outrageous. Then a retreat would be arranged. In 1979, the Environmental Protection Agency came up with regulations declaring drilling muds, oil production brines, and crude oil residue to be "hazardous waste." When the American Petroleum Institute announced the cost would be $45.5 billion annually and a *Wall Street Journal* editorial said the regulations would soak up the profits of the entire oil industry "and then some," a bill providing for a two year "study period" was passed by Congress.[40] (At this writing, four years later, no more has been heard on the subject.)

Although it is the public's belief that pollution causes cancer that explains much of the strong public support for environmentalism, there is not even any evidence that the billions poured into meeting environmental regulations have decreased or will decrease the incidence of cancer. Earlier, we mentioned that scientists have hypothesized an environmental component in cancer as high as 80%. But the chief environmental causes of cancer, as these scientists have emphasized, are factors in the personal environment that involve individual choice, even if it is culturally induced choice. Cancer is caused by the high protein diet we eat, the cigarettes we smoke, the alcohol we drink, even worse by the way we both smoke and drink, for alcohol and cigarette-smoking operate synergistically. Population density also seems to produce tensions of various kinds that correlate with cancer. John Higginson, one of the chief figures in development of the environment-causes-cancer hypothesis, spoke out against the misinterpretation of scientific findings in 1979.

> "To make cancer the whipping boy for every environmental evil may prevent action when it does matter, as with cigarettes. I think that many people had a gut feeling that pollution ought to cause cancer. You asked me, were people dishonest? I don't think that some people were intentionally dishonest, but rather that they found it hard to accept that general air pollution, smoking factory chimneys, and the like are not major causes of cancer. I mean people would love to be able to prove that cancer is due to pollution or the general environment. It would be so

> easy to say 'Let us regulate everything to zero exposure and we have no more cancer.' The concept is so beautiful that it will overwhelm a mass of facts to the contrary.[41]

While Higginson rejected the notion of deliberate dishonesty, it cannot be dismissed out of hand. Ralph Nader, quick to spot dissembling government or industry claims, has cited the figure of 80% of cancers environmentally caused so as to leave the impression that it is pollution that is at fault. So have numerous other environmental activists. Dr. Samuel Epstein is quoted in the Friends of the Earth's ideological guidebook *Progress As If Survival Mattered* as saying: "There is now a growing consensus that the majority of human cancers are environmental in origin and that they are hence ultimately preventable."[42] True enough, but once again Friends of the Earth gives no indication that personal habits are believed to be the chief environmental culprit. A book called *Environmental Ethics* revealed peculiar ethics itself in citing a 90% figure for environmentally caused cancers, relegating to a footnote, which few people consult, the acknowledgment that the figure included factors in the personal environment.[43]

It is not hard to understand why the environmentalists fudge on these figures. The very basis of the environmental movement's broad support for demanding that the government disregard the costs of antipollution measures would be undercut if its leaders were to admit that only a small proportion of environmentally caused cancers can be traced to industrial pollution. Yet, if environmentalists were really concerned with public health, even minor successes in changing personal habits would have far more impact in cancer-prevention than the crippling regulations they have imposed on industry. As it is, environmentalists have not even been especially vocal in seeking to end subsidies to tobacco growers.

Because the concentration of effort and attention by the government on pollution and toxic substances has deflected public attention from the major preventable causes of cancer, Dr. Harry Demopoulos, professor of pathology at New York University Medical Center, has accused the government of "killing many Americans through misinformation." Demopoulos warned that "if society is to listen to the Federal government, it will be led down yet another primrose path, blaming industry, air and water pollution, for most of the cancer burden, whereas, in fact, the answers to cancer lie elsewhere . . . the selection of the wrong path is the equivalent of leading millions of Americans to certain death."[44]

For the crucial fact is that there are thresholds of tolerance. Dr.

Demopoulos has noted that the findings of the National Cancer Institute's own National Cancer Survey have been treated like an "unwanted child" because they throw into question the assumptions of the regulatory programs. In the survey, seven cities were compared, four without any heavy industry and three, Detroit, Pittsburgh and Birmingham, highly industrialized. The three dirty cities had an overall lower cancer rate, for white and black males, age-corrected, than the four clean cities. Demopoulos and his team looked at the specific kinds of cancer said to be industry-related and these too were not proportionately more prominent in dirty than in clean cities.[45]

While the environmentalists claim that cancer rates are on the increase, Philip Handler, former President of the National Academy of Sciences, points out that the reality is quite different.

> "Indeed, the United States is not suffering an "epidemic of cancer," it is experiencing an "epidemic of life"—in that an ever greater fraction of the population survives to the advanced ages at which cancer has always been prevalent. The overall, age-corrected incidence of cancer has not been increasing; it has been declining slowly for some years."[46]

All this is not to say that pollution control is undesirable. Thresholds of tolerance can be crossed. A proportion of environmentally caused cancers, even if only a small proportion, are due to pollutants, and respiratory illnesses can be exacerbated by them. Moreover, there are values other than physical health to be satisfied by clean air and water. But a sensible government program against pollution must be based on knowledge of the effects of pollution, and most of the basic research has not been done.

If the benefits need to be better understood, so do the costs. The economics of pollution-control are such that in most cases it is much more expensive to remove the last 5-10% of pollutants than the first 90-95%. While the implications for government programs are obvious, they have been ignored by Congress and the regulatory agencies with their targets of zero pollution. Up to now, environmental zealots have been successful in identifying costs as an immoral subject. Yet those costs ultimately translate into poorer health and a deterioration in welfare for the average citizen.

In his challenging *Unpopular Essays on Technological Progress*, philosopher Nicholas Rescher points out that Americans may have to learn to live with an environment less satisfactory than that enjoyed by previous generations. None of the factors that produce environmental problems—high population densities, high levels of personal consumption and a messy technology of production—are likely to change. Although a particular environmental "mess" can be cleaned up, the notion of restoring a pristine environmental state is an unrealistic dream.[47] Attempting to achieve impossible goals, environmentalists can only foster alienation from government and major institutions as they are blamed for failing to do something they should never have been expected to achieve.

The distinguished sociologist and historian of ideas Robert Nisbet sees environmentalism as a revolutionary social movement. Indeed Nisbet sees it as potentially the third great social movement of Western civilization after Christianity and socialism, and one, ironically, that strikes at the roots of that civilization. If environmentalists as such do not "hate the system," they hate what is vital to the system—the development of energy sources, with the most environmentally benign source, nuclear energy, assuming a literally demonic character. Nisbet sees the reason for the movement's fascination with the sun as "a form of spiritual purification, for there is a renascent primitivism in the environmentalist's characteristic approach to life."

It is the implicit revolutionary nature of present day environmentalism that has made it, as we shall see, so attractive to political and social radicals. They see it as a lever for mobilizing masses who can be seduced into implementing their own agenda if it can be suffused with an environmentalist aura. As Nisbet points out, and as we shall document, the processes of syncretism have operated for environmentalism (as they did for Christianity and socialism) and it too "has brought to its own passion the passions of a large number of groups not primarily interested perhaps in the physical environment."[48]

REFERENCES

1. Irving Kristol, *Two Cheers for Capitalism,* New York, Basic Books, 1978, p. 45
2. Steven Roberts, "The Better Earth," *The New York Times Magazine,* March 29, 1970
3. Ibid.
4. Ibid.
5. *New York Times,* April 22 and April 23, 1970
6. Ibid., March 29, 1970
7. Mary Douglas and Aaron Wildavsky, *Risk and Culture: An Essay on the Selection of Technological and Environmental Dangers,* Berkeley, University of California Press, 1982, p. 10
8. *New York Times,* May 7, 1970
9. Ibid., February 24, 1970
10. William Tucker, "Environmentalism and the Leisure Class," *Harper's,* December 1977

11. H.E. Stokinger, "Sanity in Research and Evaluation of Environmental Health," *Science*, November 12, 1970, p. 665
12. Bruce A. Ackerman and William T. Hassler, *Clean Coal/Dirty Air or How the Clean Air Act Became a Multibillion Dollar Bail-Out for High Sulfur Coal Producers and What Should Be Done About It*, New Haven: Yale University Press, 1981, pp. 36-37
13. Ibid., p. 85
14. Ibid., p. 103
15. Ibid., pp. 62, 72
16. Paul Langerman, "The Clean Air Act," Heritage Foundation Backgrounder, August 2, 1982, p. 15
17. Ibid., p. 20
18. Aaron Wildavsky, "Richer is Safer," *The Public Interest*, Summer 1980, p. 30
19. Douglas and Wildavsky, op. cit., pp. 6-7
20. Quoted in Paul Johnson, "Sick Man of the West," *Policy Review*, Fall 1980, p. 130
21. Ibid., p. 132
22. *Access to Energy*, August 1980
23. William Tucker, "Environmentalism: The Newest Toryism," *Policy Review*, Fall 1980, p. 150
24. William Tucker, *Progress and Privilege*, New York, Doubleday, 1982, p. 73
25. Ibid., p. 83
26. Ibid., pp. 55-56
27. Ibid., p. 132
28. *U.S. News & World Report*, June 6, 1983, p. 53
29. Peter Metzger, "The Coercive Utopians," Public Service Co. of Colorado, pp. 18-19
30. *Wall Street Journal*, Dec. 12, 1978
31. William Tucker, *Progress and Privilege*, op. cit., p. 133
32. Peter Metzger, op. cit., p. 35
33. William Tucker, *Progress and Privilege*, op. cit., p. 180
34. Ibid., p. 182
35. Ibid., p. 184
36. Rice O'Dell, *The Environmental Awakening*, Cambridge, Mass. Ballinger Publishers, 1980, p. 149
37. Quoted in Ibid., p. 149
38. *Forbes*, February 19, 1979, p. 34
39. William Tucker, *Progress and Privilege*, op. cit., pp. 4-5
40. *Wall Street Journal*, May 9, 1979
41. "Cancer and the Environment: Higginson Speaks Out," *Science*, September 28, 1979, p. 1364
42. Hugh Nash, ed., *Progress as If Survival Mattered: A Handbook for a Conserver Society*, Friends of the Earth, 1977, p. 96
43. Albert J. Fritsch, *Environmental Ethics*, New York: Anchor Books, 1980, p. 130
44. "Environmentally Induced Cancer: Separating Truth from Myth," A Talk by Dr. Harry Demopoulos to the Synthetic Organic Chemical Manufacturing Association, Oct. 4, 1979
45. Ibid.
46. Quoted in Douglas and Wildavsky, op. cit. pp. 55-56
47. Nicholas Rescher, *Unpopular Essays on Technological Progress*, Pittsburgh: University of Pittsburgh Press, 1980, p. 26
48. Robert Nisbet, "Modern Man and the Obsession," *The American Spectator*, Vol. 16, No. 5, May 1983, p. 10

IV

The New Left Discovers Environmentalism

A number of characteristics of the environmental movement made it a ripe—indeed irresistible—target for utopians, not so much concerned with a world totally purified of pollution, as with creating a perfect social order.

As the environmental movement gathered force in 1970, the campus based New Left, obsessed with the evils of American society, of which it believed the war in Vietnam was merely a symptom, was unsure how to respond to it. Some political radicals rallied promptly to the new movement. Ecology Action, which the *New York Times Magazine* selected as the subject of a feature article to typify the environmental movement, started—although the *Times* did not mention this in its article—as a splinter of the Peace and Freedom Party which ran Eldridge Cleaver for President during his Black Panther period. James Ridgeway, a long-time fellow of the Institute for Policy Studies, in his *The Politics of Ecology,* published in 1970, argued that the environmental movement should not seek reforms "for controlling pollution" but should regard the attacks on various problems of pollution as "different ways of attacking concentrated corporate power, thereby opening up the possibilities of revolutionary change, and for reorganizing society and communities on different principles . . ."[1] The principles were to be those of the anarchist utopia laid out in the work of

Institute for Policy Studies co-director Marcus Raskin, described in the first chapter.

But other political radicals saw environmentalism as middle class and reformist. They feared it would distract attention from, rather than contribute to, the destruction of imperialist-capitalist society. Indeed, at the time of Earth Day, 125 protesters from Clergy and Laity Concerned about the Vietnam War and the Fellowship of Reconciliation actually sprayed insecticide on a globe in front of the Department of Interior to protest against its environmental preoccupations.[2]

The Arab oil boycott of 1973 was the turning point in convincing the New Left of the value of the environmental movement for its own agenda. The New Left had been proclaiming for years that the American economic and socio-political system was rotten and in need of profound transformation. It could point to civil rights issues and to the Vietnam War as proof of a deep social malady and of the dangers the American system posed to the world. Economically, however, the system had performed, producing greater abundance each year for the average American. Now that a genuine threat to the functioning of the American economy had materialized, the left wing activists interpreted the pervasive economic effects of soaring energy costs as an outcome, virtually preordained, of the inherent flaws of the U.S. economy. With new authority, they could now advocate a total restructuring of economy and society.

There was much to link the political left and environmentalists, even though their reasons for taking a given perspective might not be the same. William Tucker considers environmentalism as a form of aristocratic politics, in which an upper middle class, seeking to preserve its amenities and status, prevents the economic expansion that could threaten the comforts it enjoys under the status quo. But political radicals, including the counter-cultural segments of the New Left, are also aristocratic in their disdain for the values and needs of the working man, in their pursuit of higher "non-materialist" goals, in their sense of superiority to those who do not share their values.

Both groups want minimal production of energy. The political activists wanted to minimize energy production as a means to overturn the existing political and economic order, which they saw as incapable of continuing without abundant energy. Environmentalists on the other hand, were deeply concerned about the consequences of oil shortages. They foresaw increased pressure for development of American resources, especially coal, offshore oil, and hydroelectric, all of which, in their view, would have far-reaching, undesirable environmental impact.

While political radicals were far more hostile to capitalism than environmentalists, the latter felt increasing discomfort with an economic system that sought growth. Many environmentalists were receptive to the analysis of the political utopians who argued that economic growth required fostering unnecessary appetites in the consumer to obtain corporate profits. The unnecessary products filling unnecessary appetites exacerbated pollution. And so economic growth, traditionally highly valued in American society, was portrayed by some environmentalists literally as a disease. In *The Environmental Conscience,* editor Robert Disch assails "the cancer-like expansion of the GNP" and *Environmental Ethics,* produced by the Science Action Coalition, similarly decries "the cancer of modern material growth."[3] Barry Commoner, both a recognized environmental leader and a political radical, asserts that since "environmental pollution is a sign of major incompatibility between our system of production and the environmental system that supports it," capitalism will have to go. Commoner admits that the Soviet Union also suffers from pollution, but finds that socialism is better than private enterprise for "the theory of socialist economics does not appear to require that growth should continue indefinitely."[4]

Political radicals and a segment of the environmentalists were also bound by hostility to Western civilization. Political radicals identified with a host of "liberation movements" in the Third World and saw the United States as the chief barrier to the prosperity and political health of underdeveloped lands. The environmental critique of the West, strong in the "preservationist" branch of the movement, went deeper. The wilderness movement had been suffused from the beginning with nature-mysticism. The search for purity and regeneration in uncontaminated nature involved a strong anti-urban, anti-business strain. Frederick Clements, the ecological theorist who developed the concept of biological succession and climax, concluded that the white man was a disrupter and exploiter of climax ecosystems that should not be disturbed.[5] The wilderness movement rediscovered native American culture and idealized the American Indian, who was held to have had a much finer relation to the natural habitat than the European who displaced him. There was a similar romanticization of non-Western cultures generally, which were believed to have avoided the predatory values of the commercial and growth-oriented West.

The very roots of Western culture—Western religious beliefs—were identified as predisposing it to despoil the earth. Christianity, said historian Lynn White Jr., in the most influential formulation of this perspective, was "the most anthropocentric religion the world has seen" for it insisted that "it is God's will that man exploit nature for his proper ends." The very doctrine of creation set man over and above nature by calling for unrestrained growth ("be fruitful and multiply"). As White sees it "Christianity bears a huge burden of guilt" for the ecological disasters perpetrated by science and technology, themselves "cast in a matrix of Christian theology."[6] Landscape architect turned environmental philosopher Ian McHarg was even more vehement. Referring to the biblical injunction to "subdue" the earth, he writes: "Here is the appropriate injunction for the land rapist, the befouler of air and water, the uglifier and the gratified bulldozer."[7]

For political radicals, the single most important attraction of the environmental movement was its possession of an issue capable of mobilizing masses to action—the issue of nuclear power. Like the Vietnam war, the nuclear issue could provide a lever to undermine faith in established authority and to instil a willingness to defy that authority through civil disobedience and even violent action. Nuclear energy, moreover, had the advantage of serving as the symbol of centralized economic, political and military power—everything that barred the road to achievement of the utopian community of communities of which the political radicals dreamed.

The nuclear issue was discovered belatedly by both environmental and political utopians. Even at the time of Earth Day, difficult although it is to imagine in view of the enormous emotional freight the nuclear issue has assumed, nuclear energy was scarcely an issue even for the most radical segment of the movement. (The established organizations like the Sierra Club and Audubon Society had traditionally been proponents of nuclear energy.) In *The Environmental Handbook,* prepared for the first "environmental teach-in" on Earth Day, and published by Friends of the Earth in 1970, only two of more than thirty authors referred to nuclear energy at all and those two made only a glancing reference to it. The references in both cases were unfavorable, but nuclear energy at that time took a backseat to every other environmental issue.

However belatedly discovered, to political radicals it quickly became apparent that nuclear energy offered a key to mass mobilization. As psychiatrist Robert DuPont points out, it is an issue that lends itself to arousal of phobic fears. Nuclear energy lends itself to phobic fears because it is strange; its dangers are invisible; there is a long and uncertain delay between exposure and resulting health problems; and there is an association in the collective consciousness with nuclear bombs. Anti-nuclear publicists foster these fears by jumping from one "what-if" scenario to another.[8] What if radiation leaked, what if waste disposal is impossible, what if terrorists steal nuclear material, what if there is a meltdown of the reactor core?

The sophisticated exploitation of the fears DuPoint describes is apparent in the "public service announcements" distributed by Friends of the Earth to radio stations. One goes:

> Announcer: You're looking at America's worst pollution problem. What's that? You say you can't see anything? Of course you can't. This is radio. But that's okay. You couldn't see it anyway. America's worst pollution problem is the radioactive waste that comes out of nuclear power plants.

And the spot ends: "Just remember, what you can't see can hurt you."

Nuclear energy had been operating safely (with the warm approval of the major environmental organizations) for almost two decades before environmentalists "discovered" that it endangered human survival. Peter Metzger has argued that environmentalists are enthusiastic for energy sources as long as they do not exist, and finds the source of their disenchantment in the very development of nuclear energy as a practical alternative. (He predicts the same fate for solar energy, should it become viable.) And indeed, the highly publicized campaign against nuclear power has obscured public recognition of the fact that both environmental and political utopians have been opposed to further development of *all* forms of power that are viable economically. The Natural Resources Defense Council has used its money, including almost five million dollars from the Ford Foundation alone, to hire 20 lawyers who have brought suit against projects involving most kinds of power development: nuclear, coal, oil and hydroelectric. Similarly the Sierra Club's energy platform not only opposes nuclear plants but asserts that strip mining of coal should be prohibited. (This would eliminate more than half our supply of coal.) The platform calls for a moratorium on offshore oil drilling programs, opposes geothermal operations except under restrictive conditions, and opposes the "sacrifice for water power of any . . . high quality scenic resource area."[9] The same pattern of opposition to all forms of energy development characterizes the suits of the Environmental Defense Fund, which is frank in stating in its 1973 report to members that the foremost priority of its energy program is "to slow the rate of growth in demand for energy . . . thus reducing the need for environmentally destructive generating and transmitting facilities." The entire environmental movement has opposed synfuels, which are described with typical public relations flair as "sinful."

The environmental movement is of course associated with advocacy of "renewable" energy, above all solar power. But when the Department of Energy and NASA proposed developing a $2.5 trillion system of solar collection satellites to beam microwave energy from the sun to collectors on earth, environmental groups promptly banded together in a Coalition against Satellite Power Systems. Since the complaint of these groups is constantly that the government is not investing enough in solar energy, the cost was not what upset them. Rather, in the words of one of the groups, Ralph Nader's Critical Mass project, it was that yet another energy technology would be "centralized." Even if solar power were to be developed without satellites, there is little doubt it would encounter massive protest from environmentalists. The Sierra Club has already announced reservations about solar energy, noting that it may "lead to adverse environmental impacts."[10] A letter to the editor of *Audubon* quotes solar experts as saying that a solar plant equivalent to a large coal plant would occupy 50 square miles and urges Audubon to develop a guide restricting selection of land lest there be encroachment on farms and greenbelts.[11]

The political radicals, for their own reasons, are opposed to energy development. Their goal is transformation of society into decentralized pre-industrial communities: the medieval manor without its lord. This requires radically *reduced* quantities and new forms of energy, not involving centralized generation. Genuine participatory democracy and community control will not, in their view, be possible if the community depends on a complex technology controlled by those outside the community.

The major figures who serve as a bridge linking environmental and political utopians are Barry Commoner and Amory Lovins. Commoner's research led to the banning of phosphate detergents in several states (the substitute used, sodium nitrilo-triacetate, was found to be cancer-producing and the states reversed themselves). Commoner was also the founder of SIPI, the Scientists Institute for Public Information, which paved the way for science to be used to serve the ideological preconceptions of politically-minded citizen groups. Second only in impact to Rachel Carson's *Silent Spring,* his books, *Science and Survival, The Closing Circle, The Poverty of Power, The Politics of Energy* have been among the most influential in popularizing environmentalism. Commoner is also a political utopian, going so far as to run for President of the United States on the Citizens Party ticket, which embodied New Left notions of participatory democracy with a program demanding an end to nuclear energy, nationalization of "energy industries" (referred to euphemistically as "public control"), price controls, "citizen control" of corporations etc.

Amory Lovins has probably been even more important in bridging the gap between environmental and political utopians. This is because he has made the concept of "the soft path" in energy development central to the strategy of both groups.

It has been Lovins genius to make explicit the policy implications of the late E.F. Schumacher's famous book *Small is Beautiful,* published in 1973, and still serving as scripture and proof text for environmentalist proponents of a golden age. Schumacher called for an end to the use of fossil fuel and nuclear power alike, and reliance instead on what he variously called "intermediate" and "appropriate" technology. As Schumacher puts it in the book's most famous line "Man is small, therefore, small is beautiful."[12] All that man needs to consume he should be able to produce himself from beginning to end or jointly with others in the same locality, preferably from renewable resources.

In Lovins' version, complex technology of any sort is an assault on human dignity. He insists that what he calls the "hard path" of fossil fuels and nuclear technology entails dependence on "an alien, remote and perhaps humiliatingly uncontrollable technology run by a faraway, bureaucratized technical elite, who have probably never heard of you."[13] Shortly after writing this passage Lovins was ready to dispense even with that qualifying "perhaps." In an Op-Ed essay in *The New York Times,* Lovins informed readers of their "humiliating dependence on remote bureaucrats who can simply disconnect you."

For environmentalists and political utopians the "soft path" is the key to a society both accept as ideal: one where only renewable resources are used (most important to the environmentalists) and one where each man is wholly in control of his own destiny (most important to the political utopians). As soft path disciple Kirkpatrick Sale puts it in *Human Scale,* a book whose mammoth size belies its principle that big is bad (not that the book disproves the point), society's goal must be a technology "at a scale sufficiently small so that an individual could control it, sufficiently simple so that an individual could comprehend it, and sufficiently approachable so that an individual could fix it . . ."[14]

In at least one respect the environmentalists have "radicalized" the political utopians. For while most political utopians have traditionally seen technology as a tool, in their hands a useful tool, the environmentalists have increasingly come to see the movement as a liberation movement—from modern technology. For many environmentalists modern technology is incompatible with the ecological rhythms into which it is man's task to blend. The more cautious and thoughtful environmentalists have not wanted to do away with advanced technology, but there is no mistaking their ambivalence toward it. Louis Mumford felt the environmental crisis had been brought about because "man has now committed himself to an expanding technology in which material processes override human meanings and purposes" and urged that men "tell our technology how much of it is tolerable and how much of it we will put to one side even if it exists."[15]

Others are even more equivocal in their attitude to technology. David Brower, director of the Sierra Club and then of Friends of the Earth, said: "We've got to search back to our last known safe landmark. I can't say exactly where it is, but I think it's back there about a century when, at the start of the Industrial Revolution, we began applying energy in vast amounts to tools with which we began tearing the environment apart."[16] With no equivocation at all, John Shuttlesworth, in a contribution to the Friends of the Earth manual *Progress As If Survival Mattered,* writes: "The only really good technology is no technology at all." Technology, says Shuttlesworth, is "taxation without representation imposed by an elitist species upon the rest of the natural world."[17]

The integrity of science itself is being threatened by the environmental utopians. In a major study, *Ecological Sanity,* George Claus and Karen Bolander subject to critical analysis the scientific studies which were crucial in providing support for environmentalist campaigns for the banning of DDT, of phosphate detergents, of the growth hormone DES in animal feed and of the herbicide 2, 4, 5-T. George Claus is eminently suited to the task, for he is himself an ecologist and has degrees in botany, microbiology and medicine. Claus and Bolander devote over 250 pages, the length of an ordinary book, to showing in painstaking and exhaustive detail how the studies that led to banning of

DDT totally failed to provide any evidence that DDT was a carcinogen or that it constituted a hazard to wildlife.

The decision to ban DDT was a political decision, not one based on scientific evidence. The Environmental Protection Agency appointed a hearing examiner who listened to the evidence for and against DDT from 125 witnesses over 81 days of hearings. He concluded:

> "DDT as offered under the registrations involved herein is not misbranded. DDT is not a carcinogenic hazard to man. The uses of DDT under the registrations involved here do not have a deleterious effect on fresh-water fish, estuarine organisms, wild birds or other wildlife . . . in my opinion, the evidence in this proceeding supports the conclusion that there is a present need for the essential uses of DDT . . ."[18]

But although the EPA was supposed to decide whether to ban DDT on the basis of the hearing examiner's recommendations, less than two months later William Ruckelshaus, then administrator of the EPA, banned DDT for all practical purposes for use in the U.S. Ruckelshaus had never attended any part of the hearings and later admitted he had not even read the transcript of them. Claus and Bolander note: "In failing to recognize that the Hearings had exposed most of the work indicting DDT as pseudoscience or ignorant bungling, Ruckelshaus has set a very dangerous precedent for the future of American biology."[19] (Such actions by Ruckelshaus may explain why he was an acceptable appointee to the environmental lobby after it had succeeded in ousting Reagan's first appointee, Anne Burford.)

On the surface the banning of DDT in 1972 was a victory for the environmental lobby, particularly the Audubon Society, the Sierra Club and the Environmental Defense Fund which had spearheaded the campaign against it. More fundamentally it was a victory, a decade after its appearance, of Rachel Carson's *Silent Spring*. But more basically still, it was a victory in the utopian campaign against modern technology. The pesticides, especially DDT, had enormously reduced parasitic and insect threats to food production and had permitted expansion of agriculture in underdeveloped areas where plant infestation had been a major cause of malnutrition. With DDT, modern technology was on trial, its proudest achievement held to be destructive when the entire fabric of life was considered.

Claus and Bolander describe how the system of selection of scientific articles for publication in major scientific journals has been undermined under the impact of the environmental movement. Selection of articles is based on a referee system by which articles submitted for publication are subject to peer review and those that do not meet scientific criteria are rejected. In order for the system to work, referees must be qualified, must pay close attention to the materials submitted, and must have a strong commitment to scientific method, not allowing sympathy with the "usefulness" of the findings in supporting their ideological preferences to color their judgment. But Claus and Bolander point out that articles that do not meet scientific standards have been published in such standard-bearing journals as *Science* in the United States and *Nature* in England. Once published, the flawed work becomes an unexamined building stone for further flawed studies which become the basis for political decisions on environmental issues.

The "News and Comment" pages of *Science* have been markedly affected by environmentalist opinion. Claus and Bolander observe that whatever excuse the popular press may have for engaging in modish writing on topical subjects so as to sell papers, there is no excuse for *Science*, the publication of the largest and most inclusive organization of American scientists, to engage in the same one-sided promotion of fashionable but scientifically dubious views.[20]

Almost as interesting as *Ecological Sanity* is the reception it received on its publication in 1977. Although a flood of environmentalist writing was being widely touted in the popular press and reviewed in professional journals, *Ecological Sanity* was almost wholly ignored. While ignoring *Ecological Sanity* proved an effective tactic in minimizing the book's impact, it did not make the problems Klaus and Bolander analyzed go away. When zeal replaces objectivity and environmentalist dogma substitutes for scientific honesty, trust is lost: not merely public trust, but the trust of scientists in each other. The way is ultimately paved for an enormous diversion of talent and resources into the verification of announced scientific findings. Such a legacy from the environmental movement would be a disaster not only for science but also for society as a whole, which has increasingly come to depend on scientific information for major public policy decisions.

The environmental movement has also undermined science by playing a key role in the movement to give scientific opinion a standing no higher than lay opinion on scientific subjects. The origin of this development was in the scientific information committees which mushroomed in the mid and late 1950s. These were committees of scientists who performed a valuable scientific service in alerting the public to the dangers of testing nuclear weapons in the atmosphere. Starting as a modest six page mimeographed bulletin in October 1958, *Nuclear Information,* published by the St. Louis committee, became a major vehicle for disseminating knowledge of the dangers of strontium 90 and iodine 131, dangers overlooked or minimized by government scientists. Biologists Barry Commoner and Renee Dubos and anthropologist Margaret Mead were probably the best known figures in the scientific information committees which, after their victory on the testing issue, organized nationally. In 1963, the Scientists Institute for Public Information (SIPI) was established to coordinate and guide the work of the local committees which turned their attention to a series of topics which would become the staple issues of the environmental movement: pesticides, air and water pollution, toxic wastes, uranium mining, medical technology and waste disposal, among others. The issues were publicized in the successor publications to *Nuclear Information:* first, *Scientist and Citizen* and then, *Environment.*

It was not the original intention of the scientific committees to deny the importance of scientific knowledge. The scientists of SIPI saw themselves as playing a guiding role for public-spirited citizen groups. They would provide objective information without political coloration which would enable the citizen to make intelligent policy decisions. Yet from the beginning SIPI's slogans suggested rejection of a superior standing in decision-making on scientific issues for scientists because of their deeper understanding of the issues. SIPI declared "The Scientist Informs—the Citizen Decides" and "It's Your World: Don't Leave It to the Experts." As citizen groups became increasingly important in the burgeoning environmental movement, the role of the scientist became ambiguous. The citizen groups SIPI had implored to make ethical and moral decisions about "their world" took the bit between their teeth and galloped off to define science as that which confirmed their prejudices.

SIPI itself became as much a "citizen" as a scientific organization and many of the original scientists dropped out as they saw its original purposes subverted. For Peter Metzger, the shift to attacking nuclear energy, in which he had always believed, was the final straw. Like Metzger, former members Ralph Lapp and Ian Forbes became biting critics of the new SIPI and the radicalized environmental movement. Others, like Barry Commoner, rode the new wave to become politicians.

Far from serving as guides, scientists were now automatically disqualified—unless they said what the citizen groups wanted them to say. Scientists were treated as "interested" by the citizen groups because their salaries were paid by government or industry or universities dependent on government money. Only the citizen was "disinterested" and therefore to be trusted. His "gut feelings" were to be decisive. Said one self-described "nuclear critic:" "I'm one of those people who can listen to a pedigreed scientist give me a list of statistical risks that are hard to refute, then turn around, take a reading on my own 'gut feelings' and come away disbelieving everything I have heard."[21]

This is not to say that citizen groups ceased to claim scientific support for their causes. Indeed, the decisive factor in many of their victories was public conviction that science showed that public health was at risk if environmentalist demands were not met. A small number of scientists, moreover, took an increasingly idiosyncratic view of scientific method. They were in the vanguard in identifying hazards or in devising doomsday scenarios for the demise of mankind as a result of ecologically disruptive technologies. Peter Metzger gives the example of Edward A. Martell, a U.S. army atomic weapons expert who became a senior chemist at the National Center for Atmospheric Research in Boulder. In 1975, he claimed that atherosclerotic plaques, the fatty deposits that plug up blood vessels in diseased hearts, were really radiation-induced cancers. Metzger notes that when Martell was told that this was so far-fetched it might damage his professional credibility, he replied "You're either with us or against us."[22]

While, by 1980, SIPI sought to restore its badly tarnished credibility in the scientific community, other citizen-scientist hybrids that sprang up around 1970 continued to pursue ideological science. The Center for Science in the Public Interest and Science for the People both had a frankly anti-corporate thrust. The Center for Science in the Public Interest described itself as an organization keeping "watch over business interests and corporate power's tendency to disregard the welfare of the public," while Science for the People declared that its goals included "exposing the class control of science and technology" and helping scientists "ally with other progressive forces in society" in "opposing the ideologies of sexism, racism, elitism and their practice."[23]

All this has encouraged judges to put lay opinion on a par with scientific opinion on scientific issues. The most remarkable example was the decision by a federal appeals court in Washington in May 1982 that the undamaged nuclear reactor at Three Mile Island (Unit One) could not reopen until the Nuclear Regulatory Commission had considered the psychological effect on the neighboring community. The case had been brought by a group called People Against Nuclear Energy who argued that the "post-traumatic neurosis" from which people in the area suffered would be aggravated. As *Harper's* editor Michael Kinsley noted:

> "The only effect of the new 'psychological impact' doctrine is to require the NRC to consider people's *unjustified* fears as well as their justified ones. Now unjustified fears can be quite real. But whose fault is it if people are scared sick with no basis in fact? . . . It's a wonderful arrangement. Having generated hysteria, the opponents of nuclear power are now in a position to argue that, even if they cannot prove their case, the hysteria itself is a reason to ban nuclear power."[24] (The Supreme Court, in 1983, rejected the appeals court ruling.)

As science has become the target of political manipulation, publicists for a new economic and political order have seized upon scientific concepts in an attempt to rationalize their call for an end to scientific progress. In his book *Entropy,* Jeremy Rifkin renewed a practice, discredited long ago, of applying scientific laws to the social world. Herbert Spencer had misused Darwin's laws of natural selection, arguing in his *The Study of Sociology* that it followed from those laws that philanthropy was an evil. As Spencer put it: "For if the unworthy are helped to increase, by shielding them from that mortality which their unworthiness would naturally entail, the effect is to produce, generation after generation, a greater unworthiness." The triumph of the citizen over the scientist had reinaugurated the effort to support a social agenda by giving it the inescapability and certainty of scientific laws and making it appear that failure to follow the agenda will be attended with the dire consequences that follow violation of a law of nature.

In some cases political utopians have crudely exploited the environmentalist wave. For example, the Mobilization for Survival, organized in 1977, calls itself an "environmental group." The organization was founded by Sidney Peck, according to a Congressional staff study, a member of the Wisconsin State Committee of the Communist Party in the 1960s, and Sidney Lens, once a member of the Trotskyite Revolutionary Workers League, in order to rally support for the First UN Special Session on Disarmament in 1978, and in Peck's words "to energize the growing opposition to the military."[25]

The Mobilization's membership consists of national political and "peace" organizations and local direct-action (really anti-nuclear) environmental groups. Among the national organizations are the United States Communist Party, the United States Peace Council (the U.S. branch of the Soviet-controlled World Peace Council) and peace organizations, including the Women's International League for Peace and Freedom, Women Strike for Peace, the American Friends Service Committee and Clergy and Laity Concerned.

The Mobilization gives itself an environmental veneer by saying that it works against all forms of "nuclear pollution," and wherever feasible echoes environmental pieties. Thus, in calling for the MX missile to be abandoned, the Mobilization declared the money should be used instead for solar heating. But, without environmental gloss, the Mobilization called for scrapping the Camp David accords between Israel and Egypt and substituting U.S. backing for a PLO state, and an end to "all arms sales and military assistance to foreign countries by the United States." While the U.S. hostages were being held by Iran, the Mobilization called for the United States to stop "persecuting Iranians" and to support an international tribunal to "bring the Shah to justice." It sponsored something called "Survival Summer 1980" whose goal, according to its literature, was "to redefine the obsolete concept of national security." At its 1981 national meeting the Mobilization decided to devote itself to giving the antidraft movement political direction.[26]

The Mobilization has served as a national coordinator for demonstrations. While the most famous demonstration it coordinated was the June 12, 1982 march for disarmament in New York City, which brought out three quarters of a million people, the Mobilization had conducted smaller demonstrations since its inception. In a single month, April 1979, it coordinated a Zero Nuclear Weapons demonstration in Philadelphia, a demonstration against the Diablo Canyon nuclear power plant in California, a Navajo demonstration against uranium mining in New Mexico, and a protest against the Rocky Flats nuclear weapons testing facility in Colorado. A year later its publication, *The Mobilizer,* reported that "with the strong support of the National Council of Churches," the Religious Task Force of the Mobilization was sponsoring a tour of U.S. and Japanese nuclear victims through the United States. Among U.S. nuclear "victims" were "shipyard workers who build nuclear submarines," "residents living near nuclear power plants," and "Native American uranium miners."

None of the national environmental organizations belong to the

Mobilization for Survival. But its central effort—to link the struggle against nuclear energy with the campaign against nuclear weapons—has achieved considerable success. Friends of the Earth organized a national conference on The Fate of the Earth—the title was, of course, taken from Jonathan Schell's famous book attacking nuclear weapons—which brought together the major environmental organizations. A number have formally endorsed the nuclear freeze, and even among those who have not, there is growing sentiment that disarmament should be seen as an integral part of environmental concerns.

The recent success of the nuclear freeze movement has obscured recognition that, up to 1982, disarmament groups were trying to convince the public that nuclear bombs were as dangerous as nuclear energy. Chemist George Kistiakowsky, one time chief science advisor to President Eisenhower, and chairman, till his death late in 1982, of the Council for a Livable World, observed in a February 1981 interview: "We have problems in trying to redirect the public fear of nuclear plants into fear of nuclear war."[27] *The Journal of the New Alchemists* saw the problem in a more positive light: "The best handle we have to date for focusing public attention on the larger question of the arms race is with the apparently more immediate and visible issue of nuclear power."[28] Amory Lovins took the line that the peaceful and warlike atom could not be divorced. "We cannot embrace one while abhorring the other; we must learn, if we want to live at all, to live without both."[29]

Changes in the tax laws in 1976 have accelerated the political mobilization of mainstream environmental organizations. The new laws permitted tax-exempt organizations to devote 10% of their income, up to a maximum of one million dollars a year, to lobbying. *Energy Daily* notes that organizations like Audubon and National Wildlife Preservation became transformed into activist centers as fervid as their Earth Day juniors—but with much more money.[30]

At the periphery of the environmental movement—which time and again has transformed the perspective of the center—there is a conviction that pollution is a symptom of a more profound social disorder. Just as the existing political and economic system had produced every evil from environmental degradation to racism, so, it is believed, a new social and political system could arrest the deterioration of the environment—and more. Self-proclaimed ecological anarchist Murray Bookchin, a guru, not only of the counter-cultural *Mother Earth News,* but of Friends of the Earth, has announced: "Neither sexism, ageism, racism, the 'energy crisis,' corporate power . . . bureaucratic manipulation, conscription, militarism, urban devastation or political centralism can be separated from the ecological issue." Bookchin argues that it is necessary to uncover the "toxic social causes" that have created our poisoned planet: "As long as hierarchy persists . . . the prospect of dominating nature will continue to exist and inevitably lead our planet to ecological extinction."[31] On the other hand, if the value system that supports environmental degradation is changed, writes Robert Disch, editor of *The Ecological Conscience,* "of necessity" we will eradicate "such seemingly unrelated problems" as "racism, poverty, health, aging, urban blight, and social injustice."[32]

Perhaps the most mysterious aspect of the campaign for de-development of the United States is the respectful hearing it has won. That a small sect subscribed to a belief system that calls for rolling back the Industrial Revolution would entail no surprise. We would expect to see the sect's visions of the future and roadmap for its achievement detailed in the magazines and bulletins of small groups of the faithful. But the visions of the environmental utopians are published in quintessentially establishment journals like *Foreign Affairs,* whose editor told a reporter that he was prouder of having published Amory Lovins' essay than of any other article. They are given lengthy and respectful treatment in such opinion-setting journals as *The New Yorker,* and a veritable avalanche of books detailing the sect's analysis of our problems and solutions for them have poured from virtually every major publishing house. The spokesmen for eliminating complex technology were consulted by President Carter and have been respectfully attended by committees of Congress. A number of those subscribing to the sect's solutions were put in charge of major government energy programs in the Carter administration.

One explanation for the attraction exercised by the utopians who advocate a society built upon "appropriate technology" is that the best known proponents do not clarify their political agenda and hold out deceptively rosy prospects of a better future for all, with sacrifice by none. Lovins is the most adept at promising everyone a better life through exclusive reliance on "renewable" energy.

> "A soft path offers advantages for everyone. It gives us jobs for the unemployed, capital for business people, opportunities for big business to recycle itself, and for small business to innovate, environmental protection for conservationists, better national security for the military, exciting technologies for the secular, a rebirth of religious values for the

religious, world order and equity for the globalists, energy independence for isolationists, radical reforms for the young, traditional virtues of thrift and craftsmanship for the old, civil rights for political liberals, and local autonomy for political conservatives."

Lovins has repeated this particular passage in innumerable speeches, in the introduction to his book *Soft Energy Paths,* in testimony before the Committee on Government Operations of the House of Representatives and at the Salzburg Conference on a Non-Nuclear Future. Not only is the soft path beneficial to every conceivable interest group but, according to Lovins, it is perfect for all regions and population densities. It is "ideally suited for rural villages and urban poor alike." Nor does the soft path necessarily entail any changes in lifestyle. Lovins says it can be considered "a purely technical fix . . . I am a pluralist. I don't want to force my social views on anyone." A cynic might say that Americans have long had a weakness for snake oil.

If no one is quite so lyrical as Lovins, others also promise a better future without making it clear that the benefits are to be exclusively spiritual. Solar advocate Ray Reece promises a solar-powered economy will offer "maximum stimulation of employment opportunities," and "escalation in community standard of living," as well as "reduced anxiety and stress," "higher degrees of individual and group participation in the political process," and "enhanced prospects for world peace."[33] Kirkpatrick Sale avers: "Quite simply, it is now possible, probably for the first time since the human occupation of the earth, to evolve a technology that can allow us to avoid drudgery, escape poverty, provide protection, supply nutriments and enjoy comforts, to expand personal freedom and power, and to live in ecological harmony."[34] Barry Commoner assures us that the need for total societal transformation "does not necessarily mean that . . . the people of industrial nations need to give up their 'affluent' way of life," since the needed reforms can be carried out without seriously reducing the present level of *useful* goods available to the individual . . ."[35] (Italics in original) The reassured reader is not likely to ask himself, "What is Commoner's definition of 'useful goods' and will it correspond with my own?" Dr. Aden and Marjorie Meinel, pioneers in the application of solar energy, explain the appeal of such solar advocates in terms of a deep-rooted desire of the human species to return to the Garden of Eden. But the Meinels warn: "Should this siren philosophy be heard and believed we can perceive the onset of a New Dark Age."[36]

The solar advocates must explain why, if through the application of technologically simple devices the sun could be supplying a large proportion of our energy needs, it presently supplies, as James Weber emphasizes in *Power Grab,* "in effect, zero, repeat zero percent of domestic energy production."[37] They provide an answer as appealing to public psychological proclivities as their canvas of a future agrarian idyll. Big corporations have conspired to deprive us of the sun. In an interview, Ralph Nader was asked how he would explain the energy crisis if he were to make a television documentary. Nader replied that he would show trees, cornhusks, manure, the sun, the wind. He would ask if all this energy is there, why aren't we getting it. And Nader, the man who, polls show, is trusted by more Americans than any other individual, says he would answer, it is because energy corporations only like a certain kind of energy—the kind they can effectively control. And the sun, says Nader, doesn't qualify because it "can go directly to your home, bypassing your friends at the utility and power company."[38] In this conspiratorial explanation, corporations are sabotaging the "soft path" because it threatens their profits.

Ironically, the companies are also attacked for investing in solar energy. An article in Nader's *Critical Mass* (the publication of Nader's anti-nuclear project of the same name) objects to corporate investment in development of photovoltaic cells on the grounds that solar energy should be an opportunity "to redistribute social and economic power."[39] For anti-nuclear activist Harvey Wasserman, solar energy should be "a revolutionary vehicle with which people can take charge of their own power supplies, leaving the world's richest corporations out in the cold."[40] Solar activist Ray Reece argues that government research is emphasizing "those applications of solar energy which are most compatible with the present system of capital-intensive, centralized power facilities" deterring the public "from identifying solar energy as a possible means of altering the present economic and geopolitical structure of the United States."[41] Reece's view of industry involvement in solar research is summed up in his book's title, *The Sun Betrayed.*

The dream of the solar age, as advanced by these proponents, is warm and romantic. In *Progress As If Survival Mattered,* the Friends of the Earth's David Brower promises: "Our anxiously acquisitive consumer society will give way to a more serenely thrifty conserver society.[42] But the real requirements of the solar age—the decentralized solar age—are stern. Russell Peterson, a former head of DuPont and governor of Delaware, now head of the Audubon Society, writes: "I think we shall see a shift to a technology that will put man rather than the machine at the center of industrial economics."[43] Who can object to a proposal that man be at the center of human concern? But what the utopians are saying is that man is going to be the source of energy rather than the machine. Few will find it liberating to be substituted for machines as the source of energy. So unattractive has production of energy by human means been to the human beings that supplied the energy that most societies have found it necessary to render unfree those assigned to the task of providing it. The Industrial Revolution, substituting the machine's energy for that of man, liberated men from bondage.

An activist told a meeting of Nader's Critical Mass: "Instead of the Gross National Product we should measure our progress by a General Satisfaction Index which would go up dependably every time the GNP went down." But despite such bravura, occasionally in the rosiest portraits of the future, glimmers of the practical meaning of such mellifluous phrases as "matching" energy requirements as exactly as possible to "end-use" come through. Thus Ray Reece mentions that a dentist's drill requires electricity or compressed air, while the drying of clothes requires "a cotton cord or length of wire strung up in sunlight."[44] The appliances that have contributed more to women's liberation than the movement by that name would be one of the most obvious sacrifices to "matching" energy to "end-use." What more appropriate technology for washing clothes or dishes than the age-old energy of human hands? One can imagine the utopians growing poetic over the sense of community that will be restored as women (and perhaps men as well) gather at river's edge in the sunlight to beat their clothes against the rocks.

Occasionally an honest assessment of the impact of the conserver society is made by a proponent. In *Entropy* Jeremy Rifkin admits that in the conserver society, Americans will live in a "frugal or Spartan life-style" in which "production will center on goods required to maintain life."[45]

The desperately unattractive nature of the future that the conserver society holds out, once the poetic rhetoric is stripped away, has led more forthright utopians like Rifkin to seek ways to motivate people to accept the drastic decline in living standards that will come if the utopians have their way. Rifkin turns to religion as the only force capable of making people accept the future planned for them. He sees the answer in a transformed Christianity that would emphasize the fixed character of God's creation and the inadmissibility of tampering with any part of it. This would provide "a new set of governing principles for how human beings should behave and act in the world." A stewardship doctrine would enable men and women to accept lovingly the hardships of the conserver society "because it is God's order."[46] Interestingly Rifkin turns not to the religious elements who have been most enthusiastic concerning the conserver society like the National Council of Churches and the mainline churches but to those who have been least receptive, the evangelical wing of Christianity. Presumably Rifkin is dubious that the politicized and secularized churches can provide the strong religious impulse needed, so he turns to those for whom traditional religious beliefs are still a force capable of shaping their lives. But what, from the standpoint of the reader, may be most interesting is that Rifkin cannot see Americans accepting the future the environmental utopians have in store for them on any other grounds.

Ironically, if a technological solar age does dawn, and we do not retreat to an original solar age where man and animal were the chief source of energy, harnessing the sun will probably entail the most centralized and complex of all technologies yet devised for the distribution of energy. Nor is that a bad thing. David Rossin has pointed out that the decentralized energy of the conserver society requires centralized decision-making, for where there is scarcity, inevitably there is allocation and rationing, which must be performed by central authorities.[47] Centralized energy, on the other hand, is much more likely to produce decentralized decisions on the use of that energy. Since it is the power to make decisions that most people value and not the proximity of their energy source (how many of us do in fact feel humiliated, as Lovins says we should, when we turn on a light switch?), surely most of us will choose the freedom to use energy over physical proximity to energy sources we are constrained from using.

REFERENCES

1. James Ridgeway, *The Politics of Ecology,* New York, E.P. Dutton & Co., 1970, p. 208
2. *New York Times,* March 28, 1970
3. Robert Disch, "Ecology and Social Institutions," in Robert Disch, ed. *The Environmental Conscience,* New Jersey, Prentice Hall, 1970, p. 127; Albert Fritsch, *Environmental Ethics,* New York, Anchor Books, 1980, p. 171
4. Barry Commoner, *The Closing Circle,* New York, Bantam Books, 1971, p. 280
5. William Tucker, *Progress and Privilege,* New York, Doubleday, 1982, p. 164

6. Lynn White Jr., "The Historical Roots of Our Ecological Crisis," in Garrett DeBell ed., *The Environmental Handbook,* New York, Ballantine Books, 1970, p. 23
7. Ian L. McHarg, "Values, Process and Form," in Ibid., p. 25
8. "Nuclear Phobia—Phobic Thinking about Nuclear Power: A Discussion with Robert I. DuPont M.D." The Media Institute, Washington D.C., March 1980, pp. 7-8, 12-13
9. Quoted in Nuclear Legislative Advisory Service Newsletter, June 1978
10. Ibid.
11. *Audubon,* January 1981, p. 117
12. E.F. Schumacher, *Small is Beautiful: Economics as If People Mattered,* New York, Harper & Row, 1973, pp. 30-31
13. Amory Lovins, "Energy Strategy: The Road Not Taken," *Foreign Affairs,* October 1976, pp. 91-92
14. Kirkpatrick Sale, *Human Scale,* New York, Coward, McCann & Geoghegan, 1980, p. 157
15. Louis Mumford, "Closing Statement," in Robert Disch ed., op. cit., p. 101
16. Quoted in James Weber, *Power Grab: The Conserver Cult and the Coming Energy Catastrophe* New York, Arlington House, 1979, p. 46
17. Hugh Nash ed., *Progress as If Survival Mattered: A Handbook for a Conserver Society,* Friends of the Earth, 1977, p. 40
18. Quoted in Robert Bleiberg, "Bring Back DDT," *Barron's,* June 29, 1981
19. George Claus and Karen Bolander, *Ecological Sanity,* New York, David McKay Co., 1977, p. 541
20. Ibid., pp. 250-253
21. Quoted in *Access to Energy,* Boulder, Colo., August 1, 1977
22. *Rocky Mountain News,* May 9, 1976
23. Quoted in *AIM Report,* Accuracy in Media, Washington D.C., Oct. II, 1982
24. Michael Kinsley, "Mental Cases," *Harper's,* July 1982, p. 8
25. Study is Staff Study, Committee on Internal Security, House of Representatives, 91st Congress, 2nd Session, 1970, Subversive Involvement in the Origins, Leadership & Activities of the New Mobilization Committee to End the War in Vietnam and its Predecessor Organizations, p. 2
26. *Information Digest,* Feb. 13, 1981
27. "George Kistiakowsky: Champion of Arms Control," *Chemical and Engineering News,* Feb. 2, 1981, p. 26
28. *Journal of the New Alchemists,* the New Alchemy Institute, Vol. 6, 1980
29. Quoted in *Amicus Journal,* Natural Resources Defense Council, Spring 1981
30. *The Energy Daily,* August 2, 1979
31. Murray Bookchin, "The Selling of the Ecology Movement," *WIN,* September 15, 1980, p. 1
32. Robert Disch, ed., "Ecology and Social Institutions," op. cit., p. 128
33. Ray Reece, *The Sun Betrayed: A Report on the Corporate Seizure of U.S. Solar Energy Development,* Boston: South End Press, 1979, p. 194
34. Kirkpatrick Sale, op. cit., p. 161
35. Barry Commoner, *The Closing Circle,* op. cit., p. 294
36. Quoted in James Weber, op. cit., p. 134
37. Ibid., p. 43
38. Joe Klein, "Ralph Nader: The Man in the Class Action Suit," *Rolling Stone,* Nov. 20, 1975, p. 10
39. *Critical Mass,* December 1969
40. Harvey Wasserman, op. cit., p. xii

41. Ray Reece, op. cit., p. 26
42. *Progress As If Survival Mattered,* p. 1
43. Ibid., p. 87
44. Ray Reece, op. cit., p. 192
45. Jeremy Rifkin with Ted Howard, *Entropy: A New World View*, New York, Viking Press, 1980, p. 203
46. Ibid., p. 238
47. David Rossin,"The Softy Energy Path: Where Does It Lead?" *The Futurist,* June 1980, p. 62

V

In The Public Interest

Charles Halpern, a pioneer in the public interest law movement, tells a revealing story. In the spring of 1971, sixty public interest specialists met for a two day working seminar entitled, "The Bar and the Public Interest," at Airlie House in the Virginia Hills. Halpern noted wryly that the only peaceful thing about the meeting was the landscape. It broke up in a fight between public interest lawyers representing consumer and environmental interests and black, Chicano, civil liberties and poverty lawyers who called the others "racist." The participants never even got around to dealing with the problem they had gathered to solve: how to obtain long-range financing for public interest law. The Ford Foundation rescheduled a conference on the same topic three years later and it went off without a hitch. This time only lawyers representing environmental and consumer interests were invited.

The story illustrates the most profound problem with the public interest movement, its assumption that there is a single discernible public interest. "The public interest" is the most rubbery of concepts. Political theorists have generally viewed it as a vacuous abstraction. Yet for all the term's slippery character when a definition is called for, it has immense appeal as a slogan. Who is not in favor of the public interest? But there is more to the slogan than meets the eye. Proponents of the public interest do not claim that the public interest is universally recognized. Far from it. There would be no need for advocates of the public interest if it were. The public interest is obscured, so its advocates claim, because of the assertion of "special interests." Those who understand and can define the public interest must, therefore, step forward and rescue it from the special interests that prevent its realization. And so, the public interest becomes one of the most successful devices of the coercive utopians to assert their vision of what society should look like. For lo and behold, that vision is transformed from a reflection of the tastes and values of an element of the middle and upper middle class into the public interest, i.e. the interests of us all.

The public interest movement has revived the populist tradition in American politics. As Simon Lazarus notes in *The Genteel Populists,* populism, in the tradition of Rousseau, believed in the existence of "a general will." As the populists saw it, the general will was blocked by a series of powerful special interests. It was a conception contrasting sharply with the pluralist view which has been dominant in American politics. Pluralism sees special interests as the stuff of democratic politics. The populist view is optimistic about human nature, for the will of the people is a beneficent will. The pluralist conception is more realistic. Man is seen as selfish, so government must mediate between conflicting demands. Government, itself, must be controlled by a system of checks and balances. Ironically, it is the optimistic populist view that leads to a paranoid politics. Since the popular will is good, and existing political arrangements flawed, the explanation can only be in evil conspiracies and quasi-conspiracies to thwart the popular will. Even Lazarus, who sympathizes with the new populism, confesses that while it seems amazing that the populist model of the world is so simplistic as to boil down to "the people" versus "the interests," populist leaders had consistently based their actions and programs on precisely this view of the world.[1]

The most strictly populist group within the public interest movement is Common Cause, which has devoted its primary energy to procedural changes designed to make public officials more accountable. As is often the way, the effects have in many cases been the opposite of those intended. Common Cause successfully campaigned for a ceiling on the size of contributions to political candidates, which led to the emergence of political action committees (PACs) as a major political force. Then, in 1983, Common Cause took the leadership in fighting PACs. Typically, it seized the high moral ground, calling the PACs "a new national scandal corrupting our democracy" and warning that unless the system were changed "our representative system of government will be gone" replaced "with a government of, by and for the PACs."[2] However, it is hard to avoid the conclusion that what really aroused the ire of Common Cause was that the PACs had the effect of strengthening conservative groups, not those pursuing the activist liberal goals of Common Cause.

The chief hero of the new populism is, of course, Ralph Nader, and the public interest movement differs from the other movements discussed in this book in being centered so largely on a single figure, whose followers stand almost in the relation of disciples to a master. Muckrakers had influenced an earlier American populism, but not since the Roman tribune had there been a muckraker like Nader, who institutionalized his outrage. Nader fathered a whole series of organizations, twenty-five in all, a number of which eventually spun off from the parent. By 1978 there were 100 people working full time in Washington D.C. in organizations directly controlled by Nader. Other groups formed because of his example and were often manned by his veterans. The New York Public Interest Research Group (NYPIRG), headed up until 1982 by Donald Ross, who with Nader originated the idea of these groups, alone has an annual budget of $2.6 million. In 1981, Elizabeth Whelan, of the American Council on Science and Health, reported that she had been invited by the Food and Drug Administration to a meeting for heads of consumer groups and found she was the only representative of a group whose existence had not been inspired by Nader. She should not have exempted her own group. The American Council on Science and Health would also not exist were it not for Nader: it was created to counter the influence of the groups he inspired.

Nader's meteoric rise was of course thanks to General Motors, which made him an instant hero by sending detectives to explore his private life and then confessing the misdeed. Nader's book *Unsafe at Any Speed,* which prompted General Motors to its unwise actions, attacked the automobile industry as a whole for deliberately producing unsafe cars, but singled out General Motors' 1961-63 Corvairs as especially unsafe. There has been much controversy since as to whether Nader's charges against the Corvair were justified. (At Nader's insistence an exhaustive government study was finally conducted of the Corvair, which concluded that the car was as safe as any comparable car of its period. On the other hand, although his subsequent exploits may not make him the most reliable of witnesses,

John Z. De Lorean, an executive at General Motors at the time, corroborates Nader's charges, stating the 1959-63 models—the problem was corrected in 1964—had a tendency to become unstable at high speeds.)[3]

Whether or not Nader was right about the Corvair, *Unsafe at Any Speed* is primarily interesting for revealing Nader's approach to social problems, and showing that from the start, Nader belonged in the ranks of the coercive utopians.

Two years after the publication of Nader's book, the Department of Transportation calculated that 800,000 crashes each year and 25,000 deaths, half of the total, were due to alcohol abuse. Nader could have argued convincingly that given the driver's penchant to abuse the automobile, it was incumbent upon the manufacturer to do everything possible to protect the driver, as well as the innocent passengers and drivers he threatened, from the consequences of his irresponsibility. But this is not what Nader argued. In Nader's view, the consumer's incompetence, idiosyncracies or inherent frailty are irrelevant. Nader actually attacked the National Safety Council for associating accidents with drivers. The consumer is simply the victim, his innocence matched by the diabolical scheming of the profit-hungry producer who wilfully and knowingly foists unsafe cars upon an unsuspecting public.

Much of Nader's appeal is in his portrayal of the world as a western movie. Black hats confront white hats. The black hats sit in corporate headquarters, with their henchmen ensconsed in government offices. There is power in this immense simplification. It is no accident that throughout history people have believed readily in conspiracies, for they offer comforting explanations, especially if the conspirators are disliked in any case. When the bubonic plague—known as the Black Death—struck in the Middle Ages, Jews were accused of poisoning the wells. Nader's anti-corporate crusades have much the same appeal. A handful of criminal executives in a definable number of mammoth corporations are the "special interests" responsible for all the complex ills that beset the United States. For Nader they are literally responsible for everything, from the most trivial ills to the most basic, from extortionate cab drivers to mental illness. And the motive for their malevolence is always the same—the pursuit of profit.

Nader's treatment of rising energy prices and shortages (prior to the 1983 oil glut) is typical. With fellow coercive utopian Gar Alperovitz, Nader in 1978, created a coalition called COIN (Consumers Opposed to Inflation in the Necessities). Although COIN pointed out that energy had risen in price more than any other necessity, in the statement on energy *there was not a single mention of OPEC* as a factor in raising the price of oil. The blame was put squarely at the door of the giant companies and the utilities. As the lines formed at the gas stations after the Iranian revolution, Nader remained certain that it was yet another oil company ploy. Said Nader: "Every time you see a disturbance overseas in an oil country, watch out. That's what the oil companies need as pretext to put in motion their system of manipulating shortages . . . they can get away with it, because they've got Schlesinger and Carter in Washington and they're not going to be challenged."[5] (With a U.S. President and Secretary of Energy at their beck and call, the black hats have henchmen in high places.)

The public could have whatever it wanted, at the prices it wanted to pay, were it not for the black hats. The big companies block us from the sun. Nader told the faithful who gathered for the 1978 Critical Mass conference: "Giant corporations monopolize our energy supply, and their indentured regulatory agencies will not stand idly by as consumers push for a solar energy economy."[6] Corporations cause inflation. Do economists claim that government spending is a factor? Regulation? Nonsense. In COIN's slogan "Inflation isn't a natural disaster. It's caused by the people who profit from it." Unfairly, says Nader, the burden of fighting inflation has been put on the victim rather than "the corporate perpetrators."

The small crook merely imitates the biggest crook of all, the big businessman. Nader notes that New Yorkers complain about cabdrivers. But the cabdriver "listens to those corporate executives" in the back of his cab and "gets some idea of how the big boys are stealing millions. And he tells himself that if *they're* stealing millions, he might as well get *his* share."[7] The genius of the corporation, says Nader, is to develop "an abstraction of burglary." People can't follow "thievery three stages removed" and blame the small fellow instead. Nader aide, Beverly Moore, doubled the remarkable figure of $200 billion that Senator Philip Hart of Michigan had come up with, as the amount the consumer spent unnecessarily, to conclude that corporations defrauded the consumer of $400 billion annually. The figure was ten times the profits of all manufacturing corporations or 55 cents of every consumer dollar.[8]

Nader's anti-corporate passion has produced even more ludicrous results. One of the lesser known forays of Nader's Raiders into institutional misprision was called *The Madness Establishment*. It concerned the failure of community mental health centers established with federal money. There is no question that these centers did not live up to the expectations that were raised for them, nor is this surprising. The most prevalent mental disorder is schizophrenia, which affects one percent of the population worldwide (with scant regard for a country's stage of economic development) and for which there is as yet no cure. The population of mental hospitals has, nonetheless, been radically reduced because of the discovery in the early 1950s of mood-controlling drugs. These drugs improve function but do not cure, with the result that there is a revolving door, the same patients going in and out of institutions. Apart from die-hard Freudian remnants, psychiatrists agree that serious mental disorders have a biochemical basis. But there is no room for faulty human chemistry in Nader's world. So in his introduction to his Raider's study, Nader simply gives the psychiatrists the black hat. Nader informs us that psychiatry has addressed itself to the wrong patient:

> ''What about the institutional pathologies of the corporation whose products seriously abuse consumers, factories and mines that subject workers to intolerable working conditions and hazards; unions that ig nore rank and file grievances, government agencies that do not serve their citizens in need; police, merchants and landlords who rule the slums with the heaviest of hands; courts that distribute injustice to a defenseless people; liquor and drug industries that make consumers into addicts . . . Why is there such a paucity of literature on institutional insanity and its victims?''[9]

According to Nader, psychiatrists have addressed apparently ill patients rather than truly deranged institutions because of fear of loss of income and status.

Nader has identified both the villains (in the suites) and the victims (in the streets). But how are the victims to be rescued from the villains, when the villains own the government? Nader has both a long term and a short term solution. The long term solution calls for a new man in a reconstructed society. The short term solution, to which Nader has devoted most of his practical efforts, is the creation of ''change-agents'' who will serve as pilot projects for the new man.

Nader's first change-agents were the youthful ''Nader's Raiders,'' who descended upon the various regulatory agencies and assorted other targets like the mental health centers, duPont, and the First National City Bank. But the Raiders were a limited tool, best suited for hit-and-run operations, especially since they were, for the most part, students only available on college vacations. In 1971 Nader turned his attention to Congress as a potential vehicle for social transformation, using the Raiders for the so-called "Congress Project," which was to help Congress fulfill what Nader said was its potential of being "the prime lever of change and justice in reclaiming America."[10]

The Congress Project did not transform Congress. Nader's biggest raiding party, 1000 members strong, descended on Congress to dissect it. The most ambitious of Nader's raids, its failure, admitted by Nader himself, spelled the end of them. The press blamed organizational chaos, but more fundamentally the project ran head on into that stubborn problem of how one operationally defined the public interest. In the case of the regulatory agencies, there were Congressional mandates setting forth agency goals, and agency achievement could be measured against those mandates, which were assumed to represent "the public interest." Those unfortunate mental health centers had been established with grandiose targets to which their pathetic performance could be compared. Nader was committed to providing profiles of all Congressmen up for election in 1972. But how did one measure a Congressman? Should he be judged by his diligence? By his creativeness in introducing legislation? But what if a diligent, creative Congressman voted against bills Nader believed were in "the public interest." Ultimately Congressional performance could only be evaluated in terms of social and national goals and values.

The values brought by the Congress Project Raiders were described by Stephen Brown, one of the participants. Nader told TV audiences that his Raiders identified with no political party and had not been involved in political campaigns. But Brown reported that his own private survey showed that 96.8% of the Raiders planned to vote for McGovern and only 1.6% for Nixon. Moreover a great many of the Raiders had actually worked in Democratic campaigns.[11] Since the American public voted overwhelmingly for Nixon in the elections, there was presumably a rather different view of the people's interests held by the Raiders and "the people."

Nader was in a dilemma. He was sensitive to the problem of simply compiling a volume of profiles in which praise was heaped on the ideologically compatible and dirt was dumped on the ideologically incompatible. Besides, Nader's main wrath was directed at those among the ideologically compatible who had failed to vote for his favored project of a Consumer Protection Agency. The end result was unfocussed profiles that left many Congressmen relieved. Most of the planned in-depth studies of Congressional committees were never published. A potboiler called *Who Runs Congress?*, slapped together in three weeks by three Nader lieutenants, over the protests of the rest of the Project, became a best-seller but aroused no interest in the weightier products of the Project. Cost over-runs on the Congress Project left Nader $500,000 out of pocket. After the Project, which Nader called his "B-1 bomber" in reference to the unhappy fate of the plane in the Carter administration, Nader abandoned both use of the Raiders and the notion of transforming Congress.

Several years after the Congress Project, Common Cause achieved many of the procedural transformations Nader had wanted. Common Cause successfully pressed for "sunshine laws" opening up Congressional committee procedures to the public, mandatory financial disclosures, an end to the seniority system, reduction in the power of committee chairmen etc. Yet these, too, could not transform Congress, at least not in the way Common Cause and Nader had hoped. On the contrary, by 1980, John Gardner, the first President of Common Cause, was complaining of a "marked drop in effectiveness" of Congress.[12]

Nader abandoned another lever for change as quickly as Congress. That was "the people." In 1975, after his earlier efforts to stop nuclear energy at the state level failed, Nader turned to the referendum, a tool developed in an earlier populist era to allow direct public intervention in policy-making. Nader succeeded in having anti-nuclear propositions placed on the ballot in a number of states. When the propositions failed to pass in each of them, Nader was forced back on his cadres of the public interest elite. As an abstraction, "the people" continued to figure as prominently as ever in Nader's rhetoric, but as a concrete change-agent they were quietly shelved.

Apart from the activist cadre in his employ, Nader has consistently found students the most responsive to his vision. Nader first attempted to set up institutions on campus in 1970. From small beginnings on two campuses, Oregon and Minnesota, Public Interest Research Groups (PIRGs) have expanded to 30 states and 175 campuses. PIRGs have the dual purpose of training students as activists and using student funds to provide ongoing support for professional public citizens. In 1982, New York PIRG, alone, had a staff of 200 lawyers, organizers and researchers, making it the biggest citizen activist organization in the state. Overall, PIRGs have a budget of around $6 million a year. They are a substantial force, even if they have not had the impact

Nader hoped when he foresaw the transformation of campuses into huge public interest centers supporting 4,000-5,000 public interest professionals.

Nader's utopianism is manifest in his reliance upon creation of more of the very same kinds of institutions that in his own view failed miserably before. This time, presumably, they will work because of the emergence of a new kind of man, a new type of "public citizen," who will make sure the new agencies or the transformed old agencies are not subverted or gutted by the interests they are supposed to regulate. But even those sympathetic to the public interest movement have pointed out why Nader's most treasured projects, rejected by Congress, would not have worked as he planned even had they been passed.

Closest to Nader's heart was his proposed Consumer Protection Agency. Legislation to establish it was first introduced in 1970 and after almost passing in 1973 and 1974 was decisively rejected in 1978 by the House. The House vote, moreover, came on a considerably scaled-down version of the previous bills. Nader envisaged the Consumer Protection Agency as a superagency monitoring other government agencies on behalf of the consumer. It would initiate proceedings before regulatory agencies. It would challenge the disclosure policies of agencies. It would petition for improved procedures and practices in other agencies. It would petition against "chronic nonenforcement" practices by agencies. And when it wasn't satisfied with the results of its "petitions" and "challenges," it could sue the recalcitrant agency in the courts.

While Nader and Congress battled over the extent of power to be given the agency—Nader ultimately lost the agency altogether because of his refusal to accept a compromise—Simon Lazarus has argued convincingly that it would not have mattered if Nader's bill or a watered down version had been passed.[13] In both Nader's version and that of Congress, the agency head would have been appointed by the President. But the President could not have afforded to have one of the agencies he controlled constantly challenging, attacking and suing all the other agencies he controlled. It would be an admission that the whole administrative bureaucracy for which he was responsible could not be trusted to fulfil its obligations. So long as the President controlled its direction, the new agency would learn to temper its enthusiasm in short order.

Nader's other major tool, which has also not been enacted into law, was federal chartering of corporations. (At first Nader wanted to include the 700 largest corporations, but then changed the plan to the biggest 250.) Federal chartering, in Nader's words, would "tame" the giant corporation. But Lazarus notes that Nader is assuming that if the federal government, rather than the states, chartered corporations, chartering would cease to be a formality, but would be contingent on a corporation's meeting defined public interests. Yet this would only be the case if Congress passed a host of restrictions on the behavior of corporations, restrictions it would have passed, if it had so desired, without chartering. Lazarus recalls that federal chartering was a pet project of Wall Street leaders when William Howard Taft was President. They hoped it would cement a cooperative relationship between the federal government and big business. Lazarus argues the new bureaucracy could in fact weaken existing protections against excessive corporate power, since the most damaging offenses against the free market are committed under the protective cover of regulatory statutes.[14]

Nader's real purpose in pursuing chartering legislation is to transform the nature of the corporation through federal regulation. As Nader sees the corporation, it is a species of government with an electorate (shareholders), a legislature (directors) and an executive (management). And yet, Nader complains, there is no organized opposition party to challenge existing officers. He compares the American shareholder to the Russian citizen, declaring that "the Kremlin might have learned from the corporation how to develop its processes."[15] So Nader has devised a series of proposals that would make the corporation a "democracy." Each major decision made by management would have to be ratified by the shareholders, who would have to be given all the information management had in order to make an intelligent decision. Nader would also reconstruct "the legislature" (the directors) who would also include the public affected by the corporation. Nader's hope was that these proposals would become the requirements for a corporation to receive its federal charter and any corporation that violated the charter would have its products outlawed in interstate commerce.

In *The Defense of the Corporation,* Robert Hessen has provided a comprehensive criticism of Nader's proposals. Nader's assumption, that a corporation is a government, is fallacious because a corporation cannot coerce a shareholder, whose vote is registered in the marketplace. If enough shareholders are dissatisfied, share prices plummet. To deluge the shareholder with information and force him to make each major decision that management now makes is not to increase his freedom but to destroy the reason for his investment. (It also jeopardizes his investment, because once a corporation is forced to release information useful to competitors, it loses incentive to develop new products.) Most investors are attracted to the corporation as a "sideline" investment, in which they supply capital without having to acquire the specialized knowledge to run the business. Time and energy are scarce resources and the more diversified an investor's investment portfolio, the less incentive he has closely to monitor each company. In practice then, Nader's proposals would be more likely to paralyze management, making its decisions interminably slow and uncertain (management would not know if a decision had really been made until a lengthy process of stockholder voting had been completed).[16] Moreover, although Nader speaks in the name of the shareholders whose views, he argues, are presently ignored, he scarcely speaks in their interests. As the corporation board came to be composed of representatives of consumers, the community, the workers, minorities etc.—what coercive utopian Tom Hayden calls "the stakeholders"—it takes a leap of faith indeed to believe that shareholder interests, which are in profits, would be more zealously guarded than under present arrangements. Whoever benefitted from the politicization of the corporation, it would not be the shareholding "electorate."

While Nader's most grandiose schemes have not been implemented, he has had a major impact on the whole series of consumer legislation passed in the late 1960s and early 1970s and the activists he has trained or inspired have gone into the newer regulatory agencies like the Consumer Product Safety Commission and the Occupational Safety and Health Administration, whose very creation owed much to Nader's prodding. Unlike the traditional agencies which were given authority over specific economic functions of particular industries, the new agencies have vaguer responsibilities extending across large numbers of industries. The sentiments of the new regulators are hostile toward business. A Consumer Product Safety Commission member said: "Any time consumer safety is threatened, we're going to go for the company's throat."[17] And their constituency consists largely of the public interest groups whose lobbying created the agencies for which they work. A number of older agencies like the Federal Trade Commission, the first agency to serve as target for Nader's Raiders (the Nader study called it an "aged courtesan ravaged by the pox"), have become Naderite centers. Its transformed staff worked for nine years to broaden the meaning of "unfair competition" in a suit against the major cereal companies. The staff sought to ban as "illegal" such normal business practices as development of new brands, which the staff argued produced a condition of "shared monopoly." In 1981, an administrative law judge within the Federal Trade Commission threw out the staff's entire suit, on the grounds that not a single one of the charges against the cereal companies had been proved.[18]

Because Nader pursues "the public interest," he seems to feel that his standard of behavior and that of his organizations need not conform to that incumbent upon "the special interests." Nader has been a sharp critic of the book club practice of sending the month's selection to each member who does not return a card rejecting the book. Laziness or disorganization prevents many people from mailing the card and the member thus buys more books than he would if asked to send in a card saying he *wanted* a book. Yet Nader developed a program for PIRG funding that depends precisely on this psychological mechanism. PIRGs are established on campus when a petition is signed by a majority of students or a referendum is held in which students vote for a PIRG. Subsequently, all students are automatically required to contribute to their campus PIRG as part of their college fees. (On most campuses, a student may obtain a refund if, within a certain number of weeks, he applies to the appropriate office, but few go to the bother of trying to retrieve the few dollars involved.) Every few years, there is a renewed vote on the PIRG, although since many students do not vote, a mere 25% of the student body, voting for PIRG, is sufficient to impose it on all students. It is worthy of note that Nader, in advancing the original plan for PIRG, did not want a periodic vote by changing student bodies on retention of PIRG. According to Nader's proposal, a PIRG could only be terminated after 50% of the student body applied for their money back.[19] Under such a system, Nader could well believe the PIRG would last as long as the university, for only the most determined, organized effort by students could possibly produce such a volume of students applying for refunds.

Nader becomes indignant at any tampering with the system of "negative checkoff." After students voted for a PIRG at Pennsylvania State University in 1975, the administration insisted on adopting a "positive checkoff." Students who wished to join PIRG would check the appropriate box on their registration form. Nader calculated that while the negative checkoff would bring in $270,000 a term, the positive checkoff would bring in only $10,000-30,000.[20] Undoubtedly book clubs have made similar calculations. And yet, as someone wrote indignantly to Idaho's Boise State University student paper, when PIRG was debated there, at least in a book club you are there because you want to be there, not because you were voted in by someone else.[21] Nader mounted a fierce campaign against Penn State University. He called it a "citadel of fascism" and threatened university officials and trustees with a "conflict of interest" investigation by a Nader unit.[22] When Minnesota PIRG modified its negative checkoff, providing an item on the registration form that said, "If you choose not to pay the PIRG fee, check here," a Nader aide called it "a blatant concession to the special interests."[23] Clearly, in so far as Nader has his way, PIRGs would train public citizens through a device that violates every principle of consumerism.

Recently, students in several universities have brought suit, charging that university policy forces them to support political and social causes with which they disagree. The first suit was brought in 1979 by Rutgers freshman Joseph Galda and two fellow students. While the judge who initially heard the case ruled for PIRG, on appeal the U.S. Court of Appeals remanded the case. The judge declared: "We have been presented with no convincing reason—besides the obvious motive to procure additional funding from those students who do not wish to join PIRG but who are indifferent enough to forego seeking a refund—why PIRG could not obtain its financial support through purely voluntary contributions."[24]

Although PIRGs firmly deny they are political, insisting they are non-partisan, educational groups run by students, many of the issues on which PIRGs lobby are both partisan and political and the student role, in practice, is often minor. PIRGs, for example, lobby against nuclear energy and in favor of disarmament. The most quoted PIRG study is, probably, Michigan PIRG's 1975 "The Empty Pork Barrel" which recommended an instant 25% cut in the military budget on the grounds that military spending did not generate as much employment as various kinds of non-military spending did. (The study revealed no trace of awareness that there might be any other purposes to the military budget than stimulation of the economy.) In 1982, New York PIRG published a summary of the votes of New York State representatives on national security issues, its intent clearly to encourage citizens to vote against representatives who voted for various defense systems.[25] Moreover, newspaper investigation of the New York PIRG by the Gannett News Service found that former Nader associate Donald Ross had virtual control of the entire $2.6 million annual budget and that minutes of NYPIRG meetings showed that while a 38 member student board was in charge in theory, in practice most ideas and plans were generated by Ross and his staff, with the student board serving as a rubber stamp.[26] Indeed, most of the money did not come from student fees, but from door to door solicitation, government and private grants. With neither its direction nor its funds coming primarily from students, New York PIRG, the most influential of all PIRG programs, seems difficult to justify as an educational program by and for students.

The PIRGs offer only one example of the double standard Nader employs for business as against his own "public interest" enterprises. He demands the fullest financial disclosure from corporations and government, but is chary of making such disclosures himself. He zealously protects the privacy of his donors and makes minimal disclosures about the finances of his own organizations. Public Citizen is the unit with which Nader raises money from the public. It sends out a yearly report to contributors but that report does not reveal that Nader has built up an impressive reserve fund. This can be considered prudent and reasonable for it cushions Public Citizen from possible fickleness on the part of its contributors in the years ahead. On the other hand contributors might well become considerably less generous if they knew Public Citizen had a handsome nestegg. So Nader, who clamors for ever more information from companies, omits in his report information on Public Citizen's reserve fund. (By 1978 Public Citizen's net worth was $1.52 million.)[27] Challenged, Nader has said that contributors could make their own calculations by comparing financial statements from one year to another. No doubt. But how many contributors keep, let alone compare, such reports? And how would Nader react to similar justifications by corporations suppressing potentially embarassing information?

More serious is the way Nader feels free to flout laws and regulations designed for consumer protection although it is in the multiplication of such laws that he believes consumer interests lie. Dan Burt of the Capital Legal Foundation studied the Nader network and in his *Abuse of Trust,* reports that he found "a pervasive pattern of noncompliance" by Nader groups with regulations requiring groups soliciting funds to make information about themselves available to the public. The response of Nader's Public Citizen was to say bluntly that it didn't like the laws.

> "These local laws, enacted over the years by states, cities, townships, counties and various other governmental entities, are not well conceived . . Public Citizen made the judgment that the excessive and redundant state requirements, the expense and waste of charitable resources caused by the numerous different forms . . . were so great that they constituted an unconstitutional burden on a charity's 'right to associate' which is protected by the First Amendment."[28]

One can only imagine Nader's righteous wrath if a corporation, confronted with its failure to conform to government regulations, were to retort that it believed the regulations involved unnecessarily burdensome paperwork that were contrary to consumer interests in driving up the cost of products and so it had deliberately ignored the law, which it considered "unconstitutional."

Nader's sense of superiority to the laws and rules of behavior lesser mortals are expected to obey is apparent in other ways. The Gannett News Service reported that Nader's Safety Systems Foundation and Public Safety Research Institute paid $3087 in penalties to the Internal Revenue Service for "churning"—the buying and selling of stock at an excessively rapid rate. This is a rare offense for charitable foundations. In the year that Nader's organizations paid the fine for engaging in a series of short sales and in-and-out investments, the fines paid by all foundations for this type of offense were only $8,000.[29] Some investments have raised questions of conflict of interests. The foundations Nader controls have made investments in a long list of companies affected by his attacks. For example, one of them invested in Goodyear while the Nader spinoff, the Center for Auto Safety, was attacking the Firestone radial tire.[30] An accident no doubt. But even the appearance of impropriety is something Nader might be expected to avoid. If Caesar's wife was expected to be above suspicion, how much more so Public Citizen #1.

Nader's motto seems to be "Do as I say, not as I do." He has addressed institutional money managers on their responsibility for using their investments to better society by putting economic pressure on companies that are offensive to the consumer movement. Yet Nader's groups have invested not only in companies he attacked but in utility companies that generate electricity from nuclear plants, although he has called such plants "technological suicide." Although Nader complains of the shoddy character of goods turned out by industry, his own "advocacy scholarship" has been criticized on that very ground. Robert Hessen found that 8 out of 22 footnotes in a single chapter of Nader and Green's *Taming the Giant Corporation* were "unverifiable," an error ratio of 36%.[31] Nader's demands for disclosure of any sort are strictly a one-way street. As part of the Congress Project Nader requested each Congressman to send him copies of all speeches, articles, reports and press releases of the past two years. Congressman John Erlenborn replied that he would provide the material requested on condition that Nader would supply similar material in regard to himself. Haughtily Nader refused: "Perhaps you are espousing a new premise, that when citizens decide to study their elected representatives, a trade agreement must be entered, whereby the Representative studies the citizenry."[32]

Nader's definition of the public interest clearly does not include a civilized style of discourse, for he is the most vituperative of public figures. But when attacked himself, he has sued to silence his critics. Nader called Congressman Bud Schuster of Pennsylvania, an opponent of airbags, "a pathological liar, a flack for automakers," and said that he and others who opposed airbags were the sort who would sell thalidomide to pregnant women." He described Congressman Paul McCloskey Jr. of California as a "disgusting, repulsive, slimy double-crosser." Of Howard Phillips, then appointed as head of the Office of Economic Opportunity, he commented that his "interest in the poor and sick is not much greater than that of King Kong." Of Dixie Lee Ray, then chairman of the Atomic Energy Commission, he said, "She is suffering from professional insanity."[33] Bad manners make good copy, but Nader is not prepared to accept what he dishes out. In 1976 Nader sued syndicated columnist Ralph de Toledano for $1 million. The suit was based on a sentence in a column that said Nader "falsified and distorted" evidence to make his case against the Corvair. De Toledano was interpreting the findings of the Senate committee which, at Nader's urgings, had conducted an exhaustive hearing into Nader's charges that General Motors had deliberately marketed an unsafe car and concluded Nader's charges against the Corvair and General Motors were baseless. We have noted contradictory evidence on the pre-1964 Corvair. Nonetheless, given what Nader feels free to say about people with whom he disagrees, he had no justification in suing—and in the process silencing—de Toledano. (In 1983, de Toledano finally paid $5,000 in an out-of-court settlement.)

Although expanding opportunities for participation in decision-making is a key tenet of public interest groups, especially those under Nader's control or influence, a common characteristic of public interest groups is that they offer no possibility for their members to participate in their own decisions. Not only do they provide no training ground for citizen participation themselves, but the membership has no means of pressure or influence over the self-appointed leadership. Common Cause, the largest of the public interest groups, at least tries to test the pulse of the membership by frequent polls. But in a sympathetic study of these groups, *Lobbying for the People,* Jeffrey M. Berry found that almost half the groups studied had no membership, while more than half, even of the membership groups, "do not even go to the pretense of structuring their organization in a democratic mold so that they would at least have the appearance of being open to constituency influence."[34] The autocratic nature of his organizations proved costly to Nader on at least one occasion. On behalf of Public Citizen, Nader brought suit in 1977 to overturn a Federal Drug Administration regulation. But in 1979 the U.S. District Court for the District of Columbia, noted for its sympathy to public interest suits, ruled that Public Citizen lacked standing to sue on behalf of the general public because its contributors lacked any direct control or influence over it.[35]

Control of public interest groups is vested in the staff, which may—or may not—share responsibility with a board. Berry reports that total staff dominance is most apparent in consumer and environmental groups, while in church lobbies and peace organizations boards of directors had an important role. One consumer lawyer said of his organization: "Basically, we do what grabs us." Another consumer lobbyist told Berry: "Essentially we're looking for hot pokers to stick up GM's arse." Yet another said: "I guess I do what I want." Although thoroughly sympathetic to public interest groups, Berry feels impelled to observe that "these groups, which ostensibly speak for the people do so through the voices (and deliberations) of a very few."[36]

The public interest groups themselves seem surprised and occasionally a little embarassed by the solemnity with which their claims to representing the public are treated. At a conference on public interest law held in January 1980 Abram Chayes, a Harvard law professor who is a member of the board of several public interest law groups, told his audience that they should not worry about their title to represent the public interest. Said Chayes: "Well, I don't know how we got it, I think Charles Halpern probably invented it as a con to the foundation, but it's sort of like the People's Republic. Once you get it you relax and enjoy it if it sticks. And you don't get guilty about whether you deserve it all that much or not.''[37]

A recent public opinion study of the public interest leadership by Robert Lichter and Stanley Rothman suggests that their ability to pass themselves off as the ''true'' representatives of the public must indeed be counted a ''con'' to rival ''people's republic'' as a description of the dictatorships of Eastern Europe.

Lichter and Rothman studied 157 heads and top staffers of seventy-four public interest organizations, including the Naderite conglomerate, other consumer groups, public interest law firms, Common Cause and a number of environmental organizations. It would be hard to find a group whose opinions differed more from those of the American public. While 21% of the general public describes itself as being to the ''left of center,'' a full 90% of the public interest elite described itself in this way. Even more striking, was the feeling of alienation of this elite from the American political and economic system. Forty-eight percent agreed that our institutions should be completely overhauled, and three out of four believed the very structure of our society causes alienation. Only about half believed the existing system could be salvaged at all. Almost seven times as many members of the public interest elite approved of Fidel Castro (34%) as approved of Ronald Reagan (a mere 5%). With a 50% approval rating, the Sandanistas did ten times better than Reagan and more than three times better than Margaret Thatcher (14%).

The public interest elite had no doubt of its claims to represent the public interest, however. Asked to rate ten leadership groups in terms of the influence they had on American life, they rated themselves only ninth on the list. But asked to rate the groups in terms of the influence they would *like* them to have, they ranked themselves first and banished business and the military, which they perceived to be currently at the top, to the bottom of the list.[38]

Interestingly enough, there *has* been a political party that embodies the public interest agenda. That was the Citizen's Party, whose Presidential candidate, in the 1980 elections, was environmental activist Barry Commoner. The platform could have been written by Nader. The party announced that its main issue was ''corporate power'' and the platform called for public control of energy industries, an end to nuclear power, crash development of solar energy and emphasis, in the meantime, on conservation, sharp cutbacks in military spending, guaranteed jobs for all willing to work, citizen control of corporate decisions, and price controls to curb inflation (Nader's COIN had called for price controls on "the necessities"). Nader did not endorse the Citizen's Party, confining himself to saying he supported *any* party that challenged the two-party monopoly. Nonetheless, it is worth noting that Nader's definition of the public interest, fully incarnated in the Citizen's Party, received less than 1% of the public's vote.

The public interest movement's limited ability to persuade people, and especially the enormous blow of the Reagan victory, has sent it increasingly to the courts. Nader noted: "The judiciary is the citadel for the minority view. They don't count votes in court."[39] In March 1981, Nader announced that the battleground of the consumer movement would increasingly be in the courts: "We will be using the courts more and more to challenge regulatory action or nonaction . . ."[40] It is ironic that the man who sees himself as incarnating the will of the public should be repairing to the institution most insulated from the public. But it is scarcely surprising, for in the words of one public interest lawyer: "The courts now loom as the most congenial branch of the federal government."[41] They are congenial because the judges in large measure are sympathetic to the public interest movement, especially the judges on important courts to which regulatory and environmental issues normally go, notably the District of Columbia Court of Appeals. They are sympathetic because they were chosen precisely because of their sympathy. Abram Chayes has praised public interest activist Charles Halpern for his role in shaping the federal courts system through setting up a project called the Judicial Selection Process, which during the Carter administration, in Chayes words, ensured that "the right people got on the panels or some of the right people got on the panels and some of the right people got into the hopper." Chayes observed that the opportunity "to appoint a third of the judiciary or a quarter of the judiciary has been an important opportunity which will live long beyond the 1980 elections."[42] Indeed it will. Since, over the last decades, judges have increasingly made their decisions without regard to the will of the legislature and without regard to precedent, but on the basis of what they think is "right,"[43] the presence of large numbers of social-activist judges means the public interest movement can count on out-maneuvering the popular will as revealed in the electoral process—the very public will the movement claims to represent.

As in the case of the religious and environmental utopians, the battle over the definition of consumer interests was waged before—and lost by the utopian wing of the consumer movement. Indeed, the consumer movement has a complex and fascinating history. The earlier struggle was three-pronged. On the one hand, there were those who saw consumerism as a way to eliminate the abuses of the marketplace, including fraud and the marketing of dangerous products. Others viewed consumer cooperation as a new economic form, which would eventually displace the capitalist economic system. Consumer's cooperatives would be expanded in retailing, wholesaling and manufacturing until in the end the economy would form a "cooperative commonwealth." Finally, in the 1920s and 30s, there were "consumer fronts" established by Communist Party organizers.

The careers of advocates of all three positions became entangled. For example, F.J. Schlink, who simply wanted reform of the marketplace cooperated on a famous book *100,000,000 Guinea Pigs* with Arthur Kallet, who was closely tied to the Communist Party. Both Kallet and J.B. Matthews, who believed in consumer cooperatives as a new economic form that would eventually replace capitalism, became involved with the Schlink-founded organization Consumers Research, which pioneered the testing of products, seeking to improve the consumer's position in the marketplace through better knowledge. Matthews, himself, had an extensive history of work for Communist fronts, but the last straw for him was when Kallet sought to take Consumers Research away from Schlink through a Communist-organized strike and make it into a front organization.[44] Kallet's challenge was beaten back and he formed the rival Consumers Union in 1936.

In the end it was Schlink's "reform" strategy that won out decisively. Matthews repudiated his past beliefs, making a ringing defense of the essential bond between the capitalist economic order and freedom in his *Odyssey of a Fellow Traveller* published in 1938. In that same year he testified before the House Un-American Activities Committee (the Dies Committee) on the Communist activities with which he had such ample experience, impressing the committee members so much that they made him director of research for the committee from 1939-1944. While Kallet at Consumers Union pursued an activist political strategy for several years, under his direction Consumers Union too soon became a non-controversial organization, performing the same role as Consumers Research in testing products and disseminating information in order to make the market work better.

Ironically the public interest movement is opposed to the consumer interest, which lies in maximizing choice and low prices. Nader believes consumer sovereignty is an illusion because the consumer is the helpless pawn of advertisers, allowing himself "to be conned by Proctor and Gamble and Colgate-Palmolive and Lever Brothers and all the ads that swarm through the television tube." The consumer, his wants run amok because of advertising, has to be stopped."[45]

Nader's public interest organizations are not even on the side of lower prices. Simon Lazarus has noted that Nader's attacks on multinational corporations for manufacturing products in countries with cheap labor is a betrayal of his constituency. Nader wants to forbid any product made abroad by a U.S. company from being marketed in the United States.[46] How this would further consumer interests is hard to see. (What it would do to the economies of Hong Kong, Singapore or Korea, however, is clear.)

In whose interest, then, is the public interest movement? The movement would never have had the success and resonance it has enjoyed if it were not in the interest of strategically located elites. It provides rich opportunities for bureaucratic employment as the regulatory apparatus expands. Many of the value shapers of American culture see the movement as being in their interest. It gives power to those who articulate values as against those who produce goods. The "special interests" are concentrated among businessmen, farmers and workers, while public interest exponents are found primarily among the manipulators of values—college professors, journalists, television personalities, public relations professionals. Clergymen, the traditional communicators in American society, who have seen their role as bearers of the nation's conscience eroded, are also attracted to the public interest. They see an increased role for themselves as definers of moral value.

The public interest movement has special attractions for the "noneconomic man." It appeals to students, whose economic needs are met by their parents, and increasingly by government. It appeals to the managers of many foundations, also inured from the economic world through their power to manipulate wealth amassed by previous generations. Because the public interest appeals to those who have a grip on the communication of values, its significance and impact is far greater than would otherwise be the case.

The public interest movement is also in the interests of sectors of the political left, including the traditional left which believes in centralization or even the dictatorship of the proletariat. The left values the public interest movement because it saps faith in existing institutions. Under the public interest banner, political activists have been able to achieve changes in public attitudes that eluded them when they used a more honest political vocabulary. Thus, while American socialists were never able to achieve credibility in their attacks on the free market system, Nader has easily won credibility for his own attacks, based on similar assumptions.

Above all, of course, the public interest is in the interest of public interest professionals. The shift in power relationships that Nader seeks to bring about is a shift in power to the cadres of the public interest elite. It is they who will benefit as representatives of "the people" who own or control industry, manufacturing, retail sales and all major professional services. It is they who will decide what advertisers can or cannot say about their products, what products can be marketed and what products shall not be permitted because they fail to meet standards of durability and safety or fail to satisfy "genuine human needs" as defined by the elite. Nader has suggested, for example, that the whole petrochemical industry may be inherently incapable of functioning without damage to the environment and so might need to be abolished.[47] In the transitional period, before "the people" own everything, it is the public interest elite who will decide when corporations "abuse the public interest," at which point, according to Nader, they are to be "transferred to public trusteeship and their officers . . . to jail."[48] As journalist Tom Bethell aptly remarks: "Public interest groups have a 'special interest' in reforming society . . . A comparatively small clerical class of bureaucrats, professors and public interest lawyers stands to gain even more power than it already has—at the expense of 'the special interest,' which is to say, you and me."[49]

If Common Cause could really eliminate all loopholes now allowing "special interests" to continue their contributions to campaigns, the result would be to make politicians more responsive—to the definers of the public interest of Common Cause.

Nader embraces the same utopia that has seized the imagination of the environmentalists and religious leadership. Small is beautiful. Nader asserts that ". . . we're going to rediscover smallness. We're going to rediscover it in technology—already there are movements around the world calling for an appropriate technology which is more responsive to self-control and local control. And I think we're going to see it in the movement toward recognizing that the best place to live, in the United States, is a small town."[50] Given his sparse style, except when engaged in invective, Nader waxes positively lyrical in describing life there, as "people get back to the earth, grow their own gardens . . . can feel the wind across their cheek" and "watch the sun come up."

And in that small town, where the people own the supermarkets and banks, the hospitals and manufacturing plants, they will need to spend only half the time they now do in work. The balance, presently devoted to work, can be dedicated to the exercise of civic responsibility. People will live in an ideal economic system "where it's broken down into as small parts as are economically possible, and those parts are run by the constituency for whom they were supposed to operate." If, despite everything, man turns out to be less than perfectible, Nader, characteristically ascetic even when it comes to utopia, is philosophic: "If anything happens that is harmful or corrupt, the victims have nobody to blame but themselves."[51]

REFERENCES

1. Simon Lazarus, *The Genteel Populists,* New York, Holt Rinehart & Winston, 1974, p. 146
2. *New York Times,* Feb. 6, 1983
3. J. Patrick Wright, *On a Clear Day You Can See General Motors: John Z. DeLorean's Look Inside the Automotive Giant,* Grosse Point, Michigan, Wright Enterprises, 1979, p. 54
4. Ralph Nader, *Unsafe at Any Speed,* N.Y., Grossman Publishers, 1965, p. 213
5. Alexander Cockburn and James Ridgeway, "Citizen Nader" *Rolling Stone,* August 23, 1979, p. 45
6. Opening speech by Ralph Nader at meeting of Critical Mass, Oct. 6, 1978, printed in *Critical Mass,* Oct. 1978
7. Thomas Whiteside, "Profile, A.C. Force II," *The New Yorker,* Oct. 15, 1973, p. 48
8. Alan Reynolds, "What Does Ralph Nader Really Want?" *National Review,* Feb. 28, 1975, p. 220
9. Introd. by Ralph Nader to Franklin D. Chu and Sharland Trotter, *The Madness Establishment,* New York: Grossman Publishers, 1974, p. xiv
10. Quoted in Stephen Douglas Brown, *Ralph's Nadir: On What Went Wrong with the Nader Congress Project,* Michigan: Book Haus, 1976, pp. 181-3
11. Ibid., pp. 205-8
12. *Leadership: A Sampler of the Wisdom of John Gardner,* Hubert H. Humphrey Institute of Public Affairs, U. of Minnesota, 1981, p. 29
13. Simon Lazarus, op. cit., p. 197

14. Ibid., p. 213
15. Quoted in Robert Hessen, *In Defense of the Corporation,* Stanford, Hoover Institution Press, 1979, p. 53
16. Ibid., p. 79
17. Earl P. Holt, "'Social Regulation' The New Interventionism," *Human Events,* Sept. 19, 1981
18. The *New York Times,* Sept. 11, 1981
19. Ralph Nader and Donald Ross, *Action for a Change: A Student's Manual for Public Interest Organizing,* New York: Grossman Publ., 1971, p. 74
20. David Sanford, "Nader's Vested Interest" *New Republic,* June 12, 1976, p. 12
21. *The Arbiter,* Feb. 13, 1980
22. David Sanford, "Nader's Vested Interest," *op. cit.,* p. 12
23. "'Pirgs' Clash with Trustees" *The Chronicle of Higher Education,* July 7, 1975
24. *Wall Street Journal,* Aug. 18, 1982
25. "Our Lives in Their Hands" New York PIRG, 1983
26. *Poughkeepsie Journal,* Feb. 28, 1982
27. Dan M. Burt, *Abuse of Trust,* Chicago, Regnery Gateway, 1982, p. 82
28. Statement of Public Citizen, April 13, 1982
29. Barbara O'Reilly, "Nader Tax-Exempt Groups Play the Market," Bridgewater, New Jersey *Courier News,* April 2, 1979
30. Dan M. Burt, op. cit., pp. 88-89
31. Robert Hessen, "Credible Crusader? An Assessment of Ralph Nader's Scholarship" in *Controlling the Giant Corporation: A Symposium,* Center Symposia Series No. CS-14, Center for Research in Government Policy and Business, Graduate School of Management, University of Rochester, 1982, p. 72
32. Stephen Douglas Brown, op. cit., p. 219
33. Barbara O'Reilly, "After 10 Years of Controversy Nader Remains an Enigma," *Courier News,* April 4, 1979, *Washington Sunday Star,* Feb. 18, 1973; and Ralph de Toledano, op. cit., p. 113
34. Jeffrey M. Berry, *Lobbying for the People: The Political Behavior of Public Interest Groups,* Princeton, Princeton University Press, 1977, p. 210
35. *Consumer News,* April 15, 1979
36. Jeffrey M. Berry, op. cit., pp. 201-2, 210
37. Remarks of Abram Chayes, Public Interest Law Conference, Jan. 4, 1980
38. S. Robert Lichter and Stanley Rothman, "What Interests the Public and What Interests the Public Interests," *Public Opinion,* April/May 1983, pp. 47-8
39. Joe Klein, "The Man in the Class Action Suit," *Rolling Stone,* November 20, 1975, p. 12
40. *Consumer Affairs Letter,* March 1981
41. Peter Brimelow and Stephen T. Markman, "Supreme Irony," *Harper's* October 1981, p. 16
42. Abram Chayes, op. cit., pp. 11-12
43. Brimelow and Markman, op. cit., pp. 19-20
44. J.B. Matthews, *Odyssey of a Fellow Traveler,* New York: Mt. Vernon Publishers Inc., 1938, pp. 267-68
45. "This Country is on Fire," *National Wildlife,* June-July 1971, p. 18
46. *In These Times,* April 16-22, 1980
47. Joe Klein, op. cit., p. 4
48. Quoted in Ralph de Toledano, op. cit., p. 138
49. Tom Bethell, "The 'Public Interest' Lobby," *Newsweek,* April 24, 1978, p. 23
50. Joe Klein, op. cit., p. 3
51. Ibid., p. 2

VI

America The Enemy: The Utopian Think Tanks

The coercive utopians have found an especially useful tool in the "think tank." Ironically, the first important think tanks were set up to solve military problems. Indeed the very term "think tank" was first commonly used to describe the Rand Corporation, originally an adjunct of the McDonnell Douglas Corporation. The think tank could offer the long-range perspectives that government officials simply did not have the freedom to consider, pressed as they were to deal with immediate problems. But in the hands of the coercive utopians, the think tank, whose purpose was to make the American political and economic system work better, has been used to subvert the system. The institutes, centers, councils, congresses of the coercive utopians, to use the more formal names attached to think tanks, while *pretending* to serve the traditional aim of improving efficiency, are designed to bring our institutions down.

They do this, first and foremost, by destroying public belief in the virtues of key American institutions, particularly those crucial to maintaining American power and influence in the world. An image of the United States is constructed as a rapacious imperial villain, the greatest single threat to the world's peace and prosperity. Since the United States does only evil with its power, the solution is to take away her power to do evil.

American power and influence rest partly on economic strength and the think tanks discussed in this chapter want to dismantle existing economic institutions. As a great power, the United States also depends upon its military forces, its intelligence agencies and its alliances with friendly nations. The utopian think tanks seek to weaken all of these. They have different specific targets with one institute, for example, concentrating on attacking American allies, while another assails U.S. intelligence services, and yet another, discredits every proposed new weapons system. The effort is to destroy public support for defense spending, traditional allies, the CIA and FBI, and the large corporation. Eventually, the coercive utopians hope to be able to impose their vision of a reconstructed society on a demoralized public.

Deceptiveness is crucial to the operation of these think tanks, for the public, at least important segments of it, must be made to believe that their goal is to *preserve* traditional American values and institutions. And so, the institutes offer a different persona to different audiences. Testifying before Congress, an institute may represent itself as a group of citizens whose goal is to make a given institution—the CIA, the Pentagon, the corporation—work better. In other forums, it will deny the same institution's right to exist or demand that it be changed in such a way as to be unrecognizable. Sometimes, it is impossible for the same institute simultaneously to curry favor with Congress and other "establishment" organizations and with a radical audience because its activities will be unacceptable to the more conservative audience. The same people may then set up parallel operations. The Center for National Security Studies is influential with Congress; its image is of a group concerned with the problem of finding a balance between the needs of intelligence and civil liberties. But many of the same people have been involved with *CounterSpy,* the magazine that calls for the abolition of the CIA and tries to make it impossible for it to function by publishing the names and addresses of its agents worldwide. In some cases, geography provides a key to playing different roles. The Institute for Policy Studies based in Washington D.C., set up offices abroad for its Transnational Institute. The Amsterdam base makes it possible for the Institute for Policy Studies to support exponents of violent revolution, maintain contact with international liberation groups and publish a journal of orthodox Marxist-Leninist analysis which in the United States would detract from the "liberal-progressive" image that it fosters among policy-makers.

The Institute for Policy Studies—henceforth IPS—the chief think tank of the coercive utopians, is the only one that addresses their entire range of concerns. It has fathered a number of more specialized think tanks and its personnel have gone forth to man many of the more specialized institutes and centers, both those it has created and others. IPS also has the distinction of being the first think tank of the coercive utopians. Its inception was at a White House-State Department disarmament conference in April 1961. In attendance were Marcus Raskin and Richard Barnet, both government bureaucrats. Barnet was deputy director for political research at the U.S. Arms Control and Disarmament Agency, while Raskin was a staff member of the National Security Council. The encounter between the two men could be set to the verses of "Some Enchanted Evening." Across a crowded room their eyes met. "Mark and I both grimaced at the same moment—and knew we did not belong here." They recognized in each other the same contempt for and hostility toward "the whole military-industrial establishment sitting there at one table."[1] Within two years, Barnet and Raskin had put together the necessary funding, personnel and program. The Institute began work in 1963.

IPS was able to trade on the trust then automatically placed in any institute whose purpose was to aid government in establishing policy. Evidence for this comes from the first annual report of IPS.

> "The Institute has been gratified by the enthusiastic cooperation it has received from government agencies, including the White House, the Department of State, the Department of Defense, the Office of Education, the Civil Rights Commission, the Department of Justice and Members of Congress . . . Government officials have shown great willingness to make documents available whenever possible and to meet with Fellows of the Institute to discuss policy problems."

But unlike the other institutes then trying to improve the working of government, IPS began to offer a wholly new vision of what the United States was like. At its inception IPS played host to some of the pioneer revisionist historians, including Gar Alperovitz and Gabriel Kolko, who placed the blame for the Cold War on the United States. With the rise of the student movement and related anti-Vietnam war movement in the late 1960s, the Fellows of IPS ("Fellow" being the academic title IPS gave its members) became harsher in their assault.

According to IPS co-director Marcus Raskin, the U.S. began the Cold War as part of its decision "to reach for the brass ring: world hegemony."[2] As Raskin saw American society, the ordinary citizen lived within "four overlapping Colonies" (capitals are Raskin's), each of which "hollows out man." The most important is the Violence

Colony, whose primary tool is the university, "the fundamental shield and terrorizing instrument of the state."[3] Kept in line by specialists in the techniques of violence, who "use the rest of society as their hostage" those in the Plantation Colony "work at meaningless and unreal jobs to obtain things that they are led to want" but which do not satisfy "human needs." In the Channeling Colony (otherwise known as the schools), people are "broken" into "accepting authority structures." It is here that "inmates learn to become bored, user-used and hollowed out."[4]

As Raskin sees it, the population passively accepts the violence done to it because the rulers lull it with the Dream Colony, which "provides a surrogate of action and passion for the colonized."[5] The elite also uses war as a diversion for the masses, "continuous war in the lands of the poor and wretched." Such war is designed as "a sport, a diversion at most . . . the droning of everyday life would be relieved with the purpose and determination of the leaders."[6] According to IPS Fellow Arthur Waskow, we are all "war victims," victims of the war the Establishment and corporations wage against us. Waskow seized on Nader's *Unsafe at Any Speed* to announce, "GM has been killing us. Making war on us."[7] In the view of Fellow Ralph Stavins, "the thirty-three months of Kennedy's presidency marked the makings of a totalitarian state structure and a private war."[8]

Our formally democratic institutions are worthless. Elections, says IPS Fellow Michael Parenti, are only a symbol and voting less an exercise than a surrender of sovereignty."[9] Waskow calls elections "an elaborate way of collecting power from the people and handing it over to someone else."[10] Ignorantly, Americans have celebrated a terrible past. IPS Fellows Paul Jacobs and Saul Landau devote a two volume work to showing that "racism" against every minority group is the real history of the United States.[11] As they see it, the United States is "a society whose values even George Orwell might not have imagined."[12]

Its mode of operation separated IPS from other institutes as much as its portrait of the United States. In one respect, IPS was like other institutes—it saw the importance of ideas. Raskin observed: "This country and modern nations run on ideas to a large extent" and "on the political level, you have to develop a sense that there are groups within the organized political structure—Congress or the Executive—who are interested in such ideas. Otherwise no real political transformation can occur."[13] But IPS placed equal emphasis on action, seeking to combine theory and action in what Raskin called "the project" and "the social invention." Arthur Waskow described its approach:

> "The Institute is not just an ordinary research center because it's committed to the idea that to develop social theory one must be involved in social action and in social experiment. And therefore, the Institute stands on the bare edge of custom in the United States as to what an educational research institution is, as against what a political institution is."[14]

One time Fellow Karl Hess offered a more graphic explanation:

> If this were 1773 and the city were Boston, the Institute would be holding a seminar on British Imperialism. There would be tables and charts to show the injustice of the tax on tea, probably someone from the governor's office would be invited. Then, independent of the Institute, six or seven of the Fellows would go out and dump a shipload of tea into Boston harbor.[15]

The parable, with its analogy to the American revolution, paints IPS in an attractively patriotic light, but two hundred years later the enemy, as IPS sees it, is the American government, and the equivalent of "somebody from the governor's office" would be a Congressman or White House official invited to an IPS seminar. The equivalent of the shipload of tea that is dumped by Fellows in their "private" capacity is "direct action" against the government of the United States.

During the Vietnam War, IPS Fellows were involved in direct action. A goodly number of staffers, volunteers and Fellows were arrested, with Marcus Raskin becoming one of the so-called "Boston Five," indicted for conspiring to promote draft resistance. Richard Barnet spoke at a rally in Hanoi in 1969 and his speech was used for propaganda purposes, as Barnet admits he knew it would be. "I was absolutely sure that the speech would be used, be broadcast."[16] IPS Board Chairman Peter Weiss and his wife Cora, vice-president of the Samuel Rubin Foundation, the Institute's chief financial backer, also travelled to Hanoi. Cora Weiss denied charges that American POWs were mistreated, although returning POWs subsequently testified they had experienced gross mistreatment. Arthur Waskow helped to plan the demonstrations against the Democratic National Convention in Chicago in 1968 and was involved in planning the major anti-war demonstrations in Washington.

All this is not to say that IPS neglected the research functions of an institute. Unlike many New Left activists, who despised anything but action, IPS believed research was essential as an integrated element in a total campaign of action. Much of the research of IPS and its spinoff organizations is on corporations. The Transnational Institute offers what it calls "Counter Information Services" on multinationals, imparting information that it asserts is "closely guarded behind boardroom doors or barred in secret files."[17] It also has a Multinational Monitoring Project that is "developing an international network of researchers who investigate the operations of different multinational corporations."[18] Yet more ambitious is the Corporate Data Exchange, an IPS spinoff, which provides elaborate data on all major industries. The Institute for Southern Studies, an IPS spinoff established in 1970, by its own description, was engaged in "systematically collecting, evaluating and disseminating data on the operations of over 400 corporations in the South."[19]

All this data is put to a number of uses. It is employed in economic warfare campaigns against the corporations studied. It is used in organizational campaigns against multi-nationals. For example, IPS-Transnational Institute is currently trying to organize trade unions in different countries that work for the same multinational corporation. (It has run into the problem that non-Communist trade unions are unwilling to work with Communist unions, a state of affairs which it dismisses as "Cold War politics of the worst kind."[20] It has been organizing at the level of shopfloor stewards and workers, in effect undermining non-Communist unions.) Data on corporations can also be used in targeting specific countries: in 1979, IPS created the Campaign to Oppose Bank Loans to South Africa which now works through the UN Center on Transnationals to coordinate third world pressure on countries dealing with South Africa. The information is also useful to revolutionary groups "in the field." In April 1979, IPS held meetings, first in New York then in Amsterdam. The Amsterdam meeting was attended by representatives of "liberation movements" in southern Africa, including the African National Congress, the Southwest Africa People's Organization (SWAPO) and the Zimbabwe African People's Union. Each group provided its shopping list of research needs, such as The African National Congress, the action arm of the South African Communist Party, who wanted research on South Africa's synthetic oil production project and details concerning its backing from "private sector and foreign multinationals."[21]

IPS maintains a mask of being an institute devoted to liberal values. It pronounces itself an upholder of the very system whose demise it seeks. This deceptiveness is well seen in IPS's Government Accountability Project, which was established to encourage government employees to expose wrongdoing in their agencies. IPS distributed to thousands of government employees a brochure titled: "Point Out Illegality and Waste: How Federal Employees Can Help America (Without Losing Their Jobs)." The brochure, with a red, white and blue cover, assured government employees that in providing information they would be serving "as American democracy's last line of defense against those who would corrupt our institutions." The brochure provided a "Whistleblower's Hotline" phone number. Although not identified as such, it is the phone number of IPS. The Institute testified before Congress on behalf of Whistleblower protection, and a law, partially based on model legislation introduced by the project, was passed in 1978 with virtually no dissenting votes in either House or Senate. Congressmen heaped praise on the project. Patricia Schroeder, chairman of the House Civil Service Subcommittee, said of the Government Accountability Project:

> I really want to thank this group. You really have put incredible effort into a very difficult area . . . One of the things people do not understand about this country is the interest that citizens such as yourself do have. I think it is wonderful. You just care."[22]

What IPS did with the Government Accountability Project was to reap credit for a non-controversial project while conducting a highly controversial one in its shadow. In 1978, the year in which legislation protecting Whistleblowers was passed, IPS held a two day "Whistleblowers Conference on National Security." Toward the end of the conference IPS's Ralph Stavins announced that three former CIA employees who had participated in the meetings had agreed to formation of a National Security Association or League to provide assistance to members of the intelligence community, especially those who have taken secrecy oaths and who have something they wish to disclose and need assistance.[23]

Distance also serves as a camouflage for IPS activities. In Europe IPS can publish materials not liable to come into the hands of many Americans. Its Fellows abroad include people who could not even enter the United States. For example Tariq Ali, head of the British section of the Trotskyite Fourth International, became a Fellow of the Transnational Institute. Ali has been barred not only from the United States but from France, India, Japan, Turkey, Thailand, Hong Kong and Bolivia. As head of the Amsterdam office IPS appointed Basker Vashee, a Marxist revolutionary who doubled as representative of the Zimbabwe African People's Union, the sector of the Zimbabwe Patriotic Front controlled by Robert Mugabe while he was still involved in his terrorist campaign against the bi-racial elected government of Zimbabwe.

Straight Marxist-Leninist analysis is more acceptable in Europe than in the United States, for in Europe it feeds upon fashionable anti-American sentiment in intellectual circles. The Transnational Institute's *Race and Class,* published in London, provides eclectic support for Communist revolution in the Third World. Articles in *Race and Class* support the various Soviet-backed Palestinian terrorist groups, the Communist Party of the Philippines, the Thai Communist Party ("the liberation of Thailand would expose the whole main island [sic] part of Southeast Asia to the front of social revolution") and the Burmese, Malaysian and Indonesian Communist parties.[24] When the Portugese exodus from Angola left three nationalist movements contending for power, *Race and Class* supported the Soviet-backed movement and dismissed a book that proposed a united front as "myopic Trotskyism."[25] *Race and Class* was enthusiastic about Somali socialism ("We in our country have much to learn [from] . . . Siad's thought")[26] until Somalia turned to the West. Since *Race and Class* supports Chinese-backed as well as Soviet-backed insurgencies, it is reasonable to conclude that it is dedicated less to support of Soviet foreign policy than to destruction of Western societies and values.

In the United States, the primary focus of IPS has been on policymakers. It runs seminars, a Washington School, conferences, round tables, all designed to "educate" Congressmen, their staffs and administrative officials in IPS-approved "alternative" approaches. It has been in the forefront of those advocating unilateral disarmament, all-but-elimination of intelligence services and abandonment of existing allies in favor of assorted liberation movements. The very first seminars IPS conducted for Congressmen in the early 1960s were on disarmament. IPS has repeatedly insisted that the Soviet Union is an "illusory enemy." The very titles of articles and books on defense distributed by IPS tell the story: "Our Strangelovian Suspicion of Russian Intent," "Dubious Specter: A Second Look at the "Soviet Threat," "Toward World Disarmament," "Myths and Realities of the 'Soviet Threat,'" "The Rise and Fall of the 'Soviet Threat'" etc.

The budget has been a focus of IPS efforts since the surest road to disarmament is cutting off funds for defense. At the request of 56 members of Congress, in 1978, IPS provided an alternative to President Ford's budget. IPS proposed cuts that over a ten year period would have cut the defense budget in half. Savings were to come through such steps as disengagement from NATO, long a priority target of IPS, and the Middle East. In 1981 IPS was asked by 60 Democratic Congressmen to provide an alternative to the Reagan budget. This time IPS came up with an ingenious proposal to divide the defense budget into two segments, one comprising expenditures for the direct defense of the United States and the other for global defense. IPS's Marcus Raskin indicated that such an arrangement would make it easier to put pressure on Congress to cut the second category of expenditures.

IPS has assumed a major role in the disarmament movement. One of its most innovative projects was a joint disarmament program with the Soviet Union's Institute for the U.S.A. and Canada and the USSR-USA Friendship Society, with the first session in Minneapolis in May 1983. Soviet defectors have estimated that 40% of the staff of the Institute for the U.S.A. and Canada consists of intelligence officers or individuals working under the direct supervision of the KGB and the FBI has reported that the USSR-USA Friendship Society is used by the Soviet Union for "active measures" directed against the U.S. While IPS announced that the purpose of the conference was to come up with "new ideas" on disarmament, the most apparent purpose was to convey to the American public an idea shared by all three organizations sponsoring the program, namely that the United States is primarily responsible for the arms race. In practice, the ideas with which the conference came up concerned ways in which the Soviets could play upon the vulnerabilities of Western public opinion. Randall Forsberg, generally credited with having worked out the details of the nuclear freeze proposal, explained to the Soviets that the best way for them to create a climate in which the peace movement could create political pressures in the U.S. and Western Europe would be if they made the specific gesture of destroying their old SS-4s and SS-5s. She urged the Russians to get rid of them:

> "These were retained as bargaining chips. They have no military function. It doesn't hurt the Soviet Union to give them away. This is a good time to bargain. Timing is very important. We need to delay the deployment of the new [U.S.] missiles by a year—until November of 1984, when we will elect a new government. Then you can decide what to do permanently depending on what the new government is like."

And Forsberg noted: "I want to make this statement very forcefully. I think that if all of these factors work together—the peace movements, the political leadership, and the Soviet government—in a very careful, focused, coordinated and clear way, the [U.S.] missiles can be stopped."[27] (By "political leadership" Forsberg had made it clear earlier that she meant the leadership of European parties opposed to the deployment of the U.S. missiles.)

IPS has discovered other ways to undercut U.S. defense capability. In a revealing report for an IPS publication, then Fellow David Cortright discussed the benefits of unionization in producing change in "the relations of power within the ranks." Once "the soldier has won the right to determine the conditions of his service . . . the absolutist and authoritarian foundations of military discipline have been profoundly altered." The end result, Cortright noted, is that a mass soldier organization can end in "crippling military effectiveness."[28] In his 1975 book, *Soldiers in Revolt,* Cortright wrote that "radicals must join the army... The presence of even a few hundred committed activists could have great impact on the level of servicemen's dissent."

Through its Human Rights project, IPS attacks Latin American countries friendly to the United States, for human rights violations. On the other hand, Cuba, guilty of human rights violations as serious as any of the others, is not subjected to criticism. Indeed the former director of IPS's Transnational Institute, Orlando Letelier, was apparently an "agent of influence" for the Cuban government. Letelier, one time foreign minister of Chile under the Allende regime, while working for IPS was assassinated in Washington by agents of the Chilean government. Letters found by police in his briefcase revealed that Letelier was receiving a thousand dollars a month from Cuba. Documents in the briefcase showed that Letelier was sensitive to the need to employ the language of human rights in gaining the support of liberals, but was himself hoping to introduce in Chile a regime on the model "of what has been done in Cuba."[28] Letelier was replaced as head of the Transnational Institute by Saul Landau who in 1969 had made a full length documentary entitled "Fidel", a fulsome tribute to Castro.

A letter by Landau to a Cuban friend found in the Letelier briefcase[29] suggests that Landau felt that IPS needed to place greater emphasis on internal transformation:

> "I think that at age 40 the time has come to dedicate myself to narrower pursuits, namely, making propaganda for American Socialism . . . we cannot any longer just help out third world movements and revolutions,

although obviously we shouldn't turn our backs on them, but get down to the more difficult job of bringing the message home.''[30]

The single most important project of IPS aimed at ''bringing the message home'' is the National Conference on Alternative State and Local Public Policies which IPS established in 1975 and has now become independent. While the New Left disappeared from public consciousness after the Vietnam War, most of those who had been members of the organizations, like SDS, that made up the New Left, did not disappear. A considerable number became government officials at various levels and were responsive when IPS offered them a framework in which to exchange ideas and strengthen their impact on government. One activist reported of the second annual meeting of the Conference, which was held in Austin, Texas: ''In Austin for four days, the conferees taught each other how to use establishment tricks to get at the establishment.''[31] The Conferences have devoted much of their efforts to developing ways of expanding public ownership, both of natural resources and of capital. As Ilona Hancock, herself a member of the Berkeley, California, City Council put it at one of the conferences, their aim was to ''turn the unthinkable into the inevitable.''[32]

While IPS attempts to deal with all the issues important to the utopian think tanks, there are numerous others with more limited agendas, with which IPS works closely. The Center for National Security Studies, for instance, focuses on the intelligence agencies. Formally a project of the Fund for Peace and the ACLU Foundation, the Center was actually an IPS ''social invention.'' Asked by one journalist if the Center was an IPS spinoff, Richard Barnet replied: ''Well in a sense it was. He [Robert Borosage] was here earlier, and it was an idea some of us had. I was involved in the original discussion with the Field Foundation.''[33] Once Field put up the money, Borosage, who had been a Fellow at IPS, became director of the Center, taking with him IPS Fellow George Pipkin and several other IPS staffers. Borosage remained at the Center until 1977 when he returned to IPS as its director, Barnet and Raskin electing to relinquish the burden of fundraising to become ''Distinguished Fellows.''

The Center for National Security Studies has been defined as a ''responsible'' critic of the intelligence agencies. ''Responsible'' critics were considered by those on Capitol Hill and in the media as those who sought to reform, not abolish the CIA, and whose methods were confined to public education. ''Irresponsible'' critics were defined as those seeking to abolish the CIA and the internal security functions of the FBI, and whose methods included printing the names of U.S.

agents abroad. This endangered their lives and the lives of foreign nationals who assisted them and disrupted American intelligence since exposed officers were no longer of any professional value. It also closed off cooperation with intelligence services of friendly countries, which became extremely reluctant to cooperate with the CIA. *CounterSpy* and its clone, the *Covert Action Information Bulletin,* edited by a faction from the original *CounterSpy,* were the major "irresponsible" critics, printing long lists of alleged agents. The CIA station chief in Athens, Richard Welch, was murdered after his identification as an agent in the pages of *CounterSpy.*

The difficulty with the distinction was that there was a complete identity of goals, interlocking personnel and agreement on methods between the Center for National Security Studies and *CounterSpy*. The identity of goals was evident at the first conference the Center held in 1974. IPS's Richard Barnet declared that the CIA was inherently a criminal enterprise.[34] Director Robert Borosage argued the CIA was a threat to the very existence of a republican order, which is premised on the rule of law. *CounterSpy* says the same thing, its rhetoric perhaps a little harsher.

> "The Organizing Committee [publishers of *CounterSpy*] demands the CIA and covert action be abolished not only because we recognize that the CIA serves only the multinational corporate empire which is thoroughly anti-democratic and anti-American but also because the CIA is a criminal organization."[35]

The identity of views is not surprising since so many of the same people are involved in both. Marcus Raskin was an original member of the advisory board of the Organizing Committee for the Fifth Estate. (The reason for the unusual name is offered in *CounterSpy:* "What the American people need to help focus their massive resistance to techno-fascism is an alternative intelligence community—a Fifth Estate.")[36] In 1975, the Organizing Committee set up a Speakers Bureau called Public Education Project on the Intelligence Community and the speakers list included Ralph Stavins, Marcus Raskin and Victor Marchetti of IPS and Robert Borosage, Cortland Cox, Morton Halperin and John Marks from the Center for National Security Studies.[37] The Center's John Marks wrote an article for *CounterSpy* on how to identify CIA officers under diplomatic cover which provided the guidelines for a number of subsequent exposés of agents published by the magazine.

The most egregious single figure devoted to exposing United States agents throughout the world is Philip Agee, a former CIA agent turned enemy not only of the CIA but of western democracy. Agee was the major figure in *CounterSpy* until an internal dispute led to the temporary shutdown of the magazine. In 1979, Agee announced in Havana the creation of a new magazine, *Covert Action Information Bulletin,* and *CounterSpy,* too, resumed publication under a new editor, John Kelly. Although Agee, on entering the employ of the CIA, had taken an oath not to divulge classified information, his *Inside the Company: CIA Diary* contains 26 pages of names of CIA employees and contacts around the world. He has followed this up with *Dirty Work: the CIA in Western Europe* and *Dirty Work II: the CIA in Africa* (with Lou Wulf of *Covert Action Information Bulletin*) that name over 2,000 alleged CIA employees. Agee has been deported from both England and France for his contacts with unfriendly intelligence services and his American passport has been withdrawn. Agee makes no attempt to conceal where his sympathies lie. In an interview in *Esquire* in June 1975, Agee announced: "I aspire to be a communist and a revolutionary." In an interview with the *Tagesanzeiger* of Zurich, Agee was even blunter. "The CIA is plainly on the wrong side, that is, the capitalist side. I approve KGB activities. Communist activities in general, when they are to the advantage of the oppressed." Agee found refuge in Amsterdam for awhile, his stay, according to a report on Dutch television, arranged through the intercession of IPS's Transnational office there. Agee now lives in West Germany with his recently acquired German wife.

The Center for National Security Studies has consistently defended both Agee and *CounterSpy*. When the government of England began deportation proceedings against Agee in 1977, the Center's new director, Morton Halperin, gave testimony on behalf of Agee. The Center argues that naming agents "has happened only on rare occasions—those who have made this their business are few," indeed "remarkably few." Most of the "rare instances" are the consequence of "inadvertence or the climate of distrust created by our intelligence agencies themselves."[38] As the Center sees it, then, it is the fault of the intelligence agencies themselves that former agents expose their colleagues. Robert Borosage argues that the very need to protect intelligence sources proves the CIA should not exist. The Center was enthusiastic when it believed, in the first months of the Carter administration, that Agee would be permitted to return to the United States without facing legal action. Morton Halperin wrote jubilantly, "Agee will now be coming back to lecture and that is certainly a victory for the First Amendment.''[39] (As it turned out, despite the Center's efforts, Agee was not permitted to return to the U.S. ''to lecture,'' even by the Carter administration.)

What the relationship of *CounterSpy* and the Center for National Security Studies resembles most closely is the division of labor familiar from police interrogation of suspects. The bad guy threatens and bullies while the good guy provides cigarettes and understanding. But they work in tandem for the same ends, which are achieved more effectively in combination than they could be by either working singly. Yet the Senate Select Committee on Intelligence has worked closely with the Center for National Security Studies. The Foreign Intelligence Surveillance Act of 1978 was written with the aid of the Center,[40] which was also deeply involved in helping the Committee to draft ''charters'' designed to establish the U.S. intelligence system on a new basis. (The Center continued to criticize whatever charters the Committee came up with, but succeeded in making them more restrictive than they would otherwise have been. With the advent of the Reagan administration, the effort to draft charters was at least temporarily abandoned.) While the Senate Select Committee would not have dreamed of consulting with the editors of *CounterSpy,* practically speaking they might just as well have done so.

The most successful attacks on American military defense have been conducted by IPS and the Center for Defense Information, like the Center for National Security Studies a project of the Fund for Peace, which was created when the Vietnam War was winding down, to provide a tax exempt umbrella for projects funded by liberal foundations. Like its sister organization, the Center for Defense Information obtains its credibility through claiming to support that which it attacks. Its very title suggests a positive orientation toward defense and its credibility is further enhanced because its director is a former U.S. Admiral, Gene R. LaRocque, and its deputy director a former Brigadier General, B.K. Gorwitz. Admirers have called LaRocque the Ralph Nader of the military, and the title is more apt than those who use it may realize. Just as Nader's goal is to do much more than reform corporate abuses, so LaRocque has much more in mind than eliminating ''waste'' in the armed forces. The analyses of the Center for Defense Information are cleverly presented in terms acceptable to a military audience. One Defense Department official said he values the analyses of the Center because a military program is criticized not because it is wicked, but because it will not work. Presumably in the view of the Center, every major military program proposed by the government since 1972, when the Center was founded, will not "work." It has opposed each one on grounds ranging from inefficiency to irrelevance.

To make its opposition to military innovation credible, the Center must of course minimize the Soviet threat. While virtually all military analysts have pointed to the substantial superiority in conventional forces of the Warsaw pact in relation to NATO, the Center concentrates on statistics designed to obfuscate this superiority.[41] The enormous buildup of Soviet naval forces is similarly discounted. The actions of the Soviet Union, even such apparently offensive moves as the invasion of Afghanistan, are portrayed as defensive in intent. According to the Center, the Soviets only invaded Afghanistan because they believed the United States had repudiated detente.[42] According to LaRocque, the Cubans are in Africa because "they have an affinity to the people they see who appear to be downtrodden and who need help."[43] On a trip to Cuba at the invitation of Castro in June 1980, LaRocque concluded that the Soviet impact there was minimal. He told *Cubatimes,* journal of the church-funded pro-Castro Cuba Resource Center, that "Soviet influence on Cuba's military, from what I could see, was almost nonexistent."[44] The Center explains our unreasonable fear of the Soviet Union as "emotional." The repellent quality of Soviet domestic practices makes us fearful "no matter how conservative the Soviet Union may be in their foreign policy."[45]

Not only has Soviet foreign policy been conservative, but according to the Center, it has been a total failure. The Center distinguishes between "involvement" and "influence." It admits the Soviet Union has become "involved" in many countries, but insists it has significant influence in only 19 out of 155 countries of the world and these are chiefly the world's "poorest and most desperate."[46] Yet the omissions from the Center's list of countries with "significant Soviet influence" can only be accounted remarkable. The Center does not include Iraq, North Korea, Algeria, Grenada, Zimbabwe, Nicaragua, Guinea or even Finland as countries in which the Soviet Union has influence. Yet the very term "Finlandization" has come to stand for neutralization and alignment with Soviet foreign policy as the price for formal independence. Even in countries where the Center acknowledges there is Soviet influence, it attempts to minimize its importance with results that sometimes verge on the absurd. The Center insists that the Soviet Union differs with Libya "over such basic foreign policy issues as recognition of the existence of Israel."[47] As for Cuba, the Center argues that it is a misperception to think it does the Kremlin's bidding. "The increasing Cuban-Soviet cooperation in the 1970s . . . has had no real effect on Cuban policies in Africa."[48]

The Center seeks to exploit, even to create, a gulf between the United States and traditional allies. In the fall of 1975 the Center's director used his credibility as a former admiral to produce a crisis in United States relations with Japan, telling a subcommittee of the Congressional Joint Committee on Atomic Energy that the United States did not honor agreements to off-load atomic weapons from U.S. warships before they entered Japanese harbors. LaRocque then went to Moscow as a guest of the Institute of the U.S.A. and Canada, a Soviet "think tank" with close ties to the KGB. There LaRocque, after having produced the desired furor in Japan, admitted to a correspondent for the Japanese Communist Party newspaper *Akahata* that "he had never called at a Japanese port aboard a U.S. ship which was then carrying nuclear weaponry."[49]

Taking advantage of developing pacifist and neutralist sentiment in Western Europe, the Center has acted to exacerbate fear. It sponsored "The First Conference on Nuclear War in Europe" in Groningen, Holland, the very title emphasizing the fear it was trying to heighten. LaRocque was the keynote speaker and his talk struck the theme of the conference: "It seems unfair that such war [nuclear war] will be fought over and in nations which have nothing to say about whether nuclear weapons are to be used."[50] More bluntly LaRocque announced: "If you dummies let us, we'll fight World War III in Europe"[51] and his statement was widely used by those organizing demonstrations against "Euromissiles" in NATO countries. The conference brought together a series of opponents of arms modernization in NATO, including Major General Gert Bastian, formerly a commander in the West German army. Afterwards the World Peace Council, the major Soviet international front organization, published Bastian's speech and a subsequent speech to a World Peace Council-sponsored Nordic Peace Conference. The CDI later announced plans to bring retired Warsaw pact generals to the U.S. to discuss nuclear issues.[52]

Although the Center appeals to isolationist sentiment—one fund-raising letter begins, "You have a right to be angry. Only 30% of our huge $126 billion defense budget is actually spent on defense of the United States!"—it is by no means dedicated to creating a Fortress America. According to the Center, "the United States can learn some lessons from Japan's non-military foreign policy'' and it noted approvingly that Japan spends less than 1% of its GNP on military defense.[53] Emulating *CounterSpy's* role in exposing agents, the Center in 1982 issued a report identifying the location of most of the nuclear weapons storage depots used by the U.S. army, navy and air force, the sites of two depots in New York and California serving as ''storage and transshipment points to Europe and Asia,'' 8 naval bases and depots in the U.S. used by submarines and nuclear weapons carrying ships, ICBM sites, 10 strategic air command bases, and 8 nuclear weapons factories.

Remarkably, the CDI maintains its credibility on Capitol Hill. As recently as April 1983, LaRocque, Steve Goose and Eugene Carroll, all of the CDI, testified before the Armed Services Committee on the Rapid Deployment Force and the MX missile.

But nowhere is the onslaught of the utopians so severe and extensive as it is on United States allies and friends in the Third World. The language of human rights is used to undermine countries dependent upon the United States for support, and as a ground for supporting Marxist liberation groups working to install governments that will be tied to the Soviet Union. The Carter Administration's emphasis on human rights proved an enormous boon to the utopians. As Carter first intended, the principle of human rights was to be a reproach to Communist countries, and a weapon for the United States in the battle for the hearts and minds of Third World countries. But the utopians quickly seized on human rights as a weapon against the United States. They ignored human rights violations in Communist countries. Their excuse for focussing exclusively on countries with ties to the United States was that these are the only countries we can influence.

Latin America has been a prime target of the institutes. IPS is joined by the North American Congress on Latin America (NACLA), the Council on Hemispheric Affairs (COHA), the Washington Office on Latin America (WOLA), the Center for Cuban Studies and the Cuba Resource Center, to name only the major tax exempt organizations. They in turn work together with a host of committees in solidarity with the ''national liberation struggles'' of countries ranging from Chile in the south to El Salvador and Guatemala in the north. (Titles of these committees range from the forthright Puerto Rican Revolutionary Workers Organization to the bland Latin American Civic Committee.) Personnel of one move to another, and often work simultaneously with two or more organizations. Orlando Letelier, for example, while director of IPS's Transnational Institute was instrumental in establishing both the Council on Hemispheric Affairs and the Chile Legislative Committee, for he saw the importance of establishing as many organizations as possible to reiterate the same themes. All of them shape public opinion so that aid and support will be denied to governments friendly to the United States, permitting liberation forces backed by the progressive arms of the Soviet Union (via Cuba and now Nicaragua) to take over.

We encountered the North American Congress on Latin America (NACLA) earlier in the discussion of the role of the churches in fostering revolution. In addition to publishing manifestoes from priests-turned-guerillas, NACLA functions as an intelligence agency on U.S. companies operating in Latin America, a propaganda agency against U.S. government policies and targeted Latin American governments, and a publicist for the "ideal" government of Cuba. For NACLA, even U.S. government programs apparently informed by ideals of service are iniquitous. It provided extensive coverage for the Committee of Returned Volunteers, which sought to abolish the Peace Corps on the grounds that it merely gave legitimacy to local political structures and is part of a conspiracy for "the Americanization of the entire earth."[54] One can read in the pages of *NACLA Reports* a call "to subvert the Peace Corps and all other institutions of U.S. Imperialism."[55] D.J. Kirchhoff, the President of Castle and Cooke, a multi-national corporation with major investments in Latin America, has charged bluntly: "NACLA profiles the assets and personnel of American multinationals as targets of opportunity for militants."[56] NACLA puts it more delicately, saying it is necessary "to take the information available about power in this society and turn it against that power."[57] In its research methodology guide, NACLA offers spying, penetration and theft as legitimate methods for obtaining information.[58] (Ironically it is the use of such methods by intelligence agencies that are offered as grounds for abolishing them.) *NACLA Reports* devotes considerable space to the thoughts of Fidel Castro and reprints in full the pronouncements of various Congresses of liberated peoples held in Havana.

The Center for Cuban Studies and the Cuba Resource Center are wholly devoted to fostering an appreciation of Cuban achievements and to normalizing relations with Cuba. The Center for Cuban Studies sends the faithful the speeches of Fidel and of various Cuban officials and its bulletin informs readers of the "monolithic ideological unity of the Cuban people."[59] The Cuba Resource Center, largely funded by the churches, is concerned with the significance of Cuba for liberation theology. That Cuba severely restricts the exercise of religion in no way impairs its value in this respect for churchly bureaucrats. Indeed the Fall 1981 issue of *CubaTimes*, the publication of the Cuba Resource Center, carried an interview with Father Carlos Manuel de Cespedes, secretary of the Cuban Bishops Conference, in which he complained of the difficulties Christians encountered in participating in Cuban society: "One of the regulations of statutes of the [Communist] Party requires members to be atheist . . . A believer is not permitted to be a member of the Party."[60] The Washington Office on Latin America does not produce pro-Cuban propaganda. Rather it espouses the familiar view of the radicalized church that capitalism inevitably produces repression by introducing economic inequality. It calls for economic aid to Nicaragua and cutting off of aid to El Salvador.

In working for African liberation, IPS is joined by the American Committee on Africa and its lobbying offshoot, the Washington Office on Africa, both heavily church-funded, the South Africa Catalyst Project, which pressures universities to divest themselves of investments in corporations that do business in South Africa, Trans-Africa, the national black lobby on Africa, and the Interfaith Center on Corporate Responsibility, an offshoot of the National Council of Churches, which concentrates on pressuring corporations to cease having any business dealings with South Africa.

While the Republic of South Africa is the chief target of all these organizations, prior to Robert Mugabe's assumption of power in Zimbabwe, that country received equal attention. The conduct of Mugabe's terrorist forces was defended, even extolled. When Mugabe's Zimbabwe African People's Union received unfavorable publicity for slaughtering a group of missionaries, the Washington Office on Africa claimed that the slaughter was actually arranged by the white-controlled army which had impersonated guerillas and killed the missionaries to discredit Mugabe.[61] As the Washington Office on Africa described the groups that made up the Patriotic Front, it would have been impossible for them to have hurt anyone.

> "The struggle has literally become one huge classroom under the trees where soldier-teachers are involving the people in the process of governing their own lives."[62]

In the view of the Washington Office on Africa, the men and women of the Patriotic Front were "more than simply soldiers, and the brand of socialism they profess is the sharing of all they have with the people, including their lives." Mugabe's "liberation forces," said the Washington Office on Africa "are struggling for the values Americans cherish."[63] (Survivors of guerilla raids tell a rather different story. The London Times of February 19, 1976 reported the experiences of a tribesman, Phillip Humane, 30 years old, who said a gang of about 17 guerillas had beaten his father-in-law to death. According to the *Times,* "One member of the gang then took a bayonet from his rifle and hacked off Mr. Humane's ears. After trying to cut off his nose the gang made him eat his ears. The guerillas then made his wife fetch an axe to hack off Mr. Humane's fingers and toes. He had not lost consciousness during the attack and when he asked for mercy they told him they wanted him to suffer.") The Washington Office on Africa has remained silent during the brutal suppression by Mugabe of the followers of his former associate, Joshua Nkomo.

While the Republic of South Africa obviously violates human rights, the genuineness of the concern of the various institutes for the human rights of Africans is suspect. This is not only because they whitewash the most appalling brutality on the part of the terrorist groups with which they identify, but because they show no concern for violation of rights in numerous other African countries. There are currently over six million refugees in Africa, drifting from country to country, camp to camp, that arouse no concern within the institutes. They have only one villain (now that Zimbabwe has joined the ranks of approved-regimes) and parade the familiar list of Marxist-led countries that deserve United States support—Zimbabwe, Angola and Mozambique. (Countries friendly to the United States in Africa are usually described as "neo-colonialist.")

In Asia, Communist victories have sharply cut down the need for institute activity. The Indochina Resource Center, which pressed for the liberation of Vietnam, Laos and Cambodia, has had to change its name to the Southeast Asia Resource Center. It can be expected to seek the liberation of Thailand, the Phillipines, Indonesia, South Korea and Pakistan. It will have a hard time living up to past performances, however, which include a passionate defense of the Khmer Rouge rule of Cambodia. That particular performance is important in demonstrating the extent of the deceptiveness of which these groups are capable.

Coordinator of the Indochina Resource Center from 1974-1976 was Gareth Porter, who co-authored a book called *Cambodia: Starvation and Revolution* in 1976. Its thesis was that whatever starvation there had been in Cambodia occurred as a result of U.S. policy *before* the Khmer Rouge takeover, and that since the U.S. departure the revolutionary government had made agriculture thrive as never before moving from sufficiency to "surplus" and creating "a collective framework designed to release the creative energies of the people." Porter wrote that "allegations of starvation were . . . simply an attempt to further blacken the image of successful revolution in Indochina in the wake of the U.S. defeat." As for the mass evacuation of Phnom Penh, Porter claimed it "was prompted by a concern for the most basic and urgent needs of the population." The emptying of the hospitals at gunpoint? That "was actually to save lives and give the best possible care to the sick and wounded."[64] In 1977, Porter testified before a Congressional subcommittee that no more than a few thousand had died; at that time almost two million people had been killed. (Porter's performance earned him a post in 1977 as associate Fellow at the Institute for Policy Studies, and he is still considered an "expert" on Cambodia by the *N.Y. Times* for which he wrote an Op-Ed essay in 1983.) Since Vietnam's invasion of Cambodia, no organization has been more vehement in its denunciations of the barbarities of the Khmer Rouge than the Southeast Asia Resource Center or more vigorous in its defense of the right of the Vietnamese government to maintain its position there: the Center's grounds, as ever, are its dedication to human rights.

In the Middle East, Israel is the chief target of the utopian think tanks. Liberation is to come through the Soviet-backed terrorist groups of the PLO. IPS has ties to MERIP, the Middle East Research and Information Project, whose chief problem for years was in deciding with which of the rival Palestinian terror gangs to identify. It clearly sympathized with George Habash in his struggle with Yassir Arafat, but evenhandedly published speeches of leaders of the various groups and dispensed PLO literature, buttons and other paraphanalia. MERIP has expanded its efforts to combat U.S. "imperialism" in the region generally. IPS has repeatedly provided facilities for MERIP meetings and fundraisers, and a number of IPS Fellows have served as writers and editors for its publication *MERIP Reports*. IPS Fellow Joe Stork, who voyaged to Baghdad to speak at a conference on Zionism as a Racist Phenomenon was the key figure in MERIP from its inception. (IPS has been reluctant to be identified with MERIP. When journalist Joshua Muravchik brought up the subject of MERIP in an interview with Marcus Raskin, he was told abruptly "I don't know anything about MERIP. Don't even ask me about it." Similarly Richard Barnet, asked about MERIP's use of IPS facilities, replied: "I would be surprised if they have done it in years." And Muravchik noted that Barnet did indeed show considerable surprise when he promptly pulled out a poster advertising a MERIP fundraiser at IPS two nights earlier.)[65]

Perhaps the cleverest institute to manipulate the human rights issue into a weapon against U.S. allies is the Center for International Policy, founded in 1974. Like the Center for National Security Studies and the Center for Defense Information, it is a project of the Fund for Peace. Its very structure is designed to exclude the need for examination of the human rights record of any country that is *not* friendly to the United States, for it reports only on Third World countries that receive U.S. aid. According to the Center, of the $140 billion of aid the United States has given since 1945, nearly two-thirds has gone to governments that violate human rights. The Center's one-sided character is best seen by comparing it with Freedom House, an organization also concerned with the status of human rights around the world. Freedom House issues a yearly report on the state of freedom around the world. Communist countries consistently rank at the bottom, for obviously there is no freedom of the press, speech or assembly and no mechanism by which the public can change its government. Non-Communist governments also often score very poorly, but by scoring *all* countries by a consistent set of criteria, Freedom House avoids the gross distortions fostered by evaluations of only a particular group of countries.

The Center for International Policy uses a rhetoric designed to evoke broad sympathy, as it says, "America's true national interest and security is directly tied to the fate of freedom abroad." But the giveaway that the Center has no genuine interest in freedom, merely with removing American support for anti-Communist countries, is its identification with Cuba, which scores 6 in the Freedom House scale. (The lowest possible score is 7.) Cuba's score places it one below South Korea, or South Africa, favorite targets of the Center, and on a par with Chile, which the Center regularly excoriates. But according to the Center any talk of human rights in Cuba is beside the point for the revolution *is* human rights.

> "For most Cubans, the progress of the revolution and the promotion of human rights are one and the same thing. The Cuban government operates to protect and augment what are viewed as collective rights, those of the majority. When individual rights are thought to endanger collective rights they are sacrificed, a position generally disapproved of among Western liberal democracies."[66]

As to accusations of torture in Cuban jails that have been made to international bodies, the Center concedes that inspection has not been permitted. Yet while in countries friendly to the United States this would be *prima facie* evidence that the accusations were true, the Center is merely driven to further apologetics. "Cuban officials point with pride to the low rate of recidivism among civil and political offenders which they attribute to acquiring of respect for the laws of the land and goals of the revolution."[67] There is no suggestion that Castro's jails might have a dampening effect on those political prisoners who survive the experience.

Not surprisingly, in view of the correspondence of goals between the various institutes, centers, and activist groups, there is a pattern of personnel moving from one to the other or even working simultaneously for several of them. Michael Klare offers a good example of the pattern. A Fellow of IPS and director of its "Militarism and Disarmament Project," Klare was a founder and former staff member of the North American Congress on Latin America, an Associate of the Center for National Security Studies and a visiting Fellow of the Center for International Policy, and a founder of Mobilization for Survival.

A number of the institutes attacking U.S. foreign policy argue that the real strength of the United States lies in its economy and it is our economic institutions that need to be strengthened. There are institutes, working closely with IPS, that in the name of strengthening American economic institutions, seek to convert the United States to a socialist economy. The Exploratory Project for Economic Alternatives might be described as an IPS grandchild. IPS Fellows Gar Alperovitz and Christopher Jencks established an IPS spinoff called the Cambridge Institute in Massachusetts. Alperovitz then spun off from his spinoff another center. The Exploratory Project for Economic Alternatives has worked closely with the Nader organizational complex: Nader and Alperovitz jointly established COIN, the Coalition to Fight Inflation in the Necessities, mentioned in an earlier chapter. The Project argues for public ownership of large corporations and for confronting "the need for public control over major economic decisions now in the hands of the private sector." This is described as a necessary extension of democracy. In order to survive, the Project declares, democracy cannot stand still, but must be extended to the economy.

The meaning of the term "economic democracy," which the Project uses to describe its program, was clarified at a conference organized by Ralph Nader in October 1981. The conference was entitled "Taking Charge: The Next Ten Years" which summed up rather neatly the hope of the coercive utopians. Derek Shearer, a member of the steering committee of IPS's National Conference on State and Local Public Policies told those assembled why he liked the term "economic democracy." It was, said Shearer, "the great euphemism." Shearer described the problem:

> "While we can't use the 'S' word [socialism] too effectively in American politics, we have found that in the greatest tradition of American advertising the word 'economic democracy' sells. You can take it door to door like Fuller brushes, and the doors will not be slammed in your face. So I commend it to you, for those who are willing to compromise on the use of the 'S' word."[68]

It was surely appropriate that these words were spoken at the conference of the consumer advocate who has labored to eliminate deceptive advertising. Since the public would buy "economic democracy" but not "socialism" the solution was to "sell" socialism labelled "economic democracy."

There are reasons why IPS spins off institutes so readily, providing them with seed money, institute personnel and help in obtaining tax exemption. One advantage that accrues to IPS is that the spinoffs make it appear that a variety of groups and publications have independently made the same analysis of the problems of our society and come to the same solutions. For example, *Mother Jones* is a glossy muckraking magazine that fills the gap left by the passing of *Ramparts*. One does not subscribe to *Mother Jones* but becomes a member of the Foundation for National Progress, entitling one to the Foundation's publication. In the February-March 1977 issue of the magazine, the question is raised "Who is Behind Mother Jones?" The answer is lengthy and virtuous, "no banks, no corporations, no people looking for a fast buck" but rather "men and women . . . studying, organizing, researching, investigating and documenting the problems and crises of our time." Yet according to its own financial report the Foundation for National Progress was created "to carry out on the West Coast the charitable and educational activities of the Institute for Policy Studies."[69] The advantage of all this to IPS is illustrated in an article in the issue of *Mother Jones* following its proclamation of independence. *Mother Jones* endorses its own candidates for high position in the Carter administration, including IPS co-director Richard Barnet for Secretary of State, former Fellow Gar Alperovitz as director of the Office of Management and the Budget and Congressman Ronald Dellums, IPS's staunchest supporter on Capital Hill, for National Security Adviser.[70] If an IPS publication had presented these choices, complete with pictures and laudatory biographies, they would have appeared as tasteless puffery by the Institute. Suggested by an "independent" magazine, the choices give IPS enhanced stature.

Another advantage of spinoffs is that they can take advantage of opportunities that for one reason or another are not open to IPS. From its inception IPS announced that it would not accept any government money and this remained important to its image as a wholly independent think tank. On the other hand, as more and more government money became available in the sixties, IPS saw in the spinoff a way to obtain federal money without forfeiting its image. Alperovitz and Jencks, as we noted earlier, with the aid of IPS established the Cambridge Institute. That Institute in turn mushroomed into the Center for the Study of Public Policy, the Center for Community Economic Development and the Huron Institute. The various Cambridge spinoffs then raked in millions of dollars of federal money. IPS's scruples, it must be noted, apparently do not extend to taking money from other governments. One of the papers found in Letelier's briefcase was an internal IPS memo which explored ways to accept money from foreign governments that would not "enter the books."[71]

One of the most important benefits IPS obtained from its spinoffs was a newsservice established by the Bay Area Institute in San Francisco, which spun off from IPS in 1970. A news service reaches millions of people who would never ordinarily be exposed to the IPS perspective. And they are exposed unawares because the average newspaper reader does not pay attention to the small bylines that give the source of a story. Now that it has abandoned tell-tale liturgical phrases like "fascist regimes" and "U.S. imperialism" the Pacific News Service is widely used by the straight press, including the Washington Post, the Boston Globe, the Chicago Tribune and the Los Angeles Times. Yet it remains a leftwing propaganda service. It has become so successful that coverage has been expanded from the Far East to include Africa, Latin America and the domestic United States. Part of the attraction of the service is its special sources of information. Marxist governments, which exercise tight control over information, recognize Pacific News Service as a friendly press and give it scoops, e.g. interviews with prominent figures, access to human interest stories, exposés of U.S. activities in these countries etc.

One IPS spinoff was unplanned and produced considerable embarassment. A stock market slump in the mid-1970s reduced the income of the foundations upon which IPS relied. As a result IPS codirectors Raskin and Barnet decided to cut the salaries of IPS Fellows in half (although leaving their own intact) and to place the responsibility for raising the remainder upon the Fellows themselves. Raskin and Barnet may well have felt the change would have the salutary effect of making Fellows aware of the difficulty of raising funds, at least from traditional IPS donors, for some of the projects upon which they were engaged. Arthur Waskow, for example, was "into" transforming society on the basis of alternative conceptions of Torah while Charlotte Bunch was "into" Lesbian liberation as a means for expanding human possibilities. Not only did these not fund easily, but such projects did not sit well with the IPS codirectors or the Rubin family, chief bankrollers of IPS, who, especially in the Carter years, saw immense possibilities of government penetration and coalition building with radical elements in the unions. They did not want to endanger all this by indulgence in what boiled down to middle class diversions.

To the amusement of Washington journalists who chronicled the progress of the dispute, the disgruntled Fellows sought to establish a union. Finally a separation agreement was hammered out in which IPS funded the establishment of yet another institute, also located in Washington, on the condition that its name not have any similarity to the reluctant parent. Nine IPS Fellows formed the Public Resource Center, which was to focus on organizing among "movement people" at the grassroots.

Having deceived so many, the utopian think tanks fittingly were themselves deceived by an extraordinary pair of investigative journalists, John and Louise Rees, who passed themselves off as fellow utopians. It is largely thanks to the Reeses that we know as much as we do about the various institutes that have been described here as well as groups to be discussed in subsequent chapters, including segments of the peace movement and the National Lawyers Guild. Since 1968, John Rees has published a biweekly newsletter on these groups called *The Information Digest*.

A burly Welshman with a dark red beard, John Rees came to the United States in 1963. His political evolution had already occurred in England. Coming from a staunchly—according to Rees unthinkingly—Conservative family, Rees gravitated after the war to the left-wing sector of the Labour Party. His initial disillusionment with Labour had nothing to do with its domestic programs. Rees was angered when Labour reneged on one of the principles of its constitution and supported the rearmament of Germany. Rees dropped out of any political activity, working as a newspaperman in London. His disenchantment with Labour grew, however. According to Rees: "Politically I became disenchanted with the whole European system. The British Labour Party was causing economic misery and the Conservative or Christian parties of Europe had no idea how to cope with change. I thought the American system was better."[72]

In the United States, Rees worked as a journalist and for a consultancy group, National Goals, doing work for the Peace Corps and community relations work for police departments. Within a few years, Rees found his new country plunged in racial disturbances, student riots, anti-war demonstrations, a far cry from the image he had formed. On the basis of his experiences in working to contain the Newark riot, Rees took what he described as his "dog and pony show" to police departments around the country who were being assailed by or waited in fear of being assailed by the upsurge of revolutionary fervor. The *Information Digest* began as a collection of articles and clippings from different parts of the country that Rees assembled for his audience.

Rees began to develop first hand information on revolutionary-minded groups by posing as a member. He took part in the demonstrations against the Democratic National Convention in Chicago in 1968 and found acceptance was easy. He met his future wife, then a young legal secretary, at a demonstration in New York, which she watched out of curiosity. Louise says John played his part perfectly: she was trying to figure out how to go about getting this dangerous alien deported when he told her he had "something to confess." She was still so unsuspecting that she was sure it was that "he was married." Actually there was that too: John had been through two unsuccessful marriages. This marriage however, built on shared goals and talents, an appetite for hard work, and an openness to adventure and an unconventional style of life, proved strong. When, in 1969, SDS created its first off-campus chapter in New York, the New York Crazies, which Rees describes as an anarchistic group with a taste for street fighting, the Reeses became valued members. Louise remembers, as one of her most memorable activities, slipping into the annual banquet of the League for Industrial Democracy with a group of fellow Crazies in an attempt to present a pig's head to the guest of honor, then Vice President Hubert Humphrey. John describes these laconically as "amusing times."

In 1971 the Reeses moved to Washington and established a radical bookstore called the Red House—Eight Blocks from the White House.

Louise recalls that they were undercapitalized and went under in eleven months. At that point, the United Church of Christ came to the rescue. The left, with its taste for "ripping off' the establishment, received a small taste of its own medicine from the Reeses. They established the Coordinating Center for Education in Repression and the Law, ostensibly to promote prisoner rights. The Commission for Racial Justice of the United Church of Christ gave them $4,000 for the project in 1971, a disturbing sign of that church's readiness to pour money into anything that even *sounded* radical. Louise notes that it was a legitimate legal research project, only its aim was not, as the United Church of Christ probably thought, to train prisoners as revolutionaries.

The Reeses rented a large house which filled with movement people who chipped in $55 a month for living expenses. And when the organization of radical lawyers, the National Lawyers Guild, decided it needed a full-time organizer, it turned to Louise, who had done part-time work for the Guild in New York. Her efficient conduct of her work led to her promotion to membership in the Guild's National Executive Board in 1973. Since the communal house was obviously no place from which to issue the *Information Digest,* the Reeses rented a small apartment on the outskirts of Washington in which to work. A friend let them store their growing collection of documents in his garage. The Reeses reinforced their cover by printing in the *Information Digest* reports on their own activities. Louise remarked that if you go to a conference and are the National Lawyers Guild organizer for Washington, it would be odd if a report on the conference didn't mention your presence.

I asked the Reeses how they felt toward the people with whom they lived, whose values they so little shared. Louise said there were people with whom they had rapport, but from her point of view there was always a barrier:

> "Because whether you dealt with the SDS leadership or disarmament and peace activists or the Guild or IPS one theme you found was a tremendous elitist contempt for ordinary Americans, hatred of blue collar Americans because they weren't revolutionaries, contempt for them because they didn't want to smash and destroy, contempt for their pastimes, contempt for their marriages, contempt because they were Americans. Yet these elitists wanted to take that away from them, smash it, set up a system based on China or Cuba or Vietnam or Tanzania."

The Reeses led their double life in Washington for four years, Louise even going to work on Capitol Hill for the House Committee on

Internal Security in 1973, where she worked with a glossy wig of heavy black curls that sat oddly on a face designed for the straight pulled back light brown hair normally coiled above it. In 1976, their cover was blown when William Haddad, working for New York State Assemblyman Stanley Steingut, obtained what the Reeses say was unauthorized access to state police files and found copies of the *Information Digest* there. He then asked for and obtained information on its author. When Haddad called the National Lawyers Guild for "confirmation," the days of the Reeses as revolutionaries were over.

The *Information Digest* continued. Undaunted, the Reeses continued to cover open meetings, paying their registration fees, and marching into workshops. Louise observes that sometimes they tried to throw her out "and sometimes it's sensible to leave because it serves no good purpose to remain—you won't get any information. But there are times when I'm not noticed at all." The Reeses also send others to cover meetings. And surprisingly enough, the Reeses say there are people within the groups who sometimes help them: for example, a member of a splinter whose policy was rejected may pass them information. As the campaign against the intelligence agencies reaped success after success, the Reeses became the only people in the country keeping a steady eye on the multiplicity of institutes and revolutionary groups. The Reeses note that, of the groups they follow, the only ones the FBI are even allowed to keep files on are some elements of the Ku Klux Klan (the Reeses follow the radical right as well as the radical left), the Jewish Defense League and some elements of those groups that support the IRA. For the rest, the FBI is not even allowed to read their literature, until there is evidence that they have committed a crime. According to Louise Rees, from 1976 on, the FBI did not even collect information on the Weather Underground.

Not surprisingly, the groups covered by the Reeses have been angry. The National Lawyers Guild, the Socialist Workers Party and IPS have all filed suits against the Reeses. Louise reports with amusement that a lawyer for the Guild argued the *Information Digest* had not been written by the Reeses, and that other than touching the paper on which it was written, they had nothing to do with it. The Guild was trying to prove that the *Information Digest* was really put out by the FBI. The purpose of the Guild was to try to strip the Reeses of their journalistic privileges. That ploy having failed, they were charged with an as yet nonexistent offense in law, "invasion of organizational privacy." In May 1983, the NLG dropped its action against the Reeses. The Reeses note that no one has ever brought a libel suit against them, i.e. charged them with printing anything that was untrue. Rather the groups covered by *Information Digest* seem to have a healthy respect for its accuracy. A long essay on *Information Digest* in *CounterSpy* offers some backhanded compliments. It is described as the work of "trained professionals" and the Reeses are called "extremely dangerous people."

The Reeses are as unpopular with much of the radical right as they are with the radical left. If the left feels betrayed because the Reeses were accepted so long in their midst, the radical right feels betrayed because the Reeses are conservatives who detest the right fringe groups, with their racial hatreds and mindless paranoia. If IPS gets more space than the Ku Klux Klan, it is simply a reflection of the Reeses pragmatic observation that the left in the last decade has posed a more influential threat than the right to American democracy. Nonetheless *Information Digest* is a favorite target of the radical right's Liberty Lobby, which calls John Rees "a Mossad agent" (the Mossad is the Israeli intelligence service) and Lyndon Larouche's United States Labor Party, which calls him "a KGB mole."

The Reeses offer no apologies for deceiving the left. According to Louise Rees:

> If you are going to talk about deception, the culprit is the left. We have actually functioned as a consumers rights group, a sort of political consumer's protection service. We have tried to inform the public about the political fraud practiced by these groups. If you read their public statements, their declarations of purpose, you think their only purpose is to be of service to mankind. We go behind the facade to expose what these groups are really trying to do. If it is important to know if manufacturers make deceptive claims for their products, it is far more important to the long-range health of this society that people know if they are being sold a fraudulent political bill of goods."

Information Digest is not something for the average magazine subscriber: it costs several hundred dollars a year. Nor is it something to put on the coffee table. Issues are mimeographed, run from twelve to twenty pages, and stapled together. It is, however, available to anyone who wants to subscribe. John Rees observes: "The Socialist Workers Party can subscribe and the Center for National Security Studies gets their copy and can read about themselves." Other subscribers include newspapers, magazines, television stations, universities. And from the beginning, John Rees has sent the FBI a copy of each issue.

After almost fifteen years of labor, Rees is deeply concerned. "We feel there is a revolutionary flood," he said, "and we are behind the dikes with some hands and bodies in the gap and that it's at least slowing down the process."

> "There are many more activities than there were four or five years ago. The acceleration of the revolutionary movement corresponds to what happened starting in 1966 when radical movements forced the abdication of U.S. responsibilities in Southeast Asia. The teach-in movement has begun again very successfully. We would need five times as many people as we have now and resources of many thousands of dollars to put out adequate reports. Recently the *Digest* has been forced to confine itself to major activities on the East Coast, leaving out dozens and dozens of events we should have covered. The radical left is advancing on many more areas now and the involvement has broadened to include part of the labor movement and the churches. We are simply not doing a thorough enough job at this time."

The institutes and centers whose characteristic mark is their contempt for Western democracy, its values and its institutions, have met with enormous success, largely because the pioneer work of the Reeses has not been followed up by the mass media. Not only have the mass media taken these institutes and centers at their face value, but they have constituted, as we shall see, a major sounding board for them.

REFERENCES

1. Garry Wills, "The Thinking of Positive Power," *Esquire,* March 1971
2. Marcus Raskin, *Notes on the Old System: To Transform American Politics,* New York: David McKay Co., 1974, p. 134
3. Marcus Raskin, *Being and Doing,* New York: Random House, 1971, p. 125
4. Ibid., p. xvi
5. Ibid.
6. Marcus Raskin, "From Imperial War-Making to a Code of Personal Responsibility" in Ralph Stavins, Richard Barnet and Marcus Raskin, *Washington Plans an Aggressive War,* New York: Random House, 1971, pp. 290-92
7. Arthur Waskow, *Running Riot: A Journey through the Official Disasters and Creative Disorder in American Society,* New York: Herder & Herder, 1970, p. 168
8. "Washington Determines the Fate of Vietnam," in Stavins, Barnet & Raskin, op. cit., p. 79
9. Michael Parenti, *Democracy for the Few,* New York: St. Martin's Press, 1977, p. 216
10. Arthur Waskow, "Judaism and Revolution Today," *Judaism,* Vol. 20, No. 4, Fall 1971, p. 412
11. Paul Jacobs and Saul Landau, *To Serve the Devil,* 2 vols., New York: Random House, 1971
12. Paul Jacobs and Saul Landau, *The New Radicals,* N.Y. Random House, 1966, p. 84

13. David Kelley, "For Socialist Alternatives: A Radical Think Tank is Working Within the System," *Barron's,* August 23, 1976, p. 5
14. Quoted from an article by Arthur Waskow in *New University Thought,* Spring 1968 in Institutional Analysis #2, "The Institute for Policy Studies" Heritage Foundation, May 1977, p. 4
15. Stephen Clapp, "The Intellectual Bombthrowers," *The Washingtonian,* Dec. 1969, p. 50
16. Quoted by Joshua Muravchik, "The Think Tank of the Left," *New York Times Magazine,* May 3, 1981, p. 42
17. *The Link* (IPS-Transnational Institute), Jan./Feb. 1976, p. 6
18. See Rael Jean Isaac, "The Institute for Policy Studies; Empire on the Left," *Midstream,* June/July 1980, p. 10
19. Quoted in Institution Analysis #9 "The New Left in Government," Heritage Foundation, p. 17
20. "TIE-Europe—1981" *Transnational Information Exchange No. 7/8,* Oct. 1980-March 1981, p. 11
21. *Information Digest,* Aug. 10, 1979
22. Quoted from U.S. House of Representatives, Hearings before the Subcommittee on Civil Service, 96th Congress, 2nd Session, March 4, 1980, pp. 51-2 in "Reply by Robert Borosage and Peter Weiss to Rael Jean Issac" in "The Fight Around the Institute for Policy Studies," *Midstream,* Feb. 1981, p. 38
23. *Information Digest,* May 19, 1978, June 2, 1978
24. Joshua Muravchik, op. cit., p. 108
25. "Book Reviews," *Race and Class,* Vol. 18, No. 1, Summer 1976, p. 81
26. Basil Davidson, "Somalia: Toward Socialism," *Race and Class,* Vol. 17, No. I, Summer 1975
27. *Information Digest,* June 10, 1983
28. *The Link* (IPS-Transnational Institute), February 1975
29. On the Letelier documents see Accuracy in Media's *AIM Report,* Jan. I 1977, March I 1977; April I and II 1977; May I and II 1977; July II 1977. See also *Information Digest,* April 22, 1977 and *Congressional Record,* Dec. 20, 1979, E 6287.
30. Quoted in James Tyson, *Target America,* Chicago: Regnery Gateway, 1981, p. 201
31. *Los Angeles Times,* June 21, 1976
32. *The Link,* Jan./Feb. 1976
33. Joshua Muravchik's article published in the New York Times was originally part of a much longer mss. This is from that unpublished mss. Future references to it are labeled "Muravchik mss."
34. *Information Digest,* Sept. 20, 1974
35. "Abolish the CIA and Covert Action," *CounterSpy,* Vol. 2, No. 4, Winter 1976, p. 3
36. "Build the Fifth Estate," *CounterSpy,* Vol. 2, No. 1, Fall 1974, p. 17
37. Larry McDonald, Memorandum on Participation of Organizations and Individuals Hostile to the U.S. Intelligence Community in the Activities of the Senate Select Committee on Intelligence, prepared in response to Senator Gary Hart's request for information during hearings on the nomination of Frank C. Carlucci as Deputy Director, Central Intelligence.
38. Jerry Berman, Morton H. Halperin and John Shattuck, "Protecting the Names of Intelligence Agents and the Need for a New Charter," *First Principles,* Vol. 2, No. 5, Jan.-Feb. 1980, p. 4
39. Morton Halperin, "The Carter Administration: In the Mood for Reform?" *First Principles,* Vol. 2, No. 8, April 1977, p. 16

40. Joshua Muravchik, op. cit., p. 109
41. "NATO and the Neutron Bomb," *The Defense Monitor,* Vol. VII, No. 5, June 1978, pp. 2-3
42. "American Strength, Soviet Weakness," *The Defense Monitor,* Vol. IX, No. 5, June 1980, p. 8
43. *Information Digest,* August 14, 1981
44. Ibid.
45. "American Strength, Soviet Weakness," op. cit., p. 6
46. "Soviet Geopolitical Momentum: Myth or Menace," *The Defense Monitor,* Vol. IX, No. 1, Jan. 1980, p. 4
47. Ibid., p. 15
48. Ibid., p. 23
49. John K. Emerson, "Japan," Hoover Yearbook on International Communist Affairs, 1975, Stanford, Hoover International Press, p. 361
50. *The New York Times,* April 28, 1981
51. *Information Digest,* December 25, 1981
52. Report by Anne B. Zill on peace organizations—not published
53. "Japan Under U.S. Pressure," *The Defense Monitor,* Vol. IV, No. 9, Nov. 1975, p. 1
54. *NACLA's Latin America and Empire Report,* Nov. 1969, p. 6
55. Ibid., p. 7
56. "A Response to the Editor from Mr. Kirchhoff," *The Presbyterian Layman,* Dec. 1979-Jan. 1980, p. 8
57. Ibid.
58. Ibid.
59. Center for Cuban Studies *Newsletter,* Vol. 1, No. 6, Nov. 1974
60. Moises Sandoval, "The Shepherds are Few," *CubaTimes,* Fall 1981, p. 16
61. "Zimbabwe: Winning Hearts and Minds," Leaflet put out by Washington Office on Africa, 110 Maryland Ave., NE., Washington, D.C., undated
62. Ibid.
63. Ibid.
64. George Hildebrand and Gareth Porter, *Cambodia: Starvation and Revolution,* New York, Monthly Review Press, 1976, pp. 16, 41, 56
65. Joshua Muravchik, op. cit., p. 108 and Muravchik mss.
66. Patricia Weiss Fagen, "Toward Detente with Cuba: Issues and Obstacles" *Center for International Policy Report,* Vol. III, No. 3, Nov. 1977, p. 17
67. Ibid.
68. John C. Boland, "Nader Crusade—The Anti-Business Lobby is Alive and Kicking," *Barron's,* October 12, 1981, p. 20
69. 1976 Financial Report, Foundation for National Progress
70. *Mother Jones,* April 1977
71. See note 29
72. Interview, John and Louise Rees, Nov. 14, 1981

VII

The Counterfeit Peacemakers

In 1983 a peace crusade was serving as a worthy follower of the environmental crusade of 1970: an ill-considered, fevered enthusiasm that once again depicted the end of the world around the corner. In some respects, there was more realism to the peace crusade, but in other respects, it was much more dangerous. The peace crusade was more realistic in that it was far more plausible to argue that the survival of mankind was threatened by nuclear war than to claim the earth was on the verge of extinction from poisons in the air, sea and water. It was more dangerous because it could bring about the very holocaust it sought to avert. The Soviet Union did not have to worry about mass demonstrations in Moscow and Kiev calling for an end to nuclear weaponry. (When a tiny independent movement developed, the Soviets promptly clapped the leader, Sergei Batovrin, into a mental hospital and have since expelled him from the country.) The Soviets could sit back and relish the Western mass demonstrations that would force the U.S. to "negotiate" arms limitation agreements in which the U.S. made genuine cutbacks while the Soviet Union made cosmetic arrangements. Further down that road were two possibilities: war, when the Soviet Union judged its superiority sufficiently overwhelming, or nuclear blackmail, through which the Soviets subdued the West simply by the threat of using a superiority universally recognized.

The peace crusade was triggered by the Nuclear Freeze petition, which called for a mutual freeze by the United States and the Soviet Union on the testing, production and deployment of nuclear weapons and their delivery systems. Early in 1982, nuclear freeze petitions sprouted at street corners, in front of supermarkets, on church and synagogue bulletin boards. By November 1982, freeze resolutions had swept through 446 New England town meetings, 321 city councils and eleven state legislatures. In California, a drive to put the freeze on the ballot collected the requisite 350,000 signatures in a mere two months. In the subsequent referendum, it passed, as did similar referenda in seven other states.

Every effort was made to galvanize the unimaginative. In the first week of March 1982, buildings, signs, office elevators and windows at 17th and M Street in Washington, just north of the White House, were plastered with two inch circular gummed labels which said: "Flash! Boom! You're dead!!!" The presumably startled reader was enlightened by the small print: "A small nuclear bomb explodes over the White House. Standing here, you have a 98% chance of dying immediately, from leveled buildings, intense heat, lethal radiation, or debris flying to 500 m.p.h."[1] Within a short time there were bicycle races from death, "run for your life" marathons, die-ins, lie-ins, and teach-ins. In this atmosphere, half hysteria, half carnival, Physicians for Social Responsibility fanned out across the country to spell out for audiences the physical suffering they would experience following a nuclear explosion: the starvation, dehydration, radiation sickness and infections. They emphasized their total inability as physicians to help any of the survivors. Far from urging rational civil defense measures, which the Soviets, and even a neutral country like Switzerland have taken, a film produced by Physicians for Social Responsibility included a statement that it is a breach of medical ethics for a physician to participate in planning for emergency medical services in the event of nuclear attack.

Just as environmental disaster books poured from the presses in 1970, so in 1982 publishers rode the new wave, with 40 books detailing the horrors of nuclear war. What Rachel Carson's book had been to the environmental movement, Jonathan Schell's *The Fate of the Earth* was to the peace crusade. Schell's work was conceded, even by political admirers, to be repetitious, rambling, and in sections, unreadable. But the scenario it painted, and in this lay much of its fascination, was the disaster literally to end all disasters: the extinction of mankind.

The nuclear freeze was initially coordinated by two pacifist organizations: the American Friends Service Committee and the Fellowship of Reconciliation. It quickly won the support of almost all the organizations that make up what in current jargon would be called "the peace community." These are both pacifist and non-pacifist groups devoted to reducing the prospects of war. The best established of those signing the initial "Call to Halt the Nuclear Arms Race," as the freeze was officially entitled, were Clergy and Laity Concerned and SANE (the two organizations which then provided much of the manpower for securing signatures to the freeze), Mobilization for Survival, Pax Christi (a Catholic organization), Riverside Church Disarmament Program and Women's International League for Peace and Freedom. Once the freeze had caught on, a special clearing house was set up in St. Louis.

Most Americans have a warm, if hazy, image of peace organizations, especially pacifist groups, whose dedication to nonviolence is seen as wonderful, if impractical. A closer look would produce some major surprises. The major pacifist organizations—the American Friends Service Committee (AFSC), the Fellowship of Reconciliation, the War Resisters League and the Women's International League for Peace and Freedom—are centers of radicalism, whose relation to nonviolence is highly problematical, since in practice they condone violence to achieve the goals of what the left defines as "liberation movements." The distinction between pacifist and non-pacifist peace organizations, indeed between most peace organizations and radical left wing political groups, has become a distinction without a difference.

Intrinsic to pacifism, of course, is the view that means and ends cannot be separated. Lip service continues to be paid to this principle by all the pacifist organizations. A 1980 article in the Fellowship of Reconciliation's journal states the case as eloquently as ever: "Nonviolent activists dispute the assertion that the end justifies the means: they see means and ends as one and inseparable . . The means invariably become embodied in the end, however noble, and skew and distort that end—often beyond recognition."[2] The article quotes a pithy phrase: "You can't grow a rose from a cactus seed." Similar passages could readily be produced from every pacifist group.

Perhaps the most dramatic way to see the gap between pacifist rhetoric and reality is to examine the attitude of these groups to the Palestine Liberation Organization. The world's chief terror organization, the PLO should be especially abhorrent to pacifists.

And yet the attitude of the pacifist organizations toward the PLO is one of warmth, even admiration. In 1975 the Fellowship sent a group to PLO headquarters in Lebanon. The members returned to praise the PLO officials with whom they had spoken, and were particularly enthusiastic about one whom, it was claimed, "spoke in near pacifist terms about guerilla violence."[3] One member of the Fellowship group criticized then Secretary of State Henry Kissinger, who was engaged in his famous "shuttle diplomacy" in the Middle East, for "inviting Palestinian militants to return to terrorist tactics in the absence of any peaceful alternative for justice." If the United States did not give the PLO what it wanted, the PLO had no "alternative," as the Fellowship saw it, except violence.

The Women's International League for Peace and Freedom (WILPF) seems almost obsessed with the PLO. In a recent year its journal, *Peace and Freedom,* ran ten articles on the Middle East, the purport always the need to involve the PLO. WILPF's 1979 resolution on the Middle East calls for negotiations with the PLO without any suggestion that the PLO abandon terrorism or recognize Israel's right to exist. International WILPF (for years headed by Americans, first Kay Camp, now Carol Pendell, wife of a Methodist minister in California) sent its journal's editor as the organization's delegate to a PLO conference in Lebanon. This pacifist lady described with obvious relish being "driven into town escorted by jeeps full of Palestine Liberation Army soldiers" who permitted nothing "to break our line." Her only regret, after this stimulating encounter with violence, was that "more of us could not be there to come to understand why the struggle of the Palestinian people must continue."[4]

The AFSC has done more. Its activities in Israel, ostensibly "humanitarian," provoked the Israeli government to the point where it sought to remove the AFSC's Middle East representative for pro-PLO activities. The AFSC maintains a Community Information and Legal Aid Center in East Jerusalem. While the Israeli authorities were told it would be a counselling center, it rapidly developed into a legal aid service for captured PLO terrorists. In an interview in 1979 Jean de Muralt, then its director, said: "We help the small fry. The big people have their own connections and don't need our help."[5] In the United States, the AFSC has organized lobbying efforts on behalf of the PLO and speaking tours for its propagandists.

Although the identification of pacifist organizations with the PLO is a peculiarly dramatic example of the breakdown of pacifist principles, instances of support for terrorist groups by pacifist organizations could be multiplied. Almost any third world "liberation" movement, provided that it attacks the West, can count at the very least on full moral support from the U.S. pacifist organizations whose fundamental principle, to use the words of an AFSC brochure, is that "violence can never be right."

The transformation of pacifism into anti-Americanism came under the impact of the Vietnam War. Albert Hassler, executive secretary of the Fellowship of Reconciliation from 1960 until his retirement in 1974, wrote:

> "The question for pacifists, I think, is whether in their proper sympathy for the exploited and oppressed of the world, they are willing to justify the use of killing violence to rectify the situation, when it is used by 'liberation' movements. If they are, then pacifism itself was one of the casualties of Vietnam."[6]

After the North Vietnamese violated the Paris Agreements and invaded the South, both the War Resisters League and the Fellowship of Reconciliation issued statements, neither one indicating any disapproval of the offensive. One critic charged: "The failure to condemn or to express disapproval of the North Vietnamese attacks marks the end of a credible American pacifist witness against war."[7]

With the acceptance of violence—the violence of "liberation movements"—the results of an earlier struggle within American pacifism were reversed. There are of course major differences between the conflicts in earlier decades in the environmental movement, the mainline Protestant churches, and the consumer movement and those that occurred within pacifism, for whereas in the cases described earlier those rejecting utopianism won out, pacifism is by its nature utopian. But the parallel nonetheless exists in the sense that pacifists earlier rejected those they now welcome. They once cast out the Communists who sought to manipulate them and refused all forms of cooperation with them.

The original struggle that ended in the victory of pacifist principles occurred in the 1920s and 1930s. After the Bolshevik Revolution many pacifists were attracted to revolutionary Marxism, with its promise of eliminating the *cause* of war, which was defined as social injustice, through class warfare. The conflict in the Fellowship of Reconciliation, the religiously based organization founded during World War I, that drew heavily for its membership upon the Protestant clergy, came to a head during the 1930s. The Fellowship came down on the side of nonviolence and the dissidents who accepted class war—including the Executive Secretary, J.B. Matthews, whom we have encountered as a consumer advocate—were forced to resign. Reinhold Niebuhr, too, left the Fellowship because of his conversion to belief in class war although subsequently, as we have seen, he was to become the most trenchant critic both of Communism and of pacifism.

Other pacifists learned from personal experience what happened when efforts were made to work with Communists. Norman Thomas, the socialist-pacifist leader, initially felt sympathy for the Soviet Union and opposed attempts to dissociate socialism from the Communist model. In 1936 he supported the entry of the Communist Workers Party into his own Socialist Party. Within a year the Trotskyites had moved out, having made revolutionaries out of a sizable portion of the Socialists who left with them. Shortly before World War II, fighting a last ditch battle to keep America out of the war, Thomas cooperated with the America First movement, which he detested, but refused to cooperate with the Communists (then opposed to entering the war because the Stalin-Hitler pact was in effect). To a Social Gospel minister from Brooklyn who urged that after all the Communists agreed with him on peace, Thomas replied: "The trouble is that you can never be sure Communists are for peace . . . very likely there will come a day when Hitler and Stalin fall out and, if that issue comes to war, the Communists would want us to do everything possible for Stalin." There was no difference between Communism and fascism, Thomas asserted.[8]

The lessons learned before the war held up during its aftermath. When in 1950 the first Stockholm Peace Campaign was launched through the Soviet's international front, the World Peace Council, the Fellowship of Reconciliation warned: "Communist-inspired 'peace campaigns' are not genuine" and lead "to building up the Communist party rather than pacifism or peace."[9]

But if Communism was rejected by peace organizations, the way was paved for a renewal of the relationship by the continual attrition of opposition on the part of even pacifist organizations toward violence. The career of the most influential of all American pacifists, A.J. Muste, reflects the problems endemic to American pacifism. Starting as a minister in the Dutch Reformed Church, Muste became a Quaker and a pacifist during World War I, joining the newly organized Fellowship of Reconciliation. After the war, he became a labor organizer and in 1921 took over the direction of Brookwood Labor College, which the Fellowship had helped to found in 1918. Muste's radical sympathies, which put him at odds with the American labor movement the College served, strained and then overwhelmed his pacifism. He became general secretary of the American Workers Party which merged in 1935 with the Communist League of America, the "Cannonite" faction expelled from the U.S. Communist Party as "Trotskyite" in 1928. In an essay written in 1962, Muste tried to account for this period in his life. The Left, said Muste, "had the vision, the dream, of a classless and warless world . . . This was a strong factor in making me feel that here, in a sense, was the true church."[10] But after only two years as a self-described "Trotskyist Marxist-Leninist," Muste became disillusioned with violence and returned to pacifism and the Fellowship in 1937.

The ferment left its mark. Muste developed a radical conception of pacifism which he outlined in his 1928 essay, "Pacifism and Class War." The definition of violence was expanded, as Muste declared that "the basic fact is that the economic, social, political order in which we live was built up largely by violence, is now being extended by violence and is maintained only by violence." He insisted that the violence of the status quo comprised 90% of violence and there was something "ludicrous" in the fact that public concern centered about the 10% of violence used by rebels against repression. Not only did Muste minimize the importance of revolutionary violence, but he argued it was improper even to counsel nonviolence so long as we benefit from the existing "violent" order.[11] At the time of the Vietnam War, Muste's influence was important in the shift toward acceptance of cooperation with Communists. He eased the fears of pacifists by suggesting that they were equally compromised by cooperating with those who "in practice are aligned with Western nations and are less sensitive to factors of violence, suppression and evil in American and Western culture than in the non-Western world."[12]

Muste's doctrines were profoundly influential in shaping a new conception of the role of pacifists. Conscientious objectors, particularly those who chose prison rather than the forms of alternative service offered by the government during World War II, emerged with a new conception of nonviolent tactics as the way "to shake the present order to its foundations." Prison-camp graduate George Houser, later to become head of the American Committee on Africa, an institute which supported a host of violent liberation movements on that continent, told a meeting of the Fellowship of Reconciliation's national council that his group would "like to see a really revolutionary resistance program developed soon."[13] And while the Fellowship resisted, the War Resisters League (a non-religiously based pacifist group that developed out of the Fellowship in 1923) resolved in 1947 to work for "political, economic and social revolution by non-violent means."[14]

Once pacifists had accepted a broadened definition of violence according to which governments, including democratic governments, were defined as "violent" because they implicitly had the sanctions of violence behind them, both violence and nonviolence lost any meaning. According to David McReynolds, a War Resisters League staffer, non-violence is "most deeply violated" when it is confined to the area where "the state kills people;" poor housing, racism, sexism, are equally "violent," and the violence of unemployment is as real "as napalm falling on Vietnam."[15] An article in the Fellowship's magazine claims that "where a woman is denied equal pay for equal work . . . it is an example of violence."[16] War Resisters League President Norma Becker believes that all our institutions must be overturned "because unless these institutions are eradicated," it doesn't seem likely that we "will be in a position to really practice non-violence."[17]

Catholic pacifists, smaller in number than their Protestant counterparts, have been equally influenced by these modes of thought. Catholic pacifist Gordon Zahn notes that liberation theology has restored respectability among pacifists to the doctrine of "just war" and worse still, has reduced the traditional criteria for "just war" to only two, just cause and right intention. This, says Zahn "has opened the way to virtually uncritical support not only for wars of national liberation but for the full range of guerilla tactics, not excluding indiscriminate acts of terrorism." Zahn attended a conference of the Catholic pacifist organization Pax Christi in Spain where the delegates, many of whom were caught up in the struggle for Catalonian "liberation" from "the repressive government at Madrid," refused to pass a resolution that condemned violence "from any quarter" because they feared it could be taken as an implicit criticism of the violent section of the Catalonian independence movement.[18]

Given what has happened in traditional pacifist organizations, there can be little surprise that the organizations that have sprung up since World War II to promote peace, none of which are formally pacifist, have also come to identify with violent movements. The most important to develop prior to the Vietnam War were SANE in 1957 and Women Strike for Peace in 1961, both of which arose to protest nuclear atmospheric testing. (Physicians for Social Responsibility, the experts in disaster portraits, first as a result of nuclear energy, then of bomb explosions, also dates to 1961, but became moribund until pediatrician Helen Caldicott, a vivid, intense woman, whom her critics describe as wholly reckless with facts, assumed the presidency in 1979.) The Vietnam War produced a series of organizations, the most lasting of which has been Clergy and Laity Concerned about the Vietnam War (CALC). After the war was over, it dropped the last four words in its title. CALC is now just "Concerned," chiefly about the evils of the American Empire. Thus the keynote speaker at CALC's 1982 National Assembly, Rev. James Lawson, declared: "What seems very clear is that the number one enemy of peace and justice in the world today is the United States."[19]

The emptying of meaning of "violence" and the focus of hostility upon the United States, as the "number one enemy of peace and justice," has permitted today's peace movement to become a vehicle for Soviet purposes. The Soviets have moreover been able to capitalize on the willingness for the last decade of peace organizations to work with Soviet front organizations. (During the Vietnam War years representatives of peace organizations repeatedly attended Soviet-organized assemblies for peace in Eastern Europe.) U.S. peace organizations may not set out deliberately to forward a Soviet agenda. But disarmament movements, in so far as they are influential, by their very nature, weaken Western defense and inhibit the ability and willingness of Western countries to project their forces beyond their borders. If, for whatever reason, they focus exclusively on Western disarmament and discount the existence of external threats, if they, in addition, serve as apologists for aggressive actions by the Soviet Union, they become of great service to the Soviet Union, helping it to project an image as the major force for peace in the world.

While any reference to Soviet influence on the U.S. peace movement arouses storms of indignation not only from the peace movement but from major networks and newspapers, it stands to reason the Soviets would see peace organizations as objects of encouragement and direct manipulation. There is ample evidence concerning the role of the Soviets in the European peace movement, and a number of Soviet agents have been expelled for funding peace groups. Holland has served as the testing ground in the Soviet effort since 1977. KGB agent Vadim Leonov, who maintained close links with the Dutch peace movement, passing himself off as a Tass correspondent, was expelled by the Dutch in April 1981, after he boasted in a drunken bout to a Dutch counterintelligence source: "If Moscow decides that 50,000 demonstrators must take to the streets in the Netherlands, then they take to the streets . . . A message through my channels is sufficient."[20] Vladimir Bukovsky, the Soviet dissenter who spent twelve years in the Gulag, has recounted how the World Parliament of the Peoples for Peace, convened by the World Peace Council in Bulgaria, in September 1980, called for mass demonstrations in European capitals in October 1981 in association with "UN Disarmament Week." Those demonstrations occurred and Bukovsky asks: "How on earth could the Soviets have known in 1980 about events that would take place at the end of 1981, unless they were running the whole show?"[21]

In the United States, as in Europe, Soviet efforts at manipulation have been channeled in good part through the World Peace Council. Expelled from France in 1951 and from Austria in 1957, the WPC's headquarters are now in Helsinki, Finland's dependence on the Soviet Union assuring it a permanent harbor. It should be stressed that the WPC is the most transparent of fronts, and the "peace" in its title the purest Orwellian doublethink. In 1975 it gave its highest award, the Frederic Joliot Curie Gold Medal for Peace, to Yassir Arafat. That same year it gave a lesser peace award to Lolita Lebrun as an "outstanding Puerto Rican freedom fighter . . . who has been in U.S. jails for the last 20 years."[22] (Lebrun, now free, was one of four Puerto Rican terrorists who opened fire on the U.S. House of Representatives from the visitors gallery during the Truman administration.) Another year the Joliot Curie Gold Medal for Peace was awarded to Leonid Brezhnev. The tribute to him accompanying the award was revealing of the WPC's perspective. In the words of the WPC's President Romesh Chandra:

> "The hundred of millions who stand for peace . . . see in this award a symbolic way to express their affection for Comrade Brezhnev, for the glorious Communist Party of the Soviet Union and for the entire Soviet people their gratitude for their brilliant leadership in the work for the implementation of the Soviet Peace Programme and for the carrying out of Soviet initiatives on all the urgent international issues of the day."[23]

In 1975, a nine member delegation from the WPC came to the

United States to publicize the WPC's Second Stockholm Peace Petition. The reaction of U.S. peace organizations to the WPC visit was significant. None of the peace organizations decried the delegation as a fraud and Women Strike for Peace used its standing to give the delegation credibility among American political and business leaders who knew nothing about it. Edith Villastrago, director of the Women Strike for Peace Washington office, coordinated the delegation's visit in the capitol. As a result, it was able to meet with 20 members of Congress (several of them hosted a luncheon for the delegation) and was welcomed at the Methodist Church Center by leading clergymen. The delegation was also the guest of the Institute for Policy Studies. Thanks to preparations by various peace activists and church groups, in the fifteen cities it visited the delegation met with local and state officials, spoke at church meetings, campuses, even high schools. (At University High School in Milwaukee the delegation reported that following their presentation many students asked if they could join the World Peace Council). Delegation members appeared on television and met with editorial boards of major daily newspapers. In New York City Ambassador Angier Biddle Duke, on behalf of then mayor Abraham Beame, presented delegation members with Bicentennial Medals. In both Los Angeles and Milwaukee the delegation accepted mayoral proclamations in its honor. In Detroit the delegation won a sheriff's escort and keys to the city. It also accepted a "Spirit of Detroit Award" given to the WPC for its "substantial effort to achieve peace." In South Bend, Indiana, the delegation received keys to the city and a luncheon in its honor was given by the Chamber of Commerce! In each community, and the delegation also went to Seattle, Cleveland and San Francisco, the group left behind what it described as an "ongoing WPC committee." Local Peace Councils already existed in Los Angeles and Chicago. The delegation's report mentioned that the Chicago Peace Council would continue "as always to maintain contact with the WPC."[24]

In 1978, the WPC actually held a small conference in Washington, sponsored, among others, by Kay Camp, then President of the Women's International League for Peace and Freedom, and Edith Villastrago of Women Strike for Peace. The conference endorsed American Indian claims against the U.S. and Puerto Rican independence and opposed U.S. building "weapons of mass destruction." WPC President Romesh Chandra said the presence of the WPC group in the United States, when prior to the McGovern amendment it would have been barred from entering the country, "proves that we can win."[25]

The seeds planted by the 1975 delegation in the form of WPC committees came to fruition in 1979 with the establishment of the United States Peace Council. Not surprisingly the Communist *Daily World* hailed its advent, saying the organization "may mean the difference between life and death for humanity." The peripatetic Romesh Chandra showed up for the first national conference, echoing in his speech the WPC line that liberation struggles are the peace movements of their people. In Chandra's words:

> "People ask me, 'You are a peace movement. Why do you support the armed struggles in Nicaragua, Palestine, Vietnam?' And I reply, 'The armed struggle in these countries *is* the peace movement . . ."[26]

U.S. Peace Council executive director Michael Myerson, a long time official of the U.S. Communist Party, announced at the conference that "the main threat to world peace is the U.S. military industrial machine." Congressman John Conyers, Democrat of Michigan, told the assembled participants: "It's people like you who should be members of Congress" and "From you I can see the future of America."[27]

The resolutions passed by the conference, wherever possible, packaged Soviet foreign policy objectives in such a way as to appeal to segments of American society. It appealed to the anti-nuclear energy movement by linking the need to shut down nuclear plants with "the recognition that nuclear arms production is even more dangerous and needs to be shut down also." It appealed to distinctive American preoccupations by emphasizing the threat "the draft poses to human rights." It resolved not only to work closely with existing anti-draft registration organizations but to form a G.I. and Veterans Committee "to organize the thirty million American veterans and two million G.I.s to fight for peace."

On the whole, however, the conference simply passed resolutions conforming to major Soviet objectives: support for Third World liberation movements and U.S. disarmament. It passed a resolution "In Solidarity with the Arab People of Palestine and their Central Issue: Palestine" which condemned the Camp David accords as "a cornerstone of a new U.S. offensive in the Middle East." Another resolution called for withdrawal of U.S. bases from the Philippines and an end to all aid to that country. On the other hand, resolutions called for U.S. aid to Vietnam, Laos and Kampuchea. Other resolutions urged a cut back in U.S. defense expenditures and "coalitions of peace groups." Resolutions were passed opposed to all new U.S. weapons systems.

The U.S. Peace Council established a "Peace Education Foundation" which received tax exempt status from the IRS. The Fund is headed by Abe Feinglass, a World Peace Council Presidium member and secretary-treasurer of the Amalgamated Meatcutters Union. The Fund said that it planned to explore the effects of the military budget on blacks and other minorities. The Communist Party, of course, has traditionally tried to exploit and exacerbate dissatisfactions among minority groups. At its second national conference in 1981, the U.S. Peace Council established a youth caucus, designed to reach out to junior high and high school youth with anti-draft and anti-war themes and announced development of a curriculum guide for courses on peace in public schools.

That same year the U.S. Peace Council welcomed yet another nine member delegation of the World Peace Council, which came to inspect the local peace councils it had established. Touring 15 cities this time, the delegation added to what was becoming the World Peace Council's impressive collection of keys to the city and city council proclamations.[28]

Even the symbol at the top of U.S. Peace Council literature tells the story: it is a dove shaped into a clenched fist. The clenched fist is an essential feature of Communist iconography.

Not only have the established peace organizations failed to denounce the U.S. Peace Council as a transparent effort to channel the desire for peace to serve Soviet purposes, but they have become actively involved with it. Prior to its founding conference the U.S. Peace Council issued a "Call," to help organize a peace majority in this country. Those who gave their names as sponsors of this Call in effect endorsed the U.S. Peace Council as a bona fide organization seeking peace. Yet the sponsors included the president of the Women's International League for Peace and Freedom, the executive director of SANE, the disarmament coordinator of the American Friends Service Committee, the director of the Washington Office of Women Strike for Peace (who had coordinated the 1975 WPC visit) and a leader of Clergy and Laity Concerned. For many, more than sponsorship was involved. At the U.S. Peace Council's founding conference the executive director of SANE, the disarmament director of the AFSC, an official of the Women's International League for Peace and Freedom and a representative of Clergy and Laity Concerned conducted workshops.[29] When the U.S. Peace Council took out a full page ad in the *New York Times* in

June 1979 to attack Joan Baez and others who had criticized human rights violations in Vietnam (the U.S. Peace Council ad countered that "Vietnam now enjoys human rights as it has never known in history"), it was signed, not only by assorted Communists and far leftists, but by the President and vice-President of Women's International League for Peace and Freedom and by several leaders of Clergy and Laity Concerned.

Two pacifist organizations were conspicuous by the absence of any of their representatives as sponsors of the U.S. Peace Council "Call"—the Fellowship for Reconciliation and the War Resisters League. The League did send an observer to the 1979 U.S. Peace Council conference who was sufficiently disturbed by the proceedings—she noted that Communist Party literature was "everywhere"—that she prepared a critical statement that she tried to read to those assembled. She was told by the organizers that there was "no time."[30]

Despite the initial reservations of these two groups (which have since overcome them), the U.S. Peace Council has become, on the whole, an accepted member of the "Peace Club." So has the Mobilization for Survival, which also intertwines Communist and peace organizations in its membership. Those directing the Mobilization's activities wear a variety of hats. Head of the Labor Taskforce has been Gil Green, a member of the U.S. Communist Party's central committee, whose major responsibility within the party has been coordinating relations with peace organizations. Head of the Mobilization's International Task Force has been Terry Provance, who also headed the AFSC's Disarmament Task Force and was listed by the World Peace Council as an elected U.S. member both for the 1977-1980 and the 1980-1983 term.[31]

The birth and growing acceptance of the U.S. Peace Council along with the fellow-travelling of the Mobilization for Survival coalition gives the Soviets an opportunity for direct input into the peace movement. The Mobilization for Survival carried primary responsibility for organizing the demonstrations associated with the Second UN Special Session on Disarmament until the success of the freeze campaign promised the demonstration a mammoth size beyond the capabilities of any single organization. A "June 12 Rally Committee" took over, which turned out to be just as susceptible to manipulation. Journalist Ronald Radosh, despite his sympathy with the peace movement, has described in *The New Republic* the way the rally was manipulated:

"The U.S.P.C. had one seat on its executive committee [the June 12 Rally Committee] and four other seats were held by Communists or fellow-travellers who officially represented their unions but were backed for admission by the U.S.P.C. Yet the committee refused a seat to the Democratic Socialists of America, on the ground that they are a "political grouping." The U.S.P.C. was able to get the committee—whose members were keen on unity—to tone down the official rally call so that it was not equally addressed to both the United States and the Soviet Union. In its own literature, the U.S. Peace Council described June 12 as a day in which Americans would be demanding action to 'reduce *our* arsenals.' (My emphasis)."[32]

By far the most important factor in facilitating the transformation of the peace organizations into channels that, for all practical purposes, serve Soviet interests, has been a common view of the world all the peace groups discussed here have come to share: the vision of the United States as the greatest threat to world peace and the chief agent of militarism, imperialism, racism, and economic exploitation.

There is little gap between the peace movement's prescription and that of the Soviet Union on what needs to be done to create a more just global society. The World Peace Council's publications also inveigh against the evils of imperialism, militarism, sexism, racism, all of which they too define as the peculiar property of the United States and its "puppets." It is difficult to distinguish between the foreign policy the WPC, under Soviet guidance, would like the United States to pursue, and the policy the peace organizations would like it to pursue. For example, it is hard to see what the World Peace Council would find to criticize in the Women's International League for Peace and Freedom's 1980 resolution on Puerto Rico: it called for the independence of Puerto Rico, saying that free elections were impossible because of the climate of fear created by the United States; called for U.S. indemnities to Puerto Rico; removal of bases and restoration of the land to its natural state. Given the identity of underlying views, it becomes difficult indeed for peace organizations to resist Soviet infiltration and manipulation—or even to recognize it.

The end result is an approach to peacemaking whose essence is the double standard. After the Soviet invasion of Afghanistan, the pacifist organizations, all of which make a strong point of their belief in resistance—non-violent resistance—to aggression, should have strongly supported United States responses that stopped short of violence, including the Olympic boycott and the grain embargo. In fact, they sharply opposed any U.S. efforts to counter the Soviet action. (The same thing happened after the repression of Solidarity in Poland. WILPF passed a statement attacking Reagan's "political and economic sanctions" and called on him "to restore ties with Poland and the Soviet Union to their previous levels.") Writing in WILPF's journal, international president Kay Camp, summed up the organization's view of the invasion of Afghanistan: "While military intervention is always regrettable, the Soviet interest in having close relations with a neighboring country with which it shares a 2000 mile border is understandable."[33]

The peace organizations are concerned almost exclusively with U.S. disarmament. David McReynolds of the War Resisters League says frankly that the only "politically realistic" approach is bold unilateral initiatives and the League has in fact circulated a statement calling for unilateral nuclear disarmament. The League claims because the U.S. has overwhelming military superiority over the Soviet Union, the organization's focus "continues to be on the U.S. military preparations, on the economic forces that profit from militarism and on the violation of human rights in countries controlled by the U.S." The Riverside Church Disarmament Program minimizes the Soviet "threat" which its publications customarily put in quotation marks. It relies heavily on publications and speakers from the Institute for Policy Studies, whose attacks on American institutions were described in the previous chapter. This is scarcely surprising since the program is headed by Cora Weiss, daughter of Samuel Rubin, whose Samuel Rubin Foundation, directed by Cora and her husband Peter Weiss, has long served as the major funder of IPS.

What has enabled a handful of small fringe groups, deeply hostile to American institutions, to create a genuine mass movement? A number of factors contributed to making the public receptive to a peace crusade. President Reagan's call for increased defense expenditures and the warnings of Soviet superiority in a number of crucial areas were a shock to many grown comfortable with the idea of detente and arms spending as a reduced proportion of the budget in the 1970s. Contagion from the European disarmament movement played a role. There the SS20s, as General Andrew Goodpaster has noted, have proved themselves an enormously effective weapon, for without requiring a single Soviet loss, they have terrorized Europe, plunged NATO into crisis, and led Western churchmen and others to plead for further weakness.[34]

The specific freeze proposal, which seems to have been hit upon almost accidentally, proved enormously attractive. Peace "insider" Peter Pringle reported in *The New Republic* that the freeze had its origin in a meeting called by the American Friends Service Committee in the summer of 1979. SALT II seemed doomed and the group, which included Richard Barnet of the Institute for Policy Studies, decided a totally new approach was in order: instead of arguing about numbers, why not leave them where they were? The freeze proposal was then formulated by Randall Forsberg, who had been active in the Women's International League for Peace and Freedom and had started her own think tank in Massachusetts, the Institute for Defense and Disarmament Studies.[35] The genius of the freeze proposal turned out to be its simplicity. It appealed to the fears everyone shares of nuclear war and unlike SALT II, which was incomprehensible to all but the specialist, presented a measure that the man in the street felt he could understand. Moreover, it sounded evenhanded for it called upon the United States and the Soviet Union to adopt a *mutual* freeze. The public did not consider that the freeze would not free it from the nuclear sword of Damocles, but rather exacerbate the danger, leaving U.S. delivery systems, now close to obsolescence, to face relatively new Soviet systems.

The growth of utopianism generally, in the environmental movement, the churches and the public interest movement, provided the new movement with an immediate base of converts. The churches were early targets. The Mobilization for Survival, for example, set up a Religious Task Force to mobilize church and synagogue-goers, providing advice for its secularist cadres on how to penetrate churches without having membership in them. Peace groups also circulated an "Abolitionist Covenant" in which the individual affirmed his religious commitment to live without nuclear weapons and called for a freeze as a first step. Twenty denominations, as well as the umbrella National Council of Churches, had endorsed the freeze by 1983 and the Presbyterian Church, the United Church of Christ, the Disciples of Christ, the United Methodist Church and the Episcopalian Church all voted to make "peace" their priority program. There was no mistaking the unilateralist thrust of church programs. The United Church of Christ called for a "unilateral initiative by the United States." The resource list, published by the Episcopal Church on the arms race, described 37 organizations, of which only two did not promote unilateral disarmament. (Anyone who lived through the 1930s would be hard put to avoid a sense of deja vu. *The World Tomorrow,* the journal of the Fellowship of Reconciliation in the prewar period, boasted in 1934, that "unqualified repudiation of war is now becoming commonplace in religious conferences."[36])

An even greater achievement for the peace movement was its success in drawing in the Catholic hierarchy. Early in 1982, 29 Catholic bishops signed a statement that "even to possess [nuclear weapons] is wrong." While the final draft of the pastoral letter prepared for the National Conference of Catholic Bishops did away with the more far reaching elements of the first two drafts (including categorical rejection of the first use of nuclear arms) and was thus seen by critics of the bishops' new activism as "a victory," it remains true that the Catholic hierarchy, once stalwart supporters of U.S. defense policy, feel increasingly alienated from that policy and are likely to become targets of a whole series of utopian campaigns.

Major environmental organizations were drawn in. The Physicians for Social Responsibility's Helen Caldicott urged the Sierra Club to join in, on the ground that nuclear war would destroy mammals, birds and the ozone layer. Caldicott suggested this was really her own primary concern. She said she had "come to terms with my own death," but "I just worship this earth . . . So I really care immensely if this earth is to be destroyed. And that's where the Sierra Club comes in."[37] The Sierra Club, whose ranks were swollen to 300,000 members in 1982, a 44% increase over a year earlier, accepted the challenge and appointed a standing committee on "The Environmental Impacts of Warfare." The Wilderness Society, Friends of the Earth, the Environmental Policy Center and Greenpeace all endorsed the freeze. Environmental groups saw new propaganda potentialities for their long-standing fight against nuclear power. The Environmental Policy Center began to calculate the "warhead equivalent" of commercial reactors. South Carolina's anti-nuclear energy Palmetto Alliance argued that "every time you flick a switch and it's nuclear generated electricity, you're helping to make a bomb." The Alliance noted happily that "people really respond to that."[38]

It was also important to the success of the freeze that it received Soviet encouragement, and that the Soviets made it seem likely they would accept a freeze offered by the United States. On February 23, 1981, Brezhnev, addressing the 26th Party Congress, called for a "moratorium" on the development and deployment of the new missiles the U.S. planned for Europe, and the Soviets then proposed the "freeze" be extended to intercontinental nuclear armaments. The International Secretariat of the Christian Peace Conference, which invariably echoes Soviet policy, meeting in Moscow, in January 1982, declared that "the principal task of the peace movement today is to support all efforts for a freeze on nuclear weapons as a first step toward disarmament."[39]

Peace activists in the United States had first hand experience of Soviet support for the movement. Journalist John Barron reports that Soviet KGB officers participated in the first national strategy conference of the American Nuclear Freeze Campaign in March 1981 (held less than a month after Brezhnev's own call for a "nuclear moratorium").[40] In August 1981, when the AFSC was trying to build momentum for the freeze, it staged a three day march in New England. En route, the marchers were addressed by Yuri Kapravlov, formally a counselor at the Soviet Embassy in Washington, but according to Barron, actually a KGB officer. He said that the Soviet Union had "a very favorable view of the idea of a weapons freeze."[41]

Soviet-influenced organizations have been working for the freeze. U.S. Peace Council Chairman Michael Myerson signed the initial "call" for the freeze and the U.S. Peace Council collected signatures for it. The U.S. Communist Party collected signatures for petitions asking elected officials to endorse the peace campaign, concentrating on Connecticut and other New England states.[42] Members of the World Peace Council who also served in state legislatures worked for the freeze. WPC member Irving Stolberg, now speaker of the Connecticut State Assembly, coordinated the campaign that passed the freeze proposal in the Connecticut legislature[43] and Massachusetts state legislator Mel King worked for its successful passage in his state.

Finally, the media showed the same enthusiasm for the peace crusade as they did earlier for the environmental movement and the public interest movement. While they had paid no attention to the freeze movement for the first year and a half, when it was promoted solely by the hard-core peace organizations, once the movement had picked up momentum, the media rarely if ever referred to its origins, treating it as the spontaneous outpouring of Middle America. The *Reader's Digest* and the *Wall Street Journal,* of all the media serving a mass public, were the only ones to devote any attention to the anti-American wellsprings of the freeze, and even the *Digest* was much more interested in the issue of Soviet infiltration than in the character of the *American* groups involved in the freeze.

Does the Soviet Union in fact want a freeze? Despite the advantages that would accrue to it, the answer is probably no, not if it is verifiable, i.e. with on-site inspection. John Barron has summed up concisely the advantages a freeze offers the Soviets. It would

> "instantly achieve the fundamental Soviet objective of aborting American production of the Enhanced Radiation Warhead, the MX, Pershing II and cruise missiles, and new manned bomber. It would leave Western Europe vulnerable to relentlessly expanding Communist forces—now including an astonishing 42,500 tanks and the 333 deadly SS-20 missiles. It would leave the United States with a fleet of old, obsolete strategic bombers, unlikely to penetrate Soviet air defenses, and with an aging force of fixed land-based missiles, vulnerable to a first strike by great new Soviet missiles."[44]

However, as Michael Novak has noted, a "verifiable" freeze (called for in the freeze proposal) that included nuclear research and development, as freeze proponents insist it should, would involve a massive regimen of verification beyond anything remotely sustainable at present.[45] Of course the Soviets would welcome a freeze without on-site inspection. They would enjoy the option of cheating, while confident that the U.S. would enjoy no such option, for publicity would almost certainly attend any effort on the part of the United States to do so, producing intolerable political risks to any administration.

From the Soviet point of view, a situation in which there is massive public agitation for a freeze in the United States is far better than an actual freeze. Equally desirable would be the mutual acceptance, in principle, of a freeze followed by prolonged negotiations over the content (and method of verification) of a freeze, during which time the United States would be restrained by public opinion from deploying new weapons systems or even increasing defense expenditures while the Soviet Union, wholly unconstrained, methodically continued to build up its arsenal.

There is small cause for surprise that then Secretary of State Haig said of the freeze when it first gained ground in public opinion: "It is not only bad defense and security policy, it is bad arms control policy as well." It is bad security policy because the U.S. land-based missile force would be frozen in its present vulnerability, ensuring the Soviet Union an enormous strategic advantage in any future negotiations. A freeze in Europe, targeted by SS-20s, would ensure NATO's neutralization, eventually giving the Soviet Union the kind of dominant influence it now exerts over Finland. As for the impact of a freeze on arms control negotiations, it would remove from the Soviets any incentive to negotiate arms *reductions*. Once the U.S. had unilaterally foregone all modernization programs, its negotiators would lose all leverage, and be left to rely on a Soviet spirit of generosity that has never before been revealed.

Such problems are of no interest to the peace organizations. There is no better evidence of their fraudulence than their total indifference to violations of existing treaty obligations by the Soviet Union. A genuine peace movement would be particularly concerned with insisting upon the inviolability of existing treaties, for it is upon the good faith of treaty participants that disarmament ultimately depends. The Soviets have signed treaties banning the use of bio-chemical weapons, and yet are using them in Afghanistan and providing for their use by Vietnam in Laos and Cambodia. If the peace organizations mention "yellow rain" at all, it is to dismiss the charges as unproven. The peace groups are interested only in obtaining signatures on treaties—and then monitoring compliance by the *United States*.

There is another way in which the peace groups demonstrate dishonesty. NATO has relied upon nuclear deterrence because it is comparatively cheap. The alternative is a massive buildup of conventional forces that would enable European countries to stave off a Soviet attack without resort to nuclear weapons. This would involve a far greater expenditure of funds by both Europe and the United States, as well as this country's abandoning the all-volunteer army in favor of a draft. But although the non-pacifist sector of the peace movement should thus be in the forefront in demanding increased expenditures for conventional forces, nothing could be further from their minds. In a typical statement Richard Barnet of the Institute for Policy Studies declares that "the alternative of a conventional arms buildup in the name of nuclear pacifism must be resisted."[46]

For the peace organizations, the freeze is merely a device to raise public fears and "consciousness' in order to enlist masses for further campaigns. Until convinced by its mobilizing capacity, the War Resisters League actually opposed the freeze on the grounds that it failed to make connections to "anti-racist, anti-sexist and a whole variety of other oppressed peoples' struggles."[47] Already activists are moving further down the road. Looking "Beyond the Freeze," Sidney Lens, in *The Nation,* complains that most freeze advocates, especially in Congress, believe we need "some" nuclear weapons. The peace activist cadres have moved to "abolition" calling for an "agenda for non-collaboration" with the U.S. government. (Marcus Raskin of the Institute for Policy Studies is one of this group of self-styled "new abolitionists.")[48]

The next major campaign envisaged by the peace groups is for "conversion" from military to civilian production. Increasingly, conversion is also seen by the other utopians as a valuable shortcut toward destroying the capitalist system. A typical blueprint is provided by Derek Shearer, who assumed that 4/5 of the military budget is unnecessary. Since conversion on that scale will cause severe economic dislocation, the government must step in. Its programs, according to Shearer, must "be based on the notions of community-controlled economic development and publicly owned production authorities at the state, regional and national levels." On no account should plants be turned over to private enterprise. Shearer clearly does not even want to see existing private corporations compensated, suggesting that costs "would be minimized by letting the firm go into bankruptcy." The new plants would be worker-run, with naval shipyards, for example, producing fishing vessels for fishermen's cooperatives.[49] Utopian labor leader William Winpisinger's assistant has declared that "conversion is a strategy for social change" predicated on the formation of a serious alliance between peace, environmental, religious, community and labor activists.[50] In other words, it is to be a collective project of the utopians.

In the issue of peace, the utopians have finally found the kind of issue for which they had earlier unsuccessfully searched. Toxic wastes, air pollution, hazardous chemicals, nuclear energy have each been presented as signifying "the end of the road" for mankind, but none of these carry a fraction of the plausibility of nuclear war as an authentic end of the road. Themes that Soviet fronts like the World Peace Council and the Christian Peace Conference have emphasized for years, that the only alternative to peace (as defined by these organizations, of course) is annihilation, have swept through the peace movement. Dramatic rhetoric heightens the sense of imminent disaster. An article in *Fellowship* begins: "The following interview took place at the end of time."[51] (That meant it was made shortly before publication.) A Riverside Church Disarmament Conference in November 1981 warned: "We're on the brink of extinction." In the past, pacifist movements always faced the problem of convincing the public that pacifism was a viable way to obtain national security. Even the moral case was ambiguous, for it meant abstention from force when an aggressor ravished a peaceful country. But now, the alternative is presented as being between nuclear disarmament and nuclear holocaust. This solves both the moral and security problem of pacifism, for it is absurd to talk of security or morality in the face of a situation in which there are no survivors.

As the utopians see it, once the Soviet Union perceives a United States that is disarmed, anarchist, communal, egalitarian and worker-run, its fears will be calmed and it will at last feel secure. They are sure—almost sure—that will be the result. Just in case they are wrong, they have an answer. They call it transarmament, which means nonviolent resistance and noncooperation with foreign invaders. They assure us it will make effective occupation of this country "impossible." Indeed, an article in a War Resisters League journal suggests that it is time for the United States to start thinking about the nonviolent defense of the country.[52]

REFERENCES

1. *New York Times,* March 6, 1982.
2. "An Introduction to Nonviolence," *Fellowship,* March/April 1980, p. 4.
3. Questions about American intervention and increased arms shipments led the Fellowship of Reconciliation to undertake a wide-ranging tour of the Middle East this past summer. About the tour . . . undated document, approx. Nov. 1975.
4. *Pax et Libertas,* December 1981, p. 8.
5. Rael Jean Isaac, "The Seduction of the Quakers," *Midstream,* November 1979, p. 27.
6. Albert Hassler, "60 Years," *Fellowship,* December 1975, p. 17.
7. Paul Marx, "The Peace Movement: Alive but not Well," *Christian Century,* December 3, 1975, p. 1105.
8. Bernard K. Johnpoll, *Pacifists' Progress: Norman Thomas and the Decline of American Socialism,* Chicago: Quadrangle Books, 1970, pp. 227, 236.
9. Lawrence S. Wittner, *Rebels Against War: The American Peace Movement 1941-60,* New York: Columbia University Press, 1969, p. 205.
10. A.J. Muste, "Saints for this Age," in Nat Hentoff, ed., *The Essays of A. J. Muste,* New York: Clarion Books, Simon and Schuster, 1970, p. 423.
11. "Pacifism and Class War," in Ibid., pp. 179-81.
12. "Crisis in the World and In the Peace Movement," in Ibid., p. 477.
13. Lawrence S. Wittner, op. cit., p. 152.
14. Ibid., p. 153.
15. David McReynolds, "Analysis of the Continental Walk," sent out by War Resisters League with letter dated November 1976; see also *WRL News,* November-December 1975.
16. "An Introduction to Nonviolence," op. cit., p. 5.
17. *WRL News,* January-February, 1976.

18. Gordon Zahn, "The Bondage of Liberation: A Pacifist Reflection," *Worldview*, March, 1977, p. 21.
19. *CALC Report*, September 1982.
20. John Barron, "The KGB's Magical War for 'Peace'" *Reader's Digest*, October 1982, p. 232.
21. Vladimir Bukovsky, "The Soviet Role in the Peace Movement," in *The Apocalyptic Premise*, Ernest Lefever and E. Stephen Hunt, eds., Ethics and Public Policy Center, Washington, D.C. 1982, p. 188.
22. *Peace Courier*, publication of the World Peace Council, June/July 1975, p. 3.
23. "World Peace Council Highest Award to Leonid Ilyich Brezhnev," Information Centre of World Peace Council, Helsinki, Finland, p. 10.
24. "World Peace Council Tours U.S.A." Information Centre of the World Peace Council, Helsinki, Finland, pp. 3-28.
25. John Rees, ed., *The Soviet Peace Offensive*, Western Goals Foundation, Alexandria, Virginia, 1982, p. 40.
26. *Information Digest*, November 23, 1979.
27. Ibid.
28. *Peace and Solidarity*, U.S. Peace Council, May-June 1981.
29. *Information Digest*, November 23, 1979.
30. *WRL News*, January-February 1980.
31. Since attention was drawn to his membership in articles in The *American Spectator, Wall Street Journal*, and *Reader's Digest*, Provance has claimed that in each case he was elected without his knowledge.
32. Ronald Radosh, "The 'Peace Council' and Peace," *The New Republic*, January 31, 1983, p. 16.
33. Kay Camp, "On Afghanistan and the New Cold War," *Peace and Freedom*, March 1980.
34. Quoted in Michael Novak, "Arms and the Church," *Commentary*, March 1982, p. 41.
35. Peter Pringle, "Disarming Proposals," *The New Republic*, April 21, 1982, p. 14.
36. Charles Chatfield, *For Peace and Justice: Pacifism in America 1914-41*, Knoxville: University of Tennessee Press, 1971, p. 125.
37. Robert Irwin, "Nuclear War as an Environmental Issue," *Sierra*, November/December, 1981, p. 74.
38. Mark Hertsgaard, "The Atomic Horsemen," *Mother Jones*, Feb./March 1982, p. 33.
39. Release of the CPC Information Department, Prague, Czechoslovakia, No. 295, January 26, 1982.
40. John Barron, "KGB's Magical War," op. cit., p. 236.
41. *Information Digest*, August 14, 1981.
42. *Review of the News*, December 8, 1982, pp. 45-6.
43. *Information Digest*, March 12, 1982.
44. John Barron, *KGB Today: The Hidden Hand*, New York, Reader's Digest Press, 1983, p. 278.
45. Michael Novak, "Moral Clarity in the Nuclear Age," *National Review*, April 1, 1983, p. 390.
46. Richard Barnet, "Ritual Dance of the Superpowers," *The Nation*, April 9, 1983,
47. Jon Saxton, "Nuclear Freeze Campaign: Disarmament in a Vacuum," WIN, December 1, 1981, p. 14.
48. Sidney Lens, "Beyond the Freeze: The Nuclear Abolitionists," *The Nation*, March 5, 1983, p. 269.

49. Derek Shearer, "Swords into Plowshares," *Working Papers*, Vol. I, No. 2 Summer 1973, pp. 4-10.
50. Dave McFadden, "Labor's Stake in Conversion," n.d.
51. James Douglass, "Living at the End of the World," *Fellowship*, January/February 1979, p. 3.
52. *WRL News*, March-April 1980, p. 4.

VIII

Reaching For Power

The coercive utopians make no secret that their aim is power. Even the title of Ralph Nader's 1981 conference, which brought together representatives of most utopian groups, minced no words: it was called "Taking Charge—the Next 10 Years." Their efforts are bent toward—and around—the ballot box at all levels of government. Heather Booth, head of the Midwest Academy, a training center for new generations of activists, says that the "power to help throw out unresponsive elected officials and put in our own people" is essential. She acknowledges "you may have to waffle and be less clear on certain positions" (an oblique acknowledgement that "the people" may not like the utopians' plans for them if fully apprised of what they are) but "you can't really enforce the gains you've won" outside of politics.[1] In the 1980 elections, the utopians made a bid for the Presidency as environmentalist leader Barry Commoner headed the Citizens Party. More seriously, they have made repeated efforts to take over the Democratic Party, in the 1960s through the so-called "New Politics" that was able to make George McGovern a Presidential candidate, and most recently through the now-defunct Progressive Alliance, which operated within the party under the guiding hand of the Institute for Policy Studies.

Major environmental organizations have shifted their emphasis from lobbying to electing public officials. Many have formed Political Action Committees and in an initial effort budgeted over $2 million for support of political candidates in the 1982 elections. A pioneering effort in New Jersey, in which the Sierra Club, Friends of the Earth, Environmental Action, the Solar Lobby and others pooled resources to create the New Jersey Environmental Voters Alliance, considered itself successful in that all of its candidates for Congress and state-level positions won in the primaries and six of eight won election.[2] The money spent in such campaigns has much more impact than similar sums expended by industry because the environmental organizations can field thousands of volunteers. The nuclear freeze, which turned out to have enormous fund-raising appeal, has also been used to channel votes to approved candidates.

At the state and local level the utopians have established vote-seeking organizations. The most important state-level organization aimed directly at political power is Tom Hayden's Campaign for Economic Democracy (CED) in California, which is closely tied to the network of radical institutes springing from the Institute for Policy Studies. Probably the best-publicized victory of a CED candidate was that of Ruth Yanatta Goldway, who became mayor of Santa Monica on the basis of a rent control campaign. Once the CED candidates controlled the city council, they not only passed the most restrictive rent control ordinance in the country, but turned the city council into a forum for debates on national issues. Dubbed locally "The People's Republic of Santa Monica," the city lost its utopian mayor in 1983 after an election campaign in which one of the main issues was whether Santa Monica should have its own foreign policy.[3] (Goldway is married to former IPS Fellow Derek Shearer who suggested that his fellow utopians use "economic democracy" rather than the "s" word—socialism.)

More frequently, utopians avoid the ballot box. The Conference on State and Local Public Policies, which began as a "social invention" of the Institute for Policy Studies, is a networking organization for New Left activists, both elected and appointed, in state and local governments. It offers them "alternative" programs, some of them explicitly borrowed from Eastern Europe and Cuba, all of which involve government taking control of some aspect of the economy—utilities, banks, housing, etc.

But the favorite method of the utopians, in staking out a claim to power, is to establish a community action organization. Typically, these consist of a small group of activists representing at most tiny minorities, who *claim* to represent majorities. Their techniques are based on those developed by the late Saul Alinsky, on whose book *Rules for Radicals,* all utopian community organizers base their campaigns.

In his book Alinsky took as an example the claim by a group called FIGHT to represent the Rochester ghetto, and on this basis to "negotiate" with the Kodak company, Rochester's chief employers. FIGHT had not organized the ghetto but this was irrelevant: what FIGHT wanted was not to organize the constituency it claimed to represent but to get its opponents to *act* as if it did. FIGHT's object was to make Kodak recognize it as the bargaining agent of the ghetto and from that point on, FIGHT would be able to present itself as the ghetto's representative on a host of issues with government, business etc. Community action organizations thus playact for high stakes: the media are the "audience" which can bestow the prize of recognition on the actors. By accepting the activists' claims to represent whatever group they announce they represent, the media can cause the target of the group sufficient annoyance or embarrassment that it seems politic to deal with the activists, thus ratifying the legitimacy of their claim and launching their organization on its career.

Not surprisingly, these groups have relatively few members. The best known groups, with clones in several states, are the "Fair Share" organizations—e.g. Massachusetts Fair Share, Oregon Fair Share—and ACORN, the Association of Community Organizations for Reform Now, which has branches in a number of states, particularly in the south and west. The number of staff in community action organizations often runs approximately one to a hundred claimed members, and as far as people really active in the organization is concerned, staff size is almost identical with the activists. Such community groups are, therefore, a type of public interest group, differing only from the ones discussed earlier in that they claim to be "grass roots" organizations. Like the Naderite groups, they are totally dominated by staff, necessarily so, since the "leaders" have no political base.

Their lack of real support does not prevent these organizations from making the most grandiose claims and demands. ACORN, which is wholly dominated by Wade Rathke, a one-time activist in SDS and organizer for the National Welfare Rights Organization, has come out with "A People's Platform" calling for the standard incongruous utopian mix of nationalization and "neighborhood control." Although it claims no more than 25,000 members in 18 states, ACORN has no hesitation is describing itself as the representative of the majority of this country's 200 million people. The People's Platform declares: "We are the majority, forged from all minorities. We are the masses of many, not the forces of few." And the platform goes on arrogantly: "Enough is enough. We will wait no longer for the crumbs at America's door. We will not be meek, but mighty. We will not starve on past promises, but feast on future dreams." The means to accomplish this, in the words of ACORN's own handbook, is "by grabbing hold of the reins of political power." In one typical (in this case unsuccessful) power grab, ACORN demanded that the Colorado Democratic party include ACORN members in the delegation to its 1980 national convention and put ACORN members on all state and national party committees.

Such grass roots participation as is secured, is won on a basis that has nothing to do with the real goals of the organization. ACORN, for example, goes into a community—"parachutes" into it in the phrase of one critic—and organizes on the basis of issues with local appeal that it knows it can win: putting in a new stop sign, cleaning up a vacant lot. Obtaining members on the basis of such activities and the promise of more like them, ACORN then uses its members for its own agenda. A disillusioned ACORN staffer said: "We were manipulating under the guise or organizing. I was pushing my own agenda on people and they didn't know what was being done to them."[4] In the pages of *Social Policy*, an ACORN official was frank: "Our interest is not in specific or immediate reforms; instead, our purpose in such participation is to build political power." Because of the lack of real popular support, community action groups like ACORN depend heavily upon government, foundation and church funding.

Training centers have grown up that specialize in giving people the skills to "seize" representative status, and with it political power, in a community. All are based on Alinsky's teachings. The Midwest Academy, headed by former SDS leaders Paul and Heather Booth, the Institute for Social Justice, which is run by ACORN, and the Saul Alinsky Training Institute, are the chief training centers for community organizers. Their training materials are permeated by a sense of the importance of "guerilla theatre" in the reach for power. The Midwest Academy's training manual offered the advice "Give people a 'taste of blood,' Push your opponents so hard you can see them squirm." Similarly, it said: "You may want to assign some people to be *'incit-*

ers' and move about to heat up the action getting people angrier and encouraging them to show their anger. You may at other times want some *'calmers'* to stand near people who may be disruptive to the focus of the action.'' Hundreds of VISTA volunteers were trained at government expense by the Midwest Academy.

While these are alternative schools, utopians have begun to develop activist training centers within established institutions. The City University of New York, for example, has opened a new law school under the leadership of Charles Halpern, whom we encountered earlier, and who had headed the public interest law firm, the Center for Law and Social Policy. Halpern has announced the new law school will downplay traditional admissions standards in favor of examining ''each applicant's life experiences.'' It will have a curriculum wholly different from that of traditional law schools and will produce lawyers who ''serve the public interest.'' The taxpayers will be creating these new cadres of activists, since tuition fees are lower than those of any other law school in the city, the state providing the subsidy.

Nader is a fertile source of devices by which the utopians can achieve control without bothering with the ballot box. He notes that majorities are not needed: 100,000 people in a Congressional district who acted as an energetic vanguard would be enough to ensure Congress conformed to ''the public interest.'' A superb tactician, Nader specializes in the political ju-jitsu that uses the resources of American institutions against themselves. For example, Nader succeeded in persuading the legislatures of several states to institute consumer utility boards. This Nader brainchild forces utilities to collect dues from customers which are then used to attack the utilities. Nader wants to expand the idea of the board to insurance, rental housing, supermarkets etc, with companies or landlords collecting money to be used against themselves. The problem with boards of this sort from the standpoint of the consumer is that, controlled by coercive utopians, they are concerned only with price, not with availability, whether of energy, housing or food. Indeed, the utopians *desire* scarcity, for scarcity is the key to their future ability to establish control, allocating resources according to their concept of what is good for the public.

Nader was also the pioneer in viewing ''public,'' i.e. utopian, control of the extensive financial holdings of mainline churches, public and private pension funds, state and local bank accounts and federal trust funds as a lever to transform the economic system. Peter Drucker, himself no utopian, noted that the employees of American business owned at least 25% of equity capital in the United States, more than enough for the control of U.S. business. At present most of the half trillion dollars in worker pension funds are invested in American industry by the private financial institutions that manage them. Any group that could obtain control simply of pension funds and invest them, in the words of utopian theorists Martin Carnoy and Derek Shearer, according "to a different set of priorities" would be able to work a revolution.

The long-range goal of the utopians is to invest all these funds in programs that provide what Carnoy and Shearer call "a social return on investment."[5] Thus far, most of the efforts of organizations like the Interfaith Center for Corporate Responsibility, have been lavished on "divestment." Using its control over some church investments, the ICCR puts pressure on companies that invest in South Africa, build nuclear power stations, manufacture nuclear or other weapons, or make infant formula or other products that are defined as undesirable to cease doing so. The positive side of divestment is to redirect investment to socially desirable targets so as to strengthen the alternative models that prefigure the new social order. Investment would go into community development corporations, producer and consumer cooperatives and worker-owned and managed enterprises. Pilot projects have been established. For example, the Institute for Community Economics channels money into "socially approved" investments, including producers of alternative energy, community land trusts and collective agricultural experiements. (The utopians want to convert argiculture into subsistence farming, reducing by law and penalties the size of agricultural holdings. Once again there will be minimal use of energy, much greater reliance being placed on "organic" fertilizer and human labor.)

Carnoy and Shearer note that the major problem is that there are insufficient numbers of appropriate investments to make large-scale capital shifts to them possible at present. In the meantime, the utopians channel as much money as possible into groups that raise consciousness of "oppression" among farmers and workers and seek to link them together. These efforts have been sufficiently successful for the *New York Times* to run a long report, in June 1983, on the new coalitions being forged under the aegis of groups like Rural America between financially troubled farmers and workers "against powerful big interests."[6] Rural America, whose avowed purpose is "to help people gain control over their lives and communities (i.e. help the utopians gain control in the name of "the people") publishes a journal by the same name which serves as a networking tool for activists engaged in consciousness-raising among farmers. Church hunger programs have become an important source of funds for such activist groups. (There is a certain irony in programs designed to alleviate hunger being used to overturn the most productive agricultural system in the world in favor of collectivized or subsistence farms which, judging by experience, can only increase the incidence of hunger.)

The utopians also see the crucial importance of taking control of technology. They would rid us of all those whose claims to authority are validated by supposed superior knowledge. The denial of the role of expert knowledge has reached its culmination in the crusade against nuclear energy and nuclear weapons where those expert in the arcane complexities of nuclear physics or weapons systems are dismissed in favor of the superior instincts of "the people." The utopians have their own "experts" but these often have little formal training. Amory Lovins never finished college. Hazel Henderson, a favored "economist," dropped out of school in England at 16 and says her knowledge of economics comes from her experience in jobs as a dress packer, hotel switchboard operator and airline ticket clerk as well as from "reading."

Technology, in any case, is something utopians do not like or understand. In a thoughful essay in *Reason* (some of the most telling criticism of the coercive utopians, interestingly, has come from this libertarian journal), Paul Ciotti says that in his experience, the utopians—he calls them "leftists"—"feel as if they can't cope with the physical universe." Ciotti writes:

> "I remember once, 10 years ago, sitting in a Berkeley park listening to an antiwar rally, the culmination of which was a speech by Tom Hayden. At one point the mike went dead, whereupon the moderator variously tapped on it, blew in it, and juggled the connections until suddenly the sound returned. 'The spirit of the people is greater than man's technology,' he announced, whereupon the crowd responded with loud cheers. That was the way people used to think in Berkeley (and many still do.) They saw technology as some kind of malevolent magic that can only be overcome by an even greater force—the mystical spirit of the people."[7]

The utopians have understood that the way to control technology is to control the people who create and understand and use technology.

Through political action, in which the utopians are as skillful as they are technologically inept, they can decide what technology is necessary and what is not, what is "appropriate," and what is not. The Institute for Policy Studies' Marcus Raskin proposes asking the technologists: "'Now that you (we) know that you can build it why should we?'" and holds out the hope that "technological ignorance and its liberating mechanisms may force children and adults to regain the basis of understanding with each other."[8]

The utopians realize that energy is the key to modern industrial society and that is why, as *Energy Daily* editor Llewelyn King points out, they want to put a "tourniquet" around centralized energy development.[9] Once they control energy the rest of the social machinery will come under their control. They have reassuring phrases for their planned takeover of technology. Derek Shearer, pioneer of "economic democracy," has come up with another euphemism: he calls it "democratic participation in technological development."[10] Hazel Henderson calls it developing technologies that are harmonious with the environmental system and that can liberate human potential.

Increasingly the utopians have looked for ways to band together so as to increase their political impact. Issues on which strong public emotion can be aroused are particularly welcomed as coalition-builders. The fight against the Nestle company for marketing infant formula in Third World Countries was especially useful in uniting the utopians and mobilizing a broad public behind them. To be sure, there had been abuses in promotion of formula among mothers who could not afford it and then did not prepare it properly, but the intent of the utopians in using the issue was not reform. The intent was stated by a coordinator for INFACT (the Infant Formula Action Coalition) at a meeting organized by Clergy and Laity Concerned on "The Human Costs of Corporate Power."

> "It's not just babies, it's not just multinational corporations, it's class conflict and class struggle . . . I think ultimately what we're trying to do is take an issue-specific focus campaign and move in conjunction with other issue-specific campaigns into a larger, very wide, very class-conscious campaign and reassert our power in the country, our power in this world."[11]

The Reagan electoral victory played a major role in fostering utopian alliances. It was greeted by the utopians as a well-nigh millenial disaster. The National Council of Churches, itself, recognized as unprecedented its 1981 resolution "The Remaking of America?" which outlined the major elements, domestic and foreign, of the Reagan policy and described the entire program as "contrary to the best insights of both Christian faith and the national creed." A Friends of the Earth lobbyist said the administration's energy and defense policies "may be the backdrop for President Reagan's plans to wage nuclear war during the 1980s." A fund-raising letter from Nader's Public Citizen said the organization had expected reforms to be dismantled but "didn't expect all out war against the American people" and warned of a return "into the Dark Ages."

In this climate Heather Booth of the Citizen/Labor Energy Coalition urged the utopians assembled at Nader's 1981 national conference "to mobilize in coalitions and alliances with other groups . . . to clarify the underlying element of the common target in the corporate domination of our lives through the corporations and their political handmaidens." Although the mainstream environmental organizations, in the words of a former executive of the Wilderness Society, had been wary "of snuggling too close to questionable (in their minds) leftist organizations,"[12] even the Audubon's President, Russell Peterson, spoke of the need "to maximize our grassroots clout and do it in partnership with environmental and citizens groups, labor organizations and church groups."[13]

The interaction and cooperation between different utopian groups provides them with new methods and new issues. One activist reported that the environmental movement had a major impact on the peace movement in giving it a new approach with the "local health angle" and a new weapon in the environmental impact statement.[14] Peace, environmental and church groups have joined forces to demand that the government prepare environmental impact statements for defense projects. For example, Environmental Action and Catholic Action, supported by 46 "citizen groups," filed suit against the government to compel an environmental impact statement on building of a storage area in Hawaii that they argued, *might* be used to store nuclear weapons.[15] Peace movements, with their hostility to American military preparations, see environmental impact statements as a means of obtaining information about defense installations that is otherwise held secret. Anne M. Gorsuch, head of the Environmental Protection Agency in the first two years of the Reagan administration, reported that she had seen the Soviet effort to capitalize on this peace movement effort. Describing a United Nations environmental meeting in Nairobi at which she represented the U.S., Gorsuch said:

> "At the Nairobi conference, the Soviet Union was very anxious to put nuclear disarmament studies into the environmental action plan. It was an effort to leverage their way into our national defense. You can imagine having U.N. 'environmental' people running around saying, 'Your government agreed to let us study disarmament and the first thing we want to do is see everything concerning your installations.'"[16]

Peace movement and environmental movements have borrowed issues from one another as well. Clergy and Laity Concerned, a peace organization, decided to link nuclear power to its anti-nuclear weapons program and to campaign for a moratorium on both. Friends of the Earth has become as much a peace as an environmental organization. At its international meeting in 1981 (Friends of the Earth has branches in 29 countries), it decided to make the "threat of nuclear annihilation" the center of its program concerns. A Sierra Club task force urged the organization to create a standing committee to review military projects.

No branch of the utopians joins coalitions as easily and demands so little control in return for its cooperation as the mainline churches. The churches will aid virtually any group engaged in "progressive" efforts. For example, the United Methodists provided office space, staff, a letterhead and $4,000 in cash to a 1981 conference on South Africa initiated by a Soviet front organization, the International Committee against Apartheid, Racism and Colonialism in Southern Africa. Roy Beck, a journalist with the *United Methodist Reporter*, the largest independent Methodist newspaper, already in New York on another assignment, decided to attend the conference because, as he reported, so many United Methodist officials and bishops had their names on the promotional literature.

Beck found to his surprise that the conference steering committee was innocent of Methodists but included a number of members of the central committee of the U.S. Communist Party. The whole climate of the conference, Beck noted, was one of intense hostility to the United States. The final declaration of the conference "In Solidarity with the Liberation Struggles of the Peoples of Southern Africa" urging that "mass support" be organized for the African National Congress and SWAPO (both Soviet-backed terrorist organizations) went out on stationery of the United Methodist Office for the United Nations. While the conference was also sponsored by radical institutes and peace organizations, a conference organizer confided to Beck that she did not believe the conference "could have happened without the United Methodists who month after month were helping out."[17]

Church Women United, the national ecumenical movement of Christian women, has joined with the Women's International League for Peace and Freedom (which even journalist Ronald Radosh, in a generally sympathetic portrait of the peace movement in *The New Republic,* admits has been led by "nonfailing fellow travelers"[18]) in an appeal to church women to join a program called STAR (Stop the Arms Race). An innocent enough sounding acronym, it was the slogan of the World Peace Council's 1975 Second Stockholm Appeal campaign, repeated as a litany in its documents. To Make Detente Irreversible—Stop the Arms Race, To Defend the Peace and Build a New World—Stop the Arms Race.

The utopians have forged frameworks for common action: the most important are the Coalition for a New Foreign and Military Policy and the Mobilization for Survival, described in previous chapters. The Coalition for a New Foreign and Military Policy, an outgrowth of the Coalition to Stop Funding the [Vietnam] War, was inaugurated in 1976 at the initiative of the United Methodist Church. Bringing together a number of mainline churches, the National Council of Churches, radical institutes, most of the peace organizations and support groups for Third World liberation movements, the Coalition lobbies on behalf of "a demilitarized U.S. foreign policy." During the Carter administration the Coalition developed the Transfer Amendment, which called for funds taken from military programs to be allocated for projects meeting, in the utopians' favorite stock phrase, "human needs."

The Mobilization for Survival is more radical than the Coalition in that it includes groups, like the Communist Party and the U.S. Peace Council, refused entry to the Coalition. But Coalition representatives showed up for the Mobilization's founding conference in April 1977 and the two organizations have worked closely together ever since.

Since both the Coalition and the Mobilization in turn join coalitions, the base of utopian participation widens still further. The Mobilization has worked closely with the Nader groups on various anti-nuclear energy projects and they jointly coordinated the massive demonstration in Washington, D.C. demanding instant shut-down of all nuclear power plants that followed the accident at Three Mile Island. Both the

Coalition and the Mobilization have participated in the annual Critical Mass conferences organized by Nader to plan strategy for the anti-nuclear energy campaign. And, of course, both the Coalition and the Mobilization have been active in a whole variety of coalitions working on disarmament. The broadest utopian coalitions have been formed on an ad hoc basis and center on the themes that energize all the utopians—hatred of corporations, of nuclear energy, of nuclear weapons, and of the Reagan administration.

The nuclear disarmament movement has been important in drawing in even mainstream environmental organizations, providing them with an opportunity to focus on the religious aspect of the environmental ethos. The sanctity of the earth is seen by environmentalists as such that national survival, even human survival, becomes petty by comparison. While the way environmentalists formulate their concerns may sound absurd, they are the basis upon which the formidable resources of these movements are mobilized. An article in *Audubon Magazine,* in March 1982, laments the disastrous consequences of nuclear war: "What would become of the forests of the Amazon if a reconstructing world displayed an insatiable demand for timber? With millions of Americans homeless and industry in need of rebuilding, could we protect our own forests and rivers and open spaces?" And, of course, the churches have thrown themselves into the movement with unexampled fervor. By 1982 most of the mainline churches had made "peace" their priority issue.

The anti-Reagan campaign has produced such typical utopian efforts as "The First National Let Them Eat Cake Sale." Over fifty organizations, including peace, community action, anti-nuclear energy, public interest, church and alternative-energy groups, undertook to organize such sales in their communities, and the national advisory board was a Who's Who of prominent utopians. In a progress report sent out to supporters on May 3, 1983, the director, Peter Harnik (coordinator of Environmental Action) announced that the organization had received tax-deductible status and observed: "If the I.R.S. gives us their blessing, can the foundations be far behind?" The idea behind the "cake sale" program was to raise money and "consciousness" simultaneously for the utopian proposition that military spending should be drastically cut to alleviate social problems and that the Reagan administration was as callous as Marie Antoinette. Publicity was to be assured through sending press releases in the form of cakeboxes.

Liberation movements in the Third World are a perennial magnet to the utopians, although the coalitions formed in their support are partial ones, confined for the most part to the institutes, peace and church organizations, working with radical left political groups. Second only to South Africa come "Palestine" and Central America. Church leaders, institute intellectuals and peace organizations have coalesced with Arab propagandists in the PLO support organization, the Palestine Human Rights Campaign, in the Coalition for Peace and Justice in the Middle East and in the series of LaGrange conferences, organized by the Palestine Human Rights Campaign in association with church activists. For Central America, the utopians have constructed coalitions to support the Sandanista government of Nicaragua and to attack the governments of El Salvador and Guatemala. CISPES, the Committee in Solidarity with the People of El Salvador ("the people," needless to say, are the guerillas) brings together peace groups (Sandy Pollack of the central committee of the U.S. Communist Party and the U.S. Peace Council is on the steering committee), church representatives (The Interreligious Task Force, composed of religious leaders of different faiths, is based at National Council of Churches headquarters in New York), and radical institutes, including the North American Congress on Latin America.

The radical institutes figure as elements in virtually all the utopian coalitions. One function the institutes serve is in providing research, ideas, articles, books and films to the utopians. The Interfaith Center on Corporate Responsibility, in drawing up the resolutions to be presented at stockholder meetings in opposition to nuclear energy, weapons development, and investment in South Africa, Guatemala etc. relies on research provided by the North American Congress on Latin America and the Institute for Policy Studies, both of which have made elaborate studies of corporations. The Coalition for a New Foreign and Military Policy draws heavily on the Center for Defense Information and on the Institute for Policy Studies. The Nader projects use the work of the Exploratory Project for Economic Alternatives, now renamed the National Center for Economic Alternatives. The Institute for Policy Studies has provided much of the material used by the Riverside Church Disarmament Program, which can in fact be regarded as an IPS offshoot.

But the intellectuals of the institutes are the nerve center of the utopian movement in a more important sense: they provide the analysis through which all the individual issues pursued by the utopians are shown to be interrelated. Their cause is shown to lie in the needs of the capitalist system and their cure in its transformation into a decentralized "reconstructed" society built around appropriate technology. The utopians are careful to emphasize that "appropriate technology" by itself is insufficient. As one put it:

> "Unless complementary political changes are introduced at the same time, technological solutions, however appropriate, are unlikely to provide adequate solutions by themselves. . . . Truly appropriate technology can only come from the demands of the people by whom and for whom it is to be used, once they have successfully realized their own political and economic strength."[20]

In other words only after the utopians have taken over can technology be used "appropriately."

There is considerable coordination of utopian efforts behind the scenes. In October 1981, a national conference of utopians was held in Nyack, New York at the headquarters of the Fellowship of Reconciliation. Specific projects were farmed out to environmental, peace, religious, public interest and institute representatives.[21] A month after the Nyack conference, the Natural Resources Defense Council, in the past almost wholly funded by the Ford Foundation, brought together different representatives of the same utopian spectrum. This time the projects centered on heightening grass roots awareness of the link between civilian nuclear power and nuclear arms, opposition to development of breeder technologies, and forging links between groups with similar interests. Various combinations of organizational representatives were assigned to lobbying and legislative work, to "public education," to media work and to international coordination. The minutes of the meeting reported that the group assigned to international work, which included staff people from the Environmental Policy Center, Nader's Critical Mass, and the Women's International League for Peace and Freedom, would "contact friends in Europe, especially Great Britain to discourage sale of plutonium to the U.S."

Much of the coordination is conducted openly but the public is unaware of it because the media shows little interest. The huge demonstration, in June 1982, in support of the UN Special Session on Disarmament, was treated as a spontaneous grass-roots protest. It had of course been carefully planned and adherents mobilized for over a year by a series of organizations working together in the June 12 Rally Committee. This included the full range of peace organizations (including the U.S. Peace Council); Friends of the Earth and Greenpeace from the environmental movement; a series of religious organizations; several state PIRGs representing the Naderite public interest movement: and the North American Congress on Latin America, one of the institutes most vigorous in its assaults on U.S. "imperialism."

Cooperation, whether within a single utopian strand or between them, is radicalizing for the more mainstream groups. The most militant environmental groups are the local anti-nuclear alliances like Clamshell (which disintegrated in one of the sectarian battles characteristic of the extreme left), Shad, Palmetto, Bailly etc., all of which belong to the Mobilization for Survival and specialize in civil disobedience and various forms of "direct action." While Nader's Critical Mass is careful to work within the law, it has cooperated with the local militants, providing, in its words, "information, advice and moral support." Anna Gyorgy, the current director of Critical Mass, comes from a background of participation in the pro-Castro Venceremos Brigades and leadership in the Clamshell Alliance. Migration of staff from smaller, more militant organizations to larger, more "moderate" ones is typical. Naturally, such staff can only exert an influence for greater militance.

The movement of personnel is also important because it makes bonds easier to establish between organizations and facilitates common campaigns, coalitions and consultations. A few examples will have to suffice for what could be a lengthy chronicle of personnel shifts. Steve Daggett of the Institute for Policy Studies staff became Budget Priorities Coordinator of the Coalition for a New Foreign and Military Policy. Bob Chlopake, who served as director of Nader's National Public Interest Research Group, became a senior staffer for Friends of the Earth. Jeff Brummer went from the Clamshell Alliance to Environmental Action. David Talbot left the Environmental Action Foundation's Utility Project to become editor of the Foundation for National Progress' publication *Mother Jones*. (The Foundation for National Progress was set up, according to its own financial report, "to carry out on the West Coast the charitable and educational activities of the Institute for Policy Studies.")

Utopian organizations are also linked by individual leaders who take a role in a whole series of them. To take a single example, Richard Barnet, long time co-director of IPS, has served on a series of boards of utopian organizations. Specifically, he has been a member of the board of trustees of the Council on Hemispheric Affairs, a sponsor of the Chile Committee for Human Rights, a member of the advisory board of the Center for National Security Studies, a sponsor of the Cuba Resource Center, a member of the board of the Council on Economic Priorities, a member of the board of the Organizing Committee for the Fifth Estate, publishers of *CounterSpy,* and co-founder of World Peacemakers, a church disarmament group, for which Barnet's writings literally serve as a "bible."

It is doubtful if staff attitudes differ greatly between ostensibly militant and mainstream organizations. A revealing glimpse into the attitudes of at least some staff in a "moderate" environmental organization, The Wilderness Society, is provided by the emergence of a remarkable group called Earth First, which has sought alliances with peace and radical political groups. It was formed by the "issues coordinator" of the Wilderness Society, Dave Foreman, and its nucleus consisted of the former educational director of the Wilderness Society, its former Wyoming representative and a former official of Friends of the Earth. The group's slogan was "Reclaim the roads and plowed land." Its goal was not merely to halt dam construction but to tear down existing dams "freeing shackled rivers" and recreating American wilderness out of "millions and tens of millions'" of presently settled land.[22]

The utopians seek to expand their base of support to the ordinary church and union member. We noted in the chapter on the environmental movement the emphasis utopian intellectual Jeremy Rifkin put on the churches as the only institution that could provide the motivation and discipline for the harsh ethic of the conserving society. Rifkin looked primarily to the evangelical churches whose leaders have been least responsive to the utopian's call, because he felt they alone could instill a willingness to sacrifice for faith. With the exception of evangelical pockets like the Sojourners movement, which works closely with World Peacemakers, the utopians have had to rely on mobilizing mainline churches, whose leadership, of course, is part and parcel of the utopians. The importance of the peace movement has been that it enabled the utopians to reach more deeply into the grass roots of the mainline churches and into the Roman Catholic church as well, opening up the possibility of making converts on issues that, at least to the utopian mind, are inextricably related.

The utopians have found labor unions, a prime target of their efforts, much less receptive than the churches. The unions had their brush with

Marxist utopianism in the 1930s. Communists were purged from the unions they had nearly captured, retaining their grip only on isolated unions and locals. Burned by that experience, traditional labor leaders have not been receptive to the appeals of the new utopians. A few labor leaders—William Winpisinger of the International Association of Machinists is an example—have been wooed by promises that money taken out of the defense sector will produce more jobs in civilian production, by promises of support for labor demands against management, and perhaps, most important, by the offer of a stature within the utopian movement they could not expect to win within Labor.

Nonetheless, the utopians harbor high hopes of making greater inroads into labor. Plant closings and corporate migrations are exploited by the utopians to advance theories of worker ownership and "participatory democracy" in the workplace. When the Lykes Corporation closed its Youngstown, Ohio Campbell Works, Richard Fernandez of Clergy and Laity Concerned came in as a community organizer; IPS Fellows entered to raise "consciousness;" and Gar Alperovitz of the Exploratory Project for Economic Alternatives, with the support of local churches, was able to obtain a $300,000 grant from the U.S. Department of Housing and Urban Development to study the feasibility of community-employee ownership of the plants.[23] (The conclusion of HUD, although not, of course, of the Exploratory Center, was that the estimated necessary investment of $525 million in government funds was not feasible.) If the National Education Association, at once the largest and the most radical union, succeeds in its effort to enter the AFL-CIO, the utopians would greatly enhance their position within labor.

Hopefully, workers will remain skeptical of utopian promises. Kerry Ptacek, publications director of the Institute for Religion and Democracy, was active in the 1960s, in SDS. The son of a worker and with experience in union organizing, he concluded that participatory democracy, which he had believed would give workers greater control over their lives and work, was illusory.

> "I realized that workers would be the real losers. I saw how decisions were made in the movement by the small elite that didn't mind spending ten, eleven hours at a single meeting, exhausting and waiting out the others. Workers don't want to spend their lives that way. With participatory democracy *all* the decisions would be made by an elite. The only way workers can have a voice in the decisions that affect them is

> through representative democracy, through intermediate associations."[24]

And Ptacek noted what had motivated a friend of his to leave the movement: "One day he asked himself if he would want the kind of people he knew there to have control over his life. The prospect was so terrible he quit the movement overnight."

In their drive for power, the utopians are driven by a terrible sense of urgency. They are in the grip of acute, almost apocalyptic fears. At their prodding, we careen from the Great Cranberry Scare to the Cyclamate Fright to the Radiation from Color TV Danger to the Mercury in Tuna Scare to the Cancer Surge to the Radioactive Waste Storage Catastrophe. Our human rights, as they see it, are violated by our exposure to risks. The logic of weighing risks and benefits, according to favored utopian scientist John Gofman is "the way of the Nazis."[25] The risk of nuclear holocaust, upon whose horrors the utopians dwell in such meticulous detail, has served as a fitting climax to the parade of imminent catastrophes, a true end-of-the-road, dwarfing all others.

And yet, terrible as the dangers are seen to be, the utopians harbor an enormous optimism, a sense that everything is possible once they are put in charge. For, as they see it, the dangers are all of our own making. It is *we,* or at least the government we have permitted to represent us, who have made the world a dangerous place. For the utopians, the answer to every problem is instantly available, dependent only on the will to implement it. Is energy scarce and expensive? There is limitless energy from the sun, ours to have now, if we are willing to follow the utopians into battle with the corporations that keep the sun away from us. Does pollution accompany industrial development? We have only to "dedevelop" and avoid complex technology. Does nuclear holocaust threaten? We have only to put the nuclear genie back in the bottle. Does the Soviet Union threaten us? We have only to cease making them fearful by our provocations.

As the utopians coalesce, Robert Nisbet foresees the emergence of a mass movement akin to the Green Party in West Germany, including environmentalists, political radicals, public interest advocates, church leaders, community organizers, and youthful college graduates, radicalized by their training in universities where "what was created by the New Left in the raging 1960s has become a permanent part of the academic landscape."[26]

But whatever form the utopian alliances take, as subsequent chapters will show, one thing is certain; the utopians will not lack for funds or for media endorsement of their claims to represent "the public interest."

REFERENCES

1. Heather Booth, "Left with the Ballot Box," *Working Papers for a New Society*, Vol. VIII, No. 3, May-June 1981, pp. 17-18
2. Jim Jubak, "Warming Up in New Jersey," *Environmental Action*, Dec. 1981/ Jan. 1982, pp. 21-23
3. *New York Times*, April 17, 1983
4. *New Spirit*, March 1979, p. 22
5. Martin Carnoy and Derek Shearer, *Economic Democracy*, Armonk, N.Y., M.E. Sharpe Inc., 1980, p. 112
6. *New York Times*, June 5, 1983
7. Paul Ciotti, "Socialism—On the Street Where You Live," *Reason*, April 1981, p. 36
8. Marcus G. Raskin, *Being and Doing*, New York, Random House, 1971, p. 355
9. Llewelyn King, "Nuclear Power in Crisis: The New Class Assault," *The Energy Daily*, July 14, 1978, p. 7
10. *Environmental Action*, April 1981, p. 11
11. Quoted in "The Dilemma of Third World Nutrition: Nestle and the Role of Infant Formula," distributed by Nestle, 1983
12. Dave Foreman, "Earth First!" *The Progressive*, October 1981, p. 42
13. *New York Times*, April 19, 1981
14. Gail Robinson, "The War Hits Home," *Environmental Action*, September 1981, p. 18
15. *Environmental Action*, February 1982, p. 4
16. John Rees, "The Amazing Anne M. Gorsuch," *Review of the News*, June 16, 1982, p. 47
17. Roy Beck, "UM Endorsed Event Seemed Controlled by Pro-Soviets," *United Methodist Reporter*, Oct. 23, 1981
18. Ronald Radosh, "The 'Peace Council' and Peace" *The New Republic*, January 31, 1983, p. 14
19. John Barron, *KGB Today: The Hidden Hand*, New York, Readers Digest Press, 1983, p. 247
20. David Dickson, "The Politics of Alternative Technology," in Alexander Cockburn and James Ridgeway eds., *Political Ecology*, New York, Times Books, 1979, p. 369
21. Report, Nuclear Weapons Facilities Task Force, National Conference, Oct. 23-25, 1981 Nyack, New York; see also *Information Digest*, Dec. 25, 1981
22. David Foreman, op. cit., pp. 39-42
23. Leon Howell, "Youngstown: Putting the Pieces Together," *Christianity and Crisis*, June 12, 1978, pp. 152-5
24. Interview, November 1982
25. John Gofman, "Opinions in Indian Country" *Americans Before Columbus*, Vol. 9, No. 2, 1981, p. 3
26. *Our Country and Our Culture: A Conference of the Committee for the Free World*, New York, Orwell Press, 1983, p. 39

IX

Donating The Rope

The annual budgets of the organizations established by the coercive utopians, taken together, run into the hundreds of millions. And only a small portion of that money comes from members of utopian organizations or individuals who respond to their fund-raising appeals. Most of the money, unbeknownst to him, comes from the average citizen. Government funds the utopians, which means the average citizen pays through his taxes. Foundations fund them, which also means the average person pays, if more indirectly. Since it is calculated that for every $1.20 given by tax exempt foundations, the treasury loses $1.00, the taxpayer has to make up for what the foundation does not pay in taxes. Churches fund the utopians, which means the churchgoer pays through his donation to the church collection plate. To a lesser extent, corporations fund them, which means the stockholder pays in the form of foregone dividends.

To understand how government and foundations came to look upon the enterprises of the utopians as a sound social investment, it is necessary to look back to the War on Poverty. In *Maximum Feasible Misunderstanding,* his chronicle of the community action programs launched by the Johnson Administration, Daniel P. Moynihan points out that by the 1950s social scientists had reached a consensus that the problems of urban centers stemmed from the decline of community.

This belief was accompanied by an upsurge of confidence in social science—in its ability to manipulate social factors for the common good.

The social scientists were given their chance to experiment upon the social order because a President of the United States decided—and as Moynihan sees it, did so almost arbitrarily—to place poverty at the center of his legislative program. The problems of the suburbs, a competing theme, narrowly lost out within the circle of decision-makers around Kennedy. Moynihan writes of Kennedy's election, that it "brought to Washington as officeholders, or consultants, or just friends, a striking echelon of persons whose profession might justifiably be described as knowing what ails societies and whose art is to get treatment underway before the patient is especially aware of anything noteworthy taking place."[1] And the remedy they prescribed was the creation of conditions which would produce autonomous communities in which people, especially poor people, in whom it was agreed the decline of community produced the greatest social pathology, might control the decisions that affected their lives. The Community Action Program emerged as the centerpiece of the War on Poverty. It was designed to create community among the poor by ensuring "maximum feasible participation" of the poor in all areas of social life, from education to housing to crime control.

The same perspectives that shaped the government's developing War on Poverty influenced major foundations. This was scarcely surprising since, whether as staff or consultants, foundations used people with the same background as those who entered government. In fact, their authorities were in many cases the very same people. The most important foundation to enter the community building enterprise was the Ford Foundation. While only a fraction of its income from 3 billion dollars in assets was put into community building, that investment, starting in the late 1950s, had dramatic effect. Probably the best-known of Ford's efforts was the Ocean Hill-Brownsville school decentralization pilot program of 1968 in New York City, which resulted in severe ethnic conflict between blacks and Jews. And this was to be all too typical of community action programs. The groups between whom conflict was heightened varied, but harsh rhetoric became characteristic. Community action turned out to be a recipe less for building community than for building community conflict.

Less predictable than the radicalization of those who were chosen by professionals to represent the poor was the radicalization of the professionals themselves. Professor of social work Richard Cloward was a particularly good example of this tendency. His book, *Delinquency and Opportunity,* coauthored with Lloyd Ohlin, was seminal in developing the theories upon which government and foundation action rested. Cloward became steadily more hostile to the system he had first wanted to open to all.[2]

Community action programs rapidly fell from Presidential favor in the wake of urban ghetto riots. In Newark, for example, employees of the local community action program participated in the demonstration that triggered the 1967 riots and a director urged blacks to arm themselves against whites.[3] In addition, there was growing conflict between community action programs and local government. But while the high hopes that these organizations would create community or eliminate poverty vanished, they survived, assuming the quality of "normalcy" and becoming incorporated into the structure of civic government.

Community action programs left behind more than ongoing institutions receiving federal, foundation, and even corporation funding. Their more important legacy was in changing the conception of a number of important foundations concerning their role, shifting their focus from preserving social institutions—whether in the arts, education or social services—to changing them. And in so far as the community action program created within the federal bureaucracy programs which construed their mission as social change, the way was left open to redefinitions of what the nature of that social change would be.

With the advent of the Carter administration, leaders of the coercive utopians were given control of a series of government bureaucracies. For example ACTION was handed over to the direction of Sam Brown, a former anti-Vietnam war activist. Brown appointed as director of VISTA (Volunteers in Service to America) Margery Tabankin, another anti-Vietnam war activist who visited Hanoi during the war and participated in Soviet sponsored "peace" meetings abroad in the Vietnam years.[4] Prior to coming to ACTION, Tabankin directed the Youth Project, a funnel for tax exempt money to go to radical groups, many of them not tax-exempt, including anti-nuclear energy groups, anti-intelligence groups, support groups for third world liberation movements, anti-utility company groups, groups seeking to turn over a large territory in a number of states to Indian tribes, gay rights groups, prisoners unions, community organizing groups like ACORN, groups for the "liberation" of mental patients, etc. Although the Youth Project supposedly funds only "grass roots" organizations, in 1982, it provided over $50,000 for the IPS.

James Burnley, who replaced Tabankin as head of VISTA during the Reagan administration, noted that under Sam Brown's leadership of ACTION: "If you were a member in good stead of the New Left you were guaranteed help if you had an organization."[5] Brown spelled out new criteria for programs using VISTA volunteers in the Federal Register in 1978. The criteria spoke of "establishment of a grassroots advocacy system" and "supporting grassroots advocacy organizations." Brown established "National VISTA grants" and most of the $4 million from those grants went to organizations of the utopians. Thus ACORN, with its "People's Program" for achieving power and its Alinsky-style confrontational tactics, was the first recipient of a National VISTA grant. It obtained $470,475. Since as an avowedly political organization ACORN was barred from obtaining VISTA volunteers, it established a subsidiary called CORAP (Community Organization Research Action Project). Senator John Ashbrook charged CORAP was a deliberate fiction to conceal the fact that the money was going to a political organization.[6] Sixteen ACORN organizers were promptly converted to the VISTA payroll. As a result of the storm of criticism, ACORN's CORAP was not given a renewal of its grant, but the cutoff was more apparent than real. It continued to get money from the state level after its national grant was terminated.[7]

Money and volunteers flowed from VISTA into the organizations of the utopians. The Youth Project received over 60 VISTA volunteers and cash awards of over $800,000. Massachusetts Fair Share, an organization similar to ACORN, received $310,000. Nader's PIRGs received $1,000,000; Tom Hayden's Laurel Springs Institute, a training center for activists in the Alinsky style, many of whom then worked for Hayden's Campaign for Economic Democracy, received $200,000; and the Midwest Academy, yet another Alinsky-type school, received $600,000 for training VISTA volunteers.[8] The Midwest Academy's training manual, with its "give them a taste of blood" approach was described earlier and presumably provided admirable preparation for many of the projects to which VISTA volunteers were then assigned.

A whole series of government agencies vied with one another in pouring money into the utopians. Some utopian-run organizations received half or more of their budgets from the government. For example, the Western Action Training Institute, yet another training school for organizers, this one devoted to the proposition that resource development by corporations in the Intermountain West constitutes "social and cultural genocide" received from the Department of Justice alone

$172,578 in 1979.[9] The Citizen/Labor Energy Coalition, an anti-corporate coalition led until 1981 by Heather Booth, who doubled as President of the Midwest Academy, received $200,000 from the Community Services Administration and 8 volunteers and $30,000 from VISTA for the stated purpose of organizing up to 500 "low income consumers into energy activists."[10]

Many utopian organizations obtained money simultaneously from a variety of federal agencies. Nader's PIRGs received money not only from ACTION but from the Department of Education, the Federal Trade Commission, and the Environmental Protection Agency. In 1980, the American Friends Service Committee, pilot of the nuclear freeze proposal and antagonist to U.S. policy worldwide, received just under $600,000 from a variety of government agencies. The Center for Community Change, creator of the Youth Project and source of assistance to countless activist groups, received approximately $2 million from the Department of Labor, $600,000 from the Community Services Administration, over $600,000 from the Department of Housing and Urban Development and just under $1½ million from the Department of Justice. The National Council of Churches received almost half a million dollars a year for three years in a row during the Carter years, twice from the Department of Labor and once from the Department of Energy. Its half million from the Department of Energy was designed for an "energy education project," which the NCC said was unique in approaching energy production "as a social rather than . . . technical or economic issue." The NCC promised in its application that the churches would be active participants in the Citizen/Labor Energy Coalition, just mentioned, and itself the recipient of at least seven federal grants. Given the NCC's denial of the legitimacy of nuclear energy and its advocacy of "appropriate technology" there seemed little doubt as to the NCC's views on the "social" implications of energy production. The NCC also received $15,000 from the National Endowment for the Arts in 1980 for a film sympathetically portraying "social change and evolution" in rigidly repressive Marxist Mozambique.

Environmental organizations most opposed to energy development received federal funds. Friends of the Earth received the relatively minor sum of $30,000 from the Department of Energy in 1979; the Sierra Club received $669,000 from the Environmental Protection Agency between 1978 and 1980 and additional sums from the Department of Energy and the National Endowment for the Humanities; and the Natural Resources Defense Council did best of all, obtaining from the Environmental Protection Agency, between 1978 and 1981, almost one and a half million dollars.[11]

Sometimes the sums government agencies invested in projects were small but are noteworthy nonetheless because the projects are so obviously designed to attack American values and institutions. For example, the Department of Energy gave $10,000 to defray costs of the militantly anti-capitalist Black Hills International Gathering which, as one participant explained, was designed "to unite communities around the world to break the economic and environmental domination by multinational corporations that threaten our very survival." The closing workshop featured a call by a founder of the American Indian Movement for a "national liberation front" on Third World models to be created in the U.S. to "free the land and free the people."

In January 1981, shortly before the end of the Carter administration, the National Endowment for the Humanities gave $45,000 to AMCOM Productions to support the writing of 2 thirty minute scripts for a series of programs on the history of the American Communist Party, scheduled to cost in all $800,000. The proposal made it clear the film was to be a glorification of the Communist Party, for it spoke of the party's "significance for radicalism and democratic values" and stated that its ideals "are among the noblest ever to have inspired mankind." It is little wonder that the proposal could promise that the "Communist Party itself had agreed to cooperate with this project."[12] In February 1981, immediately before Reagan's accession, the National Endowment for the Humanities gave ACORN over $200,000 for programs on the history of social movements for low to moderate income people. Again, not much imagination is required to imagine the tenor of such programs.

Direct grants have not been the only form in which government money has reached the utopians. "Intervenor funding," both formal and informal, is another avenue. Formal intervenor funding refers to paying individuals or groups to participate in rule-making procedures of government agencies. Congress has authorized only two agencies, the Federal Trade Commission and the Environmental Protection Agency, to provide intervenor funding, but other agencies have provided such funding on the assumption they have an "implied authority" to do so. Although Congress has specified that intervenor funds are to go only to individuals who cannot otherwise afford the costs of testifying, the agencies have interpreted this rule liberally.

They have funded wealthy groups on the grounds that they have committed their funds elsewhere. For example, the Sierra Club, despite its multi-million dollar budget, shared in a $28,000 intervenor fee.[13] It is difficult to see on what basis some of the groups qualify as representatives of the public or as expert sources of information. Americans for Democratic Action received $177,000 to intervene in rule-making proceedings on topics ranging from funeral costs, to health spas, to over-the-counter drugs.[14] The Federal Trade Commission alone has given out almost $2,000,000 in intervenor funding since 1975.

Informal differs from formal intervenor funding in that it is not confined to rule-making; it includes funds given to groups representing "the consumer interest." In the Carter years, the Community Services Administration's Energy Advocacy Office and the Department of Energy's Office of Consumer Affairs were two of the major informal intervenor programs. Typical of the Community Service Administration's efforts was its $260,000 grant to create the People's Organization for Washington Energy Resources (POWER) in Olympia, Washington. A consumer group without members or dues, it engaged in such activities as sending protestors dressed up as light bulbs to utility rate hearings.[15] POWER was part of a nationwide "Energy Advocacy Program," which according to an internal document of the Community Services Administration, was designed "to bring about changes in existing laws and administrative regulations related to energy matters which disproportionately affect or discriminate against the poor."[16] Why Congress should want to fund an administrative agency to fund groups to attack the laws passed by Congress is a question the Community Services Administration did not address. The various Energy Advocacy Projects all saw their chief role to be attacking utilities in rate proceedings. The Department of Energy's Office of Consumer Affairs financed meetings across the country in which "the people" attacked utility companies; they were billed as "information-gathering" sessions. In Colorado, the literature inviting people to participate put out by National People's Action, led by Gail Cincotta, which organized 10 meetings across the country with DOE money was so inflammatory that any additional government funding had to be withdrawn.

Another variety of government funded "intervenors" are public interest lawyers whose fees are paid by the federal or state government. Lawyers in such suits against the government have been awarded fees of up to $125 an hour. Single cases can bring fees—paid by the taxpayer—of hundreds of thousands of dollars. For example, in March 1982, the state of Colorado was ordered to pay the American Civil Liberties Union $742,000 in attorney fees and expenses for successfully bringing suit on behalf of prisoners in Canon City, Colorado.[18] These fees are paid on the basis of Congressional authorization to judges to order the government to pay legal fees to attorneys who sue and win under almost a hundred environmental, civil rights and consumer laws.

The one restraint on public interest law has been that in cases when a suit was lost, the lawyers received no fees. Lawyers were thus reluctant to bring suits without legal merit. But now, public interest lawyers have begun to demand payment even when they lose a case. In a precedent-setting case, a judge awarded a group of environmental lawyers $230,400 for a case, after they had lost it on appeal. The case, originally brought in 1979, tried to stop the Department of Interior from leasing properties in the Beaufort Sea off Northern Alaska because of alleged dangers to the bowhead whale. The lower court judge, who had originally ruled in favor of the public interest lawyers, was the one who then awarded them fees, despite the fact they had by now *lost* the case. He not only allotted them up to $125 an hour but clamped on an additional 15% for loss of purchasing power in the intervening time.[19] Yet, as the *Wall Street Journal* noted editorially, if the Federal government is to write blank checks for suits against itself which even the courts reject, it invites paralysis.[20] The *Journal's* criticism has the more force because the purpose of a suit can be simply to ensure sufficient delay to make a project economically unfeasible. If such suits are to be federally funded after their defeat in the courts, the public interest movement will have veto power over development without any cost to itself.

During the Carter years, the utopians devised a number of schemes to secure, in Peter Metzger's words, "continuous funding for the Movement."[21] Aware that future administrations might be less prodigal toward them, they sought ways to siphon off large sums from funds allotted by Congress to aid the poor. Metzger calls their arrangements "Robin Hood in reverse" since middle class lawyers and activists take the money intended for the poor. The most dramatic scheme, in which the Community Services Administration was involved in pirating for activist lawyers and other utopians $18 million, intended by Congress to help pay the winter utility bills of poor people, will be discussed in the next chapter. In addition, when Congress allocated $87.5 million, taken from the windfall profits tax imposed on oil companies, to help households it felt might "fall between the cracks" of the initial program to help poor people pay their fuel bills, the Community Services Administration's regional energy coordinator promptly spoke of "creative ideas" for using the money. The creative idea was to change language in the Federal regulations to make "advocacy" (i.e. money spent on lawyers and activists) an eligible expenditure.[22]

Nor was the Community Services administration the utopian's only hunting ground. The Department of Energy had collected $200,000,000 by fining oil companies for infraction of its Byzantine pricing laws. It announced it would take $25 million of the money it had obtained from Getty Oil and return it to the poor. But "the poor" the Department of Energy had in mind were the public interest lawyers and community activists.[23] The Department of Energy had similar plans for the rest of the $200 million and issued a notice in the Federal Register asking for groups to submit "alternative funding" proposals for distributing the money. Needless to say, the Naderite conglomerate and similar groups responded with plans for consumer advocacy and "alternative" energy. The Consumer Energy Council of America and nineteen other activist organizations actually filed a lawsuit to demand that the Department of Energy set up a "trust fund" to fund consumer advocates and activist lawyers on a permanent basis.[24] For the utopians this was social jujitsu: they would use money earned by oil companies to attack them in perpetuity, or at least until they came under control of the utopians.

In the last days of the Carter administration, the utopians who had been brought into the bureaucracies, fearing the Reagan administration would call a halt to their activities, literally flung money at "Movement" causes. The Office of the Inspector General conducted an audit of the records of the Community Services Administration to see whether it was true, as was rumored, that an inordinate amount of money had been dispensed between Reagan's election and his inauguration, i.e. in the six weeks between Nov. 5, 1980 and January 19, 1981. The audit found that money had been spent with such frenetic haste that much of it had been given without proper authorization. For example, in all of 1980, the Office of Community Action awarded $41 million in grants and on January 19, 1981, the day before Reagan's inauguration, awarded $15 million, or 36% of all the money it dispensed in 1980. The Office of Energy Development awarded $41.5 million in grants in all of fiscal 1980 and in two days, January 17 and

January 19, 1981, it awarded over $18 million. During all of fiscal 1980, the Office for Policy, Planning and Evaluation awarded $3.5 million in grants. On two days, January 16 and January 19, 1981, it awarded $1.6 million or 46% of that amount. The audit found that of nine grants totalling $11 million awarded on January 19, 1981, only one had been presented to the Project Review Board as required by agency procedures.[25] Typical of the kinds of grants given was $3,700,000 bestowed on January 19, 1981 on the utopian favorite, the National Center for Appropriate Technology. The money was given despite the fact that an audit had showed the organization was poorly run, its record-keeping so grossly inadequate it was difficult to find out what happened to much of the money it received.[26]

Although the utopians feared their funding would end under Reagan, the flow was staunched, not stopped. ACTION was probably the agency which underwent the most thorough house-cleaning under Reagan. One feature of Sam Brown's control of the agency was the subversion of the intent that VISTA work with poor people. Community activist organizations prefer to organize working and lower middle class populations whom it is easier to mobilize for issues that are of concern to the utopians—property tax changes, anti-corporate campaigns, alternative energy promotion. With ACTION under the control of Tom Pauken and VISTA (scheduled to be phased out altogether) headed by Jim Burnley, the roster of project applications for VISTA showed a whole series of activist groups marked "disapproved" with the laconic notation "Community organizing is not a priority of this administration."[27] Under Anne Gorsuch, the Environmental Protection Agency also ceased funding the most radical environmental groups.

Housecleaning in other agencies was much less thorough with the result that grants continued to go to the utopians. The Community Services Administration was shut down but many of its programs continued to be funded by the Department of Health and Human Services and by block grants made to the states. Under Reagan, the Department of Health and Human Services continued, for example, to fund the Western Action Training Institute, which considers economic development in the West a form of "genocide." Similarly the Department of Education provided millions of dollars to activist groups through its Women's Educational Equity Act Program. One of the most remarkable groups to receive money under the program was the Council on Interracial Books for Children which received the second installment of a $244,000 grant in July 1981 for publication of a basal reader for third graders. In its guidelines for selecting bias-free texts and story books, the Council describes why it feels current material is unsuitable:

> "Implicit in all of the textbooks surveyed is the assumption that the U.S. society is a true democracy—the distortion which results is serious, for by calling our government and economic systems 'democratic,' the textbooks deny the realities of capitalism and all that goes into it—classes, conflicting class interests, and the ongoing struggle between those few who control wealth and those many who are trying to share wealth."[28]

The Council explains: "We are not interested in seeing different people win a place in the status quo, the present social structure. We are challenging the structure because it promotes anti-human values."[29]

The funding patterns of the Department of Energy under Reagan showed an uncomfortable resemblance to those under Carter. The DOE gave $68,500 to the Institute for Policy Studies offshoot, the Conference on Alternative State and Local Public Policies, which presses for government takeover of banks, utilities, housing etc;[30] $179,644 to the Environmental Action Foundation (Environmental Action is distinguished for its attacks on corporations in the so-called Dirty Dozen and Filthy Five campaigns); $19,999 to the Environmental Defense Fund; $10,000 to the Citizen/Labor Energy Coalition and $120,000 to the National Center for Appropriate Technology.

The familiar pattern of utopian groups and projects picking up funding from a variety of government agencies continued. The American Friends Service Committee obtained $150,000 from the Department of Education in 1981 and an additional $150,000 from the National Endowment for the Humanities for an "interpretive history" of the U.S. military in Puerto Rico. The proposal makes it clear that the purpose of the study is to show how the U.S. military deformed all aspects of Puerto Rican life.[31] Similarly the Center for Community Change received $1,250,000 in 1981 from a combination of government agencies.[32]

Sometimes the government funds operations directly hostile to U.S. policy conducted in the framework of apparently non-controversial institutes. David Asman, a policy analyst for the Heritage Foundation, has done in-depth studies on two recipients of millions of federal dollars: the Wisconsin Land Tenure Center and the African-American Institute. He discovered that the Wisconsin Land Tenure Center had knowingly appointed a Marxist activist, Peter Marchetti, to supervise a study of land reform in Sandinista Nicaragua. As of June 1982, total expenditures on the Nicaragua project coordinated by Marchetti exceeded $900,000 and the papers from the project presented a skewed portrait of the Sandinistas as dedicated to "pluralism." A program to train Nicaraguans in technical skills at the Land Tenure Center became a Marxist indoctrination program.[33] Similarly Asman found that the African-American Institute, established in 1953 to provide African nations with Western-trained elites, had become radicalized, with funds from the student scholarship programs going heavily to members of the African National Congress and SWAPO while students from anti-apartheid black organizations that are not Communist were excluded. Similarly the guest lists for the Institute's conferences were heavily weighted toward African Marxist governments and terrorist organizations while Africans of different political sympathies were excluded or invited in token numbers.[34]

Part of the difficulty the Reagan administration encountered was that so many in the bureaucracy were in sympathy with utopian visions and the utopian critique of existing institutions. The panels that review grants, both in Washington and regionally, are often stacked with individuals who are part of utopian networks. Grown accustomed to government support for their activities, the utopians have come to believe that it is incumbent upon government to give them the resources with which to attack it. Should a less hostile President be elected, the money sluices can be expected to open fully once again.

Foundations are the second major source of funding for the utopians. Robert F. Goheen, one time President of Princeton University and later head of the Council on Foundations told a Congressional hearing in 1973, "there is no basic philosophy in foundations other than an often tacit commitment—a very important tacit commitment—to the values and institutions of the society which permit things like foundations to function."[35] Actually, as we shall see, that generalization does not hold. There are foundations that quite self-consciously use the wealth amassed by virtue of the existing system to overturn it.

The number of foundations that devote almost all their resources to funding the utopians are few: a much larger number give a portion of their income, sometimes only a small percentage, to utopian enterprises. Nonetheless, when a large foundation contributes only a small part of its resources, the sums can be substantial. Overall, foundations contribute many millions to the utopians each year.

There are a few foundations which give them the lion's share of their grants. Among these are: Akbar, Field, Henry P. Kendall, Fund for Tomorrow, New World, Norman, Rubin, Capp Street, Louis Rabinowitz, Stern, Ottinger, Shalan, and the Rockefeller Family Fund. In addition, there are a number of relatively small funds started in the early 1970s, most of which have little or no endowment and depend upon annual contributions by a number of wealthy individuals. These include: Vanguard, Haymarket, North Star, Liberty Hill, McKenzie River Gathering and Bread and Roses. These small funds together contribute only $1.5 million a year to the utopians, much less than Field alone, but they see themselves as pioneers of a developing funding movement which they hope will grow dramatically.

What motivates those who have benefitted most from the present economic system to seek its destruction? There is no single answer. In a few cases the explanation seems to lie in hostility to the government and/or Communist sympathies. Daniel J. Bernstein, a Wall Street broker who founded the DJB Foundation (now defunct), was quoted as saying that "the chief enemy of mankind" is "the injustice of governments and of the United States government in particular."[36] Samuel Rubin, whose Samuel Rubin Foundation both before and since his death has served as the Maecenas of the Institute for Policy Studies and its offshoots, registered as a member of the Communist Party in elections shortly before World War II.[37] The much smaller Louis Rabinowitz Foundation was originally devoted to promoting Jewish culture, but after the founder's death fell under the control of his nephew Victor Rabinowitz, who has served as a lawyer for the Castro government since 1960. The Rabinowitz Foundation became the subject of considerable attention during the Vietnam War for financing a National Lawyers Guild project (Victor Rabinowitz served as President of the Guild) to promote military disobedience in the Pacific area.[38]

More frequently foundations are propelled into the arms of the utopians by their desire to be trendsetters. The raison d'etre of foundations is to contribute to human welfare and foundations aspiring to be trendsetters vie with each other in seeking out new and imaginative forms of service. Hospitals, museums, colleges, symphonies have become traditional and conventional types of philanthropy. A small or medium-sized foundation will never make a mark in the foundation world by continuing on this well-worn path. Support of the institutes and kindred groups designed to produce "systemic change" promise to put the foundation with limited resources on the "map" as a daring pioneer of the new, the challenging and the significant. As fashions in progressive circles change, these foundations respond rapidly. In 1982, a survey of peace organizations revealed that they had received $20 million from private foundations and individual philanthropists.[39]

A forty year old trendsetter that still prides itself on being the bellwether of the progressive foundation flock is the medium-size ($15 million in capital) Field Foundation. Established by Marshall Field of the retailing and publishing empire, to deal with problems of "race and poverty" particularly as they affect children, the foundation for years has spent most of its money on efforts to abolish the CIA, end existing American alliances and cut U.S. defense spending. Leslie Dunbar, until 1980 executive director of the Field Foundation, offered the rationalization that there had been no change in the foundation's pursuit of its mandate, for it had merely realized that its responsibility to children extended to the world in which children grew up.

Foundations like Field become captive to the definitions of what is progressive provided by the utopians. An interesting illustration of this comes from the ultimate resolution of a conflict that developed within the Field Foundation board. Several members, including its long-time president Morris Abram, became concerned about the activities of the Institute for Policy Studies. Never the recipient of large grants from Field, IPS ordinarily received $10,000 to $15,000 a year. Vague anxieties that Abram had experienced, on noting IPS had submitted a human rights complaint to the UN against the United States were reinforced by the appearance of two articles by one of the authors of this book, Rael Jean Isaac, on the Institute. When the Field board met in June 1980, at Abram's urging, it decided to postpone a decision on a grant application by IPS. This was sufficient for the director of the foundation, who felt his authority threatened, to resign. Dunbar went to the Center for National Security Studies, whose attacks on U.S. intelligence services were described in the chapter on the institutes.

But the Field board knew of no alternative direction in which to take their "progressive" foundation. If the board refused to fund IPS on the grounds that it represented values at odds with those the foundation sought to support, it would have had to reassess its entire grant-giving program. While the IPS grant was not large, Field provided grants ten to fifteen times as large annually to the IPS offshoot, the Center for

National Security Studies and gave grants to numerous organizations hard to distinguish from both in perspective, like the Center for Defense Information, discussed in the chapter on the institutes, the Exploratory Project for Economic Alternatives and the Youth Project. To make any sense, termination of IPS funding would have required cutting off most of those whose names filled the pages of Field's annual report on its grantees.

Such a recognition seems to have dawned upon board members, for when the board next met the majority decided to fund IPS after all, even though by now they were even better informed about it. Political scientist Joshua Muravchik had completed a long study for the *New York Times Magazine*, and although the article had not yet been published, its findings were made available to the board. Furthermore, the board also had information on the extent to which leading IPS Fellows and IPS publications had supported the PLO. The board's decision to fund IPS was the more interesting in that the decisive vote on behalf of IPS within the split board was cast by Justine Wise Polier, daughter of the famous Zionist leader Rabbi Stephen Wise, and herself long considered a supporter of Israel. One of the members of the minority that remained opposed to the IPS grant subsequently resigned, and in 1981, Morris Abram was forced off the board, his opposition to quota systems acting as a final irritant to the others.[40] Lacking any independent ability to design and define programs that would fit their original mandate, the board determined to keep the foundation's progressive credentials intact no matter what that entailed. Justine Polier became President of the Field board on Abram's departure. Predictably, as "peace" became the fashionable utopian theme, Field became one of the first to adjust its funding priorities devoting to it $416,000 of its $2.5 million grant budget or 20% of the total in 1982.

A competing bellwether is the Stern Fund, which shares its executive director (and funding patterns) with the Ottinger Foundation. Stern's beneficiaries have included the Organizing Committee for the Fifth Estate, publishers of *CounterSpy*, and the People's Bicentennial Commission, described earlier. The Commission seems to have been inspired by John Rossen, described in the *Chicago Tribune* as a "former downstate Communist organizer" who was "doing his best to see to it that Americans see only red during their red, white and blue Bicentennial celebration."[41] The Washington offices of the Commission were started by Jeremy Rifkin, who declared that "the revolutionary heritage must be used as a tactical weapon to isolate the existing institutions and those in power. . ."[49] Thanks in part to Stern money (the National Endowment for the Humanities also provided funds), the People's Bicentennial Commission obtained more media coverage than did the official Bicentennial Commission appointed by the President. Many of the same organizations that receive Field money obtain money from Stern. The Institute for Policy Studies and its various spinoffs receive annual grants as does the American Friends Service Committee and the Youth Project, also traditional Field beneficiaries.

The Rockefeller Family Fund, set up by a number of Rockefeller "cousins," is another foundation that self-consciously seeks a vanguard role. Its Report for 1980 declares that in its fourteenth year the Fund is "trying to maintain the venturesome character it has sought since its inception." The Report specifies that the foundation favors projects of young organizations with outstanding leadership "particularly those which have the promise of creating new solutions or new institutions of wide-ranging social impact." Clearly, no symphony orchestras need apply. The grants are similar to those of Stern and Field, although, as with every foundation, there is a special emphasis on some areas. In 1980, the Rockefeller Family Fund contributed $10,000 to the New Alchemy Institute, publisher of *The New Alchemist,* whose very title is revealing of its anti-technological bent. It also has been interested in women's issues, funding, for example, the Women's Commission in Exile, a dramatic title for a group of women who lost their jobs when the governor of Massachusetts disbanded a commission he had first appointed.

The Rockefeller Family Fund has moved massively into the peace campaign with $250,000 worth of grants in 1983 or 25% of its grants budget. Recipients include such imaginative organizations as Physicians for the Prevention of Nuclear War, which has as its co-Presidents Dr. Bernard Lown of Harvard and Dr. Eugene Chazov, Soviet Deputy Minister of Health. The membership list balances participating U.S. doctors with members from the USSR Academy of Medical Sciences. But as Harper's editor Michael Kinsley noted, this "posits a loony international symmetry." The Soviet doctors are not likely to apply "their chosen therapy of getting 'respected and well-informed people to discuss publicly the facts about nuclear war' in a society where the tradition of the op-ed page is not highly developed." That the Soviet Union sees the group as a useful propaganda tool is suggested by then President Brezhnev's message to the American organizers: "You may rest assured that your humane and noble activities aimed at preventing nuclear war will meet with understanding and support in the Soviet Union.''[43]

For all the typical character of the Rockefeller Family Fund grants in the context of ''progressive'' foundations, there is something particularly dramatic in money from the Rockefeller family, symbol of successful capitalism, going to the utopian movements that would destroy it.

The involvement of members of the Rockefeller family in such funding points up another element in the complex of motivations that lead men and women of inherited wealth deliberately to undermine the system that gave them what they have: feelings of guilt or anger toward the money that has set them apart since birth. John D. Rockefeller's great grand-daughter, Marion Weber, asked how she would pass her money to her children, replied: ''I hope the social revolution will come soon and take away from us the necessity of having to deal with it.'' Her cousin Peggy Rockefeller joined the Students for a Democratic Society in college.[44]

The young people who created the smaller funds like Haymarket, Vanguard and Liberty Hill are absorbed in the problems wealth has caused them. Haymarket was started by George Pillsbury of the Minnesota banking and flour fortune and Liberty Hill by Sarah Pillsbury, George's sister. In a revealing book called *Robin Hood Was Right,* some of those who have donated to the funds described their emotional difficulties in coping with wealth. A few were disturbed by it from early childhood. One describes how, in visiting her grandmother, she would sit on the floor of the chauffeur-driven car because she was so embarrassed. ''I had this thing about social class, that if you are rich, you are bad.''[45]

The funds provide a framework for those with common problems to meet and an outlet for the anger of these young people, who blame many of their personal problems on their wealth. George Pillsbury explains: ''There are meetings of rich kids. There are meetings where people, again, like myself and Peggy (Peggy Stearn, an heir of the Sears fortune) go to, 20 or 30 of us, and talk very frankly and candidly and personally about having inherited money, and as a problem.'' Pillsbury added: ''I mean money does create problems. And I guess some of those personal problems are also motivations for why we're getting involved with the community funds.''[46]

In another era, psychiatrists might have been the chief beneficiaries of maladjustment on the part of wealthy young people. But this generation has had the benefit of the utopian analysis of United States institutions which these young people have "bought" in its entirety. The Haymarket People's Fund's annual report for 1976 reports that those who give to the fund

> ". . . know that something is very wrong with a political/economic system that sterilizes women in third world countries and gives cancer to workers with polyvinyl chloride at home; require military juntas to police Latin America and Tactical Patrol Forces and SWAT squads to maintain the peace in our cities; uses violence to sell TV, status to sell cars, naked women to sell anything while dulling our consciousness with varying doses of methadone, mental institutions, fundamentalist religion, television and massive athletic spectacles."

And so the heirs to the founders of companies that have come to symbolize the American capitalist system including duPont, Gulf, and Western, IBM and General Motors have set out to remake "America the Evil," or, to use the words of a Haymarket annual report "a sexist and racist system which puts profits for a few people before the needs of the majority."[47] George Pillsbury says: "I want to spend my money to remake the system that created the fortune."[48] Paul Haible, who obtained the earnings from a $1 million trust fund based on the duPont chemical fortune on his twenty-first birthday, says: "My family's money was made unjustly. . . . I don't believe in the inequities of a system that creates a small number of people with a large amount of wealth."[49] Haymarket's annual report is blunt in saying that the fund is "dedicated to eliminating rich people."[50]

These small funds outdo the "progressive" foundations. Even their structure is different. Haymarket, and most of those who have followed in its pioneering footsteps, are run by boards composed of members of the kinds of groups that are being funded, and they make the decisions as to where the money shall go.

The money goes largely to groups that would have difficulty in obtaining funds even from Rubin, Stern or Field. For example, California's Vanguard funded a prostitute's union called COYOTE, standing for Call Off Your Old Tired Ethics and a Network Against Psychiatric Assault led by former mental patients opposed to both shock and chemical therapy. Liberty Hill aided a Women's Film Collective in producing a movie about Lesbian working mothers. New England's Haymarket funded State and Mind "to fight psychiatric and psychological oppressions," the North East Prisoners Association and a series of other consciousness raising programs for prisoners to help them understand, in Haymarket's words "the social, political and economic conditions which systematically cause poverty, alienation and crime." Organizations of lesbians and gays, tenants unions, anti-draft groups, anti-nuclear groups, support groups for third world liberation movements, all these are the staple fair of Haymarket and the rest of the regional funds built on its model.

Not content with funding such organizations Haymarket established a separate organization in 1975, called Rank and File. In announcing the new organization Haymarket noted that the Haymarket People's Fund was tax-exempt, which forced it to follow the IRS guidelines for a public charity, and prevented it from funding "the most significant political work." Rank and File, contributions to which are not tax deductible, was established to fill the gap. Rank and File has contributed funds to "The Black Panther School of Freedom Fighting," the Clamshell Alliance, the Nicaragua Solidarity Committee, the Alternative Energy Coalition, New Unity ("to build a democratic worker-controlled economy and society") etc. Actually, it is difficult to distinguish between the groups funded through Rank and File and those supported through the tax-exempt parent. Haymarket itself, reports funding several chapters of the Puerto Rican Solidarity Committee, a support group for the Puerto Rican Socialist Party, whose program is to liberate Puerto Rico from U.S. "imperialism" and set up a Cuban-style government. It is hard to see how these groups differ in character from the Nicaragua Solidarity Committee funded by Rank and File.

In their zeal to spend all their money upon the groups that would destroy the present oppressive cultural, economic and political system, the funds had personnel problems. Vanguard confesses that it did not pay its employees social security or health insurance. Only after a staff uprising did Vanguard alter its ways. A founder admits: "Unfortunately they had to make us realize that they did not have the same resources to fall back on that we did."[52]

Even in their choice of peace groups these funds outdo the typical "progressive" foundation. Mfundi Wundla of the Funding Exchange, established by these funds as a donor-advising service, reports: "I'm interested in people who can't get money from 'straight' foundations—groups like Mobilization for Survival, or the Coalition of Black Trade Unionists Concerned about Nuclear Disarmament. There are lots of Third World movements that are desperate for funding, for example in the Pacific and in Micronesia."[53]

More common than the foundations which donate all or most of their money to the utopians are those which contribute a portion of their funds, in some cases only a small proportion, to them. Ford is the largest foundation of this type and given its huge resources, its contribution to the utopians in absolute terms is very large. Ford has almost single-handedly bankrolled the public interest and environmental movements and has contributed substantially to the radical institutes. To take only a few of the largest grants, Ford gave $2 million to the Naderite Center for Law and Social Policy in 1980 and $1.8 million to Public Advocates in San Francisco between 1978 and 1980. The most activist environmental groups received huge sums: in 1978, the Natural Resources Defense Council alone received $1.5 million. The radical institutes have received smaller sums. In 1979 Ford contributed $150,000 to the Fund for Peace, of which the Center for Defense Information, the Center for International Policy and the Center for National Security Studies (all discussed in the chapter on the institutes) are projects. Ford has also funded the IPS spinoff, the Institute for Southern Studies (ISS), the Highlander Research and Education Center, which works closely with ISS, the Washington Office on Latin America and the Center for Cuban Studies, the Castroite propaganda operation described earlier. Ford has even given money to MERIP, whose journal supports Middle East Arab terror groups (with which even IPS has feared public association) and to the National Conference of Black Lawyers, U.S. affiliate of an international Soviet front, the International Association of Democratic Lawyers (Ford gave it $25,000 in 1982).

Ford, moreover, is the grandparent of what is presently the single most important funding apparatus of the utopians, the Youth Project, which disburses $6 million a year, and was mentioned earlier as a recipient of government funds. In cooperation with the United Auto Workers, Ford in 1968 established the Center for Community Change, which two years later created the Youth Project. The two shared headquarters for some time. Ford continued to fund both: it gave the Center for Community Change $650,000 in 1975, $350,000 in 1978, and $374,000 in 1980, and to the Youth Project gave $200,000 in 1978. (The name derives from the requirement that individuals must be under 30 to be selected for the board.)

Other foundations give varying proportions of their income to the utopians. The Rockefeller Brothers Foundation, founded in 1940 by the five sons and daughter of John D. Rockefeller, Jr., donates heavily to environmental organizations, including the most militant of them. It also gives money to IPS spinoffs. For example, in 1979 it gave $60,000 to the Bay Area Institute "for expansion of the Pacific News Service which disseminated in-depth analyses and reports on major issues shaping the future of the United States to national news outlets."

Among the number of sometime contributors to the utopians are the nine foundations which belong to Joint Foundation Support Inc., which advises them on appropriate "social change-oriented programs." The grants are to the typical IPS spinoffs as well as to IPS itself, to public interest law groups and to the most anti-development of the environmental groups. Among the other large number of occasional contributors to the utopians are Joyce, J.M. Kaplan, Piton, Edna McConnell Clark, Scherman, Mary Reynolds Babcock, John Hay Whitney, Compton, San Francisco, Public Welfare and Janss. The Janss Foundation is particularly interesting. Its founder, Edwin W. Janss, Jr. was a member of the IPS board of trustees for several years. Richard Neuhaus, a Lutheran minister who was a leader of Clergy and Laity Concerned during the Vietnam war years, reports that Janss, speaking of his beautiful California home, told him that when the revolution came, the houses of his neighbors would be people's palaces. "But I'm going to live in mine."[54] Janss' son Larry was a member of the IPS staff in the early 1970s. In addition to contributing to IPS, Janss has funded various IPS spinoffs.

In some cases foundations that give only a small part of their resources to the utopians seem not to realize what they are doing. Katherine Mountcastle was director of the Mary Reynolds Babcock Foundation for twenty-eight years and trustee of the A. Smith Reynolds Foundation for sixteen. She was invited by North Carolina Senator John East to attend a meeting at which Tom Pauken, recently appointed by Reagan to head ACTION, passed out a list of what he described as "leftist groups funded by VISTA." Mrs. Mountcastle was angered to see that one of the groups listed was a grantee of her foundation. She was so upset by what she heard that she testified on behalf of VISTA before a Congressional committee shortly thereafter. Mrs. Mountcastle explained that in her view community-based organizations are "as American as New England town meetings." She said:

> "These groups have kept our society from revolution and they have kept it from hardening of the social arteries. They are a way to provide

> widest public participation in the improvement of life for all of us. Again, I emphasize—they are the essence of our democracy."[55]

Mrs. Mountcastle simply could not believe that there might be community organizers who would seek to destroy rather than strengthen the American economic, political and social system.

In 1976 Henry Ford II, who had served on the board of the Ford Foundation, and had for years accepted the need for the "social application of the art of jujitsu" advocated by Ford Foundation national affairs director Paul Ylvisaker, had lost his earlier illusions. In his letter of resignation from the board he wrote:

> "The foundation exists and thrives on the fruits of our economic system. . . It is hard to discern recognition of this fact in anything the foundation does. . . I'm not playing the role of the hard-headed tycoon who thinks all philanthropoids are Socialists and all university professors are Communists. I'm just suggesting to the trustees and staff that the system that makes the foundation possible very probably is worth preserving. Perhaps it is time for the trustees and staff to examine the question of our obligations to our economic system and to consider how the foundation as one of the system's most prominent offspring, can act most wisely to strengthen and improve its progenitor."[56]

The utopians are not content with the large sums they garner annually from foundations: they believe they are entitled to all the money foundations dispense. And in the typical fashion of the utopians, they have established an organization to attack the present system of private philanthropy. Called the National Committee for Responsive Philanthropy, it developed in response to a 1973 Commission on Private Philanthropy and Public Needs established by John D. Rockefeller III, which became known as the Filer Commission after its chairman, John H. Filer, head of the Aetna Casualty Corporation.

The "donee group," as the National Committee for Responsive Philanthropy was originally known, was composed of a number of leaders of utopian organizations: Margery Tabankin, then head of the Youth Project; Pablo Eisenberg, President of the Center for Community Change; Charles Halpern, Director of the Council for Public Interest Law as well as members of community-organizing groups. It managed to obtain financing from the Filer Commission to attack it on the grounds that the Commission was giving "inadequate consideration" to such fields as "public interest law, consumer and environmental organizations,'' the groups whose interests the donee group represented.

The donee group did not merely want more for its own members; it demanded a total restructuring of philanthropy so as to be assured that the groups it represented received *everything*. The donee group demanded that government take over total responsibility for the charitable functions presently supported by foundations. Private philanthropy would then be able to devote itself to ''support of organizations monitoring, overseeing or seeking changes in government, industry and other established institutions.''[57] In other words, the role of private philanthropy would become to challenge existing institutions.

The donee group proposed changes in the structure of foundations that would ensure they had no choice. Private foundations would be transformed into ''public'' institutions by transferring control of virtually all foundations to boards, two-thirds of whose members would be representatives of ''the public''—with quotas for women, minorities etc.[58] The proposals are similar to those of Ralph Nader for ''democratizing,'' i.e. politicizing, the corporation. The same requirements would apply to corporate philanthropy. However, the donee group sought to expand the utopian war-chest still further by assessing an additional 2% tax on corporations, which could be offset by gifts to charity. But the corporation would have no control over how the money was spent: decisions would be made by boards on which self-styled representatives of the ''public interest'' had a majority. With the help of the Center for Community Change, the donee group became ''institutionalized'' as the National Committee for Responsive Philanthropy.

The third major source of funding for the utopians are the churches, especially the mainline Protestant denominations and the Catholic Church's Campaign for Human Development. How much church money goes to them is impossible to say. Unlike other tax-exempt organizations, churches do not need to file reports with the government on how they spend their money. In most cases the national bureaucracies of the churches are also not accountable to the membership. Nonetheless there is sufficient evidence to make it obvious that the sums are substantial.

Thanks to the pioneering work of David Jessup more is known about the United Methodist Church's funding of utopian groups than about their funding by any other church. As we noted earlier, apart from the United Methodists, none of the mainline denominations have a policy of full financial disclosure. However, evidence of church funding of the utopians trickles out. Recipients sometimes acknowledge gifts and many of the groups that receive money from churches must themselves file annual statements with government agencies disclosing the source of their income (although these forms as filled out often provide little information). The Indochina Resource Center, whose director testified before Congress that the Khmer Rouge was motivated by concern for the population's welfare in emptying Pnom Penh, acknowledged that the bulk of its money in 1974 and 1975—$50,000 and $60,000 respectively—came from the United Methodist Church.[59] The National Campaign to Stop the B-1 Bomber mentioned several donations it had received from churches, including the United Church of Christ. Earlier we mentioned the acknowledgement by the South Africa conference controlled by the U.S. Communist Party of funds received from the United Methodist Church and the National Council of Churches. And sometimes gifts become known as a result of inadvertence on the part of the church leadership. For example, the ten thousand dollars which the United Presbyterian Church gave to the Angela Davis Defense Fund came out thanks to the unexpected probing of a delegate at a national meeting.

A number of utopian groups depend almost wholly upon the mainline churches for financial support. The Coalition for a New Foreign and Military Policy's annual report reveals that it is funded almost exclusively by its member churches although it also includes as members numerous secular organizations. That coalition is one of the two major umbrella organizations of the utopians. Similarly the Washington Office on Latin America and the Washington Office on Africa, both of which reveal a pronounced double standard in relation to human rights violations by countries friendly to the U.S. and by Marxist regimes, are both funded almost wholly by the mainline churches.

Much of the contribution made by churches is not in the form of money but in services of various kinds: staff time, telephone, stationery, literature distribution etc. An official of the United Methodist Board of Church and Society told *Human Events* reporter Max Friedman that the United Methodist Church often took organizations under its wing, providing a bank account, bookeeping, office space and other in-kind services. The Indochina Resource Center, apologists for the Pol Pot regime, according to Friedman, not only received money but equally important, its tax-deductible status through the United Methodist Church.[60]

Another service the churches have provided is the laundering of money. The National Campaign to Stop the B-1 Bomber was a registered lobby, and thus donations to it were not tax deductible. But Clergy and Laity Concerned, in raising money for the Campaign, sent out a fund-raising appeal with a footnote which said "Checks payable to the Washington Square Methodist Church are tax deductible."[61] Another letter said: "CALC is working with the National Council of Churches on this program. If tax deductibility enables you to make a larger gift, your check may be made payable to the NCC."[62] The Internal Revenue Service had investigated the National Council of Churches several years earlier and found that, in 1971, Clergy and Laity Concerned received $250,000 of its $700,000 budget through the tax deductible channel of the NCC. The NCC claimed, and the IRS accepted the claim, that this kind of contribution of a tax exempt status to a second party did not violate the IRS rules governing the involvement of tax-exempt groups in political activity because it did not involve a "substantial part" of the NCC's revenues.[63] Nonetheless it certainly involves the churches in a subversion of congressional intent which is to make contributions to lobbying organizations taxable.

Some of the grants the mainline churches give the utopians are not hidden and yet involve an element of deception in that the churchgoer is helped to misunderstand the nature of the program to which he is giving. For example, many of the mainline denominations have hunger programs to which church members are asked to contribute. Typically the literature accompanying appeals for funds shows a needy child and specifies how much rice $10 can buy. Yet although the United Presbyterian Church alone raised almost $3 million in 1979 for its hunger program, less than 20% of that amount went in direct relief.[64] While much of the remaining 80% went to worthwhile projects, funds also went to the utopians. The Institute on Religion and Democracy estimated that over $300,000 in 1981 went to utopian organizations. Much of the money went to groups that blame commercial agriculture for the underdevelopment of poor nations and advocate "socialist experiments" like those of China, Cuba, Vietnam and Nicaragua.[65] As the IRD's Kerry Ptacek points out, there is considerable irony in this, for if there ever was a race won by capitalism, it has been in the area of agriculture, where at worst, socialism has caused famine, at best, simple agricultural stagnation. Presbyterian hunger money has also gone to the North American Congress on Latin America and MERIP, whom we have already encountered in connection with their support for revolutionary violence in Latin America and the Middle East, respectively.

Similarly the National Council of Churches coordinates an Ecumenical Domestic Hunger Project Network consisting of 105 projects that receive money from churchgoers responding to hunger appeals in member churches. Here an even larger portion of the money goes to utopian projects. Mary Ellen Lloyd, coordinator of the network, has described some of the projects funded. The Interlink Press Service "alerts people to third world needs;" the Politics of Food Taskforce is a network in Rochester that "banded together to affect the political process;" the Food Law Center consists of "lawyers who deal with land issues;" National Land for People is "primarily a politicizing group" concerned that so much profitable land in California is "owned by enormous companies and agribusiness;" even something called the Free Store, which provides clothing, furniture and food cheaply, also "has a strong component of teaching people how to battle the system."[66] Most of the other ninety-nine projects are in a similar mold. One of them, the Corporate Data Exchange, started by three NACLA staffers and originally listed as an IPS-Transnational project, collects data on corporations useful in campaigns against them. Presumably the activists who run these projects believe that if they can destroy "the system," the end of hunger will automatically follow.

The Catholic Church has also been a major contributor to the utopians through its Campaign for Human Development. The Campaign's annual budget, collected through a special appeal within parishes, is approximately $7.5 million a year and it has raised $90 million since its inception in 1970. Fr. Marvin Mottet, its director, was a member of ACORN and explains that the Campaign for Human Development is not designed to provide direct services to the poor: "Why you know, passing out food and clothing—that's a bottomless pit." Rather, he says, the Campaign is "organized for institutional change."[67]

The largest grants have gone to community-organizing projects of the Alinsky school: the largest single recipient has been the Industrial Areas Foundation, founded by Alinsky, with ACORN the second. The Campaign has contributed one-sixth of ACORN's national budget over the years, giving $200,000 in 1982. Apart from a series of Alinsky-type community action organizations the Campaign has founded groups like "Organizing Former Mental Patients," "End Racism in Public Service," "Southern Prisoners Defense Committee" and "Original Tribal Lands Withdrawal and Return."[68] It is hard to see how the activities of the Campaign's recipients benefit the poor more than direct services. The Campaign gave the Dallas chapter of ACORN $50,000 in 1979. That same year the chapter urged members to soak the computer bill card they received from their utility in hot water and iron it before returning it so that it could not be machine-processed. Members were also told to overpay by a penny and demand credit. This sort of guerilla theater is satisfying to the utopians but of little help to the poor.

An unusual program providing substantial sums to the utopians is the so-called "Veatch program" of the North Shore Unitarian Church in Plandome, New York. Established in 1959 in honor of Caroline Veatch, it was originally designed to "assist Unitarian fellowships and churches and other Unitarian efforts designed to foster and promote Unitarianism." A decade later the congregation voted to expand the Veatch program's activities to "worthy community, state and national programs." The end result has been that much of the $6 million donated annually by the Veatch program goes to utopian projects. Indeed so wide is the range of grantees that more than any other single granting source, the Veatch program supports a veritable Who's Who of the utopian organizations discussed in this book. Among the peace groups it funds SANE, the Riverside Church Disarmament Project, the American Friends Service Committee, and Clergy and Laity Concerned and of the Institutes it funds the Institute for Policy Studies, the Center for International Policy, the Center for National Security Studies and the Bay Area Institute's Pacific News Service. It also funds anti-nuclear energy organizations, community action groups, including ACORN, the Coalition for a New Foreign and Military Policy, the Naderite PIRGs, the Youth Project, and a variety of anti-corporate groups.[69]

Corporate philanthropy is the fourth—and probably the smallest—source of funding for the utopians. What is remarkable is that corporations should give them any money at all. In the case of foundations there is at least some distance between the original profit-making enterprise and the ultimate beneficiaries, intent on creating conditions in which such enterprises will no longer be able to exist. When corporations give money, whether directly or through foundations they set up, those presently running the enterprises are responsible for funding decisions, and the money comes from the pockets of the corporations' stockholders.

To some extent, corporations respond to what amounts to utopian blackmail. A typical utopian project, Gail Cincotta's National Training Information Center, engaged in Alinsky-style tactics against insurance companies. Aetna awarded the group $225,000[70] and it moved on to employing the same tactics against oil companies. Thus far the oil companies have not responded in Aetna's fashion to these tactics.

In a sense what is involved here is a short-sighted response in terms of perceived self-interest. Bad publicity and harassment can be avoided at a price which seems worth paying. Similarly railroads have given financial support to environmental groups seeking to make those who use waterways pay special fees to compensate for the pollution they cause. The railroads see these demands as a way to make themselves more competitive with water transport. They do not look to the longer-range goal of some of the environmentalist groups they support, which is to choke off all development, ultimately affecting railroad traffic as well.

The oil companies have resisted the National Training Information Center, but they have engaged in their own form of attempted cooptation through their investment in public television. So heavy has been their investment that PBC (the Public Broadcasting Corporation) is dubbed by insiders the Petroleum Broadcasting Corporation. The reasoning is that the antagonism of the utopians and those who resonate most to their criticisms will be eased by fostering a "positive image" through funding the programs these groups like to watch. It is dubious if the investment has the intended result.

There are corporations which serve as progressive bellwethers much in the manner of Field and Stern among the foundations, although thus far at least they have fewer followers among corporations than Field and Stern among foundations. Probably the corporations best known for their "innovative" philanthropy are the Aetna Casualty Corporation and the Cummins Engine Corporation, a leading manufacturer of truck diesel engines. Aetna's glossy report on its corporate giving program "Taking Part" says that Aetna urges its managers to consider public issues they can address "creatively." This translated into giving $1.8 million in 1980 to "non-traditional recipients" including "social change-agent organizations, grass roots neighborhood organizations and other groups that help increase the involvement of disadvantaged segments of society." Aetna funds a familiar list of utopian organizations, especially those involved in community organizing. Perhaps the most remarkable recipient, in terms of promoting interests diametrically opposed to those of Aetna shareholders, is the San Francisco based New School for Democratic Management, a project of the Foundation for National Progress, which was in turn established, according to its own financial statement "to perform the work of the Institute for Policy Studies on the West Coast." The purposes of the school have been defined by one of its founders, Derek Shearer. "Our Alternative Business School is not just about learning better skills. It is an ideological challenge to the rest of society" on issues such as "why workers do not run their own firms" and "why there are no workers and consumers on corporate boards of directors." Shearer believes the Italian Communist Party should serve as a model for the school because of its "strong cooperative movement and a number of successful enterprises and newspapers" as well as the "model of city management" it provides for the city of Bologna.[71] Aetna gave the school $15,000 in 1980.

An almost equally remarkable recipient of Aetna money is the National Committee for Responsive Philanthropy whose goals, as we have seen, include taking control of corporate donations from corporations and giving it instead to representatives of the "public interest" on the grounds that corporations can hardly be expected to underwrite the needs of Americans who want "to redistribute and deconcentrate" wealth.[72] Of course Aetna may feel that "public interest" representatives could hardly improve on its own performance.

The Cummins Engine Corporation's report echoes Naderite philosophy to the extent of referring to "stakeholders," a Naderite notion, rather than "shareholders" in the corporation. The Cummins report says that "managing Cummins is the art of balancing competing stakeholder claims responsibility." (That Cummins should acknowledge "competing" claims is interesting since the public interest movement never suggests publicly that there can be competition between those who represent the public interest.) Cummins gives to organizations like the Center for Community Change, the Interreligious Foundation for Community Organizations (IFCO), the Pacific News Service, the American Friends Service Committee, the National Committee for Responsive Philanthropy, even the National Conference of Black Lawyers, which, it will be remembered, is affiliated with the international Soviet front, the International Association of Democratic Lawyers, and the National Black United Front, whose "anti-Zionism" poorly conceals its hostility to Jews. Its leader, the Rev. Herbert Daughtry, on a visit to Iraq, declared: "The same elements that make life miserable for us in the United States, make life miserable for our brothers and sisters in other parts of the world."[73]

A corporate foundation that funds the utopians almost exclusively is the Playboy Foundation. Given the maverick character of Playboy Enterprises' chairman, Hugh Hefner, and the unusual nature of the product, this is not surprising. Prisoner Support Coalitions, the Institute for Policy Studies and its offshoots, Nader organizations, gay rights groups, "peace" groups like Clergy and Laity Concerned, are all Playboy Foundation recipients. More remarkably, especially since the Foundation's literature asserts that its money is given "to implement the principles of the Playboy Philosophy," the major recipients of the Foundation are what are labelled "women's rights" groups, almost all of which are women's liberation groups. Midge Decter has noted that given the history of Playboy Magazine and associated enterprises as a target of demonstrations by the women's liberation movement, the grants might well be termed "blood money."[74]

While corporations with philanthropic programs like Aetna, Cummins and Playboy are rare, the number of corporations that give minor sums to the utopians is much larger. Perhaps the most egregious recipient of funding from a whole series of corporate household names is the Youth Project, which channels money to the most extreme groups within all the utopian sectors. Predictably Aetna donates, but so does the Carnegie Corporation, General Mills Foundation, Phillips-Van Heusen Foundation, the Helena Rubinstein Foundation, the United California Bank-Contribution Committee, McDonald's Foundation, the Monsanto Fund, Best Products Foundation and the Carheart Corporation. The Center for Community Change, which created the Youth Project, has also received substantial corporate support, receiving $30,000 from Atlantic Richfield in 1981 and in the same year $25,000 from Levi-Strauss, $15,000 from Travelers Insurance and $100,000 from Aetna. Militant environmental and consumer groups and projects of the radical institutes also receive occasional corporate support. Atlantic Richfield contributed $7,500 to the New School for Democratic Management in 1980; General Mills Foundation contributed $5,000 to the National Committee for Responsive Philanthropy and the International Paper Foundation gave $5,000 to the Environmental Action Coalition.

But probably the largest corporate donations to the utopians go to groups or programs that seem to aid minorities. The African-American Institute, discussed earlier, received funds from Corning, Borg-Warner, Exxon and Gulf Oil, the latter contributing a substantial

$55,000 in 1981. The Martin Luther King Center for Non-Violent Social Change, which opened in 1982, was an immediate corporate favorite, receiving $400,000 from the Ford Motor Co., $100,000 from Atlantic Richfield, $30,000 from the Amoco Foundation, $30,000 from Exxon and smaller amounts from a large number of corporations. The Center's name, and the fact that the famous civil rights leader's widow served as its President, undoubtedly inspired confidence in corporate officers. Yet as David Asman showed in a study for the Committee for the Free World, the Center's work, from its own account, is clearly imbued with the standard utopian premises: military spending is bad; the Reagan administration is villainous; major "social change" is essential; and the struggle for human rights is the struggle of third world Marxist liberation movements. Similarly several Hispanic organizations with utopian agendas including the National Council of La Raza and the Puerto Rican Legal Defense and Education Fund receive considerable corporate funding.[75]

But most corporations avoid the utopians, who are understandably dissatisfied with what they receive and view corporate charitable donations as a potential huge prize. Corporations have now edged out foundations as a source of philanthropic dollars, contributing approximately $2.7 billion annually. Part of that money—$400 million—shows up in the $1.4 billion given annually to the various United Ways, the federated charity to which Americans contribute at both the corporate and government workplace. While in the long term the utopians would like, as we have seen, to wrest control of the corporate philanthropic dollar from the corporation, turning it over to boards made up of people like themselves, in the short term, they have focussed on obtaining funds through United Ways.

Through law suits, press releases, Congressional lobbying, conferences and articles, the Committee for Responsive Philanthropy has sought to force the inclusion of "advocacy organizations" among the charities to which contributions may go at the workplace. The advantage of receiving funds through United Way, or through competing federated campaigns the utopians want to see established at workplaces, is that collection costs are minor (often absorbed by the employer) and the funds taken in are large. Typically, raising money at the workplace costs only 4-8¢ on the dollar while other techniques cost 25-30¢ per dollar. Moreover drives in business and government obtain up to a 40% response while direct mail is lucky to yield a 5% return. If the United Way (or Community Chest—the names of federated drives differ) raises the funds, the burden of fund-raising is lifted from the utopians, an eventuality particularly welcomed at a time when the government funding on which they had learned to rely has been dwindling.

The method taken by the utopians has been to launch an all-out attack on the United Way. They have called it a "charity OPEC" and accuse it of serving simply as a corporate tax dodge. The National Committee for Responsive Philanthropy charges the United Way with "static funding patterns" that deprive "new, leading edge organizations, now being formed more rapidly than ever in the nation's history."[76] Boston sociologist David Horton Smith, a member of the original "donee group" wrote a paper distributed by the National Committee which said: "United Ways are first and foremost a politicized type of organization. They are highly visible in the community, and their control is of interest to the local community power structure. They closely reflect the prevailing power structure of their larger environment, both locally and nationally."[77] (There is a certain unconscious humor in these charges, given that the goal of the National Committee is precisely to "politicize" workplace charity, directing it away from direct services to what the Committee calls "public needs.")

While a few local United Ways have succumbed to pressure, for the most part the federated funds have resisted what they see as the potential destruction of the system they have successfully built up since 1949.

Despite the revolutionary demand of the utopians, as set forth by the National Committee for Responsive Philanthropy, to redefine charity as political advocacy, they have had considerable success with the media, which has sympathetically echoed their charges of "monopolistic practices" against United Ways and with the courts. In South Carolina an organization called "The Other Way" brought together 19 political advocacy groups including the South Carolina Committee Against Hunger, the Utility Reform Coalition, the American Civil Liberties Union and a group called Pie in the Sky. It obtained access to corporate and federal government workplaces. The pattern of recent court decisions has on the whole supported the demands of advocacy groups to inclusion in workplace fund-raising drives.

While in the short term the utopian groups will obviously benefit, the longer term result is likely to be destruction of workplace philanthropy as it becomes the source of increasing controversy. The experience of the Combined Federal Services Campaign is instructive. Established in 1961 to give Federal employees a central fund-raising program on the pattern of United Way, it raises $87 million annually, or approximately $800 for each charity on the list. The utopians brought suit in federal court to open up the list and they won.[78] But while this opened the way for the Natural Resources Defense Council, the National Organization of Women Legal Defense and Education Fund and other groups favored by the utopians, it also opened the way for groups of a competing political perspective. The National Right to Life Education Fund, an anti-abortion group, the National Right to Work Legal Defense Fund, the Pacific Legal Foundation, the Capital Legal Foundation and the Conservative Legal Defense and Education Fund all demanded and won a place. The inclusion of the National Right to Work Legal Defense Fund caused an uproar in the AFL-CIO which decided not to call a boycott but to urge members to designate the groups which would receive their contribution, making sure no money went to the Right to Work organization.[79] The end result of politicizing workplace charity in the way the utopians have successfully begun to do can only be to undermine the whole system of federated charity with its long record of efficient fund-raising

We have of course discussed funding of left-wing groups and it may be objected that we have ignored the funding of anti-democratic groups on the right. But at this point in time this is much less of a problem. Irwin Suall, Fact Finding Director of the Anti Defamation League of B'nai Brith, which has traditionally been much more concerned with the threat from the right than that from the left, says: "It is my distinct impression that right wing extremist groups get much less support from foundations than do left extremists."[80] The same is true for the other sources of funding that have been described here.

Lenin is supposed to have predicted that capitalists would sell the rope with which they would eventually be hung. And the great economist Joseph Schumpeter analyzed the ways in which capitalism produced, fostered and protected its critics. Nonetheless both might have been surprised by the success of the utopians. Lenin never predicted capitalists would donate the rope and Schumpeter did not foresee that the capitalist system would provide "grants" to its executioners.

REFERENCES

1. Daniel P. Moynihan, *Maximum Feasible Misunderstanding,* New York, The Free Press, 1969, p. 23

2. Ibid., p. 94
3. Ibid., p. 156
4. Tabankin was trained by Alinsky's Industrial Areas Foundation. She represented the National Student Association at the Moscow-controlled World Peace Assembly and visited North Vietnam during the war under the auspices of the People's Coalition for Peace and Justice, described by the House Committee on Internal Security as "tightly controlled by the Socialist Workers Party." See "The New Left in Government," Institution Analysis No. 9, The Heritage Foundation, November 1978, p. 22
5. *The Sunday* (Boulder) *Camera,* June 14, 1981
6. Report No. 96-164, Domestic Volunteer Service Act, 96th Congress, 1st Session, House of Representatives, Testimony of Rep. John Ashbrook, p. 70, 76, 77
7. Letter to editor, *Commercial Appeal,* Memphis, Tennessee, Jan. 31, 1982
8. "The New Left in Government; Pt. II" Institution Analysis No. 17, Heritage Foundation, February 1982, pp. A14-A15.
9. The phrase "social and cultural genocide" was used by Western Action Training Institute in its application for funds from the Campaign for Human Development dated January 31, 1979.
10. A Vista grant given to cover the span 12/29/79-10/28/81 provided eight volunteers with this organizing target.
11. Anna Gyorgy, "International Nuke Notes," *WIN,* Oct. 1, 1981.
12. Proposal submitted by AMCOM Productions to National Endowment for the Humanities. NEG Grant Reference No. PN-20182-81-0439.
13. Remarks for Senate Commerce Committee Hearing on Intervenor Funding by Senator Alan K. Simpson, September 19, 1979
14. Ibid.
15. H. Peter Metzger, "Government-Funded Activism: Hiding Behind the Public Interest," Presented at 47th Annual Conference. S. E. Electric Exchange, March 26, 1980. Publ. by Public Service Co. of Colorado, Denver, Colorado, p. 19
16. H. Peter Metzger and Richard A. Westfall, "Government Activists: How They Rip Off the Poor," First presented at Commonwealth North, Anchorage, Alaska, August 19, 1980 (Updated April 1, 1981) p. 18
17. *Rocky Mountain News,* March 10, 1981
18. *Rocky Mountain News,* March 25, 1982
19. *Wall Street Journal,* May 18, 1981
20. Ibid.
21. H. Peter Metzger and Richard A. Westfall, op. cit. (updated) p. 5
22. H. Peter Metzger, "Government Activists" (not updated) p. 23
23. Metzger and Westfall, "Government Activists" (updated) pp. 36-37
24. Ibid., p. 38
25. Report of Office of Inspector General, Community Services Administration Audit Report No. 3-81-905, March 27, 1981. Available at Conservative Caucus Foundation, Vienna, Va.
26. Ibid.
27. Ibid.
28. The Council on Interracial Books for Children, Institution Analysis No. 18, *The Heritage Foundation,* Wash. D.C., p. 1
29. Ibid., p. 2
30. Grant #FGP 1-80CF10083, Grant date 2/21/81-3/20/81
31. Available at Conservative Caucus Foundation, Vienna, Va.
32. The data were compiled by the Conservative Caucus Foundation from Freedom of Information inquiries concerning government agencies, including the Department of Labor, Department of Energy and Community Services Administration

33. David Asman, "The Wisconsin Land Tenure Center," Institution Analysis No. 22, Heritage Foundation, Wash., D.C., Jan. 1983, pp. 3-7
34. David Asman, "The African-American Institute," Institution Analysis No. 23, Heritage Foundation, Wash., D.C., March 1983, pp. 5-7
35. Quoted in William T. Lanouette, "The Private Foundations with a Very Public Role," *National Journal,* Feb. 17, 1979, p. 260
36. *New York Times,* May 1, 1975
37. John Train, "Invective from the Left," *Forbes,* Aug. 3, 1981, p. 110
38. "Organized Subversion and the U.S. Armed Forces: Hearings Before the Subcommittee to Investigate the Administration of the Internal Security Act and Other Internal Security Laws of the Committee on the Judiciary," U.S. Senate, 94th Congress, 1st Session, Part I, the U.S. Navy, Sept. 25, 1975, pp. 26, 66-69.
39. Susan K. Reed, "Nuclear Anonymity," *Foundation News,* January/February 1983, p. 45
40. Statement of Morris B. Abram, President of Field Foundation to the Board of Directors and Members of the Field Foundation, Oct. 12, 1981
41. "The Attempt to Steal the Bicentennial: The People's Bicentennial Commission: Hearings before the Subcommittee to Investigate the Administration of the Internal Security Act and Other Internal Security Laws of the Committee on the Judiciary," United States Senate, 49th Congress, Second Session March 17 and 18, 1976, p. 88
42. *Information Digest,* April 4, 1975
43. Michael Kinsley, "The Doctor's Plot" *The New Republic,* April 11, 1981, p. 14
44. Dan Rottenberg, "Some Ways the Rich Part with their Millions," *Parade,* March 22, 1981, p. 10
45. *Robin Hood Was Right: A Guide to Giving Your Money for Social Change,* Vanguard Public Foundation, 1977, p. 4
46. Transcript "Today Show" Interview with George Pillsbury and Peggy Stearn, August 4, 1980
47. Haymarket People's Fund 1979 Annual Report, p. 9
48. Dan Rottenberg, op. cit., p. 10
49. Ibid.
50. Haymarket People's Fund 1976 Annual Report, p. 3
51. Report for 1979, Rank and File Inc., Boston, Mass.
52. *Robin Hood Was Right,* op. cit., p. 32
53. Susan K. Reed, op. cit., p. 47
54. Interview, Richard Neuhaus, March 20, 1982
55. Statement of Mrs. Katherine B. Mountcastle, U.S. House of Representatives Committee on Government Operations, Subcommittee on Manpower and Housing, March 24, 1982
56. *New York Times,* Jan. 12, 1977
57. "Private Philanthropy—Vital and Innovative or Passive and Irrelevant" *The Donee Group Report and Recommendations, Research Papers Sponsored by the Commission on Private Philanthropy and Public Needs,* Vol. I, Leonard H. Filer, chairman, Department of the Treasury, 1977, p. 59
58. "National Committee for Responsive Philanthropy" Institution Analysis No. 8, Heritage Foundation, August 1978, pp. 6-7
59. Unpublished study by Max Friedman, "Radical Lobbying: A Historical Precedent"
60. Ibid.
61. Letter is dated Fall 1975 and signed by Don Luce and Rich Boardman
62. Letter is dated Spring 1975 and also signed by Don Luce and Rich Boardman
63. Max Friedman, op. cit.

64. *Presbyterian Layman,* April/May 1981, p. 12
65. *Religion and Democracy,* Newsletter of the Institute on Religion and Democracy, July-August 1982
66. Telephone interview, Mary Ellen Lloyd, January 18, 1982
67. Interview with Fr. Marvin Mottet by Paul Fisher, *The Wanderer,* June 18, 1982, p. 9
68. "Where There's A Thirst for Justice," Campaign for Human Development Report 1978
69. Annual reports of the Veatch Program of the North Shore Unitarian Church are available at the Foundation Center, New York City
70. *Response,* published by the Clearinghouse on Corporate Social Responsibility, March 1981, p. 4
71. Derek Shearer, "Economic Alternatives—Fundamental to Political Alternatives," *National Conference Newsletter,* Conference on Alternative State and Local Public Policies, No. 9, Nov. 1977
72. Quoted in Kenneth A. Bertsch, *Corporate Philanthropy,* Investor Responsibility Research Center, p. 28
73. New York *Amsterdam News,* April 5, 1980
74. *Contentions,* published by the Committee for the Free World, April-May 1982, p. 4
75. David Asman, study on corporate funding for the Committee for the Free World (in press)
76. "National Committee for Responsive Philanthropy," Institution Analysis No. 8, op. cit., p. 14
77. Ibid., p. 13
78. *New York Times,* July 24, 1982
79. *New York Times,* August 3, 1982
80. Interview, Irwin Suall, May 23, 1983

X

Utopians In Government

The coercive utopians have found a new use for government bureaucracies—to subvert the constitutional arrangements of the country. While the public continues to assume it has control over policy through electing representatives whose actions can then be endorsed or repudiated at the polls, the new breed of bureaucrats simply disregards the legislative mandates under which government agencies operate to pursue their own goals.

The utopian bureaucrats see their role quite differently from traditional bureaucrats. Bureaucracy has had a bad press, and no one disputes the fact that traditional bureaucracy developed undesirable traits. Bureaucrats live by the rules and rules do not account for all cases. In addition to the suffering caused to those who do not conform to unimaginatively applied criteria, there is the loss of vigor in the bureaucratic system: flexibility and initiative are not rewarded, but rather meticulous adherence to routine, which has become an end in itself. The original goals of the bureaucracy can be lost sight of, as the smooth functioning of the bureaucratic apparatus and its preservation take the place of the broad purposes the bureaucracy was established to fulfill. The ills sometimes caused the virtues of modern bureaucracies to be forgotten: they were uncorrupted, at their best efficient, and those who filled bureaucratic posts saw themselves as loyal executors of the statutes and regulations they were entrusted to administer.

But when the coercive utopians take up bureaucratic posts, they see themselves not as agents of legitimate elected authority, but as executors of the will of "the people" as they intuitively understand it. Utopian bureaucrats thus feel free to reshape, circumvent and disregard the laws they are assigned to administer. They do so with perfect good conscience, for they see themselves as incarnating the popular will and pursuing the common good. A fine expression of this attitude was the final act of utopian bureaucrat Paul Bloom on his last day in office as a lawyer in the Department of Energy. Without any authority for his action, Bloom simply gave away $4 million in public funds to four charities. In an ecumenical gesture, he gave $1 million each to the National Council of Catholic Charities, the National Council of Churches, the Council of Jewish Federations and the Salvation Army.[1] This modern Robin Hood told the groups to use the money to help the poor with their fuel bills.

While the utopians found their way into government administration in the 1960s, attracted especially to the Office of Economic Opportunity (later the Community Services Administration), it was not until the Carter administration that they were given leading roles in a whole series of bureaucracies. Writing in *Fortune,* during Carter's first year, journalist Juan Cameron identified sixty consumer, environmental and public interest activists who immediately moved into sub-cabinet posts and influential White House spots. While the environmentalists initially secured more key posts than any other group—seven staff members from the Natural Resources Defense Council alone received high ranking government posts—Peter Metzger estimates that before the administration's end, several hundred utopians were installed in key positions.

Carter's appointments even extended to the America-the-Enemy think tanks and to warriors against American imperialism. Brown and Tabankin of ACTION were mentioned earlier. Ilona Hancock, of the steering committee of the Institute for Policy Studies' National Committee on Alternative State and Local Public Policies, became director of the Western Region of ACTION. Hancock had won national attention when she was elected to the city council of Berkeley, California and refused to recite the pledge of allegiance as long as there was "racial discrimination, police brutality and joblessness,"[2] necessitating, one presumed, a permanent inability to salute the flag. John Froines was appointed as Deputy Director of the National Institute for

Occupational Safety and Health. Froines, along with Abbie Hoffman and Tom Hayden, was a member of the "Chicago 7," the group whose trial became famous for deliberate disruption of the courtroom in an effort to undercut respect for the American system of justice. IPS trustee Sidney Harmon became Undersecretary of Commerce and Consultant to the Center for International Policy. David Aaron became Deputy Assistant for National Security Affairs.

Utopians in high places brought in others as consultants and assistants to swell their ranks in lower echelons. Morton Halperin, Director of the Center for National Security Studies, the institute whose role in undermining U.S. intelligence capabilities was described earlier, wrote of the transformation that had occurred within three months of Carter's inauguration.

> "The clearest sign of change is the people. When an ACLU delegation called first on the Attorney General and later on White House issues coordinator Stu Eisenstadt, we were surrounded by old friends who were the staff assistants of Bell and Eisenstadt and used to toil with us from the outside on these issues."[3]

The decision to make the severest critics of government performance the executors of government policy was not in itself particularly remarkable. Carter was, by no means, the first leader to have concluded that critics have thought carefully about the failures of existing approaches and systems and may well have a better way to achieve common goals. That this was the general assumption seems clear from a remark of Secretary of Agriculture Bob Berglund. When Berglund showed up at a Capitol Hill hearing flanked by Carol Tucker Foreman, a former consumer movement leader appointed Assistant Secretary of Agriculture, and Robert Greenstein, formerly an activist with the Community Nutrition Institute, now special assistant to the Department, one Congressman could not conceal his surprise, which was apparently aroused no less by the physical transformation of Greenstein, in shirt, tie and jacket, than by his presence with the Agriculture Secretary. While Greenstein flushed, apparently at the reference to his altered appearance, Berglund remarked: "For years he was a critic of the Department of Agriculture. We thought he was so good we brought him on board."[4]

What Carter did not realize was that the goals of the utopians were of a very different nature from the traditional consensual goals of Americans. The utopians were motivated by an aesthetic-moral vision of egalitarian small-scale societies in which technology and production were fitted in a manner "appropriate" to the level of understanding and competence of small and stable communities. For the utopians, the traditional emphasis on providing the American public with plentiful consumer goods merely fed false materialist values and strengthened the centralized industrial system that prevented the development of the desired new social forms. The utopians were opposed to economic growth and as Peter Metzger has thoroughly documented in his essay, "The Coercive Utopians," after which this book is named, within a year of Carter's assuming the Presidency, his utopian appointees had succeeded in stopping development cold.

In one agency after another, the new bureaucrats worked to bring energy and industrial development to a halt. In the Department of Interior, the newly installed utopians actually handed over control of coal leasing on federal lands to the Natural Resources Defense Council. The stage had been set by a suit which the NRDC had brought against the Department of Interior in 1975. But Metzger points out that once attorneys from the NRDC and the Sierra Club (which had filed a series of joint suits against the government) moved into key positions in the Department of the Interior and the Justice Department, what started as an adversary proceeding became joint planning between former colleagues. As Metzger tells it, after the NRDC won its initial case:

> "using the excuse of the sure delay which would have been caused by a lengthy appeal, and the fact that the NRDC was willing to 'compromise,' the U.S. Department of Interior and Justice, now staffed with several key people ideologically associated with the plaintiffs, signed away the Government's right of appeal in this case in return for plaintiff NRDC agreeing that a very limited amount of coal leasing could commence. But in part of that agreement, signed on February 25, 1978, government lawyers actually gave NRDC an absolute veto on certain future coal leasing permitted by Interior. Thus, under the pretense of an adversary proceeding, a small group of like-minded, issue-oriented, ideologically associated lawyers privately agreed to move much of our national coal leasing authority from the government to a private environmentalist pressure group in what is clearly a flim-flam operation."[5]

The federal judge, presented with this jointly agreed-upon arrangement, disallowed NRDC's veto privilege, but permitted the rest of the agreement to stand despite the protests of Utah Power and Light, the only non-environmentalist party to the case, which argued it had been excluded from the negotiations between the NRDC and the Department of Interior.

Water development fared little better. The White House came out with an eighteen dam "hit list" prepared by Katherine Fletcher, formerly of the Environmental Defense Fund. In June 1978, the Solicitor of the Department of the Interior, without consulting state officials, shut down the Fryingpan-Arkansas water diversion project. Almost completed at a cost of $325 million, the project, it was announced, might pose a threat to the welfare of a special kind of cut-throat trout. "Incredible, unbelievable!" was the reaction of Felix Sparks, director of Colorado's Water Conservation Board.[6]

At the Environmental Protection Agency, interpretation of the Clean Air Act and its 1977 Amendments produced a virtual embargo on new industry. Metzger points out that the first casualty of the 1977 amendments to the Clean Air Act was the handiwork of Alan Merson, a Carter appointee to the EPA with a long utopian background. He stopped construction of two 700 MW coalfired power plants in Montana, a 1.4 billion dollar project. He did so on the ground that an EPA computer generated air model predicted that on some days each year EPA standards on a Northern Cheyenne Indian reservation miles away might be violated. Merson explained to the Denver Post that "economics in a sense becomes irrelevant."[7]

Carter's Council on Environmental Quality, headed by Gus Speth, formerly of the Natural Resources Defense Council, proposed requirements to force all federal agencies to assess the environmental impact in each foreign country of any project in which federal dollars were involved. Speth's proposals received reinforcement through a series of lawsuits brought by environmental organizations. They sued to stop a highway in Panama, railroad in central Gabon, a transmission line in southern Zaire, a reclamation project in Indonesia among others.

In agencies where the utopian bureaucrats were especially strong, they simply substituted their own agenda for the legislative mandates they were assigned to carry out. In the previous chapter we described the way ACTION, under the leadership of Brown and Tabankin, was transformed into a funding operation for the New Left. The Community Services Administration is another outstanding example of an agency that subverted its mandate. Created in 1974 as successor to the scandal-ridden Office of Economic Opportunity, the CSA under Carter diverted millions of dollars to utopian anti-corporate organizing in defiance of Congressional intent.

Much of the money the CSA recycled to utopian groups came into its hands as a result of the decision of Congress, in the wake of the 1973 oil boycott and the subsequent steep rise in price for oil, to cushion the impact on poor people by providing them with funds both to weatherize their homes and, through separate programs, to help pay their fuel bills. But the CSA's bureaucrats had their own ideas about the best way to aid the poor. For example, in fiscal 1977, the first year of the low-income fuel assistance programs, Congress allocated $200 million to help low-income people weatherize their homes. But a House of Representatives investigative team found the CSA used $36 million, or almost 20% of the total, for "other purposes," one of them being "energy advocacy." The House report asserted that in providing such funding, the CSA had "clearly overstepped its authority."[8]

What was "energy advocacy?" Even according to the CSA's own description, it was a strange activity to be sponsored by an agency whose purpose it was to carry out laws passed by Congress. Energy advocacy grants were designed, according to a CSA document, "to bring about changes in existing laws and administrative regulations related to energy matters which disproportionately affect or discriminate against the poor."[9] The CSA was funding programs whose very purpose was to change the laws and regulations passed by Congress.

In practice, energy advocacy turned out to be quite simply anti-utility company organizing and intervention in hearings before public utility commissions to block utility petitions for rate hikes, to promote "rate reform," and to prevent expansion of plants designed to meet future increased needs for energy. So central was intervention in utility rate proceedings to the new field of "energy advocacy" that a 1980 report to the regional executive board of the Energy Advocacy Project detailing accomplishments of the project in six western states dealt exclusively with the results of such intervention.[10]

In attacking every proposed rate hike, the CSA's energy advocates, apart from proposing "reform" of the rate structure, were forced to concentrate on those parts of utility budgets over which there is some discretion. This means primarily expansion of the system and modernization of the plant. The utopians argue that alternative energy will obviate the need for centralized energy production. Alternative energy will, at any rate, provide as much energy as the utopians believe is good for people, which as we have seen is not much energy. The newsletter of one of the energy advocacy projects featured a boxed quotation from a project associate in North Dakota. "And I for one will be happy to dance on Reddy Kilowatt's grave as soon as he is given a proper burial which will end the consumer-oriented economy he represents."[11] For the energy advocates, holding down rates by holding down production of energy is thus an unmixed blessing. They can point to their achievements as champions of the poor and look forward to phasing out centralized power production in favor of "appropriate" technology and the scaled down standards of living that are in the public's "higher" interest.

Not content with the funds it diverted to the new field of "energy activism," the CSA embarked upon schemes to capture millions more for the same and related purposes. From the standpoint of the CSA-funded agencies assigned to administer the money, they were merely acting as conduits for funds to hated utility companies. The money was designed to pay fuel bills for poor people which meant the utilities wound up with the money. The energy advocates made no secret of their unhappiness. William Schroer, testifying, on behalf of the CSA funded Colorado Energy Advocacy Office, before the Colorado Public Utilities Commission, was blunt: "We don't like having to deal with welfare programs that have to satisfy the needs of the low income with utilities."[12]

Inadvertently then, Congress had ordered teetotallers to ladle out drink. Those who wished to destroy utilities were being asked to finance them on the excuse that this benefited the poor whose bills were being paid. What happened was that CSA bureaucrats in the Community Action agencies around the country which administered the money, despite all their rhetoric of devotion to the poor, interpreted the statutes under which they operated so rigidly that they refused to aid anyone, however poor, who could not furnish a shutoff notice from a utility company. Moreover, the CSA set an arbitrary deadline of May 31, 1979, after which its agencies refused to consider requests for aid. As a result, the CSA was left with over $18 million in unspent funds at the end of the fiscal year.

At this point, government-funded lawyers from five Legal Service Corporation groups in different states brought a class action suit in the name of seven individual defendants and the Gray Panthers of Chicago, complaining that the CSA had violated both the regulations under which the fuel assistance program had been established and the intent of Congress, by their denial of aid to eligible applicants. The case was called Simer vs. Olivarez because the first of the seven plaintiffs was Elsie Simer, a 73 year old woman whose sole source of income was $287 a month in Social Security benefits. When she applied for help in meeting a $157.93 fuel bill, she was told she was ineligible because she did not have a shutoff notice. Olivarez referred to Graciela Olivarez, then head of the Community Services Administration. The lawyers from Legal Services detailed in their complaint the plight of the other plaintiffs whose requests for aid had been rejected by the CSA. Arlene Whitehouse was a blind 80 year old resident of Maine whose sole income was $211 a month; Arthur Boucher was a 70 year old home-bound resident of Lewiston, Maine whose sole income was $259 from Social Security and the Veterans Administration etc.[13]

United States District Court Judge John Grady of the Northern District of Illinois, before whom the case was brought, agreed that the CSA's regulation, requiring a shutoff notice as a condition of payment, was in violation of the Congressional statute establishing the program. He asserted that the next step would be to "certify a class," i.e. those people eligible, but refused aid by the CSA, who should get the money. But at this point, the attorneys on both sides intervened, saying that although this was what the suit had asked be done, they felt it would not be feasible and that they would prefer to try to reach an agreement between themselves. Several months later, they appeared before Judge Grady with an "agreed order" on which they wanted his signature. The CSA's lawyer assured Judge Grady that the agreement provided "a program whereby people who would meet all the requirements of the 1979 program would gain the benefits of this money. . ."[14] Assured by the lawyers for the government that the ways of spending the $18 million were in conformity with Congressional intent, Judge Grady signed the agreement.

But most of the money was earmarked for the utopians, scarcely those whom Congress had in mind by passing a program to pay fuel bills for poor people. Each of the seven plaintiffs received $250 by the terms of the "agreed order." The remaining $17,998,000 was divided up between a variety of projects suiting the identical ideologies of the CSA bureaucrats and the Legal Services attorneys. Four million was earmarked for "energy advocacy;" $2.3 million went to the National Consumer Law Center, a research "back-up" center funded by the Legal Services Corporation, which, not so incidentally, had done the early work on the suit; $200,000 was apportioned to the Citizen/Labor Energy Coalition, one of the Alinsky-style organizations discussed in an earlier chapter, for travel and other expenses connected with "coalition-building;" $2 million was assigned to solar resource centers and solar collectors; and $1 million was to go to "studies" on low income energy problems and alternative energy sources. The remaining $8 million was to be divided between energy conservation kits and a hypothermia program, these being the only uses to which the money was put that had any relation whatever to the Congressional authorizing legislation. Certainly it was hard to see how the CSA attorney could tell the judge that this was an agreement to benefit "people who would meet all the requirements of the 1979 program." The agreement even stipulated that legal services lawyers should obtain at least 50% of the $4 million allotted for "energy advocacy."[15] The pirates were making sure the treasure was divided equitably.

The money would have gone to the utopians in accordance with Judge Grady's order (as well as any other money the CSA might neglect to give to poor people, since the agreement provided that additional monies, as they became available, would be spent within the framework of the agreement) had it not been that one of Peter Metzger's assistants attended an open meeting of energy advocates in Colorado. Speakers kept referring to the new money now available to them through "Simer." Metzger investigated; revealed his findings to the *Wall Street Journal* which published them; and the Capital Legal Foundation, one of the public interest law firms established to counter the Naderite monopoly on definitions of the public interest, filed a memorandum on behalf of several U.S. Senators with Judge Grady, urging him to set aside his order endorsing the agreement between the CSA and Legal Services lawyers.

Judge Grady did so and made no secret of his opinion that he had been "had" by the CSA and Legal Services. In Judge Grady's words:

> "I believe that the parties, both by what they said and by what they did not say, misled me both as to the facts and the law. . . . A current indication of the parties' opportunistic and manipulative approach to the use of these funds is the complete turnabout they have now done in regard to the possibility of class treatment of this case. Rather than have the funds go back to the Treasury, the parties are attempting at this late date to induce the court to do something they have all along conceded was not feasible."[16]

While "Simer" did not in the end channel $18 million from the poor to the utopians, CSA bureaucrats found a host of ways to fund anti-business activism. For example, the CSA invested heavily in a favorite utopian scheme: confiscating without compensation and redistributing farm land in California. The lever to be used was a 1902 law that stipulated a 160 acre limitation for land benefiting from government-funded irrigation projects. A lot is at stake because California is the state with highest total farm income and more irrigated farm land than any other state. (Only Texas has even half as many irrigated acres as California.) The CSA funded groups made the creation of subsistence farms out of large, well-run and highly specialized irrigated holdings a "poverty issue." According to California Westside Farmers, a group that banded together against the CSA funded attack, the CSA poured what may amount to millions of dollars into the land redistribution movement. Some of it went to Legal Service Corporation groups, such as a special one year grant in 1977 of $155,590 for a "Reclamation Law Unit."[17] Westside Farmers complained that the CSA used its money to create groups and then spent more money on the excuse of "outreach" to the very groups it had initiated. Of course, those seeking land redistribution saw this effort as part of a broader effort: to realize the vision of another kind of society. Thus the publication of one of the CSA grantees, active in the crusade, lauded "simplicity, self-sufficiency, pastoral living . . . and the call to origins of the diversified, sweat-enriched family farm."[18]

Interestingly, there are studies on the outcome of U.S. government efforts in the depression to create small farming projects as a cure for poverty. A 1942 report by the U.S. Department of Agriculture surveyed the results of 176 such projects set up under a variety of government agencies. The report found that farms aided by the projects were for the most part unable to generate sufficient family income to maintain themselves or to repay any of the government loans they had received. The report said: "Experience on the projects studied indicates that subsistence homesteads do not provide relief and do not eliminate the need for it. They have not freed families at the relief level, or close to it, from the need for continued subsidy or relief of some kind."[19]

Apart from funding the utopians, the CSA squandered money on a grand scale in the Community Economic Development program. One of the development corporations the CSA singled out for special praise in its 1979 annual report, the East Los Angeles Community Union (TELACU) was exposed in a series of 1982 articles in the Los Angeles Times as a far-flung empire built on millions of dollars in federal grants that had only a glancing relationship to the Los Angeles community it was supposed to serve. The newspaper investigation found that TELACU had provided few jobs for barrio residents, but had instead invested its funds all over the country and abroad in apparent contradiction to the legislation and regulations binding it. In addition TELACU had provided lavish benefits, including homes, private loans, cars and vast travel expenses to its executives and improperly contributed to election campaigns.[20] The CSA had been conducting its own evaluation of the community development corporations without stumbling on any of these awkward facts. There was little cause for wonder because the study was conducted by utopians. The organization assigned in 1978 to perform a three year evaluation of the Community Development Corporations (including TELACU) and allotted $2,375,000 for the task was none other than the National Center for Economic Alternatives,[21] the IPS grandchild led by one-time IPS Fellow Gar Alperovitz, who with Ralph Nader created COIN, the utopian program we described earlier.

If the CSA's utopian mandate of "abolishing poverty" made it a prime candidate for infusion by utopian bureaucrats, other government departments, with mundane mandates, were transformed in the Carter years. The Department of Energy ignored its Congressionally mandated responsibility to provide a balanced public information program concerning energy, vied with the CSA in funding anti-utility groups; and, like the CSA, diverted monies entrusted to it by Congress for one purpose, to others more congenial to the new breed of bureaucrats.

The Department of Energy's public information program, by law, is required to provide a balanced picture of the state of energy resources in the nation and their future availability. A multi-million dollar effort, the program, in 1975 alone, distributed over 11 million pamphlets and provided exhibits seen by almost 16 million people. But as a House of Representatives subcommittee discovered, the picture actually offered by the program, in the Carter years, could scarcely have been more distorted. Materials on nuclear energy were simply suppressed, with over sixty existing publications of the department on the subject destroyed.[22] Scores of studies and publications on coal fared not much better. On the other hand, myriad pamphlets on "renewable, alternative, decentralized" energy were issued. The subcommittee's report noted that when a booklet on nuclear energy was finally produced by the DOE's Office of Nuclear Energy Program, it was a "sterile" presentation of the basic concepts of nuclear fission. Nonetheless, the DOE's Office of Consumer Affairs denounced it as misleading and "vulnerable to criticism from public groups."[23]

Much of the problem lay with the Office of Consumer Affairs, headed by utopian bureaucrat Tina Hobson. The subcommittee's report found that it had an extremely influential role in formulating information and educational programs on energy for the DOE as a whole and that it controlled the DOE's formal educational program, which included provision of curricular materials from kindergarten through twelfth grade. These materials were almost devoid of references to nuclear energy. A packet called "The Energy We Use," prepared for first graders, referred to nuclear energy only at the end of a play, in which the atom was depicted as giving off "poisonous waste." Through the mass media, the Office of Consumer Affairs had launched a nationwide campaign promoting solar energy, giving the impression it could play a major role in satisfying the country's energy needs in the near future. The Office of Consumer Affairs also produced a monthly publication called "The Energy Consumer" which the Congressional report said was justifiably called an "up front anti-utility publication."

The Office of Consumer Affairs provided money to a number of anti-nuclear groups and worked closely with others. In 1979, for example, it gave $131,526 to the Environmental Action Foundation. Environmental Action is one of the most militant environmentalist groups. It first attracted wide attention by producing a paperback called *Ecotage!* The book is a primer on this new activity, a neologism combining "ecology" and "sabotage." Ecotage consists of symbolically appropriate offensive and destructive actions directed against enemies of the environment. Examples offered range from smashing bill boards to despatching dead fish in the mail to stockholders in oil corporations. A simple, if conceivably lethal, suggestion was sprinkling nails over freeway interchanges. Environmental Action protected itself with a note on the book cover: "Neither Environmental Action nor the publisher suggest you go out and do any of the things described in this book." On the other hand, the last section of the book is devoted to extolling those who have actually engaged in ecotage, notably the so-called Fox in Kane County, Illinois and a group known as the Eco-Commando Force '70 in Florida.[24] The signals from Environmental Action were thus decidedly mixed.

The DOE, after Carter's initial appointee as Secretary, James Schlesinger, had departed, also branched out into anti-utility activism. Through its Economic Regulatory Administration it made grants to create State Offices of Consumer Affairs in ten states: their goal of course was to stop or reverse rate increases won by local utilities. The DOE also appropriated $2 million in 1977 to establish "State electric utility consumer offices'' to work for ''rate reform'' as well as to oppose rate increases. A pass-through arrangement allowed subgrants to consumer groups: those eligible for funding were defined as groups consisting of no less than three persons![25]

The DOE funded a series of what Peter Metzger called anti-utility training sessions in response to demands by Gail Cincotta's National People's Action. She exacted money for this enterprise from then Secretary of Energy, Charles Duncan, after occupying his office with her followers and playing with yo-yos—a reference to the Duncan yo-yo. This typified the DOE's tendency to collapse under any activist onslaught. After the Mobilization for Survival staged a sit-in at the DOE, Duncan arranged for monthly meetings with the organization,[26] despite the presence in it of the Communist Party and various fronts.

In typical utopian fashion, DOE bureaucrats were more interested in promoting solar energy than in actual solar hardware. When Congress provided the DOE with $6 million to install solar devices in Federal buildings, DOE bureaucrats diverted the money to solar propaganda. There was $246,241 for a TV program for children; $201,624 for a Florida energy conservation promotion campaign; $103,850 for International Energy Conservation month; $248,500 for a film on solar for general TV audiences; $1.2 million for a program to analyze conservation and solar activities; and $10,000 for a proposal to develop energy conservation ideas for TV situation comedies. The DOE even hung banners promoting solar energy in federal buildings at a cost of $7,900.[27] Those banners were the closest to solar energy those federal buildings came.

In 1979, Denis Hayes was installed as director of the DOE's Solar Energy Research Institute (SERI) in Golden, Colorado. Hayes had no technical credentials but as coordinator of Earth Day in 1970, Sun Day in 1978 and founder of the Solar Lobby, he had strong activist credentials. At Carter's DOE, this won him the department's first award for ''Exceptional Public Service.'' One of his chief qualifications for his new job was presumably his stated conviction that solar could provide 50% of U.S. energy needs by the turn of the century. The scientists at SERI had been making much lower estimates. Its deputy director, Dr. Michael Noland, said: ''We can and should be very proud as a nation if solar power provides seven to ten percent of our energy by the beginning of the 21st century.''[28] Under Hayes, SERI shifted its thrust from solar research to promotion, and in 1981 came out with a report asserting that solar energy and conservation could make the U.S. energy independent within 20 years. Dismissed by President Reagan, Hayes went out with the customary utopian self-righteousness. He charged that "a gang of mad mullahs" had seized power in Washington[29] and declared open war on solar energy. And although this scarcely conjured up an image of "mad mullahs," he denounced the DOE for being filled with "dull gray men in dull gray suits in dull gray offices thinking dull gray thoughts and writing dull gray reports."[30]

The conversion of research into the handmaiden of politics was not confined to SERI. Congress had designed the National Institute for Occupational Safety and Health (NIOSH) as a research agency to provide the Occupational and Health Administration (OSHA) with scientific studies and data and to conduct long-term research on the causes of occupational disease. Carter's utopian appointees, who included John (Chicago 7) Froines, a chemistry professor who founded the Radical Science Information Service, converted the agency into an enforcement arm of OSHA. NIOSH ceased to produce criteria documents on hazardous substances for OSHA. One reason, critics charged, was that they were peer-reviewed by scientific panels, a process that could be embarrassing to the researchers of an institute whose conclusions were now reached prior to conducting research. In the absence of criteria documents, OSHA simply decreed what the exposure level to a given substance should be and NIOSH tried to scrape up data to back it up.[31]

What had been a minor aspect of NIOSH's program became a major one. Congress had given NIOSH authority to enter workplaces and conduct investigations as part of its research function. In the Carter years, NIOSH developed an inspection force that worked hand in hand with OSHA, reporting all its findings to it. The credibility of NIOSH as an independent scientific research organization was destroyed as it was perceived as a covert arm of OSHA enforcement.[32]

But the agency that from its inception has most consistently defied its Congressional mandate is the Legal Services Corporation. The legal services program was a stronghold of the utopians since it began as a program of the Office of Economic Opportunity in 1965. After President Nixon vainly sought to abolish both the OEO and legal services, legal services was reconstituted as the "independent," but wholly government-funded, Legal Services Corporation in 1974. In the Carter years, it grew enormously. In 1976, the last year of the Ford Administration, the LSC budget was $92.3 million; by 1980, the annual budget had tripled to $300 million.

Although the legislative mandate of the Legal Services program was confined and reasonable—to provide "highly qualified legal assistance to those who would be otherwise unable to afford adequate legal counsel"—those who worked for it had other ideas. They saw legal services as a way to transform the social system. Some of the suits brought by Legal Services Corporation funded groups (there are 320 around the country) in 1980 illustrate this effort.

California Rural Legal Assistance, which received $5 million in 1980 from the LSC, filed suit against the University of California to halt its work on labor-saving agricultural machinery which the suit claimed would displace farm workers. Bay Area Legal Services in Tampa which received $73,740 from the LSC in 1980, filed suit against the Florida Department of Education's requirement that a functional literacy test be passed to receive a high school diploma. Pine Tree Legal Assistance of Portland, Maine, which received $1.25 million from the LSC, and the Native American Rights Fund in Boulder, Colorado, which received $238,000, filed suit jointly to restore 2/3 of the state of Maine to the Passamaquoddy and Penobscot Indians. North East Ohio Legal Services in Youngstown, which obtained $496,000 from the LSC in 1980, filed suit to force U.S. Steel to sell its mill to a tax-subsidized community-based organization. An LSC-funded program in Philadelphia filed suit on behalf of a citizens group to stop construction of the Limerick nuclear power plant and against Temple University on the grounds that it spent more on men's athletic scholarships than on women's. An LSC funded group in Michigan filed suit to force the Ann Arbor school district to recognize Black English in fulfilling its foreign language requirement.

Several of these suits clearly violate the rules that specify that LSC lawyers can only represent people whose income is no more than 125% of the poverty level. College students and citizens groups opposed to nuclear power do not fall within those income guidelines. What all the suits have in common is that they are designed to restructure American society. Halting nuclear energy, returning the U.S. to the Indians (LSC attorneys have played a key role not only in Maine, but across the country in the dramatic increase in Indian land claims), worker ownership of industry in place of private ownership, fostering of subsistence farmsteads over large-scale farming, defining school diplomas as a matter of right rather than as something earned through achievement involve fundamental changes in social policy that should not be decided without reference to the legislative process. Legal Services bypasses that process, using the courts to resolve issues according to the ideological preferences of its lawyers. And the taxpayer is not only forced to underwrite the effort to force changes of which he disapproves, but is being fooled into doing so by being told that all he is doing is to pay for the poor to have equal access to the law.

The cases we have mentioned are class actions in which suit is brought not only on behalf of the named plaintiffs but on behalf of the whole class of persons in their situation. Dan J. Bradley, president of the Legal Services Corporation from 1979-81, argued that only 2/10 of 1% of the cases handled by the LSC's offices[33] were class actions. This does not take into consideration the percentage of time or of financial resources consumed by class action litigation. For example, Florida's Orlando Sentinel reported that in 1980, while only two of the 4,000 cases handled by Greater Orlando Legal Services were class action suits, they had consumed over half of its $527,885 LSC budget.[34] A columnist for the Philadelphia Bulletin reported, in March 1981, that Community Legal Services of Philadelphia had claimed $4.5 million in legal fees for a class action suit involving 120 units of low income housing at Whitman Park. Since Community Legal Services received approximately $2.3 million a year from the LSC, it had presumably spent all its resources for two years on this single suit. If a lawyer's rate is assumed to be $100 an hour it would mean Community Legal Services had spent 45,000 hours on this single case.[35] In calculating the cost of these suits it must be remembered that most of the LSC's class action suits are brought against a branch of government, meaning that the taxpayer pays twice: he pays for the LSC suit and a generally equivalent amount for the lawyers who defend the government against the suit.

These costs are only part of the story. The cases have costs to society. For example, if high school diplomas are matters of right, and need not represent any substantive achievement, the entire structure of socially sanctioned rewards and the consensual judgment of obligations and privileges on which this society rests is undermined.

There are a number of factors which are responsible for the LSC's subversion of its legislative mandate. One is that the structure of legal services gives power and control to the provider of services rather than to the consumer.[36] Since LSC attorneys are not dependent upon client fees, they are free to reject some cases brought to them and accept, even create, others and then find the clients to fit them. Many legal services programs routinely turn away clients seeking help in obtaining a divorce, although this is the legal problem that poor clients bring with greater frequency than any other.[37] LSC lawyers are interested in cases that meet their own needs, rather than those of clients. In a study of the turnover problem in Legal Services, published in *Law and Society Review,* Jack Katz found that what chiefly distinguished young lawyers planning to enter Legal Services from those planning entry into other fields of law was their emphasis on "involvement." They expected to experience "personal growth" in their poverty law practices. But Katz notes that when poor people come to a Legal Services program they bring invitations to enter "small social worlds."[38] Within the first year then, the lawyer found that his work in the normal run of cases which poor people brought to his office had lost its novelty. Many lawyers left, leading to a high turnover rate in LSC offices. But those lawyers who managed to become involved in class action and law reform cases kept their sense of involvement, for these cases raised novel issues of interest to the broad legal community. The problems of the individual poor client were redefined so as to impinge on greater interests and broader audiences. Thus Katz points out that whether or not the lawyer originally had an ideological preference for "law reform," his interest in sustaining an experience of personal growth channeled him in that direction.[39]

A second very important factor in the subversion of Legal Services has been the massive entry of political radicals into the organization. Katz reported that a source of satisfaction some lawyers found in Legal Services was representing political radicals whose actions had symbolic importance both to their supporters and opponents. In a sympathetic study of radical lawyers, journalist Marlise Jones describes numerous cases of lawyers during the late 60s and 70s who worked at least for a time for Legal Services. She quotes one, in Chicago:

> "In Legal Services Daley controlled the money and he didn't want any criminal or civil rights cases done, or suing police officers or anything like that. So each month we'd continue doing these cases, and each month the lawyers would be reprimanded, fired, and then rehired."[40]

The principle was that the less the government in Washington knew what was going on the better. Jones also interviewed Alan W. Houseman, then director of Michigan Legal Services, who became head of the LSC's Research Institute on Legal Assistance (and now heads the Center for Law and Social Policy). Houseman explained there was:

> "a problem of Washington's trying to control more when they find out what is really going on. They don't know, and the bureaucracy in legal

> services has tried to cover up as much as possible, not because we're doing anything wrong but because we're trying to get law reform through the court system by working with aggressive, militant groups.''[41]

In referring to not doing anything wrong, Houseman was presumably referring to what he defined as ''morally'' wrong; there was no doubt LSC-funded groups violated statutory guidelines.

The radicalization of Legal Services has proceeded apace since the late sixties and early seventies. Evidence for this is that the National Lawyers Guild, the major organization of radical lawyers in the United States, according to its own report had 1,000 members in 1979 working in Legal Services programs.[42] This meant that approximately one out of six lawyers working in LSC programs belonged to the Guild. And the Guild's influence went beyond this, for Guild members also served on the local boards that set policy for the various LSC-funded groups. Several of those who rose to leading positions in the LSC were Guild members, including Alan W. Houseman.

In 1980, then-President of the National Lawyers Guild Paul Harris said that the Guild was rooted in four slogans: anti-racism, anti-sexism, anti-capitalism and anti-imperialism.[43] For the Guild the United States incarnates these ills. In his ''State of the Guild'' Presidential address Harris praised the progress that had been made and referred to the dangers remaining: ''The American Imperial eagle can no longer fly unrestricted. But it has begun to spread its ugly wings and its vicious talons.'' Harris called for U.S. imperialism to remain the main focus of the Guild's international work ''as we live in what Che Guevara accurately called 'the belly of the beast.'''[44].

The Guild's view of American justice is equally bleak. A resolution passed by the Guild's National Convention in 1981 notes that the Guild has ''observed from close quarters how the system of 'American Justice' increasingly is used to hound, attack, imprison, and execute the oppressed minorities, workers, and political activists.''[45] Not surprisingly, given this perspective, a 1973 Guild resolution cites prisons as an exaggerated reflection of the capitalist system. The Guild considers prisoners the ''revolutionary vanguard'' who will ''lead us in the streets.''[46]

If in the eyes of the Guild the American system of justice is irredeemably corrupt, there are models for emulation elsewhere. In 1980 a Guild team visited Mozambique and reported back enthusiastically about its system of justice. The team admitted the jail in Beira, designed to hold 50, was packed with 700 people literally hanging by their legs and arms between the bars, but found there was "no tension." The team also noted that none of the principles of western law were followed. Judges were elected by the legislature and directed to "function in cooperation with the Party." Neither judges, defense attorneys nor prosecutors were bound by rules of evidence. Far from causing concern, this was merely proof for the Guild team that "legal principles necessary to protect human and social rights are not immutable." In Mozambique "the people" were in power. The Guild team explained: "Laws protect those in power, and only where the people are in power are their rights truly protected."[47]

The real situation in Mozambique is revealed in the Freedom House Survey of Freedom Around the World for 1982. Out of 164 countries, there are only ten which have the lowest possible score in regard to both political rights and civil liberties. Mozambique is one of them.

The Guild's rosy view of justice in Mozambique is in accord with its view of what constitutes "progressive forces" in the world. The Guild is the major, until recently the only, U.S. affiliate of the International Association of Democratic Lawyers, described in a 1978 CIA study as "one of the most useful Communist front organizations at the service of the Soviet Communist Party." Doris Brin Walker, one-time President of the Guild, has been a vice-president of the IADL since 1970 and Lennox Hinds another Guild member who also heads the National Conference of Black Lawyers (which recently joined the IADL) is secretary. The IADL also does not believe the law should be concerned with procedural niceties. At its 1975 conference in Algiers, the IADL declared "law to be a function in the struggle against imperialism, colonialism, neo-colonialism, racism and apartheid."[48] In 1980 "zionism" joined the list of ills which the IADL vowed to extirpate as part of "our noble mission as defenders of the downcast and dispossessed."[49]

Legal Services has been a magnet for Guild lawyers. We noted that in 1979 *Guild Notes* reported that 1,000 Guild members worked for Legal Services. That same year the Guild reported a total of 6,000 members. But the proportion of Guild lawyers who work for Legal Services is higher than these figures suggest because only a little more than half the Guild's members are lawyers: 45% consist of law students, "jailhouse lawyers," i.e. prisoners, and legal workers. What this indicates is that the proportion of lawyers in the Guild who work for Legal Services is closer to 1 in 3.

While as early as 1973 Alan W. Houseman published an article in

Guild Notes referring to the tremendous potential Legal Services offers "for the support of the Movement,"[50] it was not until 1979 that the National Executive of the Guild officially made Legal Services organizing a priority. The ties have become so close that a study by Howard Phillips, one-time head of the Office of Economic Opportunity, found that there were cases where LSC offices and National Lawyers Guild offices had identical addresses and phone numbers.[51] Not all members of the Guild were enthusiastic about the Guild's emphasis on Legal Services. One member charged that the Guild was reluctant to define Legal Services for what it was, namely a bureaucratic organization "that supports the interests of the very government that exploits, murders, maims and destroys the lives of those of us who dare to struggle and who dare to win."[52]

The persistent involvement of Legal Services lawyers in political organizing and lobbying in defiance of the LSC charter is in part owing to the Guild lawyer's conception of the nature of legal work. A vice president of the Guild who worked for the LSC's California Rural Legal Assistance explained:

> "I have never 'practiced' outside of an organizational context, that is without using my legal skills to assist in an organizing drive."[53]

The reaction of Congress to repeated disclosures of Legal Services misbehavior has been to pass ever more restrictions on its activities. There are now laws stipulating that Legal Services lawyers cannot participate in criminal cases, strikes, school desegregation cases or armed forces desertion cases, among others; they are forbidden to lobby or engage in political organizing. Congress even eliminated funding for the back-up centers that were crucial to the LSC's class action suits. Nothing had any impact. After the back-up centers were eliminated, for example, they were continued anyway, the legislation being interpreted in a fashion which Edith Green, the Oregon Congresswoman who secured its passage, said was the opposite of Congressional intent.[54]

The most recent restrictions, passed in 1981 after Congress refused President Reagan's request that the LSC be eliminated, were promptly analyzed by the Guild with a view to negating their impact. Congress had now specified that membership on the boards of legal service corporations be limited to bar associations that represented the majority of attorneys in localities served by the program. This was clearly directed toward removing Guild attorneys from the boards as well as members of radical minority organizations like the La Raza Legal Alliance and the National Conference of Black Lawyers, both IADL affiliates. The Guild's campaign to have its members join local bar associations answered that problem. As for new restrictions on the kinds of cases the LSC could handle, *Guild Notes* reported: "Activists in legal services are beginning to discuss ways to resist these restrictions."[55]

While the stated purpose of Congress in setting up the Legal Services Corporation as an independent entity was to make it "free from the influence or use of it by political pressures," what Congress actually accomplished was merely to insulate it from public accountability. In June 1981 five U.S. Senators, one Congressman and an Iowa State Senator filed suit against the LSC in the U.S. District Court for Iowa. The suit charged that the LSC had deliberately violated most of the statutory restrictions that Congress had imposed on political activity by the Corporation, and provided a series of examples, among them a political rally organized by Vermont Legal Aid to protest U.S. policy in El Salvador. The response of the Legal Services Corporation was not to deny the validity of any of the charges but to insist that the same Congressional statutes cited by the Senators permitted no enforcement of their provisions. The LSC argued that under the law it was responsible for policing itself and no outsiders had a right to intervene. The court sided with the LSC, although, as the Senators' suit charged, if there was no legal means to stop the illegal activities of the LSC, this meant there was no legal duty for the LSC to perform in accordance with the law.[56] The LSC is also shielded from public scrutiny by its "independent" status. Unlike other government agencies, its 320 recipient organizations are not subject to the Freedom of Information Act.

The LSC has been able to carry on its utopian activities unchecked because of the consistent support given it by the American Bar Association. Howard Phillips notes that one reason for the support is the strategic presence of Legal Services attorneys on the committees of the American Bar Association that set its policy concerning the LSC.[57] But the major reason is that it provides thousands of jobs for lawyers, serving, as journalist Stephen Chapman has pointed out, as a welfare program for lawyers. Funds were cut back from $321 million in 1981 to $241 million in 1982, but given the astronomical growth of the agency over the previous years, this was still substantially more than what the agency received as recently as 1978.

Utopians in government work cooperatively to achieve common goals, with the LSC often acting as catalyst. Simer vs. Olivarez is a good example of that cooperation. The National Consumer Law Center, one of the LSC back-up centers, was involved in the initial planning for the suit. (Its reward in Simer was to be $2.3 million of the money.) The actual suit was brought by Legal Services attorneys who then worked closely with lawyers for the Community Services Administration to work out the agreement which Judge Grady signed—and later repudiated. As is typical of the LSC's class action suits, the ostensible plaintiffs had nothing to do with bringing the case. The *Wall Street Journal* found that few of the seven named plaintiffs in Simer had even heard of the case. The LSC has also provided the legal muscle for suits by CSA funded groups seeking to redistribute reclaimed farm land in California and elsewhere. And LSC groups have been an important part of the "energy-advocacy" movement. Legal Services provided legal representation in all major proceedings by energy advocate organizations before public service companies around the country.[58]

Of course the success of Legal Services groups, and they have had a high rate of success in the class action suits they have brought, is in part owing to the character of the courts in recent years. In a famous 1976 essay, "Towards an Imperial Judiciary?" Nathan Glazer pointed out the activist thrust of the courts which have intervened "to extend the role of what the government could do, even when the government did not want to do it." Glazer noted that judges were increasingly minded to go "to the root of the problem" even when there was no knowledge of what the root of the problem might be.[59] As Harvard Law School Fellow Gary McDowell has observed, social science speculation fills the knowledge gap. By widening the meaning of "standing," of "due process" and of "equal treatment of the laws," the judiciary has given the lower federal courts "a virtual blank check for restructuring American political and social institutions."[60]

The problem, already serious when Carter became President, became yet more intractable as a result of his appointments. Under Carter the Omnibus Judgeship Act of 1978 was passed, creating 117 new federal judgeships and 35 new judgeships in the Circuit Court of Appeals—all lifetime appointees. The Democrats, in control of House and Senate, had kept the bill on ice during the previous Republican administrations. These appointments, combined with normal attrition, allowed Carter to appoint half the Federal bench. The public interest law movement saw its opportunity, and as we noted in an earlier chapter, Charles Halpern, then of the Center for Law and Social Policy, is credited within the "Movement" for the major role he assumed in assuring that the proper personnel was appointed. Carter's judicial appointments, of whom a survey found only 3% described themselves as conservative,[61] have been called the "Trojan horse" bequeathed to subsequent administrations.

With the advent of the Reagan administration, government funds ceased to pour as generously into utopian coffers, and the utopians increasingly turned to the courts to fill the financial gap. The laws that permit judges to award fees to public interest lawyers, often regardless of whether they win or lose a suit, have become an avenue through which the Office of Management and the Budget calculates that $20 million a year now flows to the public interest movement and that $146 million may go by 1984. Moreover, the fees judges are prepared to award lawyers have escalated sharply. For example, an Indian woman teaching chemistry at the University of Minnesota claimed that sex discrimination was responsible for the university's failure to give her tenure. In July 1982 a Federal judge ordered the University to pay her $100,000. At the same time he ordered the taxpayer-funded University to pay the lawyers in the case $2 million. That amount was based on a rate for their services that went up to $375 per hour![62]

Perhaps the least noted, but most dangerous impact of the utopians has been in politicizing the use of science by regulatory agencies. William Havender, a consultant on environmental carcinogens, has described a series of shoddy studies which could not meet peer review and were contradicted by a mass of other studies that have been made the basis for agency regulations. For example, in 1969 the FDA banned cyclamates within a week of receiving a report that claimed they caused bladder cancer in rats. (Inventory losses to business as a result were estimated at over $100 million.) But although there have since been over 20 additional cyclamate studies in rats, mice and a whole series of other animals, all high-dose chronic feeding tests similar to the original, and none showed any statistically significant increase in bladder cancer, the FDA has not lifted the ban. After Abbott Laboratories petitioned to have cyclamate reapproved in 1973, the FDA waited seven years and then rejected the petition. But in doing so, the FDA made what Havender terms "stunning mistakes in its use of statistics and in its interpretation of animal cancer tests." A committee of the American Statistical Association in a letter to the FDA commissioner described the FDA's work as "foreign to everything that is taught in the statistics profession" while the Society of Toxicologists criticized the FDA's use of animal cancer tests.[63]

Similarly a study of miscarriage rates in a forested area near Alsea, Oregon, where herbicide 2,4,5 T was sprayed each spring prompted the EPA to issue an emergency order in March 1979 banning virtually all uses of the chemical. The order was issued one *day* after the EPA received the report. The study has since received 18 independent reviews by qualified scientists, including some in other countries, all of which found the study invalid. The ban remains in force; it is of course politically popular with the utopians.

Moreover, in the pattern noted by Claus and Bolander, whereby methodologically indefensible studies become the building blocks for further inaccurate work, government studies that misuse science become the basis for further false reports. For example, in September 1979 HEW Secretary Joseph Califano endorsed a government report alleging that as much as 38% of all cancer in the United States could be traced to on-the-job chemical exposure, a ten fold increase over normal estimates. It was submitted to no professional journal and subjected to no outside scrutiny. In the June 1981 issue of the journal of the National Cancer Institute, two of the world's leading cancer epidemiologists, Sir Richard Doll and Richard Peto, reviewed the methodology of the report, characterizing one methodological flaw as "indefensible" and "a confidence trick;" another as "absurd" and "a simple error to be corrected rather than a new scientific hypothesis to be considered" and yet another as a "comparison of incidence rates that seems completely unreliable." They affirmed the original scientific estimate that one to five percent of U.S. cancers are due to occupational exposure.[64] But of course the 38% figure becomes the one used as "government authority" by the utopians to press for ever more ill-considered regulations that are economically damaging without serving public health.

Agency heads are of course responding to political pressures from the public interest lobbies. These welcome studies, however unsound scientifically, that affirm dangers and reject studies, however valid scientifically, that deny there is any evidence they exist. It would be at his peril that an agency head would fail to respond instantly to a study suggesting dangers to pregnant women, while an overwhelming amount of evidence that such dangers did *not* exist will not persuade the utopians that a ban, once wrongly imposed, should be lifted, making the lifting of bans as politically unacceptable as their imposition is politically welcome. The end result, as Havender notes, is that decisions made by government agencies are "rooted in brazen tendentiousness and bias."

Thus far we have focussed on the impact of the utopians on the administrative branch of government and on specialized agencies but the utopians have also had a major impact on Congress.

A potential weakness of any democratically elected body of representatives is that those representatives are not expert in the myriad issues about which they must make decisions. In the U.S. Congress, professional expertise—outside of law—is rare. Since under these circumstances information necessarily becomes power, the utopian institutes have been able to seize their opportunity.

The vulnerability of Congressmen to the utopians is enhanced because they appear to be disinterested experts. Where there is no obvious self-interest Congressmen more often than not tend to accept the information as offered in the spirit of broad devotion to the public interest, which of course is precisely what the utopians claim to be their purpose in offering it. Actually, as we have seen, the goals of the utopians in employing their "information" are nothing short of revolutionary, for they encompass the total social and economic transformation of the country, a transformation which goes hand in hand with a redefinition of its national interests in the world.

Perhaps the single most dramatic example of the impact of the utopian think tanks on Congress is the role of the Center for National Security Studies, in cooperation with the ACLU, in persuading Congress to make it all but impossible for the Central Intelligence Agency to perform its assigned functions. When Carter became President, those who had been most influenced by the Center and ACLU were put in charge of overseeing "reform" of the intelligence agencies. David Aaron, who had served as a consultant to the sister think tank, the Center for International Policy, and had been a sharp critic of the CIA as a staffer on the Senate Committee on Intelligence, was appointed to the National Security Council, where he took over major responsibility for reorganizing American intelligence. He was joined there by others from the staff of the Senate Intelligence Committee, including Karl Inderfurth and Gregory Treverton, who had been among the most critical of the CIA and had worked closely with the

ACLU and CNSS. In the end, over 800 people were fired from the CIA, chiefly in covert action and counter-intelligence. Counterintelligence, as James Tyson notes in *Target America,* almost went out of existence. In addition to the personnel losses, a series of executive orders restricted the activities of the CIA.

The utopians, even in the inhospitable Reagan years, have hoped to persuade Congress to create a new utopian agency. They launched a vigorous campaign to secure a U.S. Academy of Peace and Conflict Resolution. It was to be built, according to the campaign's literature, upon the proposition that "there is now a science—tested and proved in actual practice—that can help make war obsolete" and that "this science can be taught, learned and applied—anywhere in the world."[65] The "science" to which the campaign literature refers is "conflict resolution." But conflict resolution is no science. It is built upon the assumption that groups can be prevailed upon to subordinate disagreements to the achievement of common goals. When disagreement runs deep, conflict resolution does not work. For example, conflict resolution between a group wishing to build a nuclear power plant and one opposed to the plant is not going to be eased by the mechanisms of conflict resolution.

As for relations between states, there has always been diplomacy, and conflict resolution has no secrets to offer diplomats. Where profound values are at stake, whether it is national survival or passionately held religio-cultural beliefs, conflict resolution, like traditional diplomacy, is at a loss.

There are innumerable programs in peace studies at U.S. universities and institutes, which have, of course, failed to come up with the "solution" to war. For proponents of the proposed United States Academy of Peace, this is not evidence that there does not in fact exist a science to end war, but that a federal institution is needed because private efforts have failed. Surely, no more touching faith in the public sector has been evidenced by the utopians than that government funding of "peace studies" can unlock the key to preventing war that eluded privately funded efforts.

Despite the intrinsic absurdities in the arguments of those who support a national peace academy, the campaign for it has the same public relations appeal that characterizes so many utopian projects. Supporting literature argues that ". . . the cost of establishing the academy and running it for the first three years would be . . . less than one tenth the price tag of a single B-1 bomber" and "any nation devoting so many millions to [military] service academies should be willing to devote a relatively small sum to a peace academy." The argument is that surely the public can spend $21 million a year for peace, when it spends so many billions on the engines of war. So persuasive have these appeals been that Congress appropriated $500,000 for a study of the proposal in 1979 and by mid 1982 156 Congressmen and Senators had gone on record as sponsors of a bill to establish it. And while the great majority were liberal Democrats, Conservative Democrats like John Stennis of Mississippi and even such Conservative Republicans as Tom Corcoran and Roger Jepsen of Iowa were among them.

For the utopians, the Peace Academy is an opportunity to obtain government money and prestige for a project they are confident of controlling and which could be used to undermine public support for defense spending. Built on the assumption techniques exist to solve all conflict peaceably, the Academy would be bound to deny the need for increased defense preparations. By reducing the ability to deter war, the Academy would only increase the probability war would occur. In the *Wall Street Journal,* economist Walter Berns observed that what Congress would be likely to get for its money was "very similar to what it is already getting from the United Nations, except this time it will have to pay 100%, rather than a mere 25% of the cost."[66]

The utopians have been looking not only to Congress and the courts as the executive branch became at least temporarily inhospitable, but to lower levels of government. They have sought to take advantage of the Reagan administration's effort to transfer spending power to the state and local level through block grants. Amory Lovins' collaborator, his wife Hunter Lovins, writes in the utopian journal *New Roots:* "I urge everyone to prepare not at a national level—we've seen how national solutions work—but at home at the local, community level."[67] At Nader's 1981 conference, Lee Webb of the Institute for Policy Studies offshoot, the Conference on Alternative State and Local Policies, which pioneered in bringing together "Movement" people in government, emphasized: "It is at [the local] level that progressives can create national models of program initiatives."[68] At the same conference Ruth Yanatta Goldway, then still mayor of the "People's Republic" of Santa Monica, described the advantages accruing from local control: "We've tripled our social services budget, including a hefty portion that goes to community organizing groups. . . ."[69]

The utopians speak in the name of "the people" to whom they promise control of all the decisions that affect their lives. But it is only after the people have been suitably "remade" to conform to the needs of a transformed system that they will be capable of such decision-making. In the meantime there are the utopians to make decisions for them. They claim to represent the people's "real" interests, in contrast to their elected representatives, who represent only "special" interests. Despite the wild disparity between their views and the public they claim to represent, the media endorses their claims. But that only shifts the puzzle: why are utopian groups so favorably treated by the media?

It is to this question that we now turn.

REFERENCES

1. *The New York Times,* February 14, 1981
2. "The New Left in Government: From Protest to Policy-Making," Institute Analysis #9, Heritage Foundation, Nov. 1978, pp. 18-20
3. Morton Halperin, "The Carter Administration: In the Mood for Reform?" *First Principles,* April 1977, p. 16
4. *New York Times,* April 20, 1977
5. H. Peter Metzger, "The Coercive Utopians: Their Hidden Agenda" Public Service Co. of Colorado, Denver, Colo. 80202, 1979, p. 22
6. Ibid., p. 26
7. Ibid., pp. 32-3
8. H. Peter Metzger and Richard Westfall, "The Great Ecology Swindle," *Policy Review,* Winter 1981, p. 77
9. H. Peter Metzger and Richard Westfall, "Government Activists: How They Rip Off the Poor," Public Service Co. of Colorado, 1981, p. 18
10. Memorandum from Dan Newman, Executive Director Region VIII Executive Board to Bruce Coles, Subject: Regional Energy Advocacy Activities, March 22, 1980
11. Regional Energy Advocacy Project Report, August 1979, p. 3
12. H. Peter Metzger and Richard Westfall, "Government Activists: How They Rip Off the Poor" op. cit., p. 22
13. In the U.S. District Court for the Northern District of Illinois, Eastern Division, Elsie Simer and others, plaintiffs vs. Graciela Olivarez, Director of Community Services Administration, Defendant, Complaint for Declarative Judgment, Mandamus and Injunctive Relief, September 24, 1979
14. In the U.S. District Court for the Northern District of Illinois Eastern Division, Elsie Simer et al, Plaintiffs v. Graciela Olivarez et al, Defendants, No. 79 C 3960 Memorandum Opinion, p. 3
15. In the U.S. District Court for the Northern District of Illinois, Elsie Simer et al, Plaintiffs v. William Allison, Acting Director of Community Services Administration, Defendants, Stipulation and Agreed Order, p. 5
16. In the U.S. District Court for the Northern District of Illinois, Memorandum Opinion, op. cit., pp. 8-9
17. "How Federal Funding Leaks to Land Redistribution Cause" A Special Report by California Westside Farmers, Fresno, California, May 9, 1979, pp. 3-4
18. Ibid., p. 14
19. Ibid., Exhibit P, p. 3

20. *Los Angeles Times,* March 28, 29, 30, April 23, May 26, 27, 1982
21. *Investing in Tomorrow: Progress Against Poverty,* FY 1978 Annual Report of the Community Services Administration, U.S. Government Printing Office, p. Axii
22. "Department of Energy's Public Information Programs: Major Changes Needed," Report of the Staff of the Subcommittee on Energy Resources and Production of the Committee on Science and Technology, U.S. House of Repres. 2nd sess. Dec. 1980, Government Printing Office, 1980, p. 18
23. Ibid., p. 29
24. Sam Love and David Obst, eds. *Environmental Action Says Ecotage!* Pocket Books, N.Y. 1972, pp. 143-70
25. Act/One: Activate Communities Today/Organize Now for Energy, U.S. Department of Energy Office of Consumer Affairs, April 1979, p. 2
26. *The Mobilizer* (Mobilization for Survival), Oct./Nov. 1979
27. *Rocky Mountain News,* May 27, 1981
28. Petr Beckmann, "Ruining the Promise of Solar Energy," *Access to Energy,* Oct. 1, 1978, p. 1
29. David Smyth, "The Dark Ages," *Westword,* Sept. 3, 1981
30. *Rocky Mountain News,* June 24, 1981
31. Hank Cox, "Carter Activists Create 'Baby Osha,'" *Regulatory Action Network: Washington Watch,* March 1981, pp. 31-34
32. Ibid.
33. Quoted in Statement of Howard Phillips to Senate Appropriations Subcommittee on State, Commerce, Justice and the Judiciary, April 28, 1982. Available from Conservative Caucus, Vienna, Va.
34. Republican Study Committee Fact Sheet: Legal Services Corporation Reauthorization H.R. 2506
35. Quoted in statement of Howard Phillips, op. cit.
36. Louis Jenkins, "The Legal Services Corporation and the Poor: Does It Meet Their Needs?" in *A Blueprint for Judicial Reform* 1981: Free Congress-Research and Educational Foundation Inc. p. 82
37. Legal Services Corporation Annual Report, 1979, p. 15
38. Jack Katz, "Lawyers for the Poor in Transition: Involvement, Reform and the Turnover Problem in the Legal Services Program" *Law and Society Review.* Winter 1978, p. 280
39. Ibid., p. 281
40. Marlise James, *The People's Lawyers,* Holt, Rinehart. New York, 1973, pp. 130-131
41. Ibid., p. 70
42. Angie Emerson, "Legal Services and the Guild," *Guild Notes,* January 1980, p. 4
43. Paul Harris, "Officer's Column," *Guild Notes,* June 1980
44. Paul Harris, "State of the Guild Speech," *Guild Notes,* April 1980, p. 15
45. *Guild Notes,* July-Aug. 1981, p. 17
46. Larry McDonald, *Congressional Record,* E5725, Dec. 9, 1981
47. "Report from Mozambique," by the Mozambique Delegation, *Guild Notes,* Nov.-Dec. 1980, p. 5
48. Larry McDonald, Dec. 7, 1981
49. *Guild Notes,* Jan.-Feb. 1981, p. 17
50. Alan W. Houseman, "Challenge to Legal Services," *Guild Notes,* May 1973, p. 4
51. "Structure, Programs and Funding of Legal Services" n.d. Available from Conservative Caucus Educational Foundation, Vienna, Va.

52. "Myers' Charge," *Guild Notes,* Jan. 1979, p. 5
53. *Guild Notes,* Jan.-Feb. 1982, p. 20
54. Louis Jenkins, op. cit., p. 86
55. Bob Hilliard, "Legal Services Restrictions Threatens More than the Poor," *Guild Notes,* July-Aug. 1981
56. Civil Action #81-277-B, Sept. 4, 1981
57. Howard Phillips, "Legal Services Should Not Be Federally Funded," *Conservative Digest,* July 1980, p. 16
58. The extent to which this is true in the mountain west is documented in the Memorandum from Dan Newman to Bruce Coles, op. cit.
59. Nathan Glazer, "Towards an Imperial Judiciary," *The Public Interest,* Fall 1975, p. 118
60. Gary L. McDowell, "A Modest Remedy for Judicial Activism," *The Public Interest,* Fall 1975, p. 118
61. Peter Brimelow and Stephen T. Markman, "Supreme Irony," *Harper's,* Oct. 1981
62. *New York Times,* Feb. 19, 1982; *Human Events* August 14, 1982
63. William R. Havender, "Science vs. Politics in Regulatory Washington, *American Spectator,* June 1983, p. 25
64. Ibid., pp. 25-26
65. Letter addressed to "Dear Fellow Human" from National Peace Academy Campaign, 110 Maryland Ave. N.E., Washington, D.C. 20002, n.d.
66. *Wall Street Journal,* August 2, 1982
67. Hunter Lovins, "Preparing for the Next Surprise" *New Roots,* Dec./January 1981, p. 64
68. John Boland, "Nader Crusade," *Barron's,* Oct. 12, 1981, p. 16
69. Ibid., p. 16

XI

The Media — Shield of the Utopians

The movements—if not the specific organizations—that have been described in this book for the most part are familiar to the reader for they are the daily fare of press and television. Yet much of what we have written may be surprising, even shocking, to the general reader. The reason for this is that the media have acted as a filter, screening out most of the information that could damage the utopians in the public view.

There are a number of factors that explain why the media, instead of providing the public with some perspective on the utopians, have made themselves a sounding board for them, absorbing and transmitting their perspective on crucial issues as objective "truth." The most important is that journalists have a broadly similar perspective on the major issues the utopians address. Journalist Robert Novak (of the Evans and Novak column) has called the media the setting where journalists, regardless of background, are welded into one homogeneous ideological mold.[1] Thomas Shepard, the publisher of *Look* Magazine until it folded in 1971, noted that with only a handful of exceptions the men and women who produced *Look* "detested big business" and "worshipped the ecological and consumerism reformers."[2]

While these observations are impressionistic, they are confirmed by surveys of the media elite. Two political scientists, S. Robert Lichter and Stanley Rothman, in 1979 and 1980, interviewed 240 journalists and broadcasters of the most influential media outlets. The survey found the media elite were markedly to the left of the American electorate as a whole. Over a sixteen year period, less than 20% of the media elite had supported any Republican Presidential candidate. Their views on issues were in striking agreement with utopian articles of faith. For example, 56% of the media elite agreed that the U.S. exploits the Third World and is the cause of its poverty.[3]

A particularly significant indication of the media elite's sympathy for the utopians came in response to questions Lichter and Rothman addressed to both the media elite and a comparative sample of the business elite. Both elites had a very similar perception of the power of different groups in society, seeing the media, business and unions as those with the greatest influence. But asked how they would *prefer* to see power distributed, the media elite put themselves at the top, followed by consumer groups, intellectuals and blacks.[4]

In part, the media elite sympathize with the utopians because they define their role in much the same way. Walter Cronkite is said to have declared that journalists identify with humanity rather than with authority.[5] Similarly Julius Duscha, a reporter who became director of the Washington Journalism Center, said "Reporters are frustrated reformers . . . they look upon themselves almost with reverence, like they are protecting the world against the forces of evil."[6]

Moreover, for all their cynicism, the media elite readily succumb to hero worship. Ralph Nader was irresistible for the role. He began as a David who bested Goliath incarnated as the biggest company of them all, General Motors. The image lived on as Nader conducted his youthful, almost children's crusades, against the great regulatory bureaucracies and major companies and banks. Nader's few ill-hanging suits, his spare single room lodgings, his avoidance of material goods and pleasures, even women, all made him a figure larger than life, totally devoted to a cause, incorruptible. To journalists, Nader was a tribune of the people, the man who assumed the role they themselves would dearly love to have played. A Nader leaflet quoted a passage from *Time:* "If there is a man in Washington who provokes pure awe and respect here and beyond the Potomac, it is Ralph Nader . . . he lives his religion, devoid of greed, filled with candor, beyond influence." Morton Mintz, the *Washington Post's* Nader-stalker, was inspired by his beat to write books whose titles could as readily have adorned Nader's covers: *America Inc.* followed by *Power Inc.* While no other single figure has captured the imagination of journalists in the same way, the utopians as a whole benefit from being viewed by journalists as people like themselves, representatives of all the people.

In the case of some of the media elite more than sympathy is involved. Some *are* utopians, sharing fully their perspective on events. Larry Stern, in a key position as national news editor of the country's second most influential paper, the *Washington Post,* was one of them. This emerged, surprisingly, at his funeral, following his sudden death in 1980, at the age of 50, of a heart attack. He was eulogized by left-wing journalist I.F. Stone, who praised Stern as a friend of Palestine and Nicaragua (i.e. the PLO and the Sandinistas) and for hating "those huge mindless institutions that devour our substance and corrupt our fundamental ideals, like the Pentagon and the CIA,"[7] (More remarkably, Stern was also eulogized by Teofilo Acosta, head of the Cuban interests section in Washington, identified by intelligence expert Robert Moss as station chief of the DGI, the Cuban intelligence service. Stern was apparently a friend of Castro's Cuba as well.) Journalist Les Whitten, who worked with Jack Anderson on the popular column, seems to have derived his political philosophy directly from Ralph Nader. He warned a high school graduating class in Maryland of the "great pirate-like corporations that swallow up the blood of the people" and informed the class that if you lined up the presidents of thirty big banks and thirty bank robbers you would have fifty-eight criminals and the only difference was that one kind did it with a gun quickly while the bank presidents did it "at 18% a year without a gun."[8]

Many in the media—including some of the elite—actually learned their craft in utopian training-grounds. A huge "underground," later called "alternative" press, burgeoned in the late 1960s, its theme that America (often spelled with a "k" wrapped in a swastika) was a fascist country. A number of journalists from these papers subsequently moved into the straight press. The best-selling novel *The Spike* described the odyssey of a reporter for *Barricades* (an obvious takeoff on the "alternative" journal *Ramparts*) whose sensational scoop exposing the CIA earns him a place on the *New York World* (clearly the *New York Times*). *The Spike's* hero Robert Hockney was presumably modelled on *New York Times* star reporter Seymour Hersh, who wrote for *Ramparts* before coming to the *New York Times* and made his name exposing the CIA. To be sure, only the first part of Hersh's career paralleled that of the fictional Hockney, for while Hockney woke up to the role he was playing on behalf of Soviet disinformation efforts, there is no evidence that Hersh's utopian perspective has changed.

Even journalists who do not start out as utopians may be drawn to them because their concerns make good copy. Utopians are endless sources of the kind of stories that sell papers. Our tuna is poisoned; the nuclear plant near our city is in danger of melt-down; nuclear bombs will destroy all life from ground zero, which is in our backyard. In addition to the inherent drama of scare stories, they have, as the utopians present them, an appealing clarity. There are good guys and bad guys, victimizers and victims. This is much more dramatic stuff than cost-benefit analyses, probability studies and theories of deterrence that are the stuff of refutation. Moreover, the utopians have solutions: shut down nuclear power plants, eliminate all pesticides, rely on the sun, endorse a nuclear freeze.

If stories told according to utopian formula make good copy for the press, they are even better suited for documentaries, television's method of exploring issues in-depth. Why this is so can be seen from a candid look into the documentary producer's world offered in 1978 by Martin Carr, a veteran in producing documentaries for all three networks. Carr noted that the producer's first step was to "arrive at a point of view." His goal was then to make the viewer feel as he felt: "If you walk away feeling differently, I failed somehow." Carr noted the obligation to provide "balance," but explained that this had to be done carefully, so as not to disturb the documentary's emotional impact. He described a documentary he had made on migrant workers in which, for balance, he had interviewed the biggest grower in Florida. But he was a charming man who could have tipped the emotional balance of the documentary in favor of his position. So Carr found another grower whose point of view was the same, but whose personality would alienate the viewer and put him on instead. As a result, Carr reports: "One could only feel a particular way at the end of the film . . . the way I felt about it."[9] The utopian point of view on most stories shapes visually striking, emotionally compelling documentaries: the good farmworker against the bad grower; the victims of disease versus the large corporation; the peasant guerilla against government-backed exploiters, etc.

On major topics such as the environment, defense, intelligence and foreign policy, the media serves as a vast sounding board for the utopians, while at the same time suppressing sounds the utopians prefer not to hear. The latter is especially important, for while there is dispute on how effective the media is in making the public think the way journalists do (after all, the public does not vote like the media elite), there is little dispute that the media determine what it is that the public thinks *about*. As an article in *The Journalism Quarterly* points out: "If newsmen share a pattern of preference as to what is newsworthy, and that pattern does not represent reality, they will present a distorted image of the world which may contribute to inappropriate decisions and policies."[10]

Nowhere are distortions in coverage more evident than in coverage of environmental issues, particularly nuclear energy, the issue on which the utopians have expended their greatest efforts. The impact of the utopian campaign against nuclear energy on the media is apparent from two systematic studies, one by the Battelle Center and one by the Media Center. The Battelle Center study covered four national periodicals, including the *New York Times,* from 1972 to 1976 and found that while in 1972 there were more positive than negative statements on nuclear energy, by 1976, negative outnumbered positive statements by 2-1.[11] (This, it must be remembered, was 3 years prior to Three Mile Island.) The Media Institute study focussed on ten years of television evening news coverage, from August 4, 1968 to March 27, 1979 (just prior to Three Mile Island). Its most telling finding concerned the "experts" used by the networks on nuclear energy. Of the top ten sources used over the years, seven were opposed to nuclear power. The source most frequently used was the anti-nuclear Union of Concerned Scientists, while the second most consulted source was Ralph Nader.[12] After Three Mile Island, earlier tendencies became even more marked. Psychiatrist Robert DuPont examined 13 hours of videotapes of news coverage on nuclear energy and found that fear was the leitmotif of the stories. Reporters continually examined what DuPont called "what if, worst case" scenarios. He found almost no mention of the risks posed by other energy sources or the need to balance risks.[13]

By 1982, the pattern of media coverage had produced serious misconceptions in the American public concerning the balance of opinion among scientists on nuclear energy. A Roper poll found that almost one in four Americans believed that a majority of scientists, "who are energy experts," opposed the further development of nuclear energy, and one in three members of the public, believed that solar energy could make a large contribution to meeting energy needs within the next twenty years.[14] Yet, an actual survey of energy experts showed that only 5% wanted to halt further development of nuclear energy (among those with specific expertise in the nuclear area 0% wanted to halt further development). No more than 2% of energy experts saw any form of solar energy making a substantial contribution to energy needs in the next 20 years.[15]

The distortions in perception can be explained by the views of science journalists, who are far more sceptical of nuclear energy than scientists. A survey of science journalists at major national media outlets undertaken by Lichter and Rothman found there was a fascinating, though scarcely surprising, connection between attitudes toward nuclear energy and political ideology. The more liberal the journalist, the more he was likely to oppose nuclear energy. Rothman and Lichter found they could define the issue more precisely. "We asked them a large number of social and political questions. The best predictor of opposition to nuclear energy is the belief that American society is unjust."[16] Moreover Lichter and Rothman found that television reporters and producers were even more hostile to nuclear energy than print journalists.

The extensive use, especially by television, of the Union of Concerned Scientists was presumably a major factor in explaining the discrepancy between what scientists think and what the public thinks they think. The public, because of its name, perceived this as an organization of scientists. But as Samuel McCracken points out in *The War Against the Atom,* its membership is obtained through direct mail solicitation of the public and the only qualification for belonging is a contribution of $15. Its executive directors in recent years have not been scientists.[17] Lichter and Rothman's random sample of 7,741 scientists turned up only one who was affiliated with the Union of Concerned Scientists. On that basis Lichter and Rothman estimate that fewer than 200 scientists among the 130,000 listed in American Men and Women of Science are affiliated with the Union of Concerned Scientists.[18] Little wonder, under these circumstances, that the organization refused Lichter and Rothman information needed to poll its membership!

McCracken observes that anyone would see the fraud if a general membership organization composed almost entirely of laymen and concerned principally with supporting bans on prayer in the schools were to call itself the Union of Concerned Clergymen.[19] Yet the media persist in using this organization of utopians, as its chief authority on nuclear energy. The media rarely calls upon Scientists and Engineers for Secure Energy, although this is an organization whose members are genuine experts on nuclear energy and includes seven nobel laureates in physics. Presumably, this is because it does not spread the utopian's message, endorsed by so many in the media, that nuclear power is immensely dangerous and the authorities are deceiving the public.

Another interesting insight into the weight of sentiment against nuclear power in the media comes from a Public Broadcasting Corporation spokesman who was castigated for the uniform imbalance of the PBC's programs. He explained that it would be difficult even to find a producer prepared to do a pro-nuclear film.[20]

On questions of defense, the media elite have also been supportive of utopian assumptions. Walter Cronkite summed up the media perspective in the 1970s when he said in 1974: "There are always groups in Washington expressing views of alarm over the state of our defenses. We don't carry those stories. The story is that there are those who want to cut defense spending."[21] The American Security Council, which during the 1970s issued reports and ran a series of conferences and seminars featuring defense experts who warned of the disrepair of the American military and the massive Soviet military buildup then going on, became convinced that there was some unwritten rule in the media that their activities would not be covered. But for the media, as a group advocating increased defense expenditures, the American Security Council was simply not defined as "news."

Survey results indicate how pervasively media coverage reflected utopian attitudes. Ernest Lefever, before starting his own Ethics and Public Policy Center, led a study team for the Institute for American Strategy which examined CBS News coverage of national defense for 1972 and 1973. The study showed that during that two year period the viewer saw only one minute on the CBS Evening News dealing with the comparative military strength of the U.S. and U.S.S.R.[22] The study found that 1400 presentations on the subject of national defense tended to support the view that threats to our security were less serious than the government thought, while only 79 contradicted that position.

With Reagan's victory, the views of those who argued more defense spending was needed could not be ignored any longer, for those views represented administration policy. CBS therefore entered the debate with a massive documentary designed to counter the administration position. Called by its anchorman Dan Rather "the most important documentary project of the decade," the five hour series in June 1981, "The Defense of the United States," was hailed by the *Washington Post* as the "first documentary epic in TV history." Its theme, as

Joshua Muravchik and John E. Haynes pointed out in their analysis of the series, "CBS vs. Defense," was that "the United States is not threatened by any external enemy, but rather by the tragic propensity of the two superpowers each to see in the other a mirror reflection of its own fears and hostilities." Muravchik and Haynes noted that in the five hours devoted to examining plans for a U.S. military build-up "there was no mention—*none*—of the Soviet buildup which precipitated it."[23]

Although the public had no way of knowing it, the program's arguments, experts, even its vocabulary were derived from the utopian organizations. To testify that current defense spending was already excessive the program used "experts" Jack Geiger and Kosta Tsipis. Tsipis is a member of the board of directors of SANE, which we encountered in the chapter on the peace movement, and Geiger is a leader of both Physicians for Social Responsibility and International Physicians for the Prevention of Nuclear War (in which Soviet physicians join with American physicians to emphasize the need for the U.S. to disarm). The viewer was not informed that they were peace movement activists, however. Geiger was identified only as professor of medicine at the City University of New York and Tsipis as professor of physics at MIT.[24]

To show that Soviet influence was already on the decline (presumably making increased defense expenditures superfluous), CBS drew on the Center for Defense Information. In the chapter on the institutes we referred to the Center's report purporting to show that Soviet influence in the world had reached an all-time low. After Defense Secretary Weinberger spoke of the need for a strong defense, Walter Cronkite undercut his statement: "Since 1960, the Soviet influence around the world actually has declined. Their so-called gains like Afghanistan and Angola take on a different perspective, particularly when measured against losses, like Egypt and China." CBS then offered a closeup of two lists of twelve nations, one showing Soviet gains and the other Soviet losses since 1960. The lists were erroneous but repeated the errors in the lists published by the Center for Defense Information.[25] The voice of the Center for Defense Information had been transformed into the voice of CBS. (In a fund-raising letter the Center boasted that all three networks had used it in a total of five major documentaries in 1981.)

The utopian campaign against the intelligence agencies depended heavily on the media for its success. The campaign began in the late

1960s, when a series of books and articles on them began to appear, many of them financed by the Fund for Investigative Journalism. The Fund was established by Philip M. Stern. The Stern Fund, on whose board he serves, is a major funder of utopian projects. But it scored its first major success when the *New York Times* ran a series of articles in December 1974 by Seymour Hersh exposing CIA involvement in illegal domestic surveillance of the anti-war movement. This precipitated a series of investigations by the specially appointed Rockefeller Commission and the Senate, which resulted in "reforms" that went far beyond correction of abuses. The CIA's ability to function in crucial areas was imperilled. At one point, eight committees of Congress, the armed services, foreign relations, appropriations and intelligence committees of both houses, had to be informed of every major CIA operation, which given the all-but-certainty of leaks by staff, meant there could be no such operations.

While U.S. intelligence agencies were a legitimate subject of media interest, the problem was that in true utopian fashion the media were interested *only* in stories that revealed intelligence activities as illegal or immoral. Reports that the intelligence services were failing to perform their task of protecting U.S. citizens were not news. When the Coalition for Peace through Strength held a conference in March 1979, entitled "Our Domestic Intelligence Crisis," it was ignored by the major media. Yet revelations that the public might have thought dramatic were made, including the fact that the Secret Service only received one fourth of the intelligence it did before the media-assisted "reforms" of intelligence agencies discouraged informants who feared their identities would be exposed in response to Freedom of Information requests. It, thus, had to recommend that the President not visit certain cities in the United States. The conference also disclosed that the Federal Employment Security program had been nullified, with members of the Communist Party or even of the Weather Underground no longer barred from federal employment, even in sensitive positions.[26] The media showed no interest in informing the public about the necessary services intelligence agencies provide to the public or about the consequences of dismantling security protections.

With all the popularity of documentaries about the malfeasances of the CIA and FBI, the networks produced nothing comparable on the KGB. This was not because the topic could not be handled. A Canadian team did an absorbing documentary called "The KGB Connections," based largely on the testimony of KGB defectors. A great critical success in Canada and Europe, it was turned down by all three networks, including ABC which had invested in its production. Challenged for its failure to show the documentary, ABC countered that it would shortly be showing its own documentary on the KGB but at this writing, over a year later, ABC had not done so. The failure to examine KGB activities by both TV and print media meant, as James Tyson points out in *Target America,* that the CIA seemed to shadow-box against a non-existent enemy. The utopian contention that covert intelligence activities were the product of deviant psychological needs of those who manned corrupt American institutions was reinforced.

Foreign policy, particularly as it touches on human rights, is yet another area in which the media almost uniformly present the utopian perspective. The reason is not simply that journalists share that perspective, although doubtless many do. Covering human rights violations in totalitarian "socialist" countries is difficult, if not impossible, for journalists. Such countries, when they do not bar journalists altogether, control their movements. This means that a major information source has to be people outside the country. Information was available on the Cambodian genocide very early, but it came from people who had escaped over the border. By 1977, *Reader's Digest* editors John Barron and Anthony Paul had produced a book, *Murder of a Gentle Land* which, based on the eye-witness accounts of hundreds of escapees, estimated that between April 17, 1975 and the end of 1976, at least 1.2 million people had died as a result of the policies of the Cambodian government.

Yet press coverage of events, unprecedented in horror since the Nazi destruction of six million Jews, was minimal. In 1976, the year in which Barron and Paul conducted their interviews, what was happening in Cambodia was mentioned on television network evening news programs only three times, with NBC never mentioning it at all. The country's two most influential papers, the *Times* and the *Washington Post,* together mentioned the subject a total of 13 times in the year.[27] In 1977, when what was happening was even clearer, the three networks had a combined total of two stories. That contrasted with 159 human rights related stories on the networks on South Africa.[28] While the *New York Times* did better in 1977, referring to the Cambodian genocide 34 times, this still contrasted sharply with 291 stories on human rights violations in South Africa. *The Washington Post* ran ten items on Cambodia; it had thirty items just on the death of Steve Biko, the black leader who died under suspicious circumstances in a South

African jail.[29] In 1978, the American Security Council made things convenient for the press corps by arranging a press conference in Washington D.C., addressed by Pin Yathay, a civil engineer who had escaped after 26 months in Communist Cambodia. Yathay reported losing 18 members of his family and provided an eye witness account of desperation and cruelty.

> "And there were many macabre incidents . . . the starving people who ate the flesh of dead bodies during this acute famine. I will now tell you a story that I lived myself . . . a teacher who ate the flesh of her own sister. She was later caught, she was beaten from morning to night until she died, under the rain, in front of the whole village as an example, and her child was crying beside her, and the mother died at the evening."[30]

A dramatic story. But not one of the networks sent a representative and while the *Washington Post* sent a reporter, the paper never carried a story.

Hedrick Smith, one time Moscow correspondent of the *New York Times*, and then chief correspondent of the Washington Bureau, has cast light on the reasons why the coverage was so poor. He noted that the *Times*—which, as one news executive asserted, is the "bible" of the other media—is not inclined to do stories on foreign countries written outside those countries.[31] This meant, for example, that while Soviet dissidents were the subject of many stories while they were in the Soviet Union, once the same people, having found refuge in the U.S., sought to draw attention to human rights violations in the Soviet Union, they found the press uninterested. When leading figures in the Soviet human rights movement like Vladimir Bukovsky and Alexander Ginzburg participated in two days of International Sakharov Hearings in 1979, that brought 60 witnesses to Washington to testify, their efforts were virtually ignored by the press. The *Washington Post* ran a story in the "Style" section called, "Remembering Russia." That was scarcely the point of the hearings. Similarly, when testimony on conditions in Vietnam was given before a House subcommittee in June 1977, including eyewitness reports of a Vietnamese imprisoned in a series of "reeducation camps," the major newspapers carried nothing.[32]

The end result is gross distortion in coverage of human rights problems; in 1977 the *New York Times* carried 48 items on human rights violations in South Korea and none on North Korea.[33] More than that, as Reed Irvine, head of the media watchdog group, Accuracy in

Media, has pointed out, what emerges is a form of collaboration between the U.S. media and the countries that most systematically violate human rights.[34]

There may have been an additional reason for the reluctance of the media to report more fully on Cambodia and Southeast Asia. In the last years of the Vietnam War, the press was an adversary of the war, and the fact that the American departure did not lead to an improved life for the people of that area, was something they were, at first, unwilling to believe, later to acknowledge. For example, *New York Times* columnist Anthony Lewis, urging a cutoff of American aid on March 17, 1975, wrote: ''What future possibility could be more terrible than the reality of what is happening to Cambodia now?'' The possibilities were beyond anything of which Anthony Lewis dreamed. While New York Times columnist Tom Wicker, in the immediate aftermath of the Vietnam War, was glad to give the press credit for forcing the U.S. out of the region, once there were boat people and millions of murdered victims in Cambodia, the press did not want to be reminded of its role. The violent reaction of CBS newsman Morley Safer to an article by Robert Elegant in the English journal *Encounter* in August 1981 is revealing. Elegant was himself a journalist in Vietnam and in the article laid bare the shabbiness of the reporting, not exempting himself from the criticism. Safer devoted a radio segment to denouncing Elegant, whose article almost none of his listeners could have seen, as worthy of the mantle of Joseph Goebbels.[35] The entire subject obviously irritated media nerves.

Coverage of human rights adhered to the utopian perspective, according to which, the world's worst human rights violator was the Republic of South Africa, followed by third world lands friendly to the United States, especially those in Latin America. As countries came under attack from internal subversion backed directly or indirectly by the Soviet Union, media focus, in true utopian fashion, was on the injustices that lead people to revolt rather than the predictable consequences of these ''wars of liberation'' in inaugurating much more repressive regimes. Karen de Young, now foreign editor of the *Washington Post,* who from Nicaragua provided warm coverage of the Sandinistas in Somoza's last period, admitted: ''Most journalists now, most Western journalists at least, are very eager to seek out guerilla groups, leftist groups, because you assume they must be the good guys.''[36] Walter Cronkite, speaking in Portland, said the U.S. should help countries such as El Salvador ''achieve their goals even if it means interim steps of socialism and communism."[37] (As Reed Irvine retorted in *AIM Report,* communism has yet to serve as an "interim step.")

With rare exceptions—NBC, in the fall of 1982, produced a film "What Ever Happened to El Salvador" that accompanied a Salvadoran army unit on patrol rather than the guerillas—network documentaries have been hostile to the government of El Salvador. Guatemala was the subject of a September 1982 CBS documentary that focussed on the theme that revolution is inevitable there as the response to tyranny backed by the United States on behalf of our exploitative business interests. On the other hand, television journalists bend over backwards in their efforts to understand the difficulties of the Nicaraguan government. A segment of ABC's 20/20, aired in June 1980, had David Marash make the patently false declaration: "Nicaragua's revolutionary justice system has been given near unanimous international praise."

The utopian influence on public television is even greater than on the networks: here they often write and produce the documentaries. For example, Philip Agee was co-producer of an anti-CIA three hour documentary, "On Company Business" broadcast in May 1980. The fund-raising prospectus sent out by the producers prior to the actual filming promised that the documentary would "show the broken lives, hatred, cruelty, cynicism and despair which result from U.S.-CIA policy" and would record "the story of 30 years of CIA subversion, murder, bribery and torture as told by an insider and documented with newsreel film of actual events."[38]

The "insider" who served as the documentary's central figure and moral hero was Agee, identified for the viewer only as someone who had worked for the CIA between 1959 and 1969. There was no mention of Agee's role in exposing the identities of U.S. agents worldwide or of his expulsion from the Netherlands, France and England. Intelligence expert Robert Moss has revealed Agee was found to have met with the Cuban intelligence station chief in London at least 30 times before he was expelled from England. If the viewer had known of Agee's record and avowed identification with communism, he might have discounted everything Agee said. The documentary's solution was to keep silent. Despite this, Public Broadcasting's director of current affairs programming, Barry Chase, described the program in a memo to all public broadcasting stations as "a highly responsible overview of the CIA's history."[39] (Chase clearly did not feel inhibited by the law establishing the Corporation for Public Broadcasting that stipulates programs funded by it must be objective and balanced if they deal with controversial issues.)

The Institute for Policy Studies' Saul Landau has written films for public television of a similar calibre. "Paul Jacobs and the Nuclear Gang" (with part of its seed money from the Samuel Rubin Foundation and Obie Benz, one of the wealthy young creators of the Robin Hood was Right species of foundations described earlier[40]) was a polemic against nuclear energy and nuclear weapons, relying primarily on emotionally charged interviews with cancer victims who believed their disease had been caused by radiation and with the members of their families. Landau also wrote "From the Ashes . . . Nicaragua," directed by Helena Solberg Ladd, who had been a lecturer at IPS. William Bennett, head of the National Endowment for the Humanities which had channeled funds for the film's production under its previous head, on seeing the film, remarked that he was "shocked, appalled, disgusted" by what he called an example of "unabashed socialist-realism propaganda."[41] Author Midge Decter, executive director of the Committee for a Free World, found even this description too mild. She noted that "we almost no longer have a working vocabulary to cover phenomena like Ms. Ladd's film."[42]

Many of the documentaries that appear on public television endorse utopian themes far more overtly than would be possible on the networks. Public Broadcasting presented, for example, a film on North Korea that could have received the imprimatur of its dictator Kim Il Sung; a hymn to Cuba called "Cuba: Sports and Revolution;" two films on China, "The Children of China" which was such good propaganda that the Chinese Central Broadcasting Administration praised it for helping American people "understand the New China" and "China Memoir" produced by Shirley MacLaine, which even Ralph Rogers, then chairman of the Public Broacasting Corporation, admitted was "pure propaganda."[43] Boston Public Television's WGBH funded a film called Blacks Britannica on British racism, which won the prize at the Leipzig Film Festival in East Germany. It was too much even for the producer at WGBH and he complained of the film's "endorsement of a Marxist point of view."[44] When he sought to edit out some of the most blatant segments, the maker of the film brought suit and the U.S. Communist Party front, the National Alliance Against Racist and Political Repression, petitioned to join the suit.[45] In the end, four minutes of the film were removed, but its Marxist message remained unmistakable.

Another utopian theme—hostility against corporations—is also reflected in the media. A Louis Harris poll in the fall of 1982 found that an "overwhelming 73%" of high level executives believed business and financial coverage on TV news was prejudiced against business.[46] The hostility is most pervasive in a surprising area—entertainment programming. A Media Institute study, "Crooks, Conmen and Clowns," found that the image of businessmen on TV series was overwhelmingly negative, with two out of three businessmen on two hundred prime time episodes shown as foolish, greedy or criminal. While on occasion a small businessman was shown in a favorable light, those running big businesses were for the most part depicted as actual criminals.[47]

While it might be argued that the businessman simply offers a convenient "heavy" in plot development, Ben Stein, in *The View from Sunset Boulevard,* shows that there is an excellent fit between the opinions of TV writers and producers and the shows they create. Stein interviewed 40 writers and producers of the major adventure shows and situation-comedies and found that even those worth millions of dollars considered themselves workers opposed to an "exploiting class." A typical flippant-serious comment was made by Bob Schiller, who wrote for Lucille Ball for 13 years and produced "Maud." He said of businessmen: "I don't judge. I think there are good lepers and bad lepers."[48] Producer Stanley Kramer could have led off a Naderite conference. He told Stein: "Everything that has to do with our lives is contaminated. The air, the streams, the food—everything is ruined."[49] It was self-evident to most TV writers that big business was responsible.

To the media, the utopians are inherently more *believable* than those who oppose them. Cynical about human motives, journalists seem unable to conceive that "public interest" spokesmen act from anything but selfless devotion to the public good. Yet Abbie Hoffman could enlighten them. He noted: "There is absolutely no greater high than challenging the power structure as a nobody, giving it your all, and winning."[50] Peter Metzger has pointed out another motivation that also has to do with heightening the individual's sense of power and self-worth. He observes that with only a few exceptions the experts cited by the utopians never made genuine scientific contributions and thus were denied the reward of recognition by their peers.[51] They have achieved the fame and status their scientific work could not gain for them through serving the needs of the utopians for men with credentials.

Journalists are ready to believe the most improbable charges against the institutions they distrust. In January 1982, the *New York Times* featured a lengthy story by Raymond Bonner concerning events alleged to have taken place a year earlier: American military advisers in El Salvador had observed a torture training session for the El Salvadoran military in which a 17 year old boy and a 13 year old girl had their bones broken prior to being killed. Bonner's sole source for the story was a deserter from the Salvadoran army. The narrative, which in its original form claimed that the American advisers were *teaching* the torture session, had appeared in a leftist Mexican paper but was such obvious Communist atrocity propaganda that it took eight months after the original publication before a taker was found among American journalists, in the form of Mr. Bonner, who offered a "sanitized" version in the *Times*.[52]

Such credulity leaves the media open to being taken in by the grossest "disinformation" forgeries. Flora Lewis, at the top of her profession as a columnist for the *New York Times,* accepted uncritically a supposed State Department "dissent document" which was distributed to newsmen. While the State Department does indeed have a "dissent channel" permitting members in disagreement with policy to have their objections heard at the highest level of the department, the document Flora Lewis accepted as authentic was marked as the product of a non-existent State Department task force. Lewis devoted her column of March 6, 1981 to the document, which attacked U.S. government policy in El Salvador. Asserting it had been "drawn up by people from the National Security Council, the State and Defense Departments and the CIA," she went on to praise the report's "solid facts and cool analysis" and closed by telling the Reagan administration that it would "do well to listen to the paper's authors before the chance for talks is lost." At this point the State Department came out with a detailed report on the forgery which the *Times* carried as a news story and Flora Lewis, her face plentifully covered with egg, wrote an apology in her March 9 column.

The attitude of the media elite to government assertions that contradict utopian views with which they identify is instant distrust. A storm broke over the *Washington Post* and the *Wall Street Journal* when it became known that the journalists of both had relied upon Philip Agee as a source for articles they wrote attacking a February 1981 U.S. White Paper, "Communist Interference in El Salvador." The White Paper summarized findings from captured documents of the El Salvador guerillas, showing the extent of clandestine military support given by the Soviet Union and Cuba to the guerillas beginning in 1979. As a result of the furor, even how the articles came to be written became public knowledge. The *Wall Street Journal's* Jonathan Kwitny told his editor of his immediate "skepticism over news accounts of the white paper."[53] The *Washington Post's* Robert Kaiser said that he had immediately been eager to explore possible deficiencies in the White Paper and so was pleased when the Post's national editor, Peter Osnos, asked him to look into the matter. And Peter Osnos revealed that he had assigned Kaiser after a call from free lance writer Jeffrey Stein who said: "Look I can't understand how you all have let that White Paper hang out there without a look."[54] (Stein was a former fellow of the Institute for Policy Studies, suggesting that the utopian grape vine operates quickly to encourage attacks on anything the utopians consider damaging to them.) For the utopians, it was crucial to discredit the White Paper, since if the American public recognized the Soviet-Cuban role in El Salvador, the carefully fostered image of the guerillas as indigenous liberal reformers might be undermined.

Philip Agee, according to Arnaud de Borchgrave, helped by his "Cuban friends," provided a 46 page attack on the White Paper which was distributed in April by the *Covert Action Information Bulletin.* This publication, it will be remembered, was started after an internal factional split at *CounterSpy,* with Agee becoming associated with the new magazine. Both the *Post's* Kaiser and the *Journal's* Kwitny obtained copies. Kaiser subsequently claimed that in an early draft of his article he had mentioned Agee as a source, but that his editor at the *Post* suggested dropping the reference as "unnecessary."[55] Kwitny was taken aback when confronted with his failure to credit Agee's paper as a source in his *Wall Street Journal* story: "I was totally unaware that it had any distribution, except to a few of his friends here."[56] He insisted that while he had read Agee's paper: "There was nothing I was drawing from him or anyone else . . . I can't really remember what was in the Agee piece." Yet in a line by line comparison, *Human Events* reporter Cliff Kincaid showed that not only did Kwitny's criticisms closely parallel those of Agee, but Kwitny even repeated a specific Agee error, referring to "labor unions" (Agee said "trade unions") when the document being analyzed was talking about the Communist Party.[57]

Perhaps the most interesting revelations concerned the wide use by journalists of the Agee apparatus and the ignorance of those in executive positions on major papers of the web of utopian organizations. Frederick Taylor, Executive Editor of the *Wall Street Journal,* came to the defense of his reporter in a long article on the editorial page entitled, "The El Salvador 'White Paper.'" Taylor declared that the *Wall Street Journal* had been accused "at the least of being the dupe of Soviet disinformation, and at the worst of taking the work of a discredited left-winger and passing it off as its own." Taylor said: "It isn't so." As proof he cited what Kwitny had told him:

> "The article originated in my own skepticism over news accounts of the white paper in February. It sprouted because of two events in April. First, having been asked to sort the files of my recently deceased Journal colleague, Jerry Landauer, I called someone who had been a longstanding source of Jerry's on intelligence matters . . . This source, John Kelly, edits a magazine, *Counterspy,* which also printed a critique of the white paper. Kelly supplied me with some leads and documents."[58]

To defend the *Journal* from charges of being a dupe of disinformation and of passing off the charges of a discredited left-winger as its own by transferring responsibility from Agee to *CounterSpy* and to inform the *Wall Street Journal's* readers that they had all along been kept informed on intelligence matters by *CounterSpy,* was, to say the least, a remarkable editorial defense. (A member of *CounterSpy's* board boasted it had been behind at least 15 stories in *The Journal* on the CIA, Indonesia, South Korea and the Phillipines.)[59]

Apparently there was a similar gap between editors and reporters at the *Washington Post.* When a *Washington Post* editorial condemned *CounterSpy's* clone, the *Covert Action Information Bulletin,* as "contemptible" and suggested its editors were less than honorable journalists, they lashed back:

> "Your diatribe only highlights the gap between the editorial offices and the reporters, for your people are among the large number of working journalists from virtually all the major printed and electronic media in the country who call upon us daily for help, research, and of all things, names of intelligence operatives in connection with articles they are writing."[60]

Occasionally, it is possible to trace a "disinformation" story through an elaborate international circuit. For example, a story alleging a CIA conspiracy behind a financial scandal involving the Nugan Hand bank in Australia was originally aired in *The Tribune,* the paper of the Communist party of Australia. It was subsequently picked up by *CounterSpy* and then by the *Wall Street Journal's* Jonathan Kwitny, who ran a front page three part series in August 1982 on what was by this time a two year old story. Dismissed in Australia when it originally appeared because of its source and the paucity of evidence, the story was now—despite the fact that Kwitny offered no new evidence—given major coverage by the Australian Broadcasting Commission as well as by mainstream Australian newspapers. Thus a story, tainted by its source when originally aired, gathers credibility as it is picked up by mainstream media and in the end serves effectively its original purpose—to sow distrust of the United States in Australia.[61]

The difficulty journalists have in believing anything the government says, that interferes with their prejudices, has become obvious to government officials. Admiral Bobby Inman, on retiring as deputy director of the CIA, spoke of his frustration at trying to convince the public of the peril of the Soviet military build-up when the press would not even believe U.S. intelligence reports that included spy satellite pictures. Inman described an intelligence briefing for the press on the Soviet and Cuban-backed military build-up in Nicaragua in which reporters were shown photos of Soviet-type military garrison arrangements, deployed Soviet T-55 tanks etc. Newspaper accounts the following day used the word "alleged" to describe the intelligence findings, suggesting that the reporters did not believe them.[62]

The media does more than *believe* the utopians: it protects them. News that could prove embarassing to the utopians is often simply not reported. Reed Irvine has christened this "the Pinsky Principle," after North Carolina journalist Walter Pinsky, who described his approach in the *Columbia Journalism Review* in 1976. "If my research and journalistic instincts tell me one thing, my political instincts another . . . I won't fudge it, I won't bend it, but I won't write it."[63] Pinsky gave as an example what he called the great untold story of the trial of Joan Little in his home state. Joan Little was an imprisoned black woman who killed her guard and defended herself on the grounds that he had tried to assault her sexually. Her story was widely reported nationally. Pinsky explained that what he meant when he said it was unreported was that reporters never described the role of the Communist Party, working through its front, the National Alliance Against Racist and Political Repression, in controlling the entire political movement surrounding the case. Pinsky says that journalists kept silent "out of concern that the information might be used in red-baiting anyone associated with the case who did not belong to the [Communist] party."[64]

ABC newsman Geraldo Rivera, in an interview with *Playboy,* confessed to practicing the Pinsky Principle in his reporting from Panama. When the Panamanian National Guard was guilty of violence at the time of the Senate vote on the Canal treaties, "We downplayed the whole incident. That was the day I decided that I had to be very careful about what was said, because I could defeat the very thing [passage of the Treaty] that I wanted to achieve."[65]

An interesting example of the Pinsky Principle was the failure of CBS in its two-part drama "Guyana Tragedy: The Story of Jim Jones," to say a word concerning Jones as a Communist. Jones had broken with the U.S. Communist Party, according to his own account, because it had turned against Stalin and "I loved Stalin." Nonetheless his feelings toward the party had clearly mellowed, for his will provided that in the absence of immediate surviving family, his estate should go to the U.S. Communist Party. Jones had also ordered that $7 million belonging to the People's Temple be transferred to the Soviet Union. When the script's author, Ernest Tidyman, was asked about the omission, he said he did not believe Jones was a Communist. Asked what Jones' political views were, Tidyman replied: "None, particularly. He was very liberal, very progressive, very community conscious."[66] Presumably, for Tidyman, giving the facts about Jones' Communism would interfere with the image he wanted to convey of Jones as an idealistic community-builder gone awry.

More recently the Pinsky Principle has been at work in the refusal of the media to examine the utopian roots of the peace movement and its links to the international Soviet front, the World Peace Council. With rare exceptions, notably the *Wall Street Journal* and the *Reader's Digest,* the mass media have portrayed the freeze as a spontaneous outgrowth of grass roots Middle America. Even when the organizations that created and promoted the freeze are credited, as in a *Newsweek* article of April 26, 1982, the identifications are superficial, giving no hint of the agenda of these organizations. For example, although Clergy and Laity Concerned is described as "a powerful force in the disarmament movement," it is identified only as a group "begun in 1965 to mobilize the religious community against the Vietnam War." There is an element of laziness in this: it is easier to ask a group about itself over the phone than to acquire its literature which would explain that CALC sees its task to be joining together those who "hate the corporate power which the United States presently represents . . ."

But more important, there is unwillingness to transmit facts that might put the utopians in an unfavorable light. Eileen Shanahan, assistant managing editor of the *Pittsburgh Post-Gazette,* observed: "I saw it at the *Washington Star* and I'm seeing it here. The present 28-35 newsroom set is antiwar to a significant degree and also antinuke."[67] When President Reagan or members of Congress made any reference to the credentials of the groups behind the freeze, the prestige media lashed out. A *New York Times* editorial, on October 6, 1982, labelled all reference to such matters an "indecent debate" and a *Washington Post* editorial, on the same date, said that to bring up such topics was a "smear."

Probably the most widespread application of the Pinsky Principle is the failure to identify utopian sources. Identification is a crucial service the media offer the viewer or reader, for without it he has no way of evaluating the information offered to him. For example, the *New York Times* reported that a National Lawyers Guild delegation to the Middle East "came away convinced that the Israeli government implements a policy of torture for the annexation of the occupied areas." Since the National Lawyers Guild was identified only as "a group of American lawyers," the reader was not helped to be properly sceptical of this information.[68] Similarly the *New York Times,* which between 1979 and 1981 carried essays by Fellows of the Institute for Policy Studies on its Op-Ed page with more than twice the frequency of any other think tank, including much bigger and better known ones, identified the Institute in each case only as "an independent research organization in Washington D.C." The suggestion was that the reader was being exposed to "independent" thought, not the radical left perspective invariably provided by Institute Fellows.

A particularly dramatic example of misrepresentation through failure of identification is the media's treatment of Wilfred Burchett. Burchett was an Australian journalist. As far back as 1967, *The Reporter,* a liberal magazine of the period, published an article by fellow Australian Denis Warner which summed up Burchett's history up to that point:

> "Stripped of his Australian passport by Canberra in 1955 and denied Australian citizenship for his three children by a second marriage—one

> born in Hanoi, one in Peking, and one in Moscow—Burchett is regarded by those responsible for Australian security as a communist and a traitor who ought to stand trial for his role in the Korean war. . .''[69]

American POWs returning from Korea had described Burchett's involvement in obtaining phony confessions from them about America's alleged use of germ warfare, some of which he had himself written and rewritten. Burchett showed up again during the Vietnam war. Senator Jeremiah Denton described being interviewed by Burchett while he was a prisoner in North Vietnam and in his book, *When Hell Was in Session,* says that Burchett lost his cool ''when I implied that he was a cheap traitor who knew in his heart that he was prostituting his talents for money in a cause that he knew was false.''[70]

In these years, Burchett's articles occasionally appeared in U.S. papers, but he was properly identified. The *Chicago Tribune* carried an essay on June 5, 1966, with the following description of Burchett: ''An Australian Communist writer, Wilfred Burchett has travelled frequently to North Vietnam. He wrote this article after returning to his Cambodian home from his latest trip. It gives a communist view of the war and its effects and it should be read as such.''

But starting in the late 1970s, Burchett's essays began to be printed without any identification that could alert the reader. *The New York Times* published his essays on the Op-Ed page, identifying him only as ''a left-wing journalist living in Paris.'' After Reed Irvine complained to Times publisher Arthur Sulzberger that this was an inadequate identification—and Sulzberger agreed—the *Times* Op-Ed page, in the following year, identified him as ''a journalist living in Paris.'' *Harper's* published a review by Burchett of a book attacking the CIA, identifying him only as ''a left-wing journalist'' and ''a personal friend of Ho Chi Minh.'' The same *Chicago Tribune* that had fully identified Burchett in 1966, introduced him to its readers quite differently on August 6, 1982: ''A man whose business is informing the world is an Australian expatriate journalist, Wilfred Burchett, now living in Paris.''

What is involved here is more than ''failure to identify.'' Implicit is a rewriting of political history. This is a major utopian target which the media abets. Communists are transformed into ''liberals.'' Joseph Barnes, foreign editor of the former *New York Herald Tribune,* who was exposed as a Communist by a series of his former colleagues who broke with the party, started to be referred to in the press as a ''liberal'' in the late 1970s. The Rosenberg case has been transmogrified. In 1978, on the 25th anniversary of the execution of the Rosenbergs for treason, Public Television served up a four year old documentary with a new introduction and epilogue, "The Rosenberg-Sobell Case Revisited." Atom spies Julius and Ethel Rosenberg were portrayed as individuals singled out for their political beliefs by a malignant government. When Accuracy in Media wrote to the President of the Public Broadcasting System to complain about the film's gross distortion of history, the reply came from the program's producer. Ignoring the long list of factual criticisms AIM had submitted, he announced loftily that the suggestion the program embodied Communist propaganda, reflected discredit on AIM.[71]

In 1982, Telefrance USA, which says that its programs reach 10 million U.S. homes, broadcast a four part French-made documentary on the Rosenberg case with the emotional title, "The Rosenbergs Must Not Die." They were portrayed as innocents railroaded by a corrupt government. Dorothy Rabinowitz, in a *Wall Street Journal* essay, noted that "no more malevolent band of fascists, scoundrels, cynics and thugs" had ever appeared on a screen than the "assortment of characters supposedly representing an American Supreme Court, an American judge and prosecutor and members of the FBI."[72] While the *New York Times* reviewer at least dismissed the program, *Cablevision Magazine* allowed that there was the "recurring paradox of how a foreigner—an outsider—may have a fuller perspective on a situation, political or otherwise, than someone more directly involved."[73]

Misidentification and the rewriting of political history produce reporting that inhibits, rather than helps, public understanding of political developments. Press coverage of Kathy Boudin, the Weather Underground leader captured during the Brink's robbery in Nyack, depicted her—to quote from a typical account in the *Boston Globe*—as a "child of privilege," "a brainy, popular tomboy who graduated with honors from the 'right' schools, the type of girl that people once described as all-American." But Kathy Boudin was a red diaper baby, the child of radical lawyer Leonard Boudin. The circle of her father's friends included many Communists and individuals sympathetic to Communism. Kathy Boudin's political development would have become considerably less mysterious if the media had not concealed relevant information.

Journalistic practices like the Pinsky Principle have grown common as journalists have changed their view of their proper role. "Advocacy," "participatory," and "activist" journalism have created new models. To some extent the "new journalism," as it is sometimes called, has developed because its literary techniques produce more dramatic copy at a time of intense competition from television, with its strong visual imagery. A "composite" prostitute (and why confuse the reader by identifying her as such) can offer a more interesting biography than any single individual. Similarly a report that suggests the writer is directly privy to the thoughts and beliefs of his subject has more impact than an article with tiresome inserts like "A neighbor said that," or "The defendant's lawyer claims that . . ."

The new journalism is also a reflection of the changing aspirations of journalists. Journalists are now in a position to set the policies of papers which they could not in an earlier era, when conservative owners set their stamp upon their property. With many more years of education than they used to have, with higher status in society, journalists are dissatisfied with a role that limits them simply to chronicling what happens. As lawyer Max Kampelman noted in a 1978 essay in *Policy Review:*

> "It is understandable that a significant segment of the media has become impatient with its limited information dissemination role. It is not easy and frequently not exciting for an intelligent person simply to report events. The tendency, therefore, has been for imaginative and socially dedicated journalists to go beyond normal reporting in order to seek fuller expression of their talents or social values."[74]

Veteran journalist Joseph Kraft notes: "Not only have we traded objectivity for bias, but we have also abandoned a place on the sidelines for a piece of the action."[75] Jim Bormann, a pioneer in broadcast news, offered a vivid illustration: he described listening to journalist Alex Kendrick telling a CBS news affiliate session that a good reporter should not be afraid, while covering a riot, to throw a few bricks himself. Kendrick urged the contemporary newsman to get involved and then report what he "felt inside."[76]

"Facts" are seen in a fresh light by the new journalism. As writer Naomi Munson pointed out in *Commentary,* while reporters had seen their job as sniffing out facts "more and more these days they have come to regard themselves, instead, in a grander light, as bloodhounds of the 'truth.'"[77] The problem with this is that facts then become, at best, a tool for revealing the truth. At worst, facts become an impediment to the "truth" which must be sloughed off, ignored, buried, so as not to interfere with the public's ability to perceive what in a "higher sense" is true. Gay Talese, a writer who was godfather to the new journalism, said its techniques allowed the presentation of "a larger truth than is possible through rigid adherence" to normal newspaper standards.[78]

One result of the new journalism was to make a scandal like the one that erupted over Janet Cooke and the non-existent eight year old heroin addict "Jimmy" inevitable. After *The Washington Post* was forced to return the Pulitzer Prize which the story had won, it tried to pass off what had happened as the victimization of a newspaper by one of its reporters. According to the Post's published account, no editor anywhere was safe from the machinations of a determined liar.

It was not so simple. Newspapers, the *Post* among them, had developed a pattern of shutting their eyes to the fictional aspects of the new journalism. When the *Daily News* accepted the resignation of its prize-winning journalist Michael Daley, a month after the Cooke scandal—he was accused of manufacturing material for an article on British army brutality in Northern Ireland—Daley remarked that he had used pseudonyms and reconstructions on many of his 300 columns and "no one has ever said anything."[79] In the case of Janet Cooke, Vivian Aplin-Brownlee, Cooke's editor on the *District Weekly,* to which she had been assigned in her first year at the *Post,* claimed that she did not believe the story from the beginning and said so to the city editor.

> "I knew her so well and the depth of her. In her eagerness to make a name she would write farther than the truth would allow. When challenged on facts in other stories, Janet would reverse herself, but without dismay or consternation with herself."[80]

What this meant was that Janet Cooke was repeatedly caught in misstatements of fact while she worked for the *Post,* but the editors, instead of firing, had promoted her.

Despite what the *Post's* ombudsman Bill Green later admitted were "rumblings" in the newsroom, the *Post* made no attempt to check the story or even to ask to see Janet Cooke's tapes or notes. A few days after the story was published *Post* reporter Courtland Milloy drove Janet Cooke through the neighborhood where she claimed Jimmy lived and he could see she did not know the area. He reported his doubts to the city editor, but the editor, as he later confessed, thought Milloy was motivated by jealousy.[81] The mayor and police officials asked the *Post* to disclose the identity of the child so he could be helped. Presumably the life of an eight year old boy hung in the balance, but the Post merely launched into high-flown rhetoric on confidentiality, leaving the police to launch an intensive, expensive, and naturally vain search.

Since the police search was finally abandoned, Janet Cooke would have been safe, had she not lied about her academic credentials. The *Post* released biographical data on their prizewinning reporter, and Cooke's claim to a Vassar B.A. she did not have, led to the unravelling of the whole fabric of invention.

The media's reaction to charges of bias is one of genuine outrage. Irving Kristol has pointed out that "the television networks and national newspapers are sincerely convinced that a liberal bias is proof of journalistic integrity."[82] CBS News President Richard Salant retorted indignantly to suggestions of bias: "Our reporters do not cover stories from *their* point of view. They are presenting them from *nobody's* point of view."[83]

Yet in the spring of 1972, a "counter-convention" of American journalists, sponsored by the journalism review *More,* was being attended by over 2,000 journalists, including such media "stars" as Dan Rather, Tom Wicker, David Halberstam and Murray Kempton. In an article describing the purpose of the meeting, *More* explained: "A growing number of people who put out the nation's newspapers and magazines and splice together the nightly news are no longer going to accept the old ways of doing things." The "new" journalists, said *More,* were "sensitive" people who turned "their attention to the kind of journalism that might help improve the quality of life rather than objectively recording its decline."[84]

How do journalists manage to believe they maintain the professional journalistic creed of objectivity at the same time they transmit, as we have seen, the utopian world view? Many journalists seem to mistake a sense of superiority for objectivity. In the fifth and final segment of CBS's series on defense, President Reagan and Chairman Brezhnev were shown making speeches denouncing each other. Cronkite then appeared, like the patient parent of quarreling children, to lament that from both the Kremlin and the White House came "angry words." Presenting the United States and the Soviet Union as mirror-image societies seems to constitute self-evident proof of objectivity to Cronkite and the media elite.

Convinced of their own objectivity, the media are arrogant and dismissive when criticized. Reed Irvine notes that when he and a group of friends who belonged to the McDowell luncheon group decided, in 1969, to start Accuracy in Media, they were convinced that if they did research on cases of media inaccuracy, those responsible would have no choice but to admit they were wrong, issue corrections, and be more careful in the future. Irvine laughs ruefully as he recalls: "We soon found out it really did not work that way."[85]

The arrogance is sometimes breathtaking, as the media unhesitatingly ignore, in their own case, the demands they make of others. For example, CBS has been the most aggressive of the networks in claiming for television cameras the right to cover any event open to the print media. Yet when CBS held its annual meeting in April 1980, while the press was admitted, television cameras were barred. William Paley, long-time chairman of CBS, declared they would be disruptive to the audience. Reed Irvine asked if he would recommend that Congress adopt the same policy and the following colloquy ensued:

Paley: I would not.
Irvine: Just CBS.
Paley: We have adopted the policy, for the time being anyway, which has been clearly enunciated today. That's all I can say about it.[86]

One journalist remarked that it was like distillers holding a meeting and barring booze.

The reaction to criticism is sometimes vituperative. Responding to an issue of *AIM Report* that clearly touched a nerve, the *Post's* editor Benjamin Bradlee wrote to Irvine: "You have revealed yourself as a miserable, carping, retromingent vigilante, and I for one am sick of wasting my time in communicating with you."[87] After looking up "retromingent," which means "urinating backward," Irvine framed the letter and hung it in the office.

All the sins of advocacy journalism, the fictions supporting a "higher truth," the selective coverage, the attacks on what are perceived as "the bad guys" and whitewashing of the "good guys" came together in a media crusade against Israel during its war against the PLO in Lebanon in 1982. In a major study for *Policy Review,* Joshua Muravchik has provided the fullest account of media distortion on a single topic since Peter Braestrup's two volume analysis of the media's coverage of the Tet offensive in Vietnam. Muravchik found variations in culpability: the *Washington Post* was much worse than the *New York Times;* NBC was worse than ABC which was worse than CBS; *Time* and *Newsweek,* on the other hand, turned in equally abysmal performances.[88] *All* the media were involved in tendentious and inaccurate reporting with one target—to make Israel look bad.

Muravchik piles high the examples of media misstatement of fact. For example, wildly exaggerated casualty reports falsely attributed to the internationally respected Red Cross (in fact they came from the nonrelated Red Crescent, an arm of the PLO run by Arafat's brother) continued to be cited repeatedly after the Red Cross had formally repudiated them. These were soon accompanied by equally inflated portraits of destruction from supposed eye witness journalists in Beirut. While all the media were guilty of this the prize may well have belonged to ABC which, in June, before the Israelis had launched any serious bombing of the city, described Beirut as a result of Israeli shelling, as resembling "some ancient ruin."

Symptomatic of the pervasive dishonesty was a photo distributed by United Press International with a caption which said it showed a seven month old baby who had lost both arms in an Israeli raid. Secretary of State George Shultz, in a statement meant to be critical of Israel, said "the symbol of this war is a baby with its arms shot off." It was a symbol not of the war, but of the media's coverage of it. Subsequent investigation showed that the baby had not been badly hurt—both its arms were intact. And while civilians, including children, were obviously hit by Israeli bombs, it so happened that in this case the time, place, and direction of bombing made it clear that the baby had been hit by PLO shelling, which the media rarely mentioned, but was also a feature of the war.

Perhaps the media bias was best revealed by the television networks' attacks on Israel for censorship. (The PLO's censorship, exercised by guns directed against unwelcome TV cameras, was never mentioned.) When ABC broke Israel's censorship by broadcasting an interview with Arafat that had been disallowed by the censor, Israel punished the network by temporarily refusing it access to Israeli television facilities. ABC accused Israel, on the air, of "an intolerable act of political censorship." Israel explained that while it exercised only military censorship on reports from Israel's side of the battle line, its extension of its facilities for reports from the enemy's side was a favor to journalists which it would not allow to be used for the PLO's political advantage. ABC had agreed to the rules and then broken them. But as Muravchik notes, while Israel's position was one with which the public might or might not have sympathized, they never heard Israel's side of the story because the networks would not report it.

Yet Israel's censorship—in wartime—was far less restrictive than that of most other countries at any time and compared very favorably with that of other Middle Eastern countries. Moreover, while despatches from other Middle Eastern countries were censored, the networks only flashed on the screen references to Israeli censorship. Eventually NBC began to flash on the screen "Cleared by Syrian censors," and CBS several weeks later followed suit. But by the end of August ABC, although it often broadcast from Syria, still made no reference to Syrian censorship while routinely using "Cleared by Israeli censors." (Ironically if Israel had kept out all foreign journalists, she would presumably have fared much better at their hands. This is what the British did during their war with Argentina over the Falklands that was going on simultaneously, and the media kept silent about "censorship.")

Given the extraordinary depths to which the media sank in the reporting on Lebanon, the analysis of the *Columbia Journalism Review* on media reporting of the war is interesting. It concluded that American journalism

> "reported what it saw for the most part fairly and accurately and sometimes brilliantly, provided balanced comment, and provoked and absorbed controversy. For performance under fire, readers and viewers could have asked for little more."[89]

Except for the remark that the coverage "provoked and absorbed controversy," which was certainly true, this could scarcely have been further from the mark. But it does underscore the extent to which the major journalism reviews, of which Columbia's is probably the most influential, have themselves become exponents of advocacy journalism. If the press is going to change its ways, it will not be because of monitoring by the major journalism reviews.

Media needs and attitudes and utopian goals dovetail nicely. From the point of view of the utopians, stories that the media may like because of their inherent drama, break down faith in authority. When ABC launched "20/20" to compete with CBS's highly successful "60 Minutes," the program was known around the studio as the "cancer scare of the week." While ABC may have pursued ratings, for the utopians, the programs reveal the wickedness or incapacity of government and corporations, which deny the reality of the dangers or fail to meet them. The media rarely report human rights violations in totalitarian societies, because they cannot gain access to them. For the utopians, these are stories that *should* be ignored, for they might interfere with their effort to mobilize public opinion against non-Communist countries threatened by those whose aim is to establish regimes of the sort that already exist in Cuba and North Vietnam.

While in theory the fondness for scare stories could make reports on the Soviet military build-up and Soviet intelligence agencies appealing, here pervasive liberal orthodoxy among journalists comes into play. It leads them to downgrade the notion that there is such a thing as a genuine Soviet threat. It also leads them to automatic sympathy with proposals that come from disarmament groups, which they become extremely reluctant to report on fully, for fear the effect would be to "unmask" them. This prevents the public from developing scepticism about the programs of these groups. The media's portrait enforces the utopian view of the world and makes the calls of the utopians for "de-industrialization," "decentralization of industry," solar roof collectors instead of central power stations, seem safer to try than they otherwise would. The utopian agenda becomes more plausible and attractive as our familiar world is seen to be threatened only by the callousness and rapacity of our own institutions.

REFERENCES

1. Quoted in *TV and National Defense: An Analysis of CBS News 1972-1973,* Ernest W. Lefever ed., Institute for American Strategy Press, Boston, Va. 1974, p. 14
2. Melvin G. Grayson and Thomas R. Shepard, *The Disaster Lobby,* Chicago: Follett Publishing Co., 1973, p. 266
3. S. Robert Lichter and Stanley Rothman, "Media and Business Elites," *Public Opinion,* Oct./Nov. 1981, pp. 42-44
4. Ibid., pp. 59-60
5. Robert Loewenberg, "Journalism and Free Speech as Political Power," *Scholastic,* Dec. 1982, p. 12
6. Quoted by Joseph Kraft, "The Imperial Media," *Commentary,* May 1981, p. 38
7. *AIM Report,* September 1, 1979
8. Ibid., June 1977
9. Ibid., Oct. 1, 1979
10. Sophie Pederson, "Foreign News Gatekeepers and Criteria of Newsworthiness," *Journalism Quarterly,* Spring 1979, p. 116
11. Stanley Rothman and S. Robert Lichter, "The Nuclear Energy Debate: Scientists, the Media and the Public" *Public Opinion,* Aug./Sept. 1982, p. 51
12. Ibid., p. 52
13. Robert DuPont, *Nuclear Phobia,* The Media Institute
14. Rothman and Lichter, "The Nuclear Energy Debate," op. cit., p. 47
15. Ibid., p. 49
16. Ibid., p. 51
17. Samuel McCracken, *The War Against the Atom*, New York: Basic Books, 1982, p. 108

18. Rothman and Lichter, "The Nuclear Energy Debate," op. cit., p. 52
19. Samuel McCracken, op. cit., p. 108
20. *AIM Report,* March 11, 1979
21. Interview with Walter Cronkite, *Utica* (N.Y.) *Press,* Nov. 13, 1974, quoted in *TV and National Defense,* op. cit., Frontispiece.
22. Ibid., p. 37
23. Joshua Muravchik and John E. Haynes, "CBS vs. Defense" *Commentary* September 1981, p. 46
24. Ibid., p. 45
25. Ibid., pp. 48-49
26. *AIM Report,* April I 1979
27. Ibid., May II 1978
28. Ibid., February I 1979
29. Ibid.
30. Ibid., March II 1978
31. Ibid., Oct. II 1979
32. Ibid., July I 1977
33. Ibid., Feb. I 1979
34. Ibid., Oct. II 1979
35. *Contentions,* newsletter of the Committee for the Free World, Dec. 1981
36. *AIM Report,* May II 1980
37. Ibid., June I 1982
38. Ibid., June II 1980
39. Ibid.
40. Ibid., March I 1979
41. *Human Events,* April 24, 1982; *New York Times,* April 9, 1982
42. *Contentions,* Committee for the Free World, April-May, 1982
43. *AIM Report,* Sept. I 1977
44. *Guild Notes,* publication of the National Lawyers Guild, April 1980
45. Ibid.
46. *Business Week,* Oct. 18, 1982
47. *Crooks, Conmen and Clowns,* Media Institute, Washington D.C., 1981, pp. ix-x
48. Ben Stein, *The View from Sunset Boulevard,* New York: Basic Books, 1979, p. 20
49. Ibid., p. 33
50. *AIM Report,* Sept. II 1980
51. Interview with Peter Metzger, January 29, 1982
52. *AIM Report,* July 11, 1982
53. *Wall Street Journal,* August 21, 1981
54. *Human Events,* July 11, 1981
55. Ibid.
56. Ibid.
57. Ibid.
58. *Wall Street Journal,* August 21, 1981
59. *Human Events,* April 9, 1983
60. *Human Events,* Sept. 26, 1981
61. Letter from Michael Danby, editor *Australia Israel Review,* Feb. 28, 1983; also *AIM Report,* Nov. II 1982
62. *Daily News,* May 12, 1982
63. *AIM Report,* April I 1978
64. Ibid.
65. Ibid., July I 1979
66. Ibid., May I 1980

67. Bob Schulman, *The Bulletin,* American Society of Newspaper Editors, Oct. 1982
68. *New York Times,* August 2, 1977
69. Quoted in *Review of the News,* September 8, 1982, p. 37
70. Jeremiah A. Denton Jr., *When Hell Was in Session*, So. Carolina: Robert E. Hopper & Assoc., 1982, Chapter 11 (no page nos.)
71. *AIM Report,* Sept. I 1978
72. *Wall Street Journal,* November 16, 1982
73. *Cablevision Magazine,* Oct. 25, 1982
74. Max Kampelman, "The Power of the Press," *Policy Review,* Fall 1978, p. 18
75. Joseph Kraft, "The Imperial Media," *Commentary,* May 1981, p. 43
76. Jim Bormann, "Honesty, Fairness and Real Objectivity—Keys to Journalistic Credibility," Keynote address to Radio and Film News Directors Association, Sept. 29, 1971
77. Naomi Munson, "The Case of Janet Cooke," *Commentary,* August 1981, p. 49
78. *New York Times,* May 25, 1981
79. Ibid.
80. *AIM Report,* May I 1981
81. Ibid.
82. *Wall Street Journal,* Oct. 14, 1982
83. *TV and National Defense,* op. cit., p. 11
84. Grayson and Shepard, op. cit., pp. 255-56
85. Interview with Reed Irvine, Oct. 24, 1982
86. *AIM Report,* May I 1980
87. Ibid., June II 1978
88. Joshua Muravchik, "Misreporting Lebanon," *Policy Review,* Winter 1982/83, pp. 18, 32, 41, 43, 46, 53
89. Roger Morris, "Beirut—and the Press—Under Siege," *Columbia Journalism Review,* Nov./Dec. 1982, p. 33

XII

Understanding the Utopians

The reader may well be puzzled by what we have reported. With rare exceptions, the utopians are well-educated, often graduates of elite colleges, well-paid, respected for their abilities, and lead interesting and comfortable lives. Why should they feel such antagonism toward an economic system that rewards them, and a political system that gives them freedom of expression? And if, for whatever reasons, there did arise a group alienated from American institutions, why do the particular movements described in this book attract them? Why should this group be so successful in mobilizing broad strata of the American public, so that they can seriously anticipate "taking charge" of this country? And perhaps most puzzling of all, why should the political form that most appeals to them be anarchism, a patently impossible ideal?

There are no simple answers, and moreover, can be no single explanation embracing Protestant clergymen and the political radicals of the National Lawyers Guild. We can merely suggest some of the factors that may be helpful in understanding why utopians from such different backgrounds feel and believe as they do, and why they have become so potent a force.

In the first chapter we noted that the utopians consisted of intellectuals, in the broad sense of those who wield the power of the spoken and written word, and those who turn their ideas into programs of action and seek to implement them. The most famous attempt to explain the antagonism of intellectuals to the capitalist system, an antagonism that goes well beyond today's utopians and has deep roots in American and Western culture generally, was made by Joseph Schumpeter. Like Marx, Schumpeter argued that capitalism carried within it the seeds of its own destruction. It would be destroyed, however, not by a class of exploited workers, but by alienated intellectuals. As Schumpeter, who today seems a better prophet than Marx, saw the process, capitalism had freed the intellectual of dependence upon political authority by giving him the printing press, a literate public able to buy what he wrote, and freedom to criticize. This freedom to criticize first served the capitalist order well because the intellectual attacked the remnants of the feudal order. But eventually the intellectual turned his criticism upon capitalism itself.

In part Schumpeter saw the intellectual's undermining of capitalism as inherent in his role—"the intellectual group cannot help nibbling, because it lives on criticism and its whole position depends on criticism that stings."[1] But there was more to it than that. Capitalism, Schumpeter argued, was deeply dissatisfying to intellectuals; the stock exchange, he noted, is a poor substitute for the Holy Grail. Schumpeter warned: "Capitalist rationality does not do away with sub- or super-rational impulses. It merely makes them get out of hand by removing the restraint of sacred or semi-sacred tradition."[2]

Once intellectuals sought transcendent meaning in a rationalistic framework, they were led to utopianism. It was here that the appeal of Marxism for intellectuals lay. Schumpeter observed that it offered "a system of ultimate ends that embody the meaning of life and absolute standards by which to judge events and actions." Marxism wove together

> "those extrarational cravings which receding religion has left running about like masterless dogs, and the rationalistic and materialistic tendencies of the time, ineluctable for the moment, which would not tolerate any creed that had no scientific or pseudo-scientific connotation."[3]

Schumpeter asserts that Marxism permitted the intellectual to be a rationalist modern and a transcendental believer in a "paradise on this side of the grave."

This view of intellectuals conflicts with the popular image of the intellectual as a relentless questioner of prevailing orthodoxies. But as sociologist Paul Hollander points out:

> "the wish to believe marks the attitudes of intellectuals as much as the need to criticize, negate, or reject. It is the alternation of these two diametrically opposed dispositions that is characteristic of intellectuals rather than a predominance of the critical impulse."[4]

Once in the grip of a desire to believe, intellectuals dull their normally sharp critical faculties.

In *Political Pilgrims,* Hollander reveals that Western intellectuals who have visited supposedly "exemplary" Marxist societies found them most attractive at the peak of their repressiveness. Intellectuals conjured up idyllic fantasies, making their pilgrimages not to observe, but to project their feelings upon the scenes they encountered. Such an acute critic of his own country as Edmund Wilson reported on Stalin's Russia in 1936: "[T]he people in the park do really own it and they are careful of what is theirs. A new kind of public conscience has come to lodge in these crowds . . ." Wilson claimed that they did not even move like other crowds, but "like slow floods of water . . . not anxious like our people, not pitted against an alien environment, but as if the whole city belonged to them . . ."[5] When the grip of the leadership relaxed even slightly, Hollander notes, the intellectual's fervor waned. Intellectuals lost their enthusiasm for the Soviet Union after the death of Stalin, for China, with the loosening up of the regime that followed the death of Mao.

Why this should be so is a fascinating puzzle. A possible explanation is that the reason these regimes attract intellectuals is because they seem to possess a transcendent authority that legitimates the use of total power for higher ends. Once that power fails, or the regime falters in its claims, even apologizes for past excesses, the intellectual loses faith in its transcendence and the bond he has felt toward it snaps.

The particularly acute pains of secularization for Jews helps to explain why they have been prominent among dissatisfied intellectuals and among today's utopians. In moving from a religiously defined to a modern existence, Jews were especially affected, because religion and nationality are fused in Judaism. Jews who lost religious identity lost national self-definition, particularly since, in spite of political emancipation, they were not permitted to assimilate psychologically and socially into the national societies of Europe and even in the United

States remained socially marginal. This sense of total displacement is conveyed by the word often used in relation to these Jews—"deracinated" which means "pulled out by the roots." Secularized Jewish intellectuals, moreover, carried over, from the religious culture they had abandoned, a heritage of messianic expectations, which could easily become translated into secular utopianism.

There is one group in the forefront of the utopians to whom Schumpeter's analysis seems to ill apply. As those who retain and uphold belief in an enchanted order, churchmen should be precisely those exempt from the problems of secularization. And yet, as we have seen, the clergy of mainline Protestant denominations have adopted the critique of secular intellectuals. While the National Council of Churches, for example, has been accused of a double standard because it frequently criticizes right wing regimes but much more rarely criticizes left wing ones, what has escaped attention is that it actually has a triple standard. By far the harshest and most frequent criticisms are directed against the United States, whose government and institutions are found guilty of the litany of sins identified by secular intellectuals—sexism, racism, imperialism, economic injustice etc. These attitudes, as we have noted, have been spreading in the Catholic hierarchy and have been making inroads, although to a lesser extent, even within such previously resistant churches as the Southern Baptists.

The appeal of the critique of secular intellectuals to clergymen was that it seemed to hold out the promise of restoring them to the "cutting edge" of moral leadership. That promise was especially important to clergy of the mainline denominations who had been at the center of the country's moral and cultural life before increasing secularization banished them to its periphery. In spearheading the critique, the clergy could restore its lost stature within the broader society. One has only to observe the extensive and respectful attention accorded the Catholic bishops by the media once they turned their attention to disarmament, and compare it to the scant attention the media accords the bishops' pronouncements on issues such as abortion, to see the rewards inherent in adopting the secular critique.

Throughout this book we have seen that the ideas of today's utopians are not new. We have also seen that utopian intellectuals, whether they created the movements, transformed them or established a beachhold in them, lost out. They lost out so decisively that their ideas were all but forgotten for a generation, appearing novel today precisely because their exponents were silenced for so long. From the onset of World War II to the student revolt of the 1960s, the utopians were in disarray. They were silenced by what Alexander Solzhenitsyn called "the crowbar of events"—the inappropriateness of pacifism as a response to Hitler, the human devastation wrought by Communism, and the enormous success of capitalism in bringing, in the post war years, unprecedented affluence to a broad public.

Historical events have also been responsible for the reemergence of utopianism, with the single most important factor probably being the civil rights movement of the 1950s. While this was not a utopian movement, but a long overdue movement of reform, it ended the generation-long truce between the majority of intellectuals and U.S. society on questions of politics. (As we shall see, on matters of culture, the truce was never established.) It did much to undermine faith in American institutions within a college generation, many of whose members became part of the movement. That the nation responded well in seeking to remedy its long history of racial injustice was not what made an impression upon the youthful participants, but the ugliness associated with the struggle for the achievement of civil rights.

The mainline church leadership, which took a major role in the civil rights movement, and was in large measure responsible for the passage of the first civil rights bills, was propelled out of its Niebuhrian "realism" by a new sense of the ingrained injustice of American society. Rather than being reassured about the United States because of its success, the leadership employed an ever more radical critique. Soon it set out to castigate and extirpate the ills of American society and to take up cudgels for every group, within or outside the country, which asserted that the United States had perpetrated injustice against it.

The Vietnam War created new legions of converts to the notion of an evil America, again especially among college students feeling personally threatened by the draft. The emerging "New Left" on campus, energized by the war, could now argue that not only was the United States internally unjust, but it was an imperialist, expansionist, militarist state intent on subjugation of liberation movements in faraway lands. The Watergate scandal became a final proof to many—not only were American institutions unjust, but American leaders were personally corrupt. More important, the Vietnam War and Watergate showed that the government could be defeated. The great imperialist juggernaut of the students' imagination was not invincible after all. It was vulnerable. Few but determined opponents could gather strength and eventually win against it.

But if all this helps to explain why hostility to American society and the urge to transform it has been concentrated in particular groups and why the ideas of defeated groups should have reemerged, it does not explain the success of the coercive utopians in becoming so great a force in the last two decades. To understand this, it is necessary to look at a post-World War II phenomenon—the emergence of what has been called the "New Class." The coercive utopians serve as the vanguard of the New Class.

Although the term "The New Class" was first coined by Milovan Djilas to describe the Communist elite, in the United States it has been used to refer to those who produce and distribute knowledge rather than material goods. Figuring prominently in the New Class are scientists and teachers, print and broadcast journalists, social scientists, planners, social workers, salaried professionals and government bureaucrats. There has been a vast expansion in the number of these and other jobs requiring communication skills as this country shifted from a production to a service, or as some have called it, an "information economy."

There was a corresponding explosion in higher education to prepare people to fill the new positions. The number of students enrolled in degree credit programs in colleges and universities has multiplied seven fold since 1940. One out of six Americans has now completed four years of college. Both what these students learned—and what they did not learn—in college, and later in New Class positions, made them responsive to utopian appeals.

Those who were to assume positions in the new growth areas gravitated to literature and the social sciences. And their literature courses were steeped in the values of "the adversary culture," a term coined by Lionel Trilling to refer to the serious writers who created the body of American literature. The critique of the adversary culture, traditionally less political than cultural, had not been affected by the "crowbar of events." Capitalism, in the view of the adversary culture, produced a "cultural wasteland," catering to the lowest common denominator, and established a cold mercantile calculus which translated all values into market prices. *American Scholar* editor and critic Joseph Epstein has pointed out that an author's alienation from American society became a touchstone for his being treated as a serious figure, i.e. having his work taught in college courses.

The social sciences expanded enormously in the period immediately following World War II, in part because they were sufficiently "soft" to accommodate students not considered suitable for higher education before its expansion. Social science courses, especially those in the proliferating sociology departments, gave a scientific aura to the notion that virtually all social problems, ranging from mental health to delinquency to inadequate school performance, were to be explained by social forces. Genetic endowment and personal responsibility were concepts outside the scope of most "social problems" courses. Under the same "scientific" cover, the social sciences prescribed solutions. Since all problems were caused by society, it followed that all problems could only be solved by society. State intervention was the inevitable remedy.

The view that *all* problems, including what were traditionally thought of as personal problems, were really social problems misunderstood, a dictum first popularized by sociologist C. Wright Mills, had enormous appeal for college students undergoing the normal problems of late adolescence. Discontents and feelings of inadequacy previously blamed upon the self, parents, chance, fate, could all be rechanneled. Mills' notion also had the effect of alienating the individual from the society he now saw as the source of all his problems. A tremendous force of animosity was brought to bear upon "the system."

Filling New Class positions, humanities and social science graduates often found views absorbed in the classroom and from peers enforced by experience. Many of the new positions involved "tutelage" of some sort. They were positions in which people were entitled to tell others how to think and act, or at a minimum, as in teaching and journalism, to shape the way in which they think and act. Typical of the positions of tutelage were the burgeoning social intervention professions, including social work and government regulation. On the one hand, positions of tutelage fed a sense of superiority on the part of the elite who provided guidance. On the other hand, they produced a sense of indignation, particularly among those most directly engaged in social intervention, by "proving" that what was learned in the classroom must be right, for there had to be something profoundly wrong with a social system that produced so many people needing help.

What the New Class did *not* learn was every bit as important as what it learned. It learned very little about how the economy of the United States actually worked. This was true even for those who took courses in economics, the least "soft" and least popular of the social sciences. Economics programs were geared to policy making in a government setting far more than to the viewpoint of a company in relation to the economy. The New Class also learned very little about other societies, obtaining no perspective from which to judge the virtues, as well as the defects, of its own society. Anthropology was an exception among the social sciences in this respect, but the lesson of anthropology, which focussed on primitive societies, was a diffuse cultural relativism, which asserted that the complex civilization and standards prescribed by Western society were not intrinsically better or "higher" than those of any primitive culture, and each culture could be judged only on its own terms.

Since the New Class, for the most part, never entered business, experience did not compensate for educational failures. To be sure, a considerable number did enter profit-making corporations—journalists are a major example—but their activities were detached from the economic aspects of running a business. The New Class could maintain its sense that it represented the "solution" part of the social order, the service sector, while the production sector, at least those at its helm, who made "profits" rather than salaries, were the source of its problems.

The movements discussed in this book, first the environmental and public interest movements, and more recently the peace movement, have had enormous appeal for the New Class. Part of their appeal, especially that of the first two, is that they offer an indictment of capitalism that turned against it what even its earlier critics had conceded were its virtues. No one had challenged the ability of capitalism to provide material benefits. Marx himself had written respectfully of the technical-industrial advances of capitalism. Marxists argued this abundance was obtained at the price of the worker's exploitation and that greater abundance would be achieved under Communism. The adversary culture had claimed many of the material benefits capitalism provided were not worth having, and the public's effort to obtain ever more of them was destructive of a higher culture. But the new environmental and consumer movement set out to show that the vaunted efficiency, innovation and high quality of product design of capitalism was a sham, and that the process of capitalist production and the products themselves were literally killing us.

The environmental movement declared that industrial pollution put the very globe at risk. (It is interesting that with all their emphasis on ecology, and the danger of tampering with any part of intricately interrelated biological systems, environmentalists never considered the industrial system from that point of view: it never occurred to them that indiscriminate tampering with it might destroy the prosperity they took for granted.) The book that launched Nader's career, *Unsafe at Any Speed,* begins with the sentence: "For over half a century the automobile has brought death, injury, and the most inestimable sorrow and deprivation to millions of people." The car, of course, was the symbol of the American love affair with technology, the proudest material possession of the average man. Nader emphasized that, in fact, it was a love affair with death. And the consumer movement, under Nader's leadership, went on to argue that product after product was dangerous, badly designed, shoddily produced.

The point was not that there was no merit to specific criticisms levelled by both movements: science and technology *did* have harmful side effects which had to be addressed. But the movements lacked all perspective, emphasizing only risks and dangers, never the benefits of technology. The New Class was oblivious to this failure because it took the achievements of technology for granted. Thus, for example, the achievements of the modern pharmaceutical and chemical industry, which gave modern medicine powerful weapons against disease and revolutionized nutrition, protecting crops through herbicides and pesticides and maintaining their quality through preservatives, could be easily ignored by the New Class. It was mindful only of their supposed dangers.

These movements were also attractive because they assigned guilt. The villain was the pursuit of profits by corporations, a pursuit intrinsic to the capitalist system. According to Nader, General Motors' Corvair was "one of the greatest acts of industrial irresponsibility in the present century"[6] and the irresponsibility lay in the unwillingness of General Motors to pay the extra amount needed to make the car safe. Similarly, pollution was treated as the moral responsibility of industry, intent on profits regardless of the cost to the general welfare. The New Class paid no price for berating the corporation for its alleged wickedness. It had the luxury of creating a guilt culture, for which its members bore no guilt—the guilt was all in the producing sector. The presence in every religion of methods by which people can confess and alleviate their sense of guilt for sins they have committed suggests this fills a deep human need. The New Class could confess the collective guilt of society while the actual penalties would be borne by others. An interesting example of this culture of guilt is the version of the Lord's Prayer offered at the 150th Annual Assembly of the Disciples of Christ in Virginia in May 1983. The assembly confessed its guilt:

> "because we are Americans
> blind with nationalistic pride, mad for revenge,
> because we ignore the existence of whole countries
> and refuse to accept borders of peace"

But the prayer immediately makes it clear that the assembly has failed "because we are subservient / and have not learned to contain tyranny / and limit the powerful . . ." It is others, after all, who are guilty; those who acknowledge their guilt in the prayer have failed in not taking a strong enough stand against the guilty ones.

Another source of the appeal of these movements is that they seem to transcend not only class but national interests. For the environmentalists, the welfare of the earth is at stake, and U.S. environmentalists have brought suit to stop projects in many parts of the world. Nader's publications involve themselves in such issues as the alleged exploitation of workers by multi-national corporations in far-off places, although such campaigns actually work against the interest of the American consumer, which is in lower prices. The movements created by the utopians appeal to the distaste for nationalism of the New Class. A Disciples of Christ seminary professor reported an experience illustrating this distaste. He invited the friends gathered in his home on July 4th to each say a few words about why he was glad to be an American and what America meant to him. A bureaucrat high in the church hierarchy, when his turn came, said he could not in conscience participate. "I am a citizen of the world" he explained. Patriotism, in short, is not a sentiment that rallies the New Class.

But while the New Class feels virtuous in an impartiality transcending the parochial bounds of the nation state, its detachment reflects its contempt for the responsibilities of citizenship. Decatur's famous line "Our country, right or wrong" is customarily taken out of context to reflect a mindless patriotism. The meaning was better stated by the famous German immigrant Carl Schurz in 1899: "Our country, right or wrong. When right, to be kept right; when wrong, to be put right." This is very different from the attitude of the New Class, whose members feel free to attack their country, while ashamed to identify with it. English writer Malcolm Muggeridge believes part of the reason the New Class incessantly attacks its own society is because it then feels no guilt for its refusal to defend it.

These movements also satisfied the quest of young people for a religious faith. In secular, rational, even quasi-scientific garb, environmentalism assumed the role of traditional religion in assigning man a place in the world and demanding behavior transcending his immediate interests. Environmentalism offered a quasi-religious discipline, demanding that family size be limited, that resources be husbanded despite present availability and that man act always in the consciousness that even his smallest action could affect the complicated interrelated web of life. Like religion, environmentalism even held out visions of heaven and hell. Man could learn to blend harmoniously into the natural rhythms of the biosphere or perish in its last convulsion, as it finally rejected the human species that had intolerably abused and degraded it.

The "solutions" offered by the environmental and consumer movement were as appealing as their analysis, for they were precisely those the New Class was in a position to enforce. These were to alert the public to the dangers posed by capitalist enterprise and to regulate that enterprise when the climate of opinion was right, when necessary, regulating it out of existence. (The nuclear industry is a case in point.) Since the New Class included the communicators and the regulators, it was in a position to perform the work of "the people" (the New Class never spoke in terms of its own interests or values) against the producers. And in the process its members could obtain power for themselves, the power that had so long resided in the "business class" which the New Class felt was in every respect less worthy than itself.

Before the growth of the New Class, the notion that intellectuals could create a base for power among people very much like themselves would have seemed laughable—to intellectuals above all. Norman Podhoretz has pointed out that, when in the 1930s, a number of intellectuals saw the Depression as a chance, as they put it, to wrest the country from businessmen, they looked to the "workers." Edmund Wilson, Sherwood Anderson, John Dos Passos, Granville Hicks, Malcolm Cowley and other important literary figures appealed to their fellow writers to vote for the Communist ticket in the 1932 Presidential elections.[7] (Of course the Communist Party in the United States was composed primarily of disaffected intellectuals, but the point was that intellectuals *saw* it as a party representing "workers.")

It was only a little over two decades ago that a few intellectuals began to see new possibilities. C. Wright Mills wrote in 1959:

> "Intellectuals have created standards and pointed out goals. Then, always, they have looked for other groups, other circles, other strata to realize them. It is time, now, for us in America to try to realize them ourselves—in our lives, in our own direct action, in the immediate context of our own work."[8]

The next year Mills was more explicit, writing that intellectuals themselves should be regarded as *the* revolutionary class of the nascent left-wing movement. It seems clear that what Mills had in mind was the power base offered by the New Class, a large educated stratum receptive to the leadership of intellectuals, sharing their values and tastes, echoing their ideas. Podhoretz argues that it was this vision of power, articulated by Mills, but sensed intuitively by others, which brought about the radicalization of intellectuals in the 1960s. They bid directly for power in the New Politics, and in George McGovern they found a Presidential candidate with whom they could identify. But the street tactics of many of the young radicals alienated a broad public, including many members of the New Class. Even some of the utopians who participated grew disenchanted. Arthur Waskow, for example, urged that guerilla street war be abandoned in favor of "guerilla politics."

The coercive utopians have taken Waskow's advice to heart. Even those among them who were radicals in the 1960s work less precipitously now—and more thoroughly. They no longer expect immediate political victory, but rather to delegitimize existing institutions and to work through a variety of organizations and with a range of interest groups. Although it is probable that only a few intellectual graduates of the New Left have read his work, the enterprise on which the utopians are embarked corresponds to that urged by Antonio Gramsci. An Italian Marxist, Gramsci criticized the classical Communist emphasis on taking power through the vanguard revolutionary party. Rather he urged the need for "building a new collective consciousness by attacking, through ideological-cultural struggle and political action, all of the 'intellectual moral' foundations of bourgeois society," and inaugurating "a thoroughgoing cultural revolution."[9]

Much of this reshaping of consciousness is already occurring. The radicalized college graduates of the 1960s moved strongly into universities and into the media, including magazines, newspapers, television and movies. This was immensely important because what once were counter-cultural challenges became accepted orthodoxies. Since the New Class is such an important segment of the serious reading public, book publishers and opinion-making journals readily adapt to their tastes. At the same time, the content of these books and magazines further radicalizes not only the New Class, but the mass public. This is because the perspective of the media that cater to a mass taste is also shaped by the elite magazines and papers. Ultimately, the university shapes the opinion of all of them. As Irving Kristol points out: "The mass media know what the Academy tells it, not more, not less, and under no circumstances will the mass media, for any period of time, entertain an opinion which the Academy dismisses." Perhaps nowhere has the ideologizing of the media been so marked—and passed with so little remark—as in the movies. Critic Richard Grenier, who has chronicled this process in the pages of *Commentary,* notes that movie reviewers do not even seem to notice the straightforward didacticism of many of the films they describe for their readers, presumably because they share their perspective.

Politically, as we have seen, the utopians have been working innovatively through community action groups, have created training schools for organizers, and have established networking groups for elected and appointed officials, voter-directed organizations like Tom Hayden's Campaign for Economic Democracy, and policy-making oriented projects like the Progressive Alliance, through which efforts were made to persuade the Democratic Party to adopt utopian programs and candidates. They have sought coalitions between different utopian branches, between secular and religious utopians, and have targeted farmers and above all, unions. The heavy New Class membership in some of the largest unions, notably those of teachers and state and local government employees, have made such coalitions ever more feasible. Finally, potentially sympathetic interest groups are wooed: feminists, gays, Gray Panthers, support groups for the "liberation" of a whole series of Western-oriented countries.

In seeking to reach beyond the New Class, the utopians are aided by the simplified formulas they have developed for solving global problems. Anxious not to let the pressure slacken, they come up with one magic key after another. No nukes (referring to energy), appropriate technology, small is beautiful, and most recently nuclear freeze have been among the keys the utopians offer to a riskless and happy future. The nuclear freeze has been the most potent key to date, offering the utopians their first chance to reach deep into Middle America.

Today's utopians show a marked sophistication over the utopians of recent generations who dismissed religion. They emphasize the role of religion in bringing about a new society. According to Arthur Waskow:

> "the 'religious' sense—that is, an urgency for reconnecting mind, body, and spirit—becomes not only a 'morally' human response to a morally dehumanizing society, but also a 'politically' liberating response to politically oppressive institutions."[10]

Secular intellectuals offer churchmen projects upon which they are urged to embark. For example, Marcus Raskin suggested that the churches "begin to operate as a secular authority whose task will be the spinning off of new political communities. Churches would fund such communities and give allegiance to them." This is heady stuff for clergymen seeking a sense of relevance in a secularized world.

We have saved the most tantalizing question for last: why should today's utopians choose anarchism as the ideal form of government when there is surely no more implausible target for a modern technological society? Yet this theme is constant in favored utopian writers. Environmentalist Murray Bookchin foresees "a new ecological society based on mutual aid, decentralized communities and "a people's technology."[11] One time chronicler of SDS, Kirkpatrick Sale, writes of the variety community greenhouses can bring to the diet, despite "the loss of Iranian caviar and Polish hams and French fraises-des-bois, not to mention in most cases Idaho potatoes, and Wisconsin cheese and Florida oranges."[12]

Part of the explanation lies in the absence of viable alternative models. The coercive utopians cannot be understood without reference to the Marxist experiments in utopia building of the twentieth century. The more societies have been built on avowedly Marxist lines, the more embarassing the socialist reality has proved to be. After the Soviet model's failure could no longer be denied, political pilgrims voyaged to Vietnam, Tanzania, Mozambique, China, Cuba—even Albania—but the Marxist ideal, seemingly detected in each of them for a time, has a way of revealing its hollowness. Economically, these experiments have been a total disaster, as those subject to collectivization refuse to produce. There is the familiar pattern of the regime being forced to countenance small private plots, which produce far more than vastly larger collectivized acreage, to prevent the total collapse of agriculture. In industry, judging from their productivity, workers in Communist countries are far more alienated from their labor than their counterparts in the West. Certainly the utopians can no longer merely invoke the name of "socialism" as a sufficient shibboleth.

Given the failure of "pure" socialist experiments, the utopians might have turned for models to the mixed economies of the Scandinavian countries or of Israel, all of which have been ruled for much of their recent history by parties that call themselves socialist, have a high degree of government involvement in the economy, a large cooperative sector, respectable productivity, a high technological and scientific level, and yet give their citizens personal freedom. But these countries lack attributes essential to models that can serve the utopians. They are European, or at least Western in culture, and the utopians reject Western culture. They are not victims of capitalist exploitation (at any rate the rhetoric of the capitalist exploitation school is never applied to Israel, although it emerged from a struggle with the British in Palestine). Most important, they are not self-proclaimed opponents of American imperialism. The models the utopians have chosen have all been anti-American. China, once it tried to forge links to the United States, rapidly lost credibility as a utopian model.

The anarchist utopia has the great advantage that no model exists to betray the faith put into it. Anarchism, which assumes small-scale frugal communities, also suits the anti-technological bent of the utopians which resonates in much of the New Class. We have noted that the New Class grew up taking the blessings of technology for granted, while becoming acutely conscious of its unpleasant consequences, including pollution, risk-taking, and the threat of unexampled destruction as a result of discoveries in nuclear fission, bacteriology and chemistry (although the latter two receive much less attention).

The implausibility, indeed the downright absurdity, of reconstructing the United States on the basis of total consensus does not give pause to the utopians, because they have learned to believe that *anything* is possible. Intellectuals are by the nature of their activity drawn toward the building of abstract models. When this is accompanied by a sense of limitless human possibility, they see no reason why the ideal schemes they draw up in their fancy cannot be blueprints for the real world. And what could be better than communities in which everyone has an equal say and nothing can be done with which each person is not in full agreement?

There is less difference between the blueprints of today's utopians and conventional Marxism than meets the eye. The "community of communities" is a long-range goal; in the meantime, the utopians seek more, not less centralized government control in order to displace the private sector. Before each individual can enjoy total control over his own life, power must be concentrated in the hands of the right people, i.e. those who will use it properly, for constructing the perfect social order. Tom Hayden told an audience in Ann Arbor, Michigan, during the Carter years, that while there was reason to distrust government bureaucracy at this point, "when we're sure we have a government we can trust, then and only then will we be able to take over the oil industry."[13] The assumption is that once the good people, i.e. the coercive utopians, run the government, it can be trusted to control more and more aspects of life.

While all this could scarcely be further from the perspective of the Founding Fathers, it is very close to classical Marxism. Our representative government was the creation of men who knew there could be no perfect order, and carefully crafted a system of separation of powers to prevent the concentration of power in any one center. But for the utopians, inherently perfect men require no rein on their freedom to act, once the proper blueprint has been devised. And it must be remembered that, only in the short term, did Marx propose a dictatorship of the proletariat, for eventually the state would wither away, leaving a changeless, perfect, classless world. There is, of course, no reason to believe the anarchist ideal of our utopians is any more likely to emerge from the intermediate stages than the classless society from Soviet dictatorship.

There is every reason to expect the utopians, rejecting the imperfect society that we have, to install something far worse—a coercive one. Perhaps the most trenchant critic of the intellectual as builder of utopia was Eric Hoffer, the longshoreman-intellectual. Hoffer wrote that "when power gives him the freedom to act, the intellectual will be inclined to deal with humanity as with material that can be molded and processed."[14] The problem is that a new order requires a new man, with motivations quite different from man as-he-is. And so, since it is beyond the power of intellectuals to create a new man, they try to build the perfect order on the backs of the recalcitrant old man. The New Man, they declare, will develop naturally under the ideal social order the utopians are creating despite all obstacles.

In the end, it is less important to know why the utopians believe as they do—something that can probably never be answered fully—than to understand the dangers that they pose. For whatever reasons they hold the strange combination of ideas that they do, in making us believe our society is not worth defending, they weaken our ability to face real external dangers. Few among the utopians deliberately carry forward the agenda of the enemies of this country, but all attack this country in its jugular—its faith in itself, its belief that what it is, and what it has, is worth preserving and defending.

REFERENCES

1. Joseph A. Schumpeter, *Capitalism, Socialism and Democracy*, New York, Harper & Brothers, 1942, p. 151
2. Ibid., p. 144
3. Ibid., p. 6
4. Paul Hollander, *Political Pilgrims*, New York: Oxford University Press, 1981, p. 416
5. Ibid., p. 115
6. Ralph Nader, *Unsafe at any Speed*, New York: Grossman Publishers, 1965, p. 2
7. Norman Podhoretz, "The Adversary Culture," in B. Bruce Briggs, ed. *The New Class?* New Jersey: Transaction Books, 1979, p. 28
8. Quoted in Seymour Martin Lipet, "The New Class and the Professoriate," in Ibid., pp. 78-79
9. Carl Boggs, *Gramsci's Marxism*, London: Pluto Press, 1976, pp. 121-2
10. Arthur Waskow, *Running Riot*, New York: Herder and Herder, 1970, p. 61
11. Murray Bookchin, "The Selling of the Ecology Movement," *WIN* September 15, 1980, p. 11
12. Kirkpatrick Sale, *Human Scale*, New York, Coward, McCann & Geoghegan, 1980, p. 408
13. Quoted in John Boland, "Anti-Capitalist Roadshow," *Barron's*, Oct. 29, 1979
14. Eric Hoffer, *The Temper of Our Time*, New York: Harper & Row, 1967, p. 91

XIII

Stemming The Utopian Tide

The election of Ronald Reagan as President in November 1980 seemed to be a repudiation of the utopians. Certainly, as we have seen, the utopians themselves saw the election as a disaster that threatened all their achievements of the previous decade, including their assumption of policy direction in key areas during the Carter years.

Given the decisiveness of the Reagan electoral victory, the ability of the utopians to prevent implementation of Reagan's policies in the areas most vital to them, and indeed to put Reagan on the defensive precisely on issues that had been central to his campaign, must be counted remarkable. Most remarkable of all was the success of the utopians in altering the entire framework of the debate on national defense. While Reagan had campaigned on a platform of accelerated defense spending in the face of a mounting Soviet threat, the utopians, through the nuclear freeze movement, were able to make the debate center on a Congressional freeze resolution and disarmament negotiations.

Second only to their success in literally turning the tables on President Reagan on defense issues, has been the ability of the utopians to maintain their monopoly on the definition of human rights violations. Early in the Reagan administration, then-Secretary of State Haig announced terrorism was the major threat to human rights internationally. Clearly, the administration hoped to continue using human rights as a principle of foreign policy, but to use it in a way compatible with its foreign policy objectives. The focus would be on the human rights violations of Communist regimes and the terrorist "liberation movements" they funded. Here too, the administration was wholly unsuccessful. Reagan's initial candidate for the post of Undersecretary of State for Human Rights, Dr. Ernest Lefever, a sharp critic of the Carter administration's approach, was forced to withdraw his candidacy after a massive utopian campaign made his confirmation by the Senate doubtful. And in El Salvador, where a terrorist movement backed by the Soviets via Cuba and Nicaragua, sought power, the utopians were able to keep the focus, not on the threat posed to U.S. national interests by another Soviet satellite in Central America, but on human rights violations by the government of El Salvador. By the spring of 1983, under pressure from the utopian coalitions, Congress had voted—and the administration had been forced to agree—that further U.S. aid would be contingent on a willingness of the government to negotiate unconditionally with the guerillas, a demand the administration hitherto had steadily rejected.

On domestic issues, the Reagan administration found itself similarly outmaneuvered by the utopians. The Administration was unable to abolish the Legal Services Corporation. It was unable to make significant changes in the environmental laws. Even interpretation of those laws was difficult to alter, except when it suited the convenience of the environmentalists. (Environmentalists were enraged when the Environmental Protection Agency announced that it would enforce the law, originally passed at their own insistence, which set December 31, 1982, as the date by which communities throughout the nation had to meet the air quality standards set by the Clean Air Act or face a variety of sanctions including banning of all new construction, withholding Federal highway funds etc. Fearing the political consequences of enforcement, the environmentalists accused the EPA of trying to torpedo the law by enforcing it.[1]) The utopians succeeded in toppling Anne Gorsuch as head of the EPA and rather than risk further confrontations, Reagan chose as her successor the first EPA head, William Ruckelshaus, a man acceptable to the environmental lobby. Although James Watt did make changes, the vehement, almost hysterical reaction of environmental and other public interest groups to his appointment as Secretary of the Interior made it difficult for the Department to act forcefully. Merely keeping Watt in the face of the environmental lobby's million signature campaign to "Dump Watt" was an administration achievement.

Unable to deliver on his promise to lift the burden of existing regulations, Reagan's chief achievement was in slowing the rate of growth in rule-making that would otherwise doubtless have occurred. Within the first few months of the administration, the President's Task Force on Regulatory Relief announced that businesses would save $18 billion as a result of regulations that had been delayed or withdrawn. Most of the relief was from regulations promulgated under Carter that had not yet been enforced. For example, the Department of Energy withdrew energy efficiency standards designed to go into effect by 1986 that would have forced producers to redesign virtually all existing models and retool production lines at a cost to the consumer of $500 million a year. The Federal Register, which publishes new rules daily, was cut in length by a third as the number of rules published was cut in half.[2]

The hostile climate created by the utopians toward what they viewed as the great symbol of "inappropriate" technology, nuclear energy, was such that the Reagan administration was helpless to deliver on its campaign promises of fostering its growth. Instead, the Supreme Court upheld the right of states to refuse to permit nuclear plants to be built on "economic" (but not on safety) grounds. For the first time, operating nuclear plants were threatened with shut-downs, as in the case of the Indian Point nuclear plants in New York's Westchester County, which were ordered to cease operation by June 1983 if a satisfactory emergency evacuation scheme could not be worked out by that date. A divided Nuclear Regulatory Commission finally allowed the plants to continue functioning despite the fact that such a scheme had not been fully worked out—and could not be since the local jurisdictions, responding to the fevered protests of the utopians, refused to cooperate.

The victories of the utopians against nuclear energy are victories not only in the ongoing utopian battle against technology, but in their campaign to undermine public faith in our political and economic institutions. Public opinion polls suggest the extent of utopian achievements in transforming consciousness. In 1968, a Yankelovich survey asked if business struck a fair balance between profits and the public interest and 70% said yes. By 1979, after a decade of the Naderite and environmental onslaught, the vote was down to 19%.[3]

As the Reagan administration sought—and failed in many areas—to make major policy changes, it discovered what Dutch journalist Jan Van Houten has pointed out: that while the right frequently wins elections, the left remains in control of pivotal institutions that shape public opinion. Moreover electoral victories are of little avail while the institutions of the consciousness industry remain in the hands of the left: the universities, the churches, and the mass media. As Van Houten notes:

> "It's in these institutions . . . where decisions are made about what will be talked about—El Salvador or the deployment of cruise missiles—or played down—Afghanistan and the Soviet arms buildup. It's where the limits of permissible political action are set, limits that few politicians can overstep with impunity."[4]

And yet, despite their grip upon the consciousness-molding institutions, the utopians have an Achilles heel. Their vulnerability lies in the gap between their goals and those of the average citizen. Exposure is what the utopians have greatest reason to fear. In the case of the churches, the wide gap between church membership and leadership means that the leadership is deeply threatened by the prospect of laymen becoming aware of what is being done with their money and in their name. The National Council of Churches reacted so vigorously merely to the *prospect* of a critical article in *Reader's Digest* and an unfriendly portrait on "60 Minutes" that the *New York Times* religion editor wrote an article about the measures it had taken to combat studies that had not yet appeared.[5] Once they *had* appeared, much of the time and resources of the Council were devoted to countering their impact on church members.

In the case of the environmental movement, particularly its more utopian branches, supporters are often unaware of the longer-range goals of the leadership. Most of those who respond to the fundraising appeals of Nader's Public Citizen see him as an advocate of the consumer for safe and reliable products, not as a central figure in the utopian effort to overthrow the present economic system. While the followers of the peace movement at this writing are in the grip of a mass enthusiasm that makes them resistant to any information suggesting its programs may actually advance the dangers they seek to avoid, ultimately the peace movement, too, stands to lose its momentum by exposure of its roots in groups deeply hostile to U.S. society.

Since, as we have seen, the media has acted as shield rather than scourge of the utopians, the burden of exposure has rested largely on the efforts of a handful of individuals. While the utopians dismiss all their critics as "right-wing," in fact, they span the political spectrum.

David Jessup, who exposed the United Methodist funding of radical political groups and went on to become one of the founders of the Institute on Religion and Democracy, as we noted earlier, is an official of the AFL-CIO and was active in the Peace Corps and in farm movement organizing. Dr. Peter Metzger was a pioneer in the environmental movement and one of the leading figures in the fight to eliminate nuclear testing in the atmosphere. He became disillusioned as he saw his fellow pioneers in the Scientists Institute for Public Information (SIPI) move on to scientifically unsound attacks on nuclear energy and realized that the target was in fact all forms of energy production. Even John Rees, who is identified with the political right, began his career as a follower of the left-wing of the Labour Party in England.

Some only reluctantly became active. Dr. Petr Beckmann, the son of Czech Communist parents (members of the party even before the Communist takeover of that country), defected to the United States in the 1960s and sought to build a new life as a professor of electrical engineering at the University of Colorado. He was pushed to action by two events: the invasion of his native Czechoslovakia by the Soviet Union in 1968 to destroy the Dubcek government, and the perception that there were forces in the United States intent on undermining the economic and political institutions that were the basis of the freedoms this country enjoyed. Reed Irvine was a government bureaucrat, an economist with the Federal Reserve System for 26 years, and became involved after watching media coverage of the student riots of the late 1960s. He felt the media gave the movement inordinate publicity and some of the demonstrations were in fact media events.

These individuals have forged their own channels of communication. Some have created newsletters. John Rees started his "intelligence" newsletter, the *Information Digest,* in 1968 and has published it twice a month ever since. Reaching a much wider public because of its much lower cost, Reed Irvine's *AIM Report* in the last few years has had its circulation go as high as 35,000 subscribers. Irvine has also used ads imaginatively, in order to reach those who had read the original faulty story with his correction of it. It is a mark of the discomfiture those ads produce in their targets that whenever they can find some excuse, the papers reject the ads or demand unacceptable changes. In one case, the *Washington Post* refused an ad on the grounds that it contained profanity. AIM was quoting the *Washington Post* editor's description of *AIM Report!* Petr Beckmann started his newsletter *Access to Energy* in 1973. Although English is not his native tongue, Beckmann has fashioned a newsletter that combines fine writing, sophisticated scientific analysis and a slashing wit. Using the press he installed in the basement of his house, Beckmann physically produces his own newsletter as well as a series of pamphlets and books under the imprint of the "Golem Press."

Newsletters have not been the only method devised by opponents of the utopians. Peter Metzger has found a novel way to publicize his findings: he writes speeches, which he delivers to a particular group, and they are then reprinted as pamphlets by the Public Service Co. of Colorado for which Metzger works as public affairs director. In the case of David Jessup, a single mimeographed report, "Preliminary Inquiry Regarding Financial Contributions to Outside Political Groups by Boards and Agencies of the United Methodist Church, 1977-1979" was the catalyst that led to the founding of the Institute on Religion and Democracy. That organization now produces pamphlets and newsletters and organizes conferences and workshops.

The best tribute to the efforts of all these individuals is the reaction to them by the utopians. So upsetting to the churches was Jessup's report that the United Methodist Church and the United Church of Christ's Board for Homeland Ministries paid $6,000 for two researchers to examine Jessup's past and the origins of the Institute on Religion and Democracy. The report turned out to be counterproductive. Christening it "The Snoop Report," Michael Novak pointed out that "two huge churches seem to wish to do for this tiny new Institute what General Motors did for Ralph Nader."[6] There was good reason for the discomfiture of the churches with Jessup's work. Taken by surprise when Jessup showed up at the national convention of the church and distributed his report, the leadership found itself unable to block a resolution raised from the floor calling for full disclosure of how church funds were spent. The importance of what Jessup had achieved was enormous. Information on church funding is a prerequisite to effecting change. In 1983 church officials tried to force the AFL-CIO to fire or silence Jessup, threatening otherwise to withhold church support for issues backed by labor.

The others have also drawn utopian fire. John Rees has been the subject of innumerable articles in the far left press, ranging from *CounterSpy* to the *Nation*. Both the National Lawyers Guild and the Institute for Policy Studies have resorted to that favorite utopian ground—the courts—in an effort to silence Rees. The utopians have made repeated efforts to deprive Metzger of his post at Public Service Co. of Colorado. In the Carter years they mobilized well-situated allies in the government to bring pressure upon his employer to fire him; it was suggested that he interfered with the cooperative relationship between government agencies and utility companies.

The media have paid repeated tribute, direct and involuntary, to the effectiveness of Reed Irvine and his Accuracy in Media. Long-time CBS head William Paley complained at the 1976 annual meeting of CBS: "We have had during the last year *fifty* long letters from Mr. Irvine—*fifty*. We have had one man practically doing nothing else but answering his correspondence."[7] At this time Irvine was still working full-time for the Federal Reserve Board and his letters to CBS were only a small fraction of those he wrote in his spare time to newspapers and networks. Once he devoted full-time to Accuracy in Media, Irvine became an even more formidable adversary. AIM has successfully pressed the networks to adopt codes of ethics. The codes are important because the media find it difficult then to defend behavior in which they can be shown to have violated their own codes.

Occasionally AIM even receives a direct, if reluctant, tribute. In 1977 Charles Seib, then ombudsman for the *Washington Post* (the growing practice of employing ombudsmen is also a tribute to Irvine's pressure), wrote: "It sticks in my craw, but I'll say it. Irvine and his AIM are good for the press."[8]

Beckmann has attracted less attention from the utopians than Rees and Metzger, something which he laments. Beckmann has performed an especially important service in focussing on those who have received least scrutiny, the scientists who put themselves at the service of the utopians. Metzger calls these people "academic barsweeps, camp followers, people who never really contributed to science and, with nowhere else to go, create fame for themselves through this type of activist public relations."[9] Beckmann dissects the work of these "scientists" with a fine scalpel. In part the utopians may avoid Beckmann because they fear his slashing pen: utopians are like others in finding ridicule the most difficult kind of criticism to bear. Nonetheless his influence is felt. In addition to educating his subscribers on the whole gamut of issues, especially the technical issues, involved in nuclear energy, as well as in other forms of energy, he has had a decisive influence on others who have entered the lists under his inspiration. Samuel McCracken, whose *The War Against the Atom* was quoted earlier, says his book would not have been written without Beckmann, the man "who first brought my attention to the state of the controversy over nuclear power, who made such good sense about it, and who continues to do so with infinite variety and detail.''[10]

What is most striking is that all these people have acted alone. Metzger is the only one with an institutional base and even here, Metzger has taken his initiatives independently and other utilities have not followed in the path he has laid out. With rare exceptions (Mobil is the most notable example), the American corporation has been almost inert under the utopian onslaught. Yet it is the corporation—and utility companies above all, because they are the source of centralized energy and vulnerable to public anger at rising energy prices—which stand on the front line facing the utopian attack. But although being under fire is supposed to concentrate the mind wonderfully, it has not had that effect on American business. Not only have corporations for the most part failed to support those confronting the utopians, but as we have seen, they have subsidized the organizations of their attackers. Schumpeter, seeing so clearly the forces undermining the capitalist system, identified

> ''. . . the very characteristic manner in which particular capitalist interests and the bourgeoisie as a whole behave when facing direct attack. They talk and plead—or hire people to do it for them; they snatch at every chance of compromise; they are ever ready to give in; they never put up a fight under the flag of their own ideals and interests . . .''[11]

A striking example of the sort of thing Schumpeter was talking about then was the payment by Edison Electric Institute, the public relations organization of the utilities, of $7,000 to Harry Reasoner in August 1981 to address the industry on the role of the media.[12] Reasoner, on ''60 Minutes,'' had done what the industry felt was a grossly unfair segment on the Clinton nuclear power plant under construction by Illinois Power Co. Typically, ''60 Minutes'' had refused to correct what Illinois Power asserted were direct misstatements of fact. But Illinois Power had exercised foresight and stationed its own cameras alongside those of CBS. It now made its own ''program'' on videotape, using footage from ''60 Minutes'' and following it with relevant segments that CBS had edited out. It was a devastating piece of media criticism. If Edison Electric wanted a discussion of the role of the media, it could have invited Harold Deakins, the Illinois Power Co. official who had shown the imagination and enterprise to station the cameras and produce the tape. But neither Deakins, nor any representative from Illinois Power, was even invited to be on the discussion panel following Reasoner's lecture. Illinois Power's only recognition came from Accuracy in Media which presented it with an award at its annual conference.

With business hoping to ride out the storm and the media dominated by those sympathetic to their perspective, exposing the utopians is an uphill battle. It is not likely to become easier soon. A study of a random sample of Columbia School of Journalism students by Linda and Robert Lichter and Stanley Rothman in the spring of 1982 found that 85% described themselves as "liberal" and only 11% as conservative. Judging from their voting patterns, even that 11% sounds high. In 1980, when 52% of American voters chose Ronald Reagan, only 4% of the students voted for him, 59% choosing Jimmy Carter and 29% third party candidate John Anderson. The students were even more critical of U.S. institutions than working journalists.[13]

But if media support for the utopians is strong, viewpoints can still occasionally be aired that the utopians reject. If a story is sufficiently dramatic, even exposure of the utopians is possible. "60 Minutes," in January 1983, aired its exposé of the activities of the leadership of mainline churches in supporting Marxist movements. (*The New Republic* noted that this was the first time since the McCarthy era that a network television program had criticized any organization for being pro-Communist.)

More commonly of course, the media ignore major stories that do not fit in with dominant perspectives. The dramatic story of the roots of the nuclear freeze movement has thus been ignored by television. As the media shun stories distasteful to the utopians, a gap is left which journals not normally considered channels for breaking major stories can fill. The *Reader's Digest,* for most of its life a popular digest of self-help pieces, inspirational stories and investigative pieces broken elsewhere, in the last couple of years has emerged as a magazine that breaks the stories other major media ignore. Soviet involvement in the nuclear freeze movement, Bulgarian involvement in the assassination attempt against the Pope, the involvement of churches in support for revolution, were all first presented to a mass audience in the *Reader's Digest*.

The difficulty of exposing the utopians, in the face of a media that with rare exceptions propagates their perspective, means that the individual citizen must become active. Several of the pioneers, we have described, in the exposure of the utopians, and other groups not mentioned, have provided means whereby individuals in local communities can help to educate others. Accuracy in Media has a speaker's bureau which sends people to interested civic groups throughout the country. The Institute on Religion and Democracy organizes workshops to educate the lay Christian in ways to work within his church to ensure accountability of the bureaucracy to the wishes of church members. Scientists and Engineers for Secure Energy, a New York city based organization, also helps to put local communities in contact with experts who can counter the fear and misinformation concerning nuclear energy spread by the utopians. If the silent majority remains silent and passive, the articulate, committed minority will determine their future. Casting a ballot once every two or four years is simply not enough.

But exposure of the utopians and citizen involvement in the education effort are only first steps. More profoundly there must be a decisive rejection of the present utopian temper, so uncharacteristic of the traditional American approach to experience. There must be a return to the stubborn wisdom of the founding fathers who knew that men were not, and could not be made perfect. As James Madison observed: "If men were angels no government would be necessary. If angels were to govern men, neither external nor internal controls on government would be necessary." There must be a return to the balky pragmatism for which Americans were famous. "Will it work?" must again become the skeptical question rudely confronting the most attractive or ingenious scheme. Surely there is no clearer sign of the abandonment of traditional American pragmatism than the burgeoning of anarchist thought, when anarchism, by every test of experience, is an absurdity.

To abandon utopianism does *not* mean to abandon efforts to achieve specific reforms. As historian George H. Nash points out:

> "[H]as there ever been a society as incessantly productive of reform movements as our own? I refer not only to such preeminent crusades as those for emancipation of the slaves, universal suffrage, and regulation of the trusts, but also to such causes as temperance, prison reform, aid to the Indians, the creation of orphanages, abolition of child labor, even the health food movement."[14]

The success of the utopians, as we have noted, has rested in good part on their ability to appeal to this American zeal for reform, to convince others they possessed the exclusive strategy for pursuing desirable goals.

Yet there are alternative, pragmatic approaches to all the problems the utopians address, precisely in the wrong way. There are alternative "market strategies" described by people like William Tucker, to deal with problems of pollution. (There is surely no greater irony than that the result of all the activities of the environmentalists has been to lead us into ever greater dependence on coal, the energy source most harmful both to the environment and human health.) Greater safety and health will not come through ever more regulation that makes products ever more costly, but through recognition of the basic principle that "Richer is safer." And the poor will not become richer through "decentralization" or "appropriate technology" but through expanding production.

It is even possible to pursue alternative strategies in the search for peace. It is instructive to compare the World Without War Council, the only traditional peace organization that has avoided the utopian contagion, with the much better known peace organizations dominating the movement today. Of course it can be argued that a world without war is necessarily a utopian target, given the fact that there has never been such a world. Nonetheless the Council tries to avoid utopianism and—anathema to utopians—to remember the need to preserve values besides the absence of war. In the words of the Council:

> "There are many today skeptical of visionary goals . . . They see the realities of power in the present international system and they are not about to risk what we have achieved in progress toward liberty and equality and security here in America in the fruitless pursuit of utopian goals."[15]

Precisely because it exposes the utopian peace organizations as groups dedicated to the abolition of capitalism far more than to the elimination of war, the World Without War Council is savagely attacked as the War Without World Council. The anger against the Council derives from the utopians' realization that its initiatives are not taken as part of a wider assault on the American political and economic system, but on the contrary may strengthen it.

The utopian pursuit of goals can readily be distinguished from genuine reform movements. The utopian believes any specific target is intimately related to much broader targets. A pure environment will abolish racism and sexism and hierarchy; a nuclear freeze will be the first step toward freeing the world from the threat posed by the discovery of the atom; worker or consumer coops will create a man free of greed or self-interest. The utopian rejects the question "Is it possible?" He asks only "Is it desirable?" and if he concludes that it is, assumes that it is necessarily possible.

Utopian groups are not burdened by complexities. Holding out the promise of a perfect society and a new man, they are able to harness the emotional energies of a major segment of the New Class, whose suppressed religious cravings are satisfied by what are essentially millenarian ideologies. The utopian message revives in secular terms the religious opposites of death and life. Death (from resource depletion, pollution, world-consuming nuclear holocaust) can be averted by accepting life (transformation of society according to utopian prescriptions). Meaning is regained for secular existence in the dedication of life to social salvation and the establishment of the just society of tomorrow. The secular millenarianism of the utopians recovers for the bearers of a secular world view the transcendence craved—but lost—with the disappearance of their faith in traditional religion. Clergymen, under psychological stress in a secular world, may experience the utopian drive as the rebirth of legitimate religious concern in a world where the old forms no longer awaken men's energies.

As in true millennial movements, it is believed that the overturn of one's own existing order will usher in the millennium. Millennial movements of the past, attempting to build a paradise on earth or to be worthy of the Judgment ushering it in, usually ended by leaving their own world in devastation. In the end the evils historians cite as causes for the movements were more firmly entrenched than before. Modern utopian demands are couched in a different language, i.e. redistribution, collective ownership, participatory democracy instead of the discarding of possessions, humbling the high and elevating the lowly, but the results can be equally disastrous.

It is not in the power of the utopians to inaugurate the perfect society of which they dream. But it may be in their power to destroy the good society in which we live. *Wall Street Journal* editor Robert Bartley has noted that these groups can bring capitalism to the point where it "will be unable to deliver on its basic promise of a progressively higher standard of living for those less fortunate than most members of the New Class. When capitalism loses the ability to increase production, the New Class will win."[16]

And while they cannot build Utopia, "dystopia," the antithesis of Utopia, men have the power to create. Long time *New York Times* correspondent, Arthur Krock, quoted a Czechoslovak student who visited the United States during the 1960s. He observed that the Americans he met were "pampered children of your permissive, affluent society, throwing temper tantrums because father gave them only education, security and freedom—but not Utopia . . ." The student, experienced in "dystopia," declared: "You simply haven't faced up to the fact that you can't build a Utopia without terror, and that before long, terror is all that's left."[15]

REFERENCES

1. *New York Times,* Dec. 26, 1982
2. *New York Times,* June 14, 1981
3. Quoted in Herman Nickel, "The Corporation Haters," *Fortune,* June 16, 1980, p. 126
4. *Wall Street Journal,* Feb. 8, 1983
5. *New York Times,* Nov. 3, 1982
6. Michael Novak, "The Snoop Report" *National Review,* Dec. 11, 1981
7. *AIM Report,* May 1976
8. *Washington Post,* Oct. 21, 1977
9. Interview, Peter Metzger, January 29, 1982
10. Samuel McCracken, *The War Against the Atom,* New York, Basic Books, 1982, p. ix
11. Joseph A. Schumpeter, *Capitalism, Socialism and Democracy,* New York, Harper & Row, 1950, p. 161
12. *Access to Energy,* Dec. 1982
13. Linda Lichter, S. Robert Lichter and Stanley Rothman, "The Once and Future Journalists" *Washington Journalism Review,* December 1982, p. 27
14. George H. Nash, "The Pyramid and the Eye," *Imprimis,* Hillsdale, Michigan, May 1983
15. Robert Pickus, "An Introduction to Camus: Neither Victims nor Executioners," World Without War Council, Dec. 1979, p. 6
16. Robert L. Bartley, "Business and the New Class," in B. Bruce Biggs, ed., *The New Class?* New Jersey, Transaction Books, 1979, p. 65
17. Arthur Krock, *The Consent of the Governed,* Boston: Little Brown and Co., 1971, p. 284

Index